JACOB ISAAC SEGAL (1896–1954)

JACOB ISAAC SEGAL (1896–1954) A Montreal Yiddish Poet and His Milieu

Pierre Anctil

Translated by
Vivian Felsen

University of Ottawa Press
2017

uOttawa

The University of Ottawa Press gratefully acknowledges the support extended to its publishing list by Canadian Heritage through the Canada Book Fund, by the Canada Council for the Arts, by the Ontario Arts Council, by the Federation for the Humanities and Social Sciences through the Awards to Scholarly Publications Program, and by the University of Ottawa.

Originally published as *Jacob-Isaac Segal (1896-1954). Un poète yiddish de Montréal et son milieu* © Presses de l'Université Laval 2012

Copy editing: Michael Waldin
Proofreading: Robert Ferguson
Typesetting: Édiscript enr.
Cover design: Édiscript enr.
Cover image: Kathleen Moir Morris, *Winter scene Montreal*, oil on canvas, circa 1929.

© University of Ottawa Press, 2017   Printed in Canada

Library and Archives Canada Cataloguing in Publication

Anctil, Pierre, 1952-
[Jacob-Isaac Segal (1896-1954). English]
    Jacob Isaac Segal (1896-1954) : a Montreal Yiddish poet and his milieu /
Pierre Anctil ; translated by Vivian Felsen.

Translation of: Jacob-Isaac Segal (1896-1954): un poète yiddish de Montréal et son milieu
Issued in print and electronic formats
ISBN 978-0-7766-2571-3 (softcover)
ISBN 978-0-7766-2572-0 (PDF)
ISBN 978-0-7766-2573-7 (EPUB)
ISBN 978-0-7766-2574-4 (Kindle)

    1. Segal, Jacob Isaac, 1896-1954. 2. Segal, Jacob Isaac, 1896-1954—Criticism and interpretation. 3. Poets, Yiddish--Québec (Province)–Montréal--Biography. 4. Yiddish poetry—20th century—History and criticism. 5. Yiddish poetry—Québec (Province)—Montréal—History and criticism. I. Felson, Vivian, translator II. Title. III. Title: Jacob-Isaac Segal (1896-1954). English.

PS8537.E444Z5613 2017   C839'.113   C2017-905934-3
                                                              C2017-905935-1

We acknowledge the financial support of the Government of Canada through the National Translation Program for Book Publishing, an initiative of the *Roadmap for Canada's Official Languages 2013–2018: Education, Immigration, Communities*, for our translation activities.

To Sherry Simon

Table of Contents

APPENDICES 1 TO 33

Translator's Note

Sans entraide et encouragement, nous peinons,
seuls. Ensemble nous progressons.[1]
Pierre Anctil, May, 2017

This is a book about a Montreal poet who wrote exclusively in Yiddish. Its author is a French Canadian anthropologist and historian, a Quebecker who for decades has made every effort to become proficient in the Yiddish language in order to study the Jewish community of Montreal. In addition to his extensive study of publications and archival material in French, English, and primarily Yiddish, author Pierre Anctil also translated from Yiddish into French entire books which he found historically significant. Selections from these books and other Yiddish sources, such as handwritten correspondence, unpublished manuscripts, and newspaper articles, appear throughout Anctil's biography of Canada's most celebrated Yiddish poet. Also included are translations of over twenty of Segal's poems, almost all of which had never before been translated into either French or English. To make it possible for readers to experience the sounds and cadences of the Yiddish language, the author provided Romanized versions of the original Yiddish poems.

Rendering this biography into English thus required translating the Yiddish passages cited, and especially the poetry, directly from the Yiddish. It was thanks to none other than Pierre Anctil that over the past twenty years I had acquired not only the requisite Yiddish translation skills, but also a substantial familiarity with much of the book's content. In 1997, I was working as a translator of French to English when I discovered by chance that a Yiddish book by my grandfather, Montreal Yiddish journalist Israel Medres, had been translated into French. Anctil's scholarly annotated translation inspired me to translate my grandfather's books into English, and resulted in my becoming a Yiddish translator. It also provided a model for all my subsequent translation work.

Over the past twenty years, I have been involved in Pierre Anctil's translations of Yiddish works by prominent mid-twentieth century Montreal Jewish cultural figures such as newspaper publisher Hirsch Wolofsky, poet Sholem Shtern, Labour Zionist activist Simon Belkin, and lexicographer Chaim Leib Fuks. Whether it was helping to track down obscure words and expressions in Yiddish, Russian, Polish or German, or reading through a draft of a French translation, I found myself entering a world I had only known from a child's per-spective—the rich cultural milieu of Montreal's Yiddish writers and intellectuals, the world of my grandfather.   It was also the milieu in which my mother, Anne Medres Glass, had spent her formative years. It sparked her life-long devotion to Yiddish, and instilled in me a deep appreciation for the language and a love of Jewish history.

The knowledge I gained about Yiddish culture in Canada, the translation skills I developed in the process, and the rediscovery of my own family history, all came together in translating this book. J. I. Segal was, after all, my grandfather's colleague. He had written the Foreword to *Montreal of Yesterday*, the book Anctil translated in 1997. He was also the father of Toronto Yiddishist Sylvia Lustgarten, my close friend and role model. To this day she continues to be a source of inspiration and wise counsel.

The vitality of the Yiddish-speaking immigrant community of Montreal in the middle decades of the twentieth century reverber-ates throughout this book. I hope that my translation conveys this vibrancy, as well as the author's passion for his subject.

Vivian Felsen,
Toronto, June 2017

Note

1.   Without mutual support and encouragement, we struggle alone. Together, we forge ahead.

Preface: A Quebec Lyric Poet

In Quebec we are rather proud of our "interculturalism"[1] and "reasonable accommodation" policies, which allow various cultural groups to live together without major conflict. Although there is the occasional tension, at least there is neither violence nor persecution. While many other parts of the world must contend with groups seeking to assert their cultural identity through the use of force, Quebec appears to be a place of peaceful harmony. Is it necessary for me to enumerate the wars and other forms of political oppression still happening today?

However, among the accommodations, there is one—I hope it is not too much of a stretch to call it an "accommodation"—that is widespread, but whose virtues are debatable. It is based on the idea that what we don't know can't hurt us. We can simply ignore those who are different, and live within our own group. Quebec was known for this attitude in the past, as exemplified by Hugh MacLennan's novel Two Solitudes.

The phrase "two solitudes," however, falls somewhat short. What do we know about the Chinese community in whose establishments we eat dim sum, or the Greeks who serve us souvlaki and kebobs? Ethnic cuisine is often sufficient to mask the rest. For example, what do we know about the Jews who, at the turn of the twentieth century, were the largest immigrant group, next to Canada's two founding nations, to settle in Quebec? That they eat kosher food, and own delicatessens! What else? Pogroms? They did not happen here, nor did the Holocaust, nor the founding of the State of Israel. What do we know about their specifically Quebec Jewish culture? To be sure, we have read the cynical novels of Mordecai Richler and heard the disillusioned voice of Leonard Cohen. Is there anything else? Is it worth the trouble?

Perhaps. A culture is also a memory, a heritage, a language, and a reverence for that language. In this book Pierre Anctil reveals to us a language we do not know, that of the Eastern European Jews who were escaping the pogroms in the Tsarist Empire, and later extermination by the Nazis during World War II. It came to us with the immigrants fleeing these persecutions. Here this culture took root and flourished, supported a newspaper, inspired painters, staged theatre productions, and endowed its language with poetry of outstanding quality that was celebrated from Warsaw to New York to Buenos Aires. If we are more familiar today with A. M. Klein, Irving Layton, and Leonard Cohen, it is because they wrote in English and their work became part of English-language Canadian literature. Yet we also have a Quebec Yiddish literature of which we know next to nothing, largely because of the language barrier. In this book Pierre Anctil introduces us to the poet Jacob Isaac Segal, one of giants of that literature. His inspiration has been termed "international" because the language in which he penned his work is enhanced by a Hebrew vocabulary, and even more so by German, and because his work evokes a community whose influence reaches well beyond the borders of Quebec. But who has sung the praises of our winters better than Segal? What a celebration of light and snow! Although undoubtedly international in origin, his poetry is nonetheless inspired by Quebec, and more specifically by Montreal. His lyricism transforms the city into a place of Jewish mysticism, inventing a new part of ourselves. A contemporary of Saint-Denys Garneau and Frank G. Scott, Segal proves himself their equal, their lesser known confrere. Pierre Anctil has given us the opportunity to get to know this Montreal poet and his milieu.

Denis Saint-Jacques, March 2012
Professor Emeritus of Quebec and French Literature,
Laval University (Université Laval)
Co-editor of *La Vie littéraire au Québec*

Note

1.   Translator's Note: For the definition of "interculturalism," as opposed to "multiculturalism," see "The Management of Diversity, Part 1: A Clarification of Terms." First of Five Reports prepared by Miriam Chiasson for David Howes and the Centaur Jurisprudence Project, Centre for Human Rights and Legal Pluralism, McGill University, August 2012.Introduction: A Clarification of Terms: Canadian MulticulturalismandQuebecInterculturalismhttp://canadianicon.org/wp-content/uploads/2014/03/TMODPart1-Clarification.pdf

Introduction

Looking back through the passage of time at my academic journey, I can state today that my interest in Yiddish culture in Montreal dates back more than thirty years to my first encounter with David Rome,[1] archivist at the Canadian Jewish Congress. As an immigrant himself, Rome was the repository of a vast body of knowledge about the great wave of Eastern European Jewish immigration and the intense Yiddish literary activity it generated in Canada—knowledge which, at the end of his life, he wished to transmit to future generations. When Rome and I began to discuss this subject at the beginning of the 1980s, most of the important figures of the Montreal Yiddish world had already disappeared, and their work had fallen into obsolescence and oblivion. Although over the years a new school of professional historians had made its appearance in the Jewish community of Canada, it was primarily preoccupied by the anti-Semitism of Canada's elite. This school turned its back on the early period when Yiddish was the everyday language of Eastern European Jews. It took me some time to understand everything that Rome had so generously shared with me about Jewish Montreal, including the fact that he must have been astonished to be welcoming a gentile into a field of research so little valued in his own community.

As I realized only later, the spark that ignited my interest in this unexplored area of Montreal literary creativity could only have come through a personal Jewish connection. With my academic background in anthropology and my interest in immigration during my doctoral studies at the New School for Social Research in New York, I understood from the outset that it was important for me to learn the Yiddish language spoken by the first Jewish arrivals from Eastern Europe. Without this knowledge, Rome intimated to me, an academic in the field of Canadian Jewish studies would be condemned to merely skimming the surface. Hence, I spent the next five years acquiring an adequate mastery of the language by enrolling in courses in the Department of Jewish Studies at McGill University, where, beginning in the fall of 1984, I began to study with Leib Tencer, a Holocaust survivor. This period more or less corresponded with the years I spent at the Institut québécois de recherche sur la culture, the IQRC, and culminated in the publication of my book entitled *Le rendez-vous manqué, les Juifs de Montréal face au Québec de l'entre-deux-guerres*, in 1988.

Several events made me aware that I was at a crossroads in my research. *Le rendez-vous manqué* was an in-depth study about the relations between French Quebec and the Montreal Jewish community. However, the book was based on historical assumptions belonging exclusively to French Canada of the 1920s and 1930s. As my Yiddish reading skills improved, I gradually understood that the question of the great Jewish migration should be posed differently, namely, based on Eastern European Jewish cultural references, rather than a Francophone Quebec perspective. In short, the time had come, once and for all, to cross the cultural and religious divide that still separated me from the Yiddish universe and its basic frame of reference. Several other factors propelled me in this direction, including the fact that *Le rendez-vous manqué* was not well received inside the Francophone academic community to which I belonged. The academic leadership of the IQRC politely let me know that it would not be desirable for me to continue in that direction. This only reinforced my decision to turn the page once and for all. In view of this peremptory rejection, I came to the conclusion that it would be preferable to distance myself from the Francophone academic world.

Beginning in 1988, with the support of a grant from the *Social Sciences and Humanities Research Council* of Canada, I chose to pursue post-doctoral research on Montreal Yiddish culture in the Department of Jewish Studies at McGill University. My subject was an exploration of the poetry of the Montreal writer Jacob Isaac Segal, an author that Rome brought to my attention and for whom I had developed a special affinity. Arriving in 1910, Segal was the first of a long line of major Jewish poets who settled in Montreal. Born in 1896 in the Russian Empire in the region of Volhynia, now part of the Ukraine, with Yiddish as his mother tongue and educated in a strictly Hasidic environment, he went on to publish a body of work that was modern in form and squarely within the Jewish cultural renaissance. Between 1918 and 1961 twelve volumes of his Yiddish-language poetry were published, all in Montreal except for two, which appeared in New York in 1923 and 1926 respectively. (see Appendix A). To delve into Segal's work is to traverse the entire Canadian Jewish literary milieu, discovering its cultural parameters, its historical trajectory, and its hopes at a time of transition when Yiddish was still the dominant language of the immigrants. The poet also opened vast new literary horizons because his work had an impact throughout the Ashkenazic Jewish diaspora world-wide, in particular on the modernist literary circles of New York, Warsaw, and Kiev, where he was considered one of the great talents of his time. To read Segal is to enter a world of rich poetic imagery and heightened sensitivity marked by the trying events in the life of the poet and his people.

During my post-doctoral studies, from 1988 to 1991, I was able to teach Canadian Jewish history at McGill University. To my great surprise, I found a way to begin translating, from Yiddish into French, fifty or so of Segal's poems, most of them from his collection entitled *Lirik*, published in Montreal in 1930. Once completed, these translations were published in 1992 by Éditions du Noroît in an annotated volume entitled *Poèmes yiddish/Yidishe lider*. It was around this time that a media controversy erupted over the PhD thesis of Esther Delisle, which focussed on the anti-Semitic proclivities of Canon Lionel Groulx and the French-language newspaper, *Le Devoir*. In the aftermath of these events, the atmosphere in the area of research on relations between Jews and French Canadians had become so stifling that I made up my mind to stop writing about this subject. Instead, I decided to focus my research on Montreal Yiddish culture, which offered me a secure refuge from tensions and confrontations which were more political than intellectual. In 1997 Éditions du Septentrion published my first translation into French of a Yiddish book which had appeared fifty years earlier, *Montreal of Yesterday* (*Montreal fun nekhtn*), by journalist Israel Medres.[2] This was an eye-witness account of the great Eastern European migration between 1905 and 1914. The author's keen observations and humorous descriptions exposed the difficulties encountered by Yiddish-speaking Jews attempting to integrate into Montreal society. In the meantime, partly to preserve my intellectual independence, I chose to embark upon a career in the Quebec public service. Thus, in 1991, I accepted a position in the strategic areas of immigration and intercultural education, where I remained for almost twelve years. By distancing myself from academic life, I was able to explore with complete freedom other works written about Yiddish Montreal. I translated some important books, including those by Simon Belkin, H. Wolofsky,[3] Chaim Leib Fuks, Sholem Shtern, and Hershl Novak. The majority of these translations into French were published between 1999 and 2010 by Éditions du

Septentrion and Éditions du Noroît. In particular, the translation of the biographical dictionary of Chaim Leib Fuks, published in Yiddish in 1980 and then in French in 2005 under the title *Cent ans de littérature yiddish et hébraïque au Canada*, allowed me to discover the scope and complexity of this subject. According to Fuks, approximately 425 writers, poets, journalists, and pedagogues, who arrived in three distinct waves of immigration and mostly remained in Montreal, once in Canada published work in Yiddish as well as in modern Hebrew. A new world had opened up for me.

In 2004, my career completely changed course when I became Director of the Institute of Canadian Jewish Studies at the University of Ottawa, where once again I had the opportunity to devote myself to teaching and scholarly articles. Four years later, in 2008, I was awarded a Killam Fellowship from the Canada Council for the Arts on the basis of a research project entitled "Parcours migrants, parcours littéraires canadiens; le poète Jacob-Isaac Segal (A Canadian Literary and Migrant Odyssey: Yiddish poet Jacob Isaac Segal)" Equipped with a better understanding of the language and the cultural context in which this Montreal writer had developed, I aimed not only to translate some of his work and provide an overview, but also to write his biography and describe the historical circumstances that made it possible for his talent to emerge. For me, this was also an opportunity to deepen my perception of the Montreal Yiddish literary milieu by following its progression from the beginning of the twentieth century to its eventual decline almost sixty years later. The work of J. I. Segal enabled me to better grasp the parameters of Canadian Yiddish writing, and assess its originality in relation to other literary traditions in the city of Montreal.

This opportunity also allowed me to expand on the idea of a Quebec literary corpus that included work produced in immigrant languages, of which Yiddish was the most significant in terms of its scope, and the depth of its historical origins. The difficulty here was not so much in showing how the Eastern European Jewish literary tradition was brought to Montreal around 1900 by specific historic events. Rather, it was the fact that the tools required to follow its development on Canadian soil were sadly lacking. We knew that Segal wrote and published in Montreal for over forty years, until his death in 1954. Nonetheless, his work was never the object of systematic attention. In addition, it had appeared in a variety of newspapers and periodicals published both here and abroad. Apart from the twelve volumes of Segal's poetry published between 1918 and 1961, including the two that were published posthumously, there was no way of obtaining a clear picture of the actual scope of his contribution in the fields of poetry, essay writing, and autobiography (see Appendix C). It would take many years and a team of researchers to comb through material that was often ephemeral and frequently difficult to access, if not impossible to locate. The difficulty was compounded by the fact that only a tiny fraction of Segal's work was ever translated. What is more, everything he wrote, without exception, was of the highest literary quality, which again underscored the immensity of the task for a contemporary researcher.

To produce results within a reasonable timeframe, a study of Segal required resorting to means other than those described above. Instead of trying to look at his work as a whole, I chose to closely examine two archival repositories housed within the Montreal Jewish Community's institutional network, namely, the holdings of the Jewish Public Library, and those of the Canadian Jewish Congress. Bear in mind that Segal belonged to a very close-knit Montreal Jewish community where the total number of institutional stakeholders was rather limited. During his career, the poet worked within a narrow cultural space that essentially included the Yiddish daily newspaper, the *Jewish Daily Eagle* (the *Keneder Adler*), the Montreal Yiddish-language schools, the Peretz School and the Jewish People's School, as well as the Jewish Public Library. In addition, his social circle was restricted mainly to his fellow writers and teachers, his regular readers, and some activists employed by Yiddish-language community institutions.

Traces of Segal's life and work were most likely to appear within the Yiddish-language organizations of Montreal. In fact, it is important to understand that Eastern European Jews spent considerable energy in Canada preserving and disseminating the history of their community, even at the time when immigration from Eastern Europe was at its peak. As early as 1939 an institutional archival repository was placed in the Canadian Jewish Congress and, after World War II, in the Jewish Public Library. These efforts, originally in the Yiddish language, soon led to the writing of comprehensive histories, including Simon Belkin's book about the Labour Zionist movement in Canada,[4] and B. G. Sack's *History of the Jews in Canada*.[5] By relying on these scholarly works and existing community resources, it was possible for me to reconstruct the career of Segal the poet through the eyes of his closest co-workers and colleagues. Furthermore, in the mid-1950s, the Segal family donated to the Jewish Public Library the entire collection of manuscripts and correspondence kept by the author from the time of his arrival in Montreal in 1910. Above all, among the holdings of the Canadian Jewish Congress Archives are the personal papers of H. M. Caiserman, General Secretary of that organization from 1919 until his death in 1950, and a close friend of the poet. Caiserman, who had witnessed Segal's first steps onto the Montreal Yiddish literary scene, had written numerous essays on this subject, and had published a 1934 anthology entitled *Idishe dikhter in kanade* (Yiddish poets in Canada). (See Appendix H.) Thanks to Caiserman's literary reviews and unpublished manuscripts about Segal's life, it seemed possible to reconstruct the poet's biography, as well as the principal elements of his creative process. Indeed, it would not be an exaggeration to state that Caiserman's career as a community activist in an extraordinary way sheds light on that of his friend the poet. For that reason, literary criticism is prominently featured in my book.

A study of Segal also raised other fundamental issues in the context of Quebec studies, beginning with the place of Montreal's Eastern European Jews in the history of ideas and artistic creativity. Segal's poetic output, remarkable in many ways, was not an isolated phenomenon produced by a single individual. On the contrary, it was inextricably linked to the appearance of a Yiddish literature of the highest quality that signalled a more far-reaching and significant development: the Yiddish language was one of the earliest harbingers of modernity in Montreal. Yiddish was in effect a vehicle for social, cultural and artistic innovation which, at the beginning of the twentieth century, had not yet emerged in the Quebec context. As Jean Baumgarten states in his history of the Yiddish language:

> [TRANSLATION] From the earliest literary texts, Yiddish writing had a unique tone, not only due to multiple crosscutting and transversal influences, but also to elements unique to the Jewish tradition. Yiddish was reserved not just for internal use in a complex range of texts, from secular literature to poetry, from Biblical commentaries to community proclamations. It also became a creative space which echoed the numerous, often contradictory developments in European culture [. . .].
>
> We are dealing with an innovative and unique aesthetic universe that reflected the needs and aspirations of Jewish readers as

much as the changes in society. This lively dialectic, consisting of unique aspirations on the one hand, and extreme responsiveness to centrifugal forces on the other, remains one of the constants in Yiddish culture.[6]

Eastern European Jews arriving in Canada, having left a Russian Empire in the throes of powerful revolutionary fervour, where they had been a minority targeted by discriminatory policies, became a catalyst for change and renewal. Although few in number, they congregated around various diasporic ideologies and effective community institutions, and almost immediately were able to give expression to their literary creativity. Because Yiddish literature encompassed many currents of thought, at times diametrically opposed, and was often influenced by the ideas of European radicalism, it also produced in Montreal a universe prone to hyperbole and pervaded by glaring tensions. Just as Yiddish writers distinguished themselves by their intense creativity and their desire to treat contemporary and often controversial subjects, they also bore the burden of the difficult consequences of immigration, social marginalisation, and racial discrimination. As Baumgarten points out, Yiddish writing frequently surprises the reader of today by its taste for the sensational, by its incisive statements, and by its descriptions of extreme situations:

> [TRANSLATION] Yiddish writers, artists and poets had to invent both a new aesthetic and new literary forms, and to find within themselves the strength to remain free. Relying on its Hebrew past and drawing on the rich sources of Jewish tradition, Yiddish literature was forged in a context where energy, positivity, but also despair, and the will to fight against the forces of attenuation and annihilation, served as a spur and a stimulus. In the Jewish world, writing made it possible to live with hope, to have faith in the future, and to combat disappearance and oblivion. In numerous situations throughout history, creating in the Yiddish language was like laughing on the brink of disaster.[7]

The shadow of Eastern Europe hovered over this young Montreal literature conceived in unique circumstances by writers who had left behind the terrible Kishinev pogrom and the still vivid memory of the failed revolution of 1905. They had suffered the severe political repression that would eventually lead to the fall of the tsarist regime. Born in the Russian Empire during an era of widespread violence, an unre-lenting struggle for survival, and daily political strife, Yiddish writing in Canada for a long time bore the stamp of a turbulent world and liberation of uncertain outcome. Hence, underlying its main achieve-ments were smouldering embers that sometimes smacked of pain and bitterness. The Yiddish writers of Montreal, particularly in the early years, lived in a cultural universe where both physical suffering and mental anguish were constant, and the fear of foundering ever pres-ent. Worried about their loved ones left behind in the old country, distressed by the idea of confronting in North America the disastrous consequences of events taking place in Europe, and isolated in a new country they barely knew, literate Canadian Yiddish speakers at times suffered unbearable pressures in their pursuit of creativity. They were the heirs of a turbulent Russian world that would leave its mark on the writing produced in Montreal for more than one generation. This was the idea which historian Jonathan Frankel tried to convey more generally with regard to Eastern European Jewry at the beginning of the twentieth century:

> They were, after all, mainly members of the 1905 generation, their formative years indelibly stamped by the revolutionary experi-ence in the Russian Empire. Strikes, demonstrations, sudden mobilization of mass support, the burgeoning of political activ-ity and party rivalry, a clandestine and semi-legal press, pogroms and self-defence units, gunrunning, street clashes with Cossacks, highly attended funerals, arrests, imprisonments and the years of exile in Siberia—all this could not but produce a crop of young people with political experience and skills totally unprecedented in modern Jewish history.[8]

In searching for a historic solution to the political tensions to which they had fallen victim in Europe and subjecting Canadian and Quebec society to their critical questioning, the Jews contributed substantially to transforming their immediate Montreal milieu, as well as the very society into which they sought to integrate. The motivation for their ideas and their actions are perfectly reflected in the work of J. I. Segal and other Yiddish writers, such as Sholem Shtern, Yudika, and N. I. Gotlib, who would inject into their writing subject matter and aes-thetic preoccupations hitherto unknown in Quebec, especially those inspired by urbanism and industrialization. As the heirs of both

Jewish tradition and Russian culture, these new citizens brought to their new home a form of writing and a way of thinking derived from the literature they first discovered on the other side of the Atlantic Ocean, often in a raw, unfinished form. In Montreal, wedged between two large linguistic groups, Yiddish speakers could explore these new themes more easily simply because they wrote in a language unreadable by the majority. They occupied a transitory geographic space, a part of the city reserved for recent immigrants, including the length of St. Lawrence Boulevard, where they were sheltered from indiscreet and malevolent looks. As they become acquainted with the poetry and biography of J. I. Segal, readers will be invited to ponder the significance of the Yiddish presence in Quebec, and the recurrent themes of Canadian Jewish history. Perhaps this will contribute to a new understanding, more inclusive and open to outside influences, of the Montreal and Quebec identity that emerged at the beginning of the twentieth century.

This book is divided into five chapters, each covering a decade in the poet's life. Since Segal put his literary talents to use primarily in Montreal, this study begins in 1910 when he arrived in the city, at a time when Eastern European immigration was at its peak. It was during this time that his first attempts at writing appeared, culminating in the publication in 1918 of his collection of poems entitled *Fun mayn velt* (From my world), the first such poetry collection in Yiddish in Montreal. In the second chapter the reader is invited to step back in time and discover the writer's Ukrainian birthplace. Born in Slobkovitz,[9] he moved while still very young to Korets, which would be transformed into a mythical place in his work. There Segal received an Eastern European Jewish education profoundly influenced by Hasidism. His difficult family situation in the town of Korets would later lead to his immigration to America. The third chapter, focussing on the 1920s, finds the poet, attracted by modernity, moving to New York in the hope of launching his literary career there. During this period, Segal formed friendships with writers who belonged to the modernist groups *Di Yunge* and *In Zikh*, without, however, losing contact with Montreal. His stay in the large metropolis was a time of fresh troubles, including the tragic loss of his eldest daughter. In chapter four, the reader will find Segal forced by the Great Depression to return to Montreal where, starting in 1930, he would become a dominant figure on the Yiddish cultural and literary scene. The beneficiary of a new wave of Eastern European immigrants during the interwar period, Montreal became a centre of Yiddish writing that attracted the attention of the Ashkenazic diaspora worldwide. Finally, the fifth chapter presents Segal at the summit of his artistic career yet emotionally devastated by the years of war and the Holocaust. Before his death, the poet took a radical turn in his work, dedicating his last poems to the vanished world of his childhood and traditional Jewish life in Korets.

Because only a minuscule part of Segal's oeuvre has been translated, I decided to include translations of poems belonging to different periods in his literary career. To introduce the reader to the language in which these poems were penned, Romanized versions of the original Yiddish are included in the Appendices at the end of this book. Also in the Appendices are biographical documents which provide valuable insight into Segal's life and the context in which he composed his poetry. While perusing the archives of both the Canadian Jewish Congress and the Montreal Jewish Public Library, I discovered clippings from newspapers and literary magazines containing articles written by Segal at various times in his career, as well as critiques of his work. These items are listed in bibliographies at the end of this book (See Appendices C and D). To date they constitute the only comprehensive compilation of Segal's work. In the Appendices, the reader will discover lists of the addresses declared by Segal as his residences in both Montreal and New York between 1917 and 1954 (see Appendix B), his poetry collections (see Appendix A), the members of the Jewish Writers Association between 1941 and 1948 (see Appendices E and F), and the members of the Board of Directors of the J. I. Segal Foundation in 1954 (see Appendix G).[10]

I would like to thank the Killam Foundation for its generous contribution and its much appreciated support. Without the support of the Killam Fellowship of the Canada Council for the Arts I would never have been able to devote myself so completely to the research and writing involved in this project over a period of two years. My gratitude also extends to the Jewish Public Library and the National Archives of the Canadian Jewish Congress for their support. Archivists Shannon Hodge and Janice Rosen moved heaven and earth to give me access to documentation that was as rich as it was rarely consulted, often difficult to decipher, and catalogued in a summary manner. Without their assistance over a period of several months, I would probably never have been able to discover certain manuscripts of paramount importance for my research that elucidate the emergence of the Montreal Yiddish literary scene. In this connection, I would like to thank Eva Raby, Director of the Jewish Public Library, and Eiran Harris, Archivist Emeritus. I also wish to thank my academic colleagues Ira Robinson, Richard Menkis, Sherry Simon and Morton Weinfeld, without whose observations, knowledge and encouragement, it is safe to say, my research would not have resulted in as complete a biography of the poet J. I. Segal. I wish to highlight the unwavering support of my wife, Chantal Ringuet, who, on numerous occasions, provided judicious advice with regard to my writing, and assisted in the translation of Segal's poetry into French. A final word of thanks to the *Centre interuniversitaire sur les lettres, les arts et les traditions* (CELAT) at Laval University for its financial support in the final preparation of this manuscript. To do justice to the complexity and scope of the Yiddish literary and cultural activity in Montreal, much work remains to be done. It is my fervent hope that this book will inspire more narrowly targeted and better documented research.

Pierre Anctil, 2012

Notes

1. Born in 1910 in Vilna (Vilnius), Lithuania, at that time part of the Russian Empire, David Rome arrived in Canada in 1921, and settled with his family in Vancouver. Educated in English, he also had a good knowledge of Yiddish when he moved to Montreal in 1942. Having served for many years as Press Officer at the Canadian Jewish Congress, in 1953 he became Director of the Montreal Jewish Public Library. In 1972, he returned to the Canadian Jewish Congress as archivist and went on to publish over sixty volumes about Canadian Jewish history under the auspices of the Canadian Jewish Archives New Series.

2. The translation was entitled *Le Montreal juif d'autrefois*.

3. H. Wolofsky, *Mayn lebns rayze; zikhroynes fun iber a halbn yorhundert idish lebn in der alter un nayer velt (Journey of My Life*, Montreal: The Eagle Publishing Company 1946), 1946.

4. Simon I. Belkin, *Di Poale Zion Bavegung in Kanada: 1904–1920* (Montreal: Actions Committee of the Labour Zionist Movement in Canada, 1956). Translated into French by Pierre Anctil as *Le movement ouvrier juif au Canada, 1904–1929* (Sillery, les éditions du Septentrion, 1999).

5. B. G. Sack, *Geshikhte fun di yidn in kanade* (Montreal: Northern Printing and Stationery, 1948). Translated into English as *History of the Jews in Canada* (Montreal: Harvest House, 1965).

6. Jean Baumgarten, *Le yiddish, histoire d'une langue errante* (Paris, Albin Michel, collection "Présences du judaïsme," No. 16, 2002), 140–141.

7. Ibid., 142.

8. Jonathan Frankel, *Crisis, Revolution and Russian Jews* (Cambridge U.K., Cambridge University Press, 2009), 219.

9.   More commonly spelled Solobkovtsy, its Russian name. Slobkovitz is the Yiddish name of this town.

10. Translator's Note: In the French edition, Appendix E consists of a twelve-page index to all of J.I. Segal's correspondence available in the Montreal Jewish Public Library archives. That index has been omitted from the English edition because it is ordered alphabetically according to the Hebrew alphabet, thus limiting its usefulness for those unfamiliar with that alphabet.

Chapter 1

Arrival in Montreal

We know very little about the circumstances of J. I. Segal's arrival in Montreal. It is difficult, for example, to determine the exact age of the poet when he stepped onto Canadian soil for the first time. No legal document attesting to his date of birth has survived. It is entirely plausible that he left his native Ukraine without official proof of citizenship. The most credible guess, based on evidence provided after the fact, is that he arrived in Montreal when he was about 13 or 14 years old. Segal's niece, Sylvia Angell,[1] believes that he left central Europe around 1910 from the port of Hamburg. There he boarded an ocean liner with the auspicious name *Montreal*, which sailed to Saint John, New Brunswick, before arriving in Montreal. We also know that he was accompanied by his mother Shifke, and his sisters, Esther and Pearl. If such is the case, we can reasonably conclude that Segal left Korets, a small town in Volhynia, in Western Ukraine, where he had lived for several years, and travelled through Poland and Germany to reach the North Sea. At that time, steamboats bound for Canada departed from a British maritime terminal so that Eastern European immigrants had to dock on the coast of England or Scotland prior to embarking upon their long trans-Atlantic voyage. Hershl Novak,[2] who had sailed to Canada in 1909, one year before Segal, also left from Hamburg after having travelled by train via Warsaw, Vienna, and Berlin. After arriving in Great Britain, he waited for several days before boarding a ship in Liverpool and sailing non-stop to Montreal.[3]

Novak, who during the 1910s would become a close friend of Segal the poet, provided a detailed description in his memoirs of the journey that had to be undertaken prior to the First World War by the many Russian, Ukrainian, and Polish Jewish immigrants who wished to settle in Canada. Taking into account the train trip across Europe, followed by a sea voyage in two distinct stages, it seems reasonable to assume that their journey took approximately two months, including two to three weeks on the high seas, under trying conditions. Despite these difficulties, most long-distance travellers in those days considered the length of time quite acceptable, and marvelled at how much maritime travel had advanced over the previous twenty years. Technological innovations resulted in lower ticket prices on all commercial ships owned by large German, French, and British companies, making the cost of a third-class ticket within the reach of the majority of travellers. At the turn of the twentieth century, regardless of social status or ethnicity, people leaving the cities and towns of Europe were able to afford the cost of a transatlantic voyage without undue hardship. It is safe to say that without these major advances, immigration from Eastern Europe would have remained more limited in terms of numbers, or would have occurred more slowly. For the young Jacob Segal, who had never been outside his immediate family circle, arriving in the great port of Hamburg must have been a momentous event. Five years his senior, Novak in his memoir described the docks of Hamburg in 1909, and his feelings upon leaving Europe forever, as follows:

> In the few hours before our departure, I wandered around the harbour. Seeing the enormous ships being loaded in preparation for their departure made a lasting impression on me. It corresponded completely with my boyish dreams about the world, a world that was immense and vast and open to all. One only had to be alert to all its possibilities. How accessible everything was, how different from the small and stifling Gerer prayer house! I, too, wanted to be a free, unfettered citizen of this great world.[4]

Currently available data lends credence to the information provided several decades after the fact by Pearl Segal. According to documents in the Canadian Government Archives, over the course of the year 1910, a steamship belonging to the Canadian Pacific Railway Company by the name *Montreal* dropped anchor three times in the port of Saint John, New Brunswick. Having sailed each time from Anvers, Belgium,[5] it discharged its human cargo in Canada on three occasions: January 12, 1910, March 10, 1910, and finally December 14, 1910. If this information is accurate, Segal and his family, after having declared their identity to a customs agent and completed the required paperwork, immediately boarded a train to traverse the approximately 800 kilometres that still separated them from their final destination, Montreal.

Another theory is that the ship sailed directly to Montreal.[6] This theory is supported by a form completed by Segal for the I. L. Peretz Yiddish Writers Association in New York in 1923, while he was living in New York working on a text to be published in a literary anthology.[7] Below the letterhead are his hand-written answers for the benefit of his American colleagues, stating that he was born on December 15, 1896, in Korets, Volhynia, and that he had arrived in America in 1910. Segal added that he had launched his literary career in 1916 at the age of 20, and that until 1922 Montreal had been his principal place of residence. There follows a list of periodicals in which his poetry and literary criticism had appeared, and the titles of his first three published poetry collections. This document constitutes the first available historical document pertaining to Segal's literary career (see Appendix 1).

Factory Work

All the documents used in this book support the following fact: Prior to 1914, entering Canada was not a great problem for subjects of the Russian Empire, and Jews were no exception. The arrival of the Segals was facilitated by the fact that they were welcomed in Montreal by family members. A few years earlier, the poet's two older brothers, Eliezer (Leyzer) and Nehemia, and two sisters, Chaya (Chayke) and Edith, disembarked in Montreal, where they remained. Segal's personal papers do not reveal why the older siblings chose to settle in Canada's largest city, or when they arrived. Understandably, the dire living conditions of the Jewish population in the Russian Empire, as well as the general climate of political oppression, played a major role in their decision. On the other hand, we do know that these young immigrants, who were probably in their early twenties when they left Eastern Europe, immediately upon their arrival began working in the clothing factories near the Montreal harbour, joining the ranks of the Jewish working class in the early stages of its development.[8] Nehemia Segal, one of the first Yiddish poets in Montreal, received more attention than his brother and two sisters, who had disembarked in the port of Montreal at nearly the same time. According to the biographical dictionary of Ch. L. Fox (Chaim Leib Fuks), he was born in August of 1878 in Korets, and arrived in Montreal in 1902, roughly eight years before his younger brother J. I. Segal. However, Nehemia's literary talent did not save him from the fate so often reserved for his generation of Yiddish-speaking immigrants. According to Fox, "for many years he worked very hard until, in 1922, he became seriously ill, and had to stop working."[9] The same fate awaited the members of the Segal family who arrived subsequently. From the time she immigrated to Montreal, Pearl, the youngest child in the Segal family, was employed in a factory that produced men's trousers. She was barely ten years of age[10] when she began working, and she worked twelve hours a day until her marriage in 1920 to a Montreal tailor by the name of Endler. According to Mirl Erdberg-Shatan, Segal's oldest sister, Esther Segal, also a gifted writer,[11] went to work at the age of thirteen in a sweat-shop housed in a dimly lit cellar,[12] while attempting to acquire an education by attending night school.[13] Pearl's account, recorded at the end of her life, provides a picture of the Segal family's economic situation before World War I:

> One night, walking home from Dufferin School,[14] which she attended two nights, she found all the furniture scattered on the sidewalk—not being able to pay the rent had caught up with them, and they had to leave their Morris[15] Street place, with no bathroom and no electricity. They lived in the back room of a relative on Morel Street for a while, and then Clark Street, below Sherbrooke, and then Laval, moving westward with the rest of the "old" immigrants, their place taken by newer immigrants.[16]

As in many other families, Segal's brothers and sisters, who, by 1910, had already established themselves in Montreal, must have contributed to the travel expenses of their family members, and helped them find work in the downtown clothing factories. The young Segal, like other immigrants arriving in the years just before First World War, almost immediately found himself working sixty hours a week in a sweatshop. In an unpublished biography of the poet written at the beginning of the 1940s, H. M. Caiserman described his situation in one short sentence: "In 1916, as a boy of 18, he left Korets, and went directly into a Montreal tailor shop."[17] Similarly Fox notes that "Segal came to Montreal, and for a number of years worked sewing pant pockets."[18] According to Caiserman, who must have gleaned this information from Segal himself, the poet first lived with his mother and sisters near the harbour, where many other newly arrived Yiddish-speaking immigrants were to be found. Plucked from the predominantly Jewish world of his *shtetl*, the young Segal had to adjust to life as a tailor in a factory in a large North American city full of people of diverse origins.

He had left a childhood spent in the comfortable home of his grand-father, David Perlmuter, to become an unskilled worker in a sector of the economy known for its slack seasons and low pay. In one of the earliest poems published by Segal in Montreal, entitled "In the Shop," he evokes the difficulties he experienced during those years (see Appendix 2).

In the Shop

> Long and lazy drag the days
> As I strain under my yoke
> Always toiling, always struggling
> My tired hands are throbbing, broke.
>
> On the tense and drawn faces
> Lies a sadness, heavy, broad.
> And each pair of eyes stares blindly
> With the deepest suffering.
>
> On and on and never stopping
> I stand and work at my machine.
> The world requires so much clothing,
> And making clothing so much blood!...[19]

In fact, for most of his time in Montreal, Segal remained dependent on the clothing industry as a source of income for himself and his family. Raised in Eastern Europe, lacking any vocational training or special skills, and unable to obtain a diploma from a recognized institution in Montreal, the poet was forced to supplement his meagre earnings both as writer and as a teacher in the Yiddish secular schools, with manual labour. During the interwar period, the poet and his wife Elke (née Rosen), whom he married at the age of 19, often took in piece work, putting the finishing touches on ready-made clothing. Since this work required neither specialized machinery nor any special skill, Segal and his wife worked from home on a contract basis several hours a week. The poet in all likelihood left his factory job shortly after the end of World War I, and quite quickly lost contact with the large factories which had been prevalent in the clothing industry since the beginning of the twentieth century. In this important sector of Montreal's economy, large production units depended on a group of smaller sub-contractors who in turn contracted out work to

J. I. Segal soon after his arrival in Montreal with his mother Shifke (right),
his grandmother (left), and one of his sisters. (Private collection
of Sylvia Segal Lustgarten and Annette Zakuta Segal.)

sweatshops that appeared and disappeared according to demand. Yet
although Segal had distanced himself from the vibrant trade union
activity and ideological exuberance that characterized the factory
environment, throughout his life he kept in close contact with the needle trades, where the majority of workers were Eastern European Jews
and Yiddish was used extensively as a language of communication.

   On the one hand, the poet's dependency on his earnings from the
garment industry kept him strongly connected to the Yiddish-speaking
immigrant world, from which, in fact, he hardly ever ventured very

J. I. Segal and Elke Rosen on their wedding day.
Studio Pismonov, St. Lawrence Boulevard, Montreal.
(Private collection of Sylvia Segal Lustgarten and Annette Segal Zakuta.)

far during his life in Montreal. In this milieu Segal found unwavering support for his work, as well as admirers willing to assist him in his literary career, in particular by raising the money to print his poetry collections. On the other hand, his reliance on factory work also restricted him, depriving him of the opportunity to enhance his social status, and enter into the world of Canadian literature. As a garment worker, Segal shared the unenviable fate of many intellectuals, writers and artists of his generation who never succeeded in breaching the barriers that kept them out of mainstream Canada's cultural life. Those not drawn to the needle trades sometimes found employment, not significantly more lucrative, in Jewish community institutions, or took jobs associated with Jewish religious practice such as rabbis, part-time Hebrew teachers, or ritual slaughterers whose services were required to meet the demand for kosher meat. Consequently, Segal lived most of his life below the poverty line, so much so that he did not really benefit from the upward mobility which propelled large segments of the Jewish population into the middle class,[20] beginning in the late 1930s.

First Attempts at Writing

Upon his arrival in Canada, the poet and other members of his family were obliged to use all their energies just to survive. They turned to one of most reliable sources of income available to immigrants in their situation, the garment industry. There, one could be hired speaking only Yiddish, and without any particular knowledge of Montreal society. Early on, however, the young Segal exhibited talent in another field. After work, during his rare hours of free time, he composed poetry in Yiddish. As a newly arrived immigrant, he began writing in complete isolation. Only his family was aware of his literary activity. The following is what Caiserman had to say in the biographical account previously mentioned:

> He lived alone, reclusive, and never met anyone in the (Jewish) community. Until late at night, by the light of a small kerosene lamp, he diligently composed poetry. Very often his mother awoke at two or three in the morning to find him writing. She would put out the light so that he would have the strength to get up in the morning and go to work.[21]

Today, almost a century later, it is difficult to pinpoint the exact moment when this literary activity in Canada began, or to assess its worth. For a long time Segal himself was silent about the circumstances that gave birth to his career as a writer. It was probably at the request of his friend Caiserman that Segal confided to him these biographical details at the end of his life, perhaps with a more in-depth biography in mind. However, it is evident that from the time he arrived in Montreal, Segal was seized with an irrepressible impulse to write, and to write only poetry. Perhaps J. I. Segal was following in the footsteps of his older brother Nehemia who was driven by the same desire. The latter had early on published some of his poetry in the Montreal Yiddish daily, the *Keneder Adler*, known in English as the *Jewish Daily Eagle*.[22] Nonetheless, it was not long before the younger brother surpassed him in terms of literary production, and seemed to have devoted his constant attention to writing. Above all, J. I. Segal gave the impression of wanting to make writing poetry an integral part of his existence. "This was the first stage of his poetic quest. In those years Segal was quiet and reserved, but he worked persistently and tirelessly to build his career."[23]

In this regard, it is important to note that the poet immigrated to Canada in the very same year that the first Yiddish book was printed in Canada.[24] In the early 1910s no one could have imagined that the Eastern European Jewish population of Montreal would steadily increase over the following two decades, nor that it would become possible for someone to achieve renown in that city as a Yiddish poet. Who could have foreseen that a limited but loyal and passionate readership would emerge between the two World Wars to welcome and sometimes applaud its favourite authors? Who would have believed that in this literary outpouring, poets would earn such remarkable esteem and visibility? Frequently found in the Old Testament and other Jewish sacred literature, poetry was perceived in the Yiddish world to be a spiritually exalted genre, so much so that it was often ascribed prophetic overtones. Poetry also echoed the spirit of modernity that infused much of Jewish literature from the time of the *Haskala*, the Jewish Enlightenment that originated in Germany at the end of the eighteenth century, and served as the point of departure for the great cultural revival that gradually spread to Eastern Europe. When Segal penned his first manuscripts in Canada, no one in the emerging Jewish community would have imagined that among the immigrants disembarking on Canadian shores there could be people with superior literary talent. At that time Yiddish printing was just making its debut in Canada.[25] Although some Yiddish pamphlets were being printed in Montreal and it was possible to purchase certain New York Yiddish newspapers in the Jewish neighbourhood, it was not until the *Keneder Adler* was founded in 1907 on St. Lawrence Boulevard near

Ontario Street, that Montreal Yiddish writing found its first vehicle for expression.

The owner of the *Adler*, Hirsch Wolofsky, soon realized that his newspaper had to cater to an ideologically diverse readership. The risk of losing a large number of its readers prevented the paper from openly supporting any particular political faction.[26] Wolofsky also deemed it worthwhile to publish in the newspaper literary pieces, such as short stories and serialized novel that would appeal to his readership. To this end, he tapped the talents of local writers, many of them young immigrants who had not previously published their work and sought no more than to see their name in print and become known in the community. Furthermore, Eastern European Jews arriving en masse in Montreal's harbour were already familiar with Yiddish literature. In the old country, many had been accustomed to reading, albeit sporadically, books and newspapers in Yiddish.[27] From the very beginning, Wolofsky attracted literary personalities such as Benjamin Gutl Sack, Israel Medres, and Israel Rabinovitch, who would become full-time staff writers for the *Jewish Daily Eagle* for the rest of their writing careers. He also attracted young aspiring writers, such as Shmuel Talpis, Abraham Aron Roback, Isaac Yampolsky, and Joel Leib Malamut[28] who worked on a free-lance basis. In fact, from its inception, an assortment of Yiddish writers of various social backgrounds converged around the *Eagle*. Without actually being aware of it, they were laying the groundwork for a specifically Montreal Yiddish literature. Enjoying Wolofsky's support, these authors realized that they were forming a rather sizeable literary circle, and that a promising future awaited them. Most of these young men had never before published their work in a Yiddish daily newspaper or a recognized Yiddish periodical. Newly arrived in America, they were already assuming the responsibilities of publishers and editors, responsibilities with which they would not have been entrusted in Eastern Europe at such a young age. Israel Medres, who came to Montreal in 1910 and worked as a full-time journalist for the *Eagle* beginning in 1922, later explained how the majority of the newcomers hired by Wolofsky became writers, and described the process which led them to embark upon a literary career.

> Almost all the Yiddish writers in those days became writers because they were intelligent readers. Before emigrating from the old country they had read scores of books and journals in Hebrew, Russian, and other languages. Once in Canada they

became involved in community activities and felt compelled to
write [. . .]
Among the intellectual immigrants were former university students from Russia or Rumania who began to write about moral
issues such as relations between brides and grooms, husbands
and wives, parents and children. Former Hebraist *maskilim*[29]
became specialists in literary criticism, cultural studies, or plays
for the theatre. Intellectual factory workers who had received
their education through party proclamations began to author
short stories or poetry.[30]

The Yiddish paper was perfectly suited to the emerging immigrant
community as well as to the talents of the writers making their first
forays into the literary world in Montreal. Since the readers were
more preoccupied with their economic situation than discovering
new works of literature, Wolofsky favoured the publication of short
literary texts, printed on a single page under an engaging headline.
He searched for writers capable of developing characters that would
evolve in serialized instalments with the aim of keeping subscribers
in suspense from week to week, or even from day to day. Because
they enjoyed tremendous prestige among the Jewish masses, poets
were welcome at the *Eagle,* where the editor-in-chief gave them pride
of place, most often grouped together on a page devoted to literature. This receptiveness to first-rate literature was further accentuated
when, in 1912, Wolofsky recruited as the *Adler's* editor-in-chief none
other than Reuben Brainin (1862–1939), a man whose international
reputation in the world of Jewish letters had preceded him. One of
the fathers of modern Hebrew literature, Brainin had championed
the Jewish Enlightenment in Vienna, Odessa, Moscow, Warsaw, and
Berlin. Moreover, he had participated in the founding of the Zionist
movement, and had helped to propagate its basic principles in
Eastern Europe. When he arrived in Montreal in 1912 at the age of
50, Brainin, already a renowned intellectual and journalist, set out to
promote the best local writers and consolidate Montreal's Yiddish cultural network. Among his other achievements were the creation of the
first Yiddish-language schools in Montreal, for which he devised the
curriculum, and the founding of the Jewish Public Library. Five years
later, in 1919, he was among those who paved the way for the emergence of the Canadian Jewish Congress, the first Canada-wide Jewish
communal institution. Beginning in 1912, Brainin recruited the best

Yiddish writers in Europe, as well as promising local talent, to write for the *Keneder Adler*.

> He brought to his readers the contribution of the best Yiddish authors, most of whom he knew intimately; including I. L. Peretz, Shalom Aleichem, Mendele Mokher Sforim (Sholem Yankev Abramovitch), Jonah Rosenfeld, Abraham and Sarah Reisen, Nahum Sokolow, Der Nister (Pinchus Kahanovich), Zalman Shneur, Micah Joseph Berdichevsky, Simon Bernfeld, Baal-Makhshoves (Israel Isidor Elyashev), D. Friedman, Hersh Nomberg, Moshe Nadir, Sholem Asch, Peretz Hirschbein and Isaac-Meir Weissenberg.
>
> Among the other contributors whom Brainin welcomed to his pages were Montrealers A. B. Bennett, young Yehuda Kaufman, Israel Figler, Leiser Mendl Bernstein, J. Kirschbaum, his brother Isaac Brainin and his son Joseph, and Ontario resident Melekh Grafstein.[31]

In the early 1910s, the Montreal Jewish literary community was abuzz with excitement. A faint echo of this vibrancy must have reached the young poet who worked from morning to night in a garment factory near the harbour. Perhaps an issue of the *Eagle* read by another worker during the lunch break had fallen into his hands. Perhaps he had benefited from the contact his brother Nehemia had established with various members of the *Eagle*'s editorial staff. In this regard, we only have the testimony of Chaim Leib Fox who states that from the time Nehemia Segal came to this country, he wrote poems in Yiddish which appeared in the *Jewish Daily Eagle*.[32]

Caiserman described J. I. Segal as a shy and solitary young man who eventually summoned the courage to submit his manuscripts to the editor of the *Eagle* in person. "Only on Saturdays would he sometimes very timidly go to Main Street to purchase a few notebooks which he filled with poems over the course of the week."[33] This continued for a while until the poet finally summoned the courage to meet Brainin and personally hand him some poems. The first meeting with Brainin could not have taken place prior to September of 1912 because Brainin was still managing the Hebrew-language New York periodical *HaDror*. Nor could it have been after December 1914, when the famous intellectual had a falling out with the owner of the *Eagle* for ideological reasons, over the future evolution of Zionism. By all appearances, Segal walked into the office of the great Zionist thinker at the earliest in 1914 when he had just turned 18 years of age and was working full-time in a clothing factory. In notes he made some thirty years later, Caiserman gave this account of the conversation between the young worker and the imposing Brainin:

> When a timid Segal finally made the decision to have his poems printed in the newspaper, Reuben Brainin was the editor-in-chief of the *Keneder Adler*. Segal, with uncertain steps, came to see him and gave him a poem entitled *Helft* [Help]. The poem was about the pogrom in Proskurov. Brainin read the poem, got up from his chair, and handed it back to the shy poet. He praised the poem and asked him to bring more of his poetry.[34]

In the Pages of *Jewish Daily Eagle*

The much desired interview yielded no immediate results, and Segal returned home with nothing other than the compliments of the great champion of the Jewish cultural renaissance. By late 1914, once Brainin had severed his relationship with the *Eagle*, the young writer had no reason to hope that his work would be published in the news-paper. The poem entitled *"Helft* [Help]," mentioned by Caiserman in his biography of Segal, appeared in 1915, almost one year later. This was apparently the first time that Segal had published any of his work in the Montreal Yiddish press (see Appendix 3).

Help

Brothers, can you see the flames,
The raging seas of blood and tears
Of those with whom you lived for years
Sharing suffering and joys.

Can you feel the great disaster,
Can you grasp the tragic fate
Of your closest friends and loved ones
How they perish, disappear.

In battle fall the strong, the sturdy,
The old are driven from their homes
Betrayed by foes to Tsar and Kaiser.
Women and young girls despoiled.

Jewish homes are razed and shattered
Fathers shot and stabbed and hanged
You, the only hope of orphans,
Don't stay deaf to their despair.

Will you leave them to their suffering
Tortured, hunted everywhere?
Won't you help the ones still struggling
In that bloody storm of hate?

How can you absolve your conscience
When you let their blood be spilled,
When you do not share your morsel,
And leave them starving in the streets.

Only you can save your dear ones
Even though you're far away.
They extend their hands and beg you:
"Save our lives as best you can!"

Save your father, mother, children.
Help them, you must not delay.
Extinguish now the deadly fires
Lest we all be swept away.[35]

There is no doubt that the poet could count on the support of Hershl Hirsh who had become the editor-in-chief of the *Eagle* and wished to pursue the same editorial policy as his illustrious predecessor. Born in the Ukraine in 1880, Hirsch had immigrated to the United States in 1904. In 1913 he was the first editor-in-chief of *Der Yidisher Zhurnal* which, despite its official English name, the *Daily Hebrew Journal*, was the Yiddish daily newspaper in Toronto. When Brainin left, Wolofsky decided to lure Hirsch to Montreal to run the *Adler*. A Hebraist and multi-talented writer, Hirsch wrote literary texts which suited the tastes of his readership and could fit, without too much difficulty, into its limited number of pages. For several years the *Eagle* was only six large pages long on weekdays, while on Sundays and certain Jewish holidays, it grew to eight pages. Fox notes that

for many years he [Hirsch] himself did translations from old Yiddish literature, and, in addition to his own poems, epigrams, satirical personal commentaries on subjects of public interest

called *feletons*, and articles on various topics, he also published his
own translations from Hebrew [into Yiddish] of liturgical verses,
prayers, and chapters from the prophets.[36]

Hirsch had tried his hand at various literary genres, including a play
entitled *Der politisher* (the politician) that was performed in Canada
and the United States, serialized novels, and two books of fables.[37]
Over the years, many of his pieces had been reprinted in the North
American Yiddish press, in particular in the *Eagle*. As soon as he
moved to Montreal, Hirsch decided to attract young writers who
were capable of improving the literary quality of the *Eagle* without
becoming a drain on its very limited budget. Among these young
writers was an unknown by the name of J. I. Segal, whose career was
launched thanks to the open-mindedness and good will of the editor-
in-chief, Hershl Hirsch.

Segal's first poem to appear in the *Eagle*, entitled *"Helft,"* described
his response to a pogrom. Here the poet was following the Eastern
European Jewish literary tradition of recording violent attacks against
Jews, in particular the pogroms perpetrated in the Ukraine under the
Cossack leader Bogdan Khmelnitsky in 1648,[38] notorious to this day
for their scale and magnitude. A few years earlier, great Jewish writers had been incited by more recent history to write about pogroms in
the Russian Empire such as those in Kishinev in 1903 and 1905, which
had a profound impact on the entire Jewish world at the time.[39] In
response to the 1903 pogrom in Kishinev, then the capital of the province of Bessarabia, for example, the celebrated poet Chaim Nachman
Bialik (1873–1934) composed a poem in Hebrew entitled "In the City
of Slaughter"[40] that had important ramifications in both nationalist
and Zionist circles. *"Helft"* was Segal's reaction to the atrocities committed by the Russian army at the beginning of World War I against
Jewish communities near the German border accused of collaborating
with the enemy. In 1915 the brutal treatment of Eastern Europe's Jews
by the Tsarist armies preoccupied the Montreal Jewish community.[41]
Undoubtedly this climate of indignation worked to Segal's advantage
when the time came to submit his poem to the editor of the *Eagle* who
was well aware of the mood of his readership.

What can be said about the first poem that J. I. Segal published?
Comprised of eight verses with a complex structure, *"Helft"* incorpo-
rates the traditional Jewish values of charity and compassion toward
victims of violence, especially in the context of anti-Jewish persecution.

Composed in a Hebraized literary Yiddish, this poem evokes the type of event in Eastern European Jewish history that until then had had no equivalent in North American Jewish life. Hence, the imagery in *"Helft"* is derived exclusively from the old country. This poem gives no indication as yet of Segal's rootedness in Canada, his interest in the Yiddish literary movements born in America, nor his desire to become acquainted with new cultural influences. In 1915 the young poet was still too much of a newcomer to Montreal for these developments to manifest themselves in his writing. The poem's level of literary maturity, however, probably led the readers of the *Eagle* to believe that that they had come across the work of a seasoned writer skilled in his craft. What is more, Segal's first poem had appeared in a daily newspaper which had never really had the opportunity to publish established local writers, with the exception of Reuben Brainin. Nor could it count on regular access to the work of authors whose renown had spread beyond the Canadian Jewish community. The majority of the *Eagle's* readers were immigrants who were not in the habit of reading work of highly original writers. In the unsophisticated milieu of Montreal Yiddish literature in 1915 at that time, how could a writer's work or talent be assessed? What criteria could the Montreal Jewish reader have applied? Who in Montreal would have been in a position to evaluate work that barely reached a few hundred people scattered throughout Canada's vast expanses? It is easy to speculate that in these years of mass immigration the *Eagle* would have been read distractedly by people consumed by their daily chores with little concern for quality when it came to the Yiddish language. Other than a small group of educated people who had inadvertently ended up in Canada, those who bought the newspaper were mostly young people unschooled in literature, at the mercy of external events, and more interested in finding objective news in a familiar cultural context.

The identity and the career of J. I. Segal were to remain a mystery for a while longer because his work was not published in the *Keneder Adler* again until November 22, 1916. On that date there appeared a short poem in three verses entitled *"In mayn shtetl"* which the editor-in-chief characterized as a "war poem." Like *"Helft,"* its theme was the destruction of Jewish life, but in a more intimate context where the poet presents himself as personally afflicted by the tragic events of World War I. This time Segal imagines he is back in the Korets of his childhood, the first expression of an attachment that would keep growing in his writing.

In My Little Town

My imagination transports me home
    To my small, faraway shtetl.
Searching through its ruins
    I find no one.

Houses, like grey mourners,
    Stand fearful, staring from afar
As though trashed without mercy
    By a shameless demon.

A black crow
    Hovering above a naked autumn tree
Stripped of each and every leaf
    Caws the mourners' prayer.[42]

In the meantime, the *Eagle* had published several short pieces with biblical motifs by Hershl Hirsch or disguised translations. During this same period there appeared a few short anonymous poems described by Hirsch as "folk songs," which were actually popular songs that the editor inserted among longer articles. From time to time the *Eagle* presented poems by two much appreciated American Yiddish populist writers, Morris Rosenfeld (1862–1923) and Mark Warshawski (1848–1907) whose work resonated with the working masses. Beginning in 1916, Shimon Nepom, a Ukrainian Jew who had been living in Canada since 1908, began carving out a place for himself on the pages of the *Eagle*, almost on a weekly basis. Although many years his senior, Nepom like Segal worked as an unskilled labourer, including as a streetcar conductor. His poetry reflected his life, dealing with subjects accessible to all in unpretentious language. Soon Segal began publishing alongside Nepom in the *Eagle*, and their work alternated while occasionally leaving room for the contributions of Hirsch and later, beginning in 1918, Joseph Leiser Kaluschiner.[43] Within the amorphous Montreal Yiddish cultural universe of the 1910s, Segal's creative and evocative use of language was very rare. In his unfinished biography of Segal, Caiserman noted that beginning in late 1916, the young clothing worker sent Hirsch a packet of poems on a weekly basis. This time, Segal's output did not go unnoticed in the Yiddish-language literary firmament that was emerging in Montreal:

A weekly column of his poetry began appearing in the *Keneder Adler*. These were poems with lyrical motifs and descriptions of nature written quite differently than his previous work, poems which created a stir in the small literary family at that time. From week to week we noticed in Segal's poetry, although still technically unsophisticated, his experimentation with new words.[44]

Caiserman also mentions that a series of Segal's poems about Passover appeared in the *Eagle* in 1917. They made a strong impression on those few people who had been fostering Yiddish writing in Montreal for some time. Since 1910, the city had become home to an informal circle of Yiddish writers at the centre of which was the anarchist sympathizer Moshe Shmuelsohn, an immigrant born in the Ukraine who had arrived in Montreal in 1907. An ordinary labourer his entire life, Shmuelsohn was motivated by a veritable passion for Yiddish literature.[45] He was also the driving force behind the first Yiddish Writers Association (*shrayber farayn*) founded in the immigrant neighbourhood near the Montreal harbour. Gathered around him were young authors such as Getsl Zelikovitch (1855–1923), Dr. Ezekiel Vortsman, and M. Kaplan. His circle also included B.G. Sack, Shimon Nepom, S. Shneyer, Nahum Perlman, and A. M. Mandelbaum, all of whom wrote in one form or another for the *Eagle*. Soon after his arrival in Montreal in 1910, Caiserman began to participate in the weekly meetings of this group which often met in Shmuelsohn's home. At this juncture it should be recalled that the *Eagle* the centre of intense community activity. Each day its offices faced an onslaught of penniless immigrants in search of work, advice, or a recommendation for a post in a community organization. In his memoirs Wolofsky provides several examples of individuals coming to him to have a Canadian government form translated, to fill out a citizenship application, or to find the means to bring their families to Canada from the Russian Empire. Similarly, the editorial staff of the *Eagle* was constantly beset by an assortment of typesetters seeking employment, journalists in search of news, writers in need of readers, and advertisers impatient to meet their deadlines. In this state of affairs, it was no wonder that a timid young poet went unnoticed.

In 1917, it took the members the first Montreal literary circle no time at all to realize that a new star had been born in the modest pantheon of Canadian Yiddish letters. No one in the Writers Association had ever heard of J. I. Segal or his story. How could such a talent have blossomed in the small world of Montreal Yiddish without any prior indications? What was the source of Segal's creative impulse? Where had he received his basic literary training? That such work could spring up all of a sudden in the still uncultivated Jewish immigrant neighbourhoods, was astonishing. Caiserman described the situation in an unpublished manuscript:

> One day we were all intrigued by the few poems which appeared in the *Canader Adler* [*sic*] by one J. I. Segal. No one knew him, but his poems which often appeared made an impression. [. . .] J. I. Segal's name became a problem of literary discussion at the weekly meetings in Schmuelsohn's home. We visited the editor of the *Canader Adler*, Mr. Hirsch, to obtain information about J. I. Segal – if old or young, Canadian or a recent arrival from overseas; but Mr. Hirsch did not know. He only knew that a young man is depositing in the office packs of poems and disappears![46]

It is not surprising that the publication of Segal's first poems created a sensation among Montreal's Yiddish-speaking literati, despite the mystery surrounding the author's identity. Members of the Writers Association that had formed around Shmuelsohn were not merely interested in noting the emergence of literary production in the city, somewhat in the manner of an objective learned society devoted primarily to the study of scholarly texts. For these individuals, Yiddish writing had symbolic value and showcased Jewish national vitality in an extraordinary way. That a new form of literature was making its debut in a place as far removed from the Eastern European diaspora as Canada meant that a strong wind was blowing all the way from distant Russia to Montreal, carrying with it the long-awaited promise of a Yiddish cultural revival. Was this not proof that Jews were in the process of liberating themselves from the political and cultural oppression they had suffered for centuries, and from its disastrous cultural consequences? According to available documents, Shmuelsohn and his colleagues saw each of Segal's early poems as the sign of a promise fulfilled, indeed the first manifestation of an accomplishment of biblical proportions: the appearance in the rarefied air of the Canadian wilderness of first-rate work finally free to express itself without any restrictions. Moreover, at the beginning of the twentieth century the Yiddish cultural universe was crowned with such glory that each book published in that language assumed prophetic proportions. Was Yiddish not the vehicle for the propagation of revolution and modern ideas among the Eastern European Jewish masses? Had it not attracted great minds capable of rallying the energies of the youth? Was it not the embodiment of a profound social transformation experienced by all of Russian Jewry? In Montreal, Yiddish gave rise to a new intelligentsia, galvanized by the attempted Russian Revolution of 1905 whose slogans were followed with intense political fervour.

The Revelation of 1917

It is understandable that in the unique circumstances in which Eastern European Jewish immigrants found themselves, a new ray of light on the Montreal Yiddish literary landscape was received with enthusiasm and satisfaction. The Yiddish-speaking milieu had such a thirst for culture that the least spark was considered of prime importance. With Segal's breakthrough, the emotion and enthusiasm emanating from Shmuelsohn's circle of literati reached their peak. Rarely was an opening salvo received with as much hope and trepidation in Montreal Yiddish letters. In a northern wilderness like Canada, where no Jewish literature worthy of that name had ever bloomed before, and where the Jews themselves were mainly immigrants who had only recently left their birthplace, Segal was quickly seen as a David on his way to slay Goliath. It seemed to his enthusiastic readers that Segal, pathetically ill-equipped, had attained the very summit of his art armed only with his courage. That the sounds of Yiddish literature could echo so confidently at the foot of Mount Royal, and that a circle of connoisseurs had been there to recognize its significance, was a phenomenon beyond comprehension. Caiserman was so moved by this unexpected turn of events that he remembered it vividly for the rest of his life. In this sense his effusive reaction reflected the outstanding accomplishment associated with artistic and literary endeavours in the Yiddish-language in those days. In fact, Caiserman never lost his youthful passion for Yiddish, a passion shared by many of his generation. Thanks to Segal, the foundation was finally being laid for a solid building that would be enlarged unexpectedly over the following decades. Who the author of the poems in the *Adler* actually was had yet to be discovered. This is what Caiserman had to say on this subject in his biography of Segal:

> It was the time when the tailors of Montreal were being organized into a Trade Union; when the author of this biography acted as a chairman of the Union, and when regular weekly meetings took

place at Coronation Hall situated on St. Lawrence Boulevard between Dorchester Street[47] and St. Catherine West. [. . .] As already indicated, the Jewish writers at the time were few — and in friendly relations. The Jewish newspaper of the Community was a rallying point for the writers.[48]

Jacob Isaac Segal and his brother-in-law Abraham Shlomo Shkolnikov (left), Montreal, 1920. (Montreal Jewish Public Library.)

The mystery surrounding Segal was solved in the most unexpected way. While Shmuelsohn's colleagues who met in his flat were searching among devotees of Yiddish culture for an individual of high intellectual stature, someone who could personify literature in the elitist Russian manner, Caiserman was told that the J. I. Segal in question was a member of his own union, a young tailor who had recently immigrated to Canada. "The Meetings of the Tailors Union were attended by hundreds of Men and Women, and an inquiry revealed that J. I. Segal was a worker in the needle industry. It was thus that we found the poet Segal."[49] The matter must have taken some time since Caiserman describes the efforts of the Montreal Yiddish authors to locate Segal as if it were a real adventure.[50] However, it is difficult to imagine two such disparate personalities as those of Caiserman and Segal. In 1917 Caiserman was one of the principal leaders of the very powerful Tailors' Union while Segal was unquestionably among the lowliest of its members. Coming to Montreal in 1910, H. M. Caiserman immediately set to work organizing a tailors union affiliated with the United Garment Workers of America (UGWA). That year, before the creation of a true labour movement, the work week in the clothing industry increased to fifty-five hours and even higher for those who worked for sub-contractors. Furthermore, the economic crisis of 1907 had destroyed several of the existing labour organizations in that sector, leaving the tailors with no means of improving their lot. Thanks to activists like Caiserman, a new membership drive took place under the auspices of the United Garment Workers of America (the UGWA), with the result that in June of 1912 its Montreal branch declared the first general strike of mens' clothing workers in the city. It was joined by nearly 5,000 employees from twenty manufacturing firms, 90 per cent of which were owned by Jews:

> From almost his first day in Canada in 1910, comrade H. M. Caiserman devoted himself to the cause of the UGWA. Although he was not a tailor by trade, he earned the respect of all the tailors thanks to his talent as an orator, his persuasive speeches, and his dedication [. . .] by 1912 he had won the loyalty of the tailors to such an extent that they elected him president of the union, a post he held for two years, excluding the duration of the general strike.[51]

According to community and union activist Simon Belkin, the 1912 strike ended after seven weeks with a number of substantial gains for the workers, including the establishment of a forty-four hour work week, the end of the practice of subcontracting by manufacturers, and an increase the amount paid for piece-work, all of which would certainly have had an impact on the family of young Segal.[52] A second general strike took place in Montreal at the beginning of 1917, at the very moment that Segal was launching his literary career. Once again the economic situation of the tailors improved. However, the garment workers' unions were not just involved in improving the material conditions of the working class. Early on their leaders were also concerned with providing their members with a communal environment that could give them the opportunity to continue their education, improve their personal lives, and better adapt to Canadian society. In fact, in Montreal in the early twentieth century, the main groupings of needle trade workers had been infiltrated by various left-wing ideologies, many of which reflected the political situation of the Jews in the Russian Empire. Cells in all the factories and sweatshops actively promoting anarchist, socialist and left-wing Zionist ideas—and later Communist ideas—were all connected to cultural and literary groups which tried to agitate among the Jewish working class. Caiserman belonged to that generation of activists. He was convinced that organizing the labour force in the needle trades required more intense cultural and political activism. For him, the unionization of Jewish works also meant a struggle to make Yiddish central to the community's evolution:

> He acted this way because he driven by a powerful belief in justice and equal rights for the workers. His aim was always to improve and ennoble the life of the Jewish neighbourhood. That is why he was so interested in the emergence and development of Yiddish culture and literature . . . He was the first professional union leader in Montreal who facilitated the inclusion of intellectual and cultural activities among the city's organized Jewish workers.[53]

While Caiserman proved to be a gifted individual with inexhaustible energy when it came to organizing, or, in Belkin's words, "a new and powerful force among Montreal's Jewish workers,"[54] Segal was the exact opposite. Several eyewitnesses from this period agree on the fact that the poet was introverted, sensitive, and entirely focussed on his writing. Israel Rabinovitch, who became the editor of the *Eagle* in 1924, described him as "a traveller lost in the desert."[55] Almost ten years older than Segal, Caiserman did not take long to grasp the benefit that the Yiddish-speaking community of Montreal could derive from the unexpected appearance of this literary talent. For that reason, he quickly undertook to introduce Segal to the small circle to which his most sophisticated readers belonged. One can easily imagine that this was the first time that the poet had left the confines of his immediate family and his acquaintances in the factory. The evening was not without its tensions. According to Caiserman:

> Segal then, was young and shy and somewhat scared. But the warm reception at the small gathering, and in the fine atmosphere, J. I. Segal relaxed. He was later asked if he had brought along a few of his poems. Instead of an answer, he placed on the table a pack of poems. It was a literary holiday. Each poem was read and commented upon and a real enthusiasm enveloped all.[56]

Nothing similar had ever occurred in Yiddish-speaking Montreal in terms of both the depth of the literary discussion and the originality of the writing.

Despite their fondness for Yiddish literature, their more advanced age, and the richness of their cultural life, several of the members of the Writers' Association found themselves in more or less the same social circumstances as the young poet J. I. Segal. Moshe Shmuelsohn, who had asked Hershl Hirsch for more information about Segal, had begun his literary career in New York. He had written novels, sketches, satirical pieces and plays for newspapers and other periodicals on both sides of the border. Most of his writing addressed popular topics or described the daily life in an Eastern European *shtetl*. When he met Segal in 1917, Shmuelson was regularly publishing traditional novellas in the *Eagle* that frequently related to his childhood in the Ukraine. Except for Simon Nepom, Shmuelson's colleagues at the Montreal Yiddish daily were writers known in the local press for their prose-writing. Moreover, several members of the Yiddish WritersAssociation had only lived in Montreal for a few years, such as, for example, Dr. Ezekiel Vortsman who was the editor-in-chief of the *Eagle* from July of 1910 until February of 1912 and worked as a journalist. Others, like A.M. Mandelbaum, were only inspired to write for a short time before devoting themselves to other more lucrative pursuits. Most of the Yiddish literature enthusiasts grouped around

Shmuelsohn did not have a clear grasp of modernism in Jewish literature. The majority treated conventional subject matter, inspired in
particular by Bible stories and other religious themes, such as the celebration of Jewish holidays, the lives of great historical personalities,
and the moral teachings of the Talmud. Brought together by chance,
these first Yiddish writers in Montreal were a rather motley crew.
Many of them left soon afterward to settle in various American cities.

Several of these authors, such as Simon Nepom, had not
received much education and were forced to spend all their energies
as unskilled labourers just to make ends meet. Hence, they wrote
sporadically and in a tone that reflected their proletarian existence.
In other words, they produced literature in which their immediate
social and ideological preoccupations were featured. Although fifteen
years older than Segal, Nepom began his career at the *Adler* at the
same time as Segal. Initially he had a fair amount of success in the
paper. However, he soon became a proletarian poet, writing about the
life of the workers, as evidenced by his first series of poems entitled
Tramvay lider (Streetcar Poems) as well as his book of poems published
in Toronto in 1926 entitled *In gerangl* (In Struggle). As for Caiserman,
who had been the president of the tailor's union without actually
working at this trade, he came to Shmuelsohn without claiming to be a
writer. Of course, he had published articles in Europe in the Rumanian
and French working-class press, and had become a major contributor
to the *Eagle* in 1910. Most of his contributions, however, were either
political or social commentary. Aware more than anyone of the limits
of his own literary ability in the Yiddish language, Caiserman instead
sought to find that rare pearl who would do honour to all of Jewish
Montreal. When Segal came to meet these men, all of whom were his
seniors, Caiserman immediately understood that the great moment
had finally arrived.

The Emergence of Yiddish Literature in Montreal

Everyone who met Segal at Shmuelsohn's home remarked that the
poet's compositions in no way resembled any of the Yiddish literature
published in Canada up until then. The poet gave the impression of
having found his own path to a dazzling modernity that had eluded
his predecessors who were either still nostalgic for life in Eastern
Europe or too preoccupied with reproducing the traditional forms
of biblical literature. Without rejecting the old country and its Jewish

values dating back thousands of years, Segal's writing resolutely positioned itself squarely in the new social conditions experienced by North American immigrants. The poet liked to contemplate the contemporary world and the North American cities, including Montreal, which for him were so amazing. His poems were also marked by lofty ethical sentiments and a novel esthetic which astonished his first audience. The latter was all the more striking for his first serious readers as they quickly grasped that what Segal had published in the *Eagle* in 1917 did not represent the full scope of his literary talent. The Writers' Association led by Shmuelsohn recognized that Segal had submitted only his shorter poems since they were more likely to find some room among the already crowded pages of the Montreal daily Yiddish newspaper. As subsequent events would show, in his boxes full of poetry he also had lengthier compositions which he immediately shared with his mentors. Decades later, Caiserman still recalled his surprise at the writing of the young Montreal prodigy: "They were a new form of poetry of a pronounced lyricism, singing of nature, of poverty, of social phenomena, in a manner which greatly excelled [exceeded] the [Yiddish] poetry of the day."[57]

In 1917, the enthusiasm that seized the members of the Montreal Writers' Association should be considered a turning point for Montreal Yiddish literature. When this unexpected revelation occurred, there was some consensus about the possible emergence of this much awaited cultural phenomenon, and its future on Canadian soil. This was the first time that such an event had taken place.

Although Shmuelsohn's circle consisted of only a dozen people, all of them immigrants who had been in the country for less than ten years, it was nonetheless attentive to the least sign announcing the presence of a Yiddish cultural life in the city. With Segal, a decisive step forward had been taken, a step which the literary circle, as modest as it was, hurried to recognize and encourage. In this country, still without significant Yiddish cultural achievements, and so far from the Eastern European centre of gravity, the fact that a young timid worker was determined to write poetry after a long day of work seemed like a miracle. Emotions reached their climax when it turned out, after closer examination, that Segal surpassed all their hopes. The Writers Association was not going to stop here, and it was decided to publish, then and there, the work that Segal had shown in part to his hosts on the evening of their first encounter. Caiserman states categorically that "it was then and there that these poems were published in the

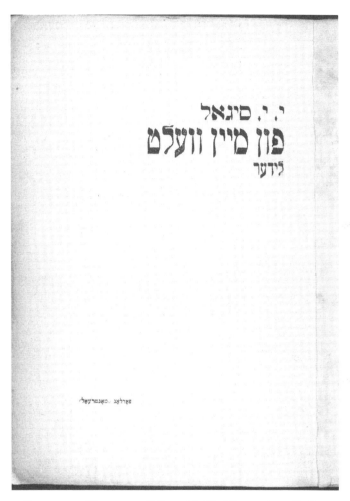

Cover page of *Fun mayn velt* (From My World), a poetry collection
published in 1918 by J. I. Segal. (Canadian Jewish Congress Archives.)

first volume of Segal—called *Vun mein Welt* (From my World)."[58] This
unforeseen event revealed the existence of a still embryonic Yiddish-
language literary project that seemed to have a brilliant future.

So it was that in the last trimester of the year 1918[59] *Fun mayn
velt*, the first collection of poems in the history of Quebec Yiddish literature, was published. This booklet of sixty-seven pages, printed at
712 St. Lawrence Boulevard,[60] was the second of its kind to appear in
Canada.[61] A few weeks later, in February of 1919, Caiserman's review
of Segal's collection was published in the monthly publication *Der*

Yidisher Arbeter (The Jewish Worker). This was the first piece of literary criticism in all of Canadian Yiddish literature.[62] As he wrote a few
years later, "It was my privilege to write and publish the very first
review on Segal's book. I then expressed the confidence that the recognized Jewish literary critics will acknowledge him as a great lyric poet
that has appeared on the literary firmament of Jewish literature."[63]
The same year that Segal's work was disseminated outside the narrow
circle of his admirers, Shmuelsohn published in New York an anthology of fiction entitled *Veltn un tsaytn: ertseylungen un skitsn* (Worlds
and eras: stories and sketches)[64] which he had previously published
in the North American Yiddish press. Very well received by the critics, this work contained short pieces about traditional life in Eastern
Europe, immigration to North America, and family life on both sides
of the Atlantic. Although it belonged more to American Yiddish literature, due to the nature of its readers, Shmuelsohn's collection was
an important contribution to Montreal's cultural environment. In his
memoirs, Caiserman states that the title of the book was suggested to
the author by none other than the poet Segal.

Those years, which saw the founding of the *Keneder Adler* (*Jewish
Daily Eagle*) and the first attempts at journalism, provided the foundation that would make possible the launching of literary careers. In
1919, following the conclusion of World War I, two outstanding figures
did not take long to make a name for themselves in the Montreal community: the poet J. I. Segal, and the literary critic H. M. Caiserman.
Thus, after almost a decade of Montreal Yiddish literature created
mostly by immigrant writers adapting to the New World, and whose
sojourn in Canada was generally very brief, it could henceforth count
on two men who were personally connected with the life of the city.
In addition, they were united by a strong friendship in which they
each played a complementary role, and which would prove essential
to the future development of Yiddish literature in Montreal. Segal, for
his part, embarked upon a long career of literary creativity that would
earn him an international reputation in the Yiddish world. Caiserman,
on the other hand, was there at the right time to interpret and place
this artistic outpouring in a Canadian Jewish context that until then
had been fluid and formless. We already know that in 1917 Caiserman
had had a front row seat when Segal met the members of the Writers
Association grouped around Moshe Shmuelsohn. This moment
constituted the launching of a literary tradition that Caiserman had
ardently wished to see blossom in Montreal, and to which he gave his

utmost attention for decades. Thanks to his critical essays and analyses, most written at a later date, we are in a better position today to follow the thread that led to the flourishing of Yiddish literature in that city. Therefore, before continuing, it seems important to present the biography of the man who made such an extraordinary and multifaceted contribution upon which the literary ascent of the young Segal essentially depended. Years later, the poet did not hesitate to thank his friend Caiserman for his vote of confidence from the very beginning:

> In Caiserman's home my early attempts at poetry found warm encouragement. Were I not afraid of appearing to be sentimental I would say he was my guardian angel. The first to bring me encouragement were H. Novek[65] and Caiserman. In those days I did so need a warm, friendly glance, the true word of an understanding person.
>
> How much this meant for me in those days of strange, frightening solitude; days when I had to go alone, make a way for myself, for no one else could help me![66]

Caiserman in Montreal

Fortunately, Caiserman has left behind numerous autobiographical documents that provide a fairly accurate picture of his first days in Canada. According to available information, he reached the port of Montreal on the evening of July 2, 1910, aboard the steamship *Montrose*, which at that time belonged to the Canadian Pacific Railway Company. Twenty-six years old when he disembarked in Canada, this young man had been active in the union movement as well as in Zionist organizations in both Bucharest and Paris.[67] In the harbour, he was met by his parents and several brothers and sisters, who had been living in Canada for some time.[68] Relatively well established, the family shared a flat on City Hall Street, a few steps north of Ontario Street. At that time their neighbourhood was outside the area of the highest concentration of Eastern European Jewish immigrants, which was further south around De la Gauchetière Street. The active members of his family worked either in the needle trades or in cigar-making establishments. Hence, the income of the Caisermans in 1910 was presumably slightly above average for the Montreal Jewish working-class. Since the majority of recent Jewish immigrants were mainly employed as tailors, upon his arrival H. M. Caiserman was encouraged by his brothers to learn tailoring and join the ranks of the thousands of Yiddish-speaking workers who spent long hours at their sewing machines. The brothers, however, had not taken into account the fiery temperament of the young immigrant from Rumania who thought it was his duty to help organize the workers in the needle trades left to their own devices after many unsuccessful attempts to unionize them. In fact, from the moment that Caiserman got off the boat in Montreal he already had aspirations of spreading the message of political radicalism and revolution among his co-religionists in the crowded sweatshops. Several years later he described his first day of work in a sweatshop as follows:

> My younger brother worked at Wolman's on Notre-Dame Street. Early the following morning, I went there with my brother who made an arrangement with the owner for me to learn tailoring there. Entering the factory, I saw about twenty people seated at sewing machines, one right beside the other. I shouted a friendly "Good morning!" and in reply received a "Drop dead!"
> I stood there in astonishment at such "poetic" friendliness, and unhappily took my place at a sewing machine beside my brother. He tried hard to teach me to sew in a straight line, but I was more interested in leaving the factory and find [sic] another occupation, where I could devote myself to organizing the tailors.[69]

At the same time, Caiserman discovered Elstein's bookstore on Ontario East, as well as the one owned by Harry (Hirsch) Hershman on nearby St. Lawrence Boulevard. In both stores one could find socialist literature and various trade union pamphlets in Yiddish.[70] Among those who congregated in these bookshops were members of the radical intelligentsia who were likely to support the young Caiserman in his quest for justice, with the major demands of the Eastern European Left still fresh in his memory. Considering how quickly he became the president of the Tailors' Union in Montreal—a matter of months—we can assume that Caiserman possessed extraordinary powers of persuasion. Less than two years later, thanks to his oratorical skills and organizational abilities, this immigrant from Rumania found himself at the head of the leading labour organization in the men's garment industry. At that point in time, the majority of the skilled workers in the clothing trades were Jewish. Every day, immediately after arriving in Montreal, dozens of Eastern European immigrants tried to find work in this growing segment of the economy. As Hershman recounted in an article dated 1927–1928, many of the immigrants on their way to Canada had passed through large cities in England, or New York, where factory owners had acquired more advanced machinery, which the Montreal manufacturers now wished to acquire in order to speed up the production process.[71] Among the working class, there were several individuals committed to the ideologies of anarchism, socialism and cooperativism who did not require much persuasion to join organized protest movements. Caiserman must have immediately felt at home in this bubbling cauldron of ideas.

Nevertheless, Caiserman was not going to stop there. During that period of new beginnings, the clothing unions were often used by Jewish ideologues for their own purposes. Zionists, Yiddishists, adherents of the various Russian socialist movements, and community activists, all took advantage of the platform provided by the labour organizations to advance their own agendas and promote their political objectives. In fact, up until the end of the 1930s, the worker's associations in the garment industry constituted the best organized and most unified sector in the Jewish community. For that reason, activists of various persuasions thronged to them. Caiserman was no exception. While he was preoccupied with improving the social and economic conditions of the working class in general, the young immigrant also was involved in a number of Montreal Jewish cultural and political movements. Among the causes spearheaded by Caiserman in the second decade of the twentieth century were the creation of the first Yiddish-language schools, the founding of a worker's public library, the formation of a labour Zionist party among the working classes, and the founding of a central organization to coordinate the harmonious development of the Canadian Jewish community. Caiserman also set up an organization to assist immigrants and refugees, and fought for ongoing support for Zionist institutions in Palestine. Of course, Caiserman was not the only one to engage in such projects. In most cases he enjoyed the lively collaboration of his colleagues who were also active in union struggles. Several accounts attest to his contribution in these key areas during the "heroic" period of Montreal Jewish history. Louis Rosenberg, who immigrated to Calgary in 1915, one of the greatest intellectuals in the Yiddish-speaking Jewish community, emphasized in 1944 that Caiserman's contribution was remarkable in a number of ways:

Ever since his arrival in Canada 34 years ago, his effervescent spirit has been active in almost every phase of Jewish public life. He had barely exchanged the pitching decks of the steamship for the steep streets of Montreal when he became one of the founders of the Jewish Public Library in 1910,[72] and later was among the founders of the Jewish Folk School and the Peretz School.

An active worker in the Poalei Zion, the Jewish National Workers' Alliance and the Rumanian Farband, with the outbreak of the first World War he threw himself into the work for the relief of Jewish war sufferers, and was one of the founders of the Canadian Jewish Alliance in 1915, and later of the Canadian Jewish Congress, which he helped to organize and of which he became the General Secretary in March, 1919.[73]

Caiserman's enthusiasm, his profound empathy, and the intensity of his rhetoric were especially evident in January of 1911 when the plan was hatched to found the first part-time Yiddish-language school for Jewish pupils to attend in the afternoons at the end of their school day in the schools run by the Protestant School Board.[74] The school was intended to teach the children of immigrants the rudiments of the Yiddish language and the progressive ideas of their parents. Situated on Dante Street near Casgrain, it was called the Mile End School after the name of the neighbourhood in which it was located. This was soon followed in May of 1913 by the opening of the National Radical School[75] on Prince Arthur, where over one hundred pupils were registered almost immediately. According to Simon Belkin, the purpose of this new school was "to inculcate in the Jewish youth a sense of belonging to the Jewish people, enable them to resist the trend toward assimilation, and instil in them a heightened notion of truth and justice in relation to their own people and to all of humanity."[76] In September 1914, when a group of dissidents decided to create the Jewish People's School (the *Folk Shule*) in the neighbourhood around Saint Urbain Street, Caiserman again put his nose to the grindstone.[77] This schism occurred after a quarrel had erupted among the members of the Poale Zion, a socialist Zionist party, about the respective places of Yiddish and Hebrew in the curriculum. Caiserman also supported the Jewish Public Library, a project that began in Montreal around 1912, with the aim of providing Yiddish speakers with an institution where they could continue their education and remain in touch with Jewish literary activity worldwide.[78] The unions representing

clothing workers, carpenters, and bakers, as well as fraternal organizations, political parties inspired by Russia, the Zionist movements,
and several renowned activists participated in the founding of this
critically important cultural institutions, including Reuben Brainin,
then the editor in chief of the *Jewish Daily Eagle*. In May of 1914, the
library finally opened its doors on Saint Urbain Street, a few steps
north of Milton Avenue. In 1917, Caiserman became one of its first
presidents.[79]

The Poale Zion and the Founding of the Canadian Jewish Congress

Caiserman's most important commitment during this period was his
involvement in a Marxist political party launched in Russia at the
time of the 1905 Revolution, namely the Poale Zion.[80] Transplanted
to Montreal almost immediately afterward by some of its young militants, it was not long before this movement had carved out an important niche for itself in the city. Founded and headed in Eastern Europe
by Ber Borochov,[81] the Poale Zion was inspired by the Zionist fervour
which had made its appearance in central Europe a decade earlier
thanks to Theodor Herzl. This party also endorsed the Marxist concept of class struggle prevalent among the Jewish masses in the tsarist
Empire. Firmly believing in the need to maintain an attachment to a
national homeland in Palestine among the Jewish workers, the Labour
Zionists in Montreal soon realized that they had to support every
Jewish institution in Canada capable of countering the ever-present
trend toward assimilation. Driven by the desire to keep intact the
nationalist sentiments of the Jewish working class, and to support the
workers in their struggle against exploitation and social injustice, the
members of the Poalei Zion lent their support to various initiatives in
Montreal aimed at promoting Yiddish language and literature, education for the masses, and secular Jewish culture in general. They were
aware that this course of action would help keep the flame of Zionism
burning in Montreal, and make it possible to pass the torch to a new
generation. Already active in the tailors' organizations, Caiserman
joined the Poale Zion in 1914, and wholeheartedly embraced Labour
Zionism. Indeed, at this time he refocussed all his activism in that
direction. Under his leadership, members of the Poale Zion infiltrated
the garment workers' unions, and became active in the majority of
influential institutions in the community. In short, the Labour Zionists

were at the forefront in laying the groundwork for a Jewish network in Montreal. Hence, with the notable exception of strictly religious institutions, the majority of Jewish organizations that were formed in Montreal during the great migratory wave were initiated by the Poale Zion. As Simon Belkin recounts in his book:

> The party associations became centres for cultural and edu-
> cational activities. The second stage of the party's existence in
> Montreal, from 1910 to 1915, can be called the period of building
> cultural initiatives, schools, public libraries, and trade unions. It
> is true that even in the early years of their existence, the party
> associations assumed a broad role in cultural activity and trade
> union work. However, only after 1910 were these efforts realized
> to their full extent.[82]

Caiserman's participation in this community strategy reached its peak when he decided to run for office as the official candidate of the Poale Zion Party in the Montreal municipal election of April, 1916, in the Saint-Louis district, located north of Sherbrooke Street and bisected by St. Lawrence Boulevard. At the time this was an extraordinary decision. Jewish socialists or labour Zionists who immigrated to North America at the beginning of the twentieth century quickly understood that the political climate on this continent did not require specifically Jewish parties, as was the case in the Russian context of political and cultural repression. By joining existing political parties, they could make themselves heard both inside and outside the Jewish community. Unlike tsarist Russia with its perpetual revolutionary climate, where Jews were victims of violent repression, Canada was a democratic and liberal country where the Poale Zion could openly attain its goals within the unions and Jewish community institutions. By 1916, the Saint-Louis district north of Sherbrooke Street had become home to a large Yiddish-speaking population. It is possible that the Labour Zionist party found it expedient at the time to make its political agenda known to Jews less familiar with radical worker militancy (like shopkeepers and pedlars) but who shared more or less the same living conditions as the more organized factory workers. It was therefore a good opportunity to reach Jewish voters who had no particular affiliation with Zionism, but who could potentially become adherents of the progressive ideals of the Poale Zion in a more general way. Caiserman immediately printed election material in three languages, including French. Here is an example of the type of message that he wanted to deliver to his constituents:

> Over the past few years H. M. Caiserman has been one of the central figures in this city's labour movement. He has fought in City Hall for effective and radical working conditions, as well as civil rights and social equality for all national groups and minorities in this city.[83]

When it came to politics, Caiserman found himself in excellent company. At the time, Jews running for office who belonged to the more affluent social classes were essentially competing for the same voters as their representatives in both the Quebec Legislative Assembly and the Parliament of Canada. On May 22, 1916, Peter Bercovitch was elected as the MLA from Montreal-Saint-Louis,[84] becoming the first Jew to sit in the Quebec Assembly. The next year, on December 17, 1917, Samuel W. Jacobs won for the first time in a federal election in the Montreal riding of Cartier. There were two administrative units sharing a Montreal urban district that was home to Yiddish-speaking immigrants. Nonetheless, as opposed to Caiserman, who was running on behalf of a radical left-wing party rooted in the Eastern European Jewish experience, Bercovitch and Jacobs had been running for the Liberal Party, a moderate group in which Jewish identity mattered little at first glance. The Zionist program of Caiserman had to be adapted, however, to a very diverse electorate. He concentrated on four main issues: "No tax increases, reduction of (public) spending, increased income (for private individuals), and (political) autonomy for the city."[85]

In his publicity campaign, he avoided any reference to his Jewish origins, even in Yiddish. "A vote for H. M. Caiserman, the worker candidate, as alderman in St. Louis Ward, is a vote for an intelligent city administration."[86] Nevertheless, it did not take long for the progressive bias of the Poale Zion to become apparent in Caiserman's election campaign (see Appendix 5). Its basic principles were audacious at the time, such as giving women the right to vote, graduated income tax, rent control, and municipalization of streetcar services, gas and electricity. Caiserman also advocated for the improvement of sanitation and health measures in Montreal, especially the pasteurization of milk and public park development in working-class neighbourhoods. When it came to culture, he went so far as to propose the construction of a municipal library, a museum of history and culture, zoos and botanical gardens, and an art museum. All these institutions were to be funded by tax revenue or the public purse. Moreover, Caiserman showed his colours with regard to labour by demanding an eight-hour workday, official recognition for unions, factory inspections, abolition of child labour, the construction of affordable housing for workers, accident insurance, and old age pensions. Despite all this, Caiserman was rejected by the voters of St. Louis Ward, including its Jewish residents. He received the fewest votes. In Montreal of 1916 the time was not ripe for the election of an openly socialist Jewish candidate.[87]

The last battle Caiserman waged during the years from 1910 to 1920 was to create the Canadian Jewish Congress, a large umbrella organization to unite the Canadian Jewish community on the basis of democratic principles and full participation. The idea had existed since the creation of the Yiddish daily newspaper, the *Keneder Adler*, in 1907, but significant obstacles prevented its realization, including the fear among affluent assimilated Jews that such an institution would be dominated by leftist and Yiddish-speaking labour organizations. The Zionists themselves were divided by class, with more recent immigrants advocating more radical methods of funding, propaganda, and organization than those employed by militants belonging to the business and commercial bourgeoisie, known in those days as "uptowners." With regard to Palestine, the Poale Zion supported the establishment of a socialist state based on agricultural collectives, whereas the Canadian Zionist Organization, under the leadership of Clarence de Sola, was for the most part content to provide fundraising and encouragement from a distance. Above all, the matter of electing representatives to a Canada-wide Jewish organization, as well as determining their responsibilities, remained unresolved. Had it not been for the outbreak of World War I in August of 1914, with its devastating consequences for the Jews of Russia, the Canadian Jewish Congress would probably never have seen the light of day during that decade. Beginning in 1915, the Montreal Yiddish-speaking community rallied to the aid of the victims of the war in Europe. These exceptional circumstances prompted the creation of a central organization that would channel the aid to destitute and starving populations displaced by military conflict. A similar fate awaited Jewish communities several months later during the Bolshevik Revolution and its aftermath, in particular the civil war in the Ukraine, from 1919 and 1921. In anticipation of such a development and in response to the general deterioration of the situation in Russia, the downtown Jews in

1915 founded the People's Relief Committee (*Folks Farband*), to which Caiserman immediately lent his full support.

In 1917, Caiserman began investing all his energy in the campaign to found a Canadian Jewish Congress. During this time, the Poale Zion and the entire labour movement joined forces in support of the formation of this umbrella organization. After much political maneuvering and community negotiation, the election of delegates by universal suffrage to the first Jewish Congress took place on March 2, 1919. On March 16 of that same year, 209 official representatives of Canadian Jewry, almost one third of them Labour Coalition activists, finally met in Montreal in the Monument National building on St. Lawrence Boulevard. This entire project rested on the shoulders of thirty-six elected members of the executive, including Caiserman, who had been chosen General Secretary of the organization. The day after it was founded, the Canadian Jewish Congress dealt with several issues, including the possible resumption of immigration from Europe, the creation and maintenance of a solid Canada-wide network of Jewish communities, the promotion of Zionism, the struggle against anti-Semitism, and support for Jewish education, as well as the plight of European Jews caught in the midst of the civil war in Russia. There were so many issues that the various Jewish pressure groups had not previously been able to address them effectively.[88] Caiserman himself had great expectations of the Congress, as revealed in comments he made during the 1940s: "The creation of Congress and the responsibilities entrusted to it by Canadian Jews constituted a sacred and historic event."[89] Nevertheless, the signing of the Treaty of Versailles in 1919, and the reestablishment of world peace, soon had the effect of diverting the attention of the majority of Canadian Jews from the new governing body of the Canadian Jewish community. Within a matter of months, the Congress was forgotten, to the great dismay of the General Secretary. With neither the financial resources nor the active support of a broad coalition, Caiserman understood that his presence in Montreal was no longer useful. That was when he made the decision to fulfil his life's dream of making *aliyah*, to go to live in Eretz Israel.

The Urgent Call of Zionism

When Caiserman made *aliyah* in July of 1921, several articles appeared in the Montreal Jewish press about his career as a community activist and the major role he had played in building Montreal's network of

Jewish institutions. In the *Canadian Jewish Chronicle*, one anonymous writer wrote:

> With the departure of Mr. H. M. Caiserman for Palestine, the Montreal Jewish community will lose one of its most prominent and active workers. There was not a movement of any size undertaken in this city that could not count on Mr. Caiserman as one of its most active supporters, and what Mr. Caiserman supported, he did with all his might."[90]

Before he left, a coalition of activists from the Poale Zion, the Jewish Folks Shule (the Jewish People's School), and the Jewish Public Library, including J. I. Segal and his wife Elke, organized an evening in his honour. At this celebration, held on July 13, 1921 in Sinclair's Hall, he was presented with a scroll inscribed in traditional Jewish calligraphy, giving it the appearance of a religious document. However, instead of Hebrew, the representatives of the various radical organizations addressed Caiserman using secular Yiddish, in the familiar second person singular, to praise his progressive achievements on behalf of the Montreal community. The Hebrew letters on this scroll, hand-drawn by a special scribe called a *sofer,* give the impression that they were interweaving the respect for the thousands of years of Jewish history with the irrepressible desire to participate in the "revolutionary vanguard and struggle for social justice." Reading it today, one becomes immediately aware of the sharp contrast between the expressly archaic form of the scroll and the adventure which Caiserman was about to embark upon in Eretz Israel, where the language of the Bible was being revived in a new form, adapted to the exigencies of modernity. In choosing this type of document, the authors of the scroll had wished to indicate that Caiserman had succeeded in positioning himself precisely on that perilous divide where a venerable Judaic past was coming into direct contact with the new aspirations of the Jewish people. The following excerpt makes reference to this.

> When you came to live among us, Jewish life in Canada, still in its infancy, was raw, amorphous, disorganized, and uninteresting. At the same time, individuals went around full of ideas. We were all young then, and passionately searching for the ways and means to realize the ideas that were so holy and dear to us all. We understood that we had to assume the responsibility for organizing the

Jewish community, the radical Jewish community. Today we can state with pride that many of those ideas were realized, and that you, with your boundless and youthful energy, were one of the key factors in our success.[91]

In an article that appeared in 1944, on the occasion of Caiserman's sixtieth birthday, J. I. Segal recalled the period when they had met for the first time, underscoring how infatuated his friend Caiserman was with Yiddish literature, in addition to being an excellent organizer when it came to building cultural institutions:

> It was at that time when we had just immigrated that I met Caiserman. Like today, of course, he was bursting with life and dreams. He was completely different from the other people active in our Jewish socialist milieu [. . .] Caiserman did not stop thinking, for even one minute of the day, about a good book, or a fresh insight or idea in the world of literature.[92]

C. H. CAISERMAN
Gen. Secretary.

Photograph of H. M. Caiserman published in March 1919 in the Canadian Jewish Chronicle on the occasion of the first meeting of the Canadian Jewish Congress. (Canadian Jewish Congress Archives.)

In the early 1920s, there was not a single Canadian Yiddish language publication that Caiserman had not read and reviewed, not a single Jewish cultural event in Montreal on which he had not commented. In addition to his work as a critic, this militant trade unionist conducted a literary salon in his home with the help of his wife Sarah Wittal Caiserman.[93] With startling sincerity and passionate devotion, Caiserman assigned to Yiddish literature a decisive role in the expression of Jewish cultural vitality and identity in Montreal that was emerging simultaneously in the new Eastern European Jewish communities being established on several continents. This quasi-religious fervour for cultural expression in

Text of the scroll given to H. M. Caiserman at the celebration in his honour at Sinclair Hall, Montreal, July 13, 1921. (Canadian Jewish Congress Archive.)

the Yiddish language governed every single one of Caiserman's ideological, as well as practical, considerations. Yiddish elicited a powerful emotional response from him. For Caiserman, nothing could replace the evocative power and irrepressible vitality of Yiddish poetry. The fact that he was also a committed Zionist and fervent supporter of modern Hebrew changed nothing. Released from its ancient ancestral underpinnings and its status of ghetto vernacular, Yiddish, for Caiserman, could henceforth soar to the highest artistic and ethereal realms of Jewish culture and nationalism. Although the times and circumstances were often difficult, the unexpected ascent of Yiddish culture required of Montreal Jews their unwavering support for the Yiddish language, and unceasing loyalty to the creators who used it in their work.

The departure of Caiserman, the mentor of young Yiddish writers, put an end to the first period of Yiddish literature in Montreal. Once the critic had left for abroad, a new cultural climate settled upon the city, and the career of his protégé, J. I. Segal, took a pronounced turn. Caiserman, however, remained in Eretz Israel for only a few months.[94] During that time, he worked at various temporary jobs and concluded a number of commercial transactions for the Canadian Palestine Trading Co., a company managed from Montreal by none other than Hirsch Wolofsky. For example, beginning in December of 1921, Caiserman worked in Petah Tikvah, the first modern Jewish agricultural settlement in Palestine and a bastion of Labour Zionism. For a while he was the controller and administrator of the American Fruit Growers of Palestine, Inc., a company that exported Jaffa oranges to the United States and whose head office was in Boston. Caiserman also tried his hand at real estate, attempting to sell lots near Tel Aviv to Canadian Jews interested in making *aliyah*. But according to a letter to an unknown correspondent in March of 1922, this venture was not very successful. "You must not imagine that the whole place is anything else but a deep sea of sand, the only advantage being that our place is situated at the edge of the sea."[95] The notes he wrote at this time reveal that he was interested in the jewelry, olive oil, softwood lumber, fabric, and railway supply businesses. Understandably, taking into account the underdeveloped economic life of Jewish Palestine, his ventures ended without achieving very much. One day, in November of 1923, Caiserman received a short telegram from his wife, who put an end to his stay in Palestine. "Come home, save business and name,"[96] she implored him. As he was leaving for Canada, Caiserman composed this self-portrait, with no indication of the role he played in the development of Yiddish culture and literature in Montreal.

> I am 37 years old, married, born in Rumania, British subject naturalized in Canada; I possess a thorough general education and a special commercial training of about 20 years practical work as Book-Keeper, Accountant, Special Cost Accountant, Statistician and Office manager.
>
> I speak, read and write the following languages: English, German, Rumanian, French, Idish [sic] and a little Hebrew (the complete study of which I have lately undertaken), and I have the expert understanding for the financial management of any sized commercial or industrial undertaking.[97]

Caiserman's boundless admiration for Yiddish language and literature, however, contained one baffling element. Before arriving in Montreal in his mid-20s, he had not used Yiddish as an adult.[98] Two unpublished autobiographical documents clearly indicate this. The first, consisting of a single page, contains answers to questions about his career as a writer, which Caiserman sent to an unknown correspondent in the 1930s, most likely someone representing a

Yiddish-language organization or publication[99] (see Appendix 6). By
his own admission, Caiserman indicates that before 1910 he had only
written in Rumanian, including for the Rumanian Yiddish Zionist
periodical *Mevasseret Zion* [Messenger of Zion]. In the Canadian
Jewish Congress Archives there is also a scrapbook containing copies
of personal letters sent by Caiserman to his parents and other relatives
between 1900 and 1912, all in Rumanian, except for one in German
to a young woman named Mina. A partial autobiography written by
Caiserman toward the end of his life conveys quite a clear picture of
the early years of this future immigrant. Born on March 19, 1884, in
Buhusi[100] near Piatra Neamt, Caiserman grew up in a Rumanian village where most of the businesses belonged to Jewish shopkeepers.
Throughout his childhood Caiserman heard Yiddish used in his family, not to mention the fact that the family was decidedly traditional
in its Jewish religious observance. Caiserman's father, Meir, went
to pray in the synagogue every Saturday. He worked in the family
business that was very connected to the village life which dominated
Rumania's economic landscape:

> My grandparents were in business partnership with my parents,
> and both families occupied a very specious [sic] home, an inn
> and grocery in the front rooms, and many rooms in the back, sur-
> rounded by an immense garden of flowers, grain, vegetables and
> various fruit trees such as apple, pear, prune, apricot, cherry and
> grape.
> Hundreds of chickens, ducks, and geese were separated from the
> dozens of milk cows, lambs and goats. In other words it was a
> house of plenty.[101]

Presumably at that time the young Hannaiah Meir spoke only Yiddish
with his parents. This did not prevent him, once in he had moved to
Bucharest, from expressing his outrage over the treatment of Jews in
his country.[102] In 1902, at the age of 17, he founded in the Rumanian
capital a Zionist society called Ahavath Zion (love of Zion),[103] with the
avowed aim of facilitating Jewish immigration to Palestine. "During
that same year anti-Semitic attacks were directed against the Jewish
population in various cities in Rumania. Many young people bit-
terly resented the attitude of the police and government authorities
and a movement was started by these young Jews to leave the country."[104] These ideas, new to Rumania at that time, made it possible for

Caiserman to speak publicly and publish articles on this theme in the local Jewish press. The same year, he personally wrote to Theodore Herzl to ask for his assistance and advice concerning immigration to Palestine.[105] It was also at this time that Caiserman became interested in the trade union movement and got involved in left-wing organizations in Rumania. Bernard Figler, his biographer, claims that his passion for radical ideas even earned him a brief stint in prison for having defended the socialist position.[106]

Whatever twists and turns Caiserman's life had taken in Europe, the fiery militant Zionist and socialist who disembarked at Montreal harbour in July of 1910, like many of his Eastern European co-religionists, had melded into a single ideal the national liberation of his people and the victory of the international revolution. Under these conditions, the utopian project of building a national Jewish homeland in Palestine seemed perfectly compatible with the idea of overthrowing capitalism, promoting the demands of industrial labourers, and working toward a more equitable distribution of wealth. For him, to struggle for one of these causes was equivalent to trying to improve the situation of all Jews, because hastening the hour of the great socialist upheaval would surely facilitate the liberation of all oppressed peoples. Early in the twentieth century this multi-faceted and ideologically nuanced approach, both revolutionary and Jewish at the same time, was almost always communicated in Yiddish, especially in the Russian Empire. Before the First World War, Yiddish was the *lingua franca* of the majority of factory Jewish workers in Eastern Europe. In most cases, these workers received their political directives in Yiddish, and struggled to improve their lives in Yiddish. No Jewish progressive political party or spokesman could ignore this means of communication, not even the Hebraists who considered Hebrew to be the universal language of Zionism and of the realization of a Jewish community in Palestine. The crystallization of all revolutionary and Jewish national causes around Yiddish conferred upon this language, until then considered strictly vernacular, immense power and prestige among the Jewish masses yearning for national liberation. This was particularly true of the Zionists who sought to attract Jewish factory workers both in the Old Country and in America. As the historian Jonathan Frankel explains:

> Another aspect of the revolution which presented the Zionists
> with a complex dilemma was the necessity to think in terms of

> mass propaganda, mass education and mass culture. Clearly
> Zionists could not compete in the new era of growing political
> consciousness unless they made far greater use of Yiddish. [. . .]
> In the years 1905–06, however, there could be no escaping the fact
> that Yiddish was the language of the moment and (it was increas-
> ingly assumed) also the language of the future.[107]

In short, at the beginning of the last century, Yiddish was simultaneously the uncontested symbol of Jewish political aspirations in Eastern
Europe as well as the optimal tool of communication for the working classes struggling for civic equality. What was considered indis-
pensable in Warsaw, Kiev, and Vilna was also imperative in Montreal
where a large Eastern European Jewish proletariat was taking shape
in the downtown clothing factories and sweatshops. During the years
of increased immigration, the strategic importance of Yiddish rapidly
manifested itself, all the more so because it was the only language
understood by almost all the recently settled Jews in Canada, most
of them from the various regions of the Russian Empire. Of course,
Russian, Polish, Ukrainian, and Rumanian were also used by the garment workers, in addition to English. However, none had the ascen-
dant symbolism of Yiddish, nor the ability to unite the Jewish masses
of Montreal. As for literary Hebrew, German, and French, they were
only accessible to a small number. On the other hand, it is not surprising that someone with as passionate a loyalty to Yiddish as Caiserman
lacked a good command of that language when he arrived in Montreal.
The years that Caiserman had spent in Belgrade where he worked in
the fields of accountancy and international business, and then as an
activist in Rumanian-language Jewish organizations, had interfered
with his practical knowledge of Yiddish, to the point where he had to
relearn it once he immigrated to Canada.

    In Montreal at that time there were plenty of places where
Yiddish was the main language of communication. There were also
a fair number of union organizations in which this linguistic vehicle rallied the activists around a common cause. For these reasons,
Caiserman did not delay in reacquiring a certain level of fluency in
the factories of St. Lawrence Boulevard. Unlike the poet J. I. Segal,
for whom Yiddish was both mother tongue and literary language,
Caiserman's attachment to Yiddish always remained a political choice,
not dictated by aesthetic considerations. Caiserman's lack of fluency
in the Eastern European Jewish vernacular is reflected most notably

in his less accomplished journalistic writing, where he is often at pains to express his thoughts. This relative unease also reveals itself in his excessive use of scholarly terminology borrowed from academic German, which distanced the author from the two most vibrant sources of the Yiddish language and its Judaic sensibility—Jewish folk imagery and traditional religious texts. Caiserman was not alone in trying to infuse Yiddish with a Germanic rhythm and tone. Reuben Brainin, who wanted to "wrench" the language from a past he deemed "deficient," and in this way contribute to a Jewish cultural renaissance in Montreal, authored the first report of the Jewish Public Library in 1914 in a literary style closer to High German than to the language spoken by the immigrants.[108]

The Failed Russian Revolution of 1905

In 1910 Caiserman and Segal were both part of a migratory wave that brought tens of thousands of Jews to Canada. During this great migration, the Eastern European Jewish population of Montreal increased on a daily basis in the neighbourhood near the harbour. At the same time, in other large Canadian centres, a Jewish prole-tariat was forming at a precipitous pace under the astonished eyes of labour leaders of every other cultural origin. During the year 1910–1911 alone, 8,729 Jews entered Canada. The majority were immigrants from Eastern Europe who, for the most part, had to pass through Montreal (see Appendix 7). Over half of them settled at the foot of Mount Royal, near other Jews who had arrived some time earlier. In 1911, Montreal's Jewish population numbered 30,000, an increase of 23,000 from the previous decade. That same year, in all of Canada the Jewish population reached 75,000, five times the number of Jews living there a decade earlier (see Appendix 8). This migration reached its highpoint in 1913, when 18,031 Jews crossed Canada's maritime boundaries. As Louis Rosenberg points out in his book *Canada's Jews*, published by the Canadian Jewish Congress in 1939, not all the migrants who entered the country remained on Canadian soil. After a few years, some of them returned to the Old Country or left for the United States.[109] Hence, in 1911, the Jews who came with the great migration from Eastern Europe were over 1 per cent of the total population of Montreal, Toronto, and Winnipeg, the three Canadian cities where Eastern European Jewish immigrants were in the process of settling. In Montreal in particular, the Yiddish-speaking immigrants in the first years of the twentieth century made the great-est demographic leap in their history. That was followed over the next decade by almost as large a surge in population. The constant increase in Jewish immigrants registered in the pre-war years con-tributed greatly to the augmentation of the total Jewish population in the country, so much so that in 1921 Quebec had 47,977 Jewish resi-dents, and 60,087 in 1931. Over the first three decades of the twenti-eth century, immigration accounted for an almost 80 per cent growth rate in the Jewish population of Canada.[110]

The source of this unprecedented influx lay outside Canada, in the intolerable situation imposed on the Jewish minority in the Russian Empire, prior to the Bolshevik Revolution of 1917. Even a superficial analysis of the data on migration in the years from 1901 to 1919 reveals that the period of greatest Jewish migration to Canada corresponds very closely to three events of premier importance in the history of the Jews in Russia, namely, the pogroms perpetrated from 1903 to 1905 in the Moldavian city of Kishinev, the Russo-Japanese war of 1904–1905, and above all, the Russian Revolution of 1905. The latter event, in particular, would shake the established order in the Empire of the Tsars to its very foundations, and serve as a catalyst for a situation where Jews were subject to constant political persecu-tion in various regions of Imperial Russia. What is more, Jews were subject to exclusionary laws in all areas of activity, and confined to the Pale of Settlement, where none of the great political centres of the Russian Empire, such as Moscow and St. Petersburg, were located. Generally excluded from the liberal professions, institutions of higher education, and official functions, Russia's Jews at the beginning of the twentieth century lived in endemic poverty. Their marginalization was aggravated by the beginnings of proletarianization in certain bur-geoning industries, such the textile industry, and the manufacture of clothing and consumer products. In these generally unfavorable eco-nomic circumstances, with powerful forces of diverse origins strug-gling to overthrow power by violent means, the Jewish population was often perceived by the autocracy as one of the principal channels through which liberal democratic values were infiltrating Russia. To these new fears, all the more visible in a climate of perpetual politi-cal struggle, were added the age-old accusations originating in tradi-tional Christian doctrine that the Jews had killed Christ. Thus, Jews could not find a place for themselves in Imperial Russian society, nor could they win the trust of the current rulers.

> They [the Russian authorities] considered the minorities to be culturally inferior, and they were especially antagonistic toward the Jews, who numbered five million. The tsarist government had long imposed economic, legal and social restrictions on the Jews that were more extensive and demeaning than the measures taken against any other group [...]. At bottom, the hostility toward the Jews derived from the belief that they were marked by "innate vices" that made their integration into Russian society impossible. The prominence of Jews in the radical movements and, to a somewhat lesser extent, in the liberal movement, was in large measure the fruit of the government's discriminatory policies.[111]

Social tensions in Imperial Russia peaked during the Revolution of 1905. Superimposed on measures explicitly directed at the Empire's Jewish population during the severe political repression of 1906–1907 (in particular at the time of the dissolution of the First State Duma in July of 1906), these tensions led to a reaction unprecedented in its scale. Jews in the Ukraine, Congress Poland, Byelorussia, Lithuania and Russia proper, especially those between twenty and thirty years of age who were unable to advance politically, economically or culturally, took the road to exile. Thus began the largest demographic shift in Jewish history up until that time. Between 1903 and 1914, when the First World War put an end to this massive outflow, two-and-a-half million Jews voluntarily left Imperial Russia to make their way to one main destination—America. Except perhaps for Orthodox Jews, or militant revolutionaries convinced of the inevitability of an imminent and victorious revolution, this great migratory outpouring affected every stratum of Jewish life in Russia. The flight from Russia was rendered possible, as we have seen, by the technological advances in rail and maritime travel, which had been unthinkable twenty years earlier, including the creation of animmigration processing infrastructure at international borders. In addition, the fact that leading European Jewish figures such as the Baron de Hirsch and Edmond de Rothschild were funding the establishment of agricultural colonies in America and Palestine, to be settled by Eastern European Jews, must also be taken into account. Above all, this mass exodus was fuelled by the desire of younger and stronger individuals to emancipate themselves from the political constraints imposed by the tsarist authorities. For that generation, it had become impossible to continue tolerating being deprived of the countless advances provided by the liberal European revolution that took place in the second half of the nineteenth century.

> The ways in which socialism and other Jewish radical political beliefs mobilized a new Jewish politics in the aftermath of the 1905 insurrection have, however, already been documented. Far less understood are the ways in which the ideals espoused by the fin de siècle Russian Jewish liberal intelligentsia, such as personal autonomy, individual economic betterment, education, professional status, rule of law, and political integration, also influenced immigrants in this period.[112]

In contemporary Jewish history, this migration of extraordinary proportions was a completely novel response to the relentless persecution experienced by Jews in the Russian Empire, as well as the political roadblocks erected by the ruling autocracy. Except for a brief period immediately following the assassination of Alexander II, in 1882, when emigration increased but on a much smaller scale, never before had such high numbers of Russian Jews been prepared to emigrate from the Russian Empire, which was then home to the largest Jewish population in the world. "The revolution's failure, deteriorating economic conditions, and the concurrent rise in anti-Jewish violence prompted them [the Jews] to rethink their commitment to the Russian Empire, setting in motion a truly monumental revolution: mass Jewish migration."[113] The sudden and unforeseen movement of hundreds of thousands of Eastern European Jews from Russia had major consequences for Jewish communities abroad, which initially received the newly arrived immigrants with anxiety and distrust. The demographic flood spread unevenly across the world, with the United States, especially New York City, receiving the lion's share. In the year 1905 alone, almost 800,000 Russian Jews were admitted into the United States, compared with 50,000 in Argentina. Other migratory currents, much more modest in size, made their way to Brazil, Mexico, Cuba and South America, while London, Paris and Berlin served as centres of temporary refuge for people on their way to further destinations. As we have seen, a minor offshoot of the great migration of 1903–1914 sailed to Montreal, the main Canadian seaport near the Atlantic coast, a city which provided fertile soil for putting down roots.

The migration of the Jews from the Russian Empire completely altered Eastern Europe's influence in the Jewish world, while contributing decisively to the growing importance of the North American continent. The arrival of large numbers of refugees beginning in 1905 brought to their host cities new Jewish populations swept up by the winds of revolution and inspired by the radical political ideas of the Russian Liberal elite. Fuelled by their insurrectionary experience, these fighters and militants took no time in transferring into their new environments in the Lower East Side or St. Lawrence Boulevard the harsh lessons they had learned in Tsarist Russia. This transfer of emotions and experiences irritated the more affluent Jews long integrated into American and Canadian society. Within a few years, the Jewish immigrant neighbourhoods in many large North American cities swarmed with anarchists, socialist, and political activists using Yiddish to recruit their freshly arrived co-religionists. Statistical studies demonstrate that in 1920 almost 35 per cent of the Jewish population in the United States had entered the country during the great migratory wave of 1905–1914. In smaller places, this percentage was sharply higher, such as in Buenos Aires, for example, where it reached 70 per cent. In Montreal, where Eastern European Jews numbered 30,000 in 1921, nearly 85 per cent had come with the great migration of 1903–1914. These percentages make it possible to measure to what extent the insurrectionary events and spirit of 1905 profoundly influenced the evolution of Montreal Jewish identity during the interwar period. In fact, this spirit remained almost completely intact until 1948, with the arrival of a new migratory influx comprised of Holocaust survivors. Essentially, during the first forty years of its existence, from 1905 to 1945, the Eastern European Montreal Jewish community was a direct beneficiary of the struggle of Russian Jews for democratic freedoms and the promotion of workers' rights. In his 1947 book, *Montreal of Yesterday*, journalist Israel Medres emphasized this crucial element:

> At social gatherings the members of the *Arbeiter Ring* used to sing revolutionary songs from the Revolution of 1905 in Yiddish or Russian. Popular among the Russian songs was the revolutionary prison song *"Solntze voskhodit i zakhodit a v'tyurme mayi tyomna* (The sun rises and sets, but my prison cell is in darkness)." During many of these social occasions money was collected to support Russian revolutionaries languishing in prison.
>
> Russian revolutionary traditions were dear to the hearts of the socialists. May Day was an important holiday which was celebrated with a parade to the Champs-de-Mars followed by a

concert and mass meeting in the Labour Temple or in Prince Arthur Hall.[114]

The Beginnings of a Jewish Proletariat in Montreal

Eastern European Jews who arrived in Montreal after 1905 were, for the most part, young men and women who had grown up in smaller cities, as well as towns called *shtetlekh*, the plural of the Yiddish word *shtetl*, where the majority of the population were Jews who were mostly artisans or engaged in local commerce. Often, these young people had spent their early life in a traditional religious Jewish environment. The advent of modernity occurred when labour organizations and left-wing Zionist groups involved in the struggle for freedom made their appearance for the first time around the turn of the century. These developments rallied Jews in Imperial Russia within a specifically Jewish framework through publications in the Yiddish language or in maskilic Hebrew, or through Russian-speaking political movements. When the time came to immigrate to America, these individuals were still midway through the process that would uproot them from the living conditions of the previous generation. While considering undertaking the voyage to the New World, several of them had already begun their education in religious institutions such as the *yeshiva* or *beysmedresh*, where traditional Judaism was taught using methods practised for centuries, while others belonged to Hasidic and Orthodox circles when they were disrupted by the call of the sea. Having been on the barricades or under fire during the revolutionary excitement of 1905, some candidates for immigration had already rejected the immutable tenets of Judaism with which they had been inculcated years earlier. Harry (Hirsch) Hershman, who arrived in Montreal in 1902, described the blending of modern ideas and Jewish religious practices among several militant anarchists as follows:[115]

> Most of the members were typical Jews . . . who debated the subtleties of socialism and anarchism with the same *nigun* [chant] used in studying the *Gemara* [the rabbinical commentaries on the *Mishna* that constitute the second part of the Talmud]. Some of them who had even studied at the Volozhin Yeshiva at meetings gesticulated strangely with their fingers while talking with their hands. For these young men the struggle of the masses was a sacred struggle.

At the beginning of the twentieth century, Russian Jews immigrated *en masse* to countries in the New World that were more open to immigration. These regions offered more economic prosperity and social mobility, giving newcomers the opportunity to see their social status rise rapidly. Of course, those migrants who had received more formal education and were better connected settled in the large capital cities of Europe. Western Europe, however, could not offer refuge to Eastern European Jews on a large scale. The adverse economic and social conditions in its cities left them ill-equipped to accommodate large numbers of newcomers. Anti-Semitic notions and opinions, notably in Germany and France, which varied in intensity depending the time period, made largescale Jewish immigration problematic. Only a country like America, which found itself in the process of accelerated industrialization and urbanization, could absorb the impact of such widespread demographic displacement. Moreover, Russian Jews, in heading to the New World, were only a tiny part of a migratory movement unprecedented in modern history. Without the American government's official Open Door policy, in effect from the 1880s up to and including the mid-1920s, the Jews of Eastern Europe would not have been able to cross the Atlantic Ocean and enter the United States so easily. Between 1881 and 1924, almost twenty million new citizens from eastern and southern Europe were admitted into the United States, mostly through the port of New York.[116] Of this number, about 10 per cent were Jews from the Russian Empire. Once settled, they gradually joined the small and more integrated American Jewish community, composed mainly of Jews of German origin, who had little choice but to welcome the Yiddish speakers into their institutions.[117]

During this period, immigration to Canada could not attain such extraordinarily high numbers because the country's level of economic development was not comparable to that of the neighbouring republic in the aftermath of the Civil War of 1861–1865. With a generally sparse population scattered across its vast territory, Canada at the end of the nineteenth century still had the uncertain status of a former British colony, and was grappling with serious political problems of its own. After 1896, the Canadian government, however, devised an immigration plan named after Sir Clifford Sifton, Minister of the Interior in the government of Prime Minister Wilfred Laurier. Its purpose was to promote Canada as an immigration destination for farmers in order to settle the immense regions recently acquired by the creation of the provinces Saskatchewan and Alberta in 1905. Under this plan the federal government subsidized and facilitated the transportation of immigrants, recruited mostly from Europe, as well as their settlement on as yet uncultivated farmland, for a period of fifteen years, that is, until the outbreak of World War I.

Between 1901 and 1910 the Laurier government succeeded in attracting to Canada almost 1,630,000 immigrants, most of whom were British, Polish, Russian, or Italian. The fact that the total population of Canada was only 6.2 million in 1911 made this sudden demographic increase all the more significant. Of the cohort admitted into the country, mostly between 1906 and 1909, Eastern European Jews were only 2.8 per cent of the total, about 46,000 people. During the following decade, mainly in the years preceding the First World War, slightly over 1,712,000 newcomers were admitted into Canada under the same conditions and from the same parts of the world, among them 29,464 Jews or 1.7 per cent of the total. At the end of this twenty-year period, the total percentage of Canadians who were immigrants grew from 4.9 per cent to 17.5 per cent, close to one fifth of the population.[118]

The exceptional set of circumstances that allowed a sizeable number of Eastern European Jews into the country had vanished by the mid-1920s. The largest migratory wave in the history of Canada in the twentieth century had allowed tens of thousands of Yiddish-speaking Jews to become part of an unprecedented demographic movement that would have a decisive impact on the evolution of Canada over the decades that followed. Although hardly significant from an international perspective, or even in terms of the worldwide Jewish diaspora, the influx of Eastern Europeans to Montreal, Toronto, and Winnipeg made possible for the first time in this country the emergence of visible and audible Jewish communities. In Montreal after 1914, Russian, Ukrainian, Byelorussian, Lithuanian, and Rumanian Jews formed a compact community in a neighbourhood near the harbour. After the armistice of 1918, this group migrated to the Mount Royal Plateau, in particular to that part of St. Lawrence Boulevard situated north of Sherbrooke Street. While the majority of farmers recruited under the Sifton Plan had made their way to central Canada, Eastern European Jews in Montreal constituted the largest immigrant group in Canada. At the same time, Yiddish became the language, next to French and English, most spoken and heard in Montreal, a status it maintained until the early 1950s.

Like most of the great demographic shifts of the modern era, the migratory movement that brought Yiddish speakers to Montreal was intense but short-lived. Within a few years, a Jewish community appeared in Montreal practically out of nowhere, without any prior signs or indications of its emergence. Who would have imagined that so many Russian Jews would be forced to take the path of exile to Montreal? How many of these migrants had given much prior thought to going to Canada? Having travelled, usually on their own and unexpectedly, from a variety of places, Yiddish-speaking immigrants arriving in Montreal realized that in the New World they were part of an identifiable "ethnic entity." Surrounded on all sides by their fellow Jews, they very quickly became engaged in founding synagogues, benevolent societies, and charitable institutions. Most often organized according to the city of origin of their members, these *landsmanshaftn* formed the nucleus of a communal network which, after 1905, was steadily expanding, thanks to the Yiddish daily newspaper, the *Jewish Daily Eagle*. Often coming from a secular background, Yiddish-speaking Jews had no difficulty in recreating in Montreal the foundations of the type of communal life they had experienced in the Old Country. Nevertheless, their new home differed in several important respects from their previous experience in Russia, including the fact that historically they were the first sizeable immigrant group to settle in that city. Likewise, the pervading liberalism in North America would prevent any recourse to authoritarian, elitist, or coercive arguments when it came to building Jewish identity and community.

The great migration of the years from 1901 to 1920 also brought to Canada, for the first time, immigrants able to write in a language other than English or French. Among the millions of people who presented themselves at Canada's gates during the massive migration, a certain percentage were educated people, journalists and writers who laid the groundwork for new bodies of literature in various languages, including German, Polish, Russian, Ukrainian, Italian and Yiddish, not to mention languages less frequently used such as Finnish, Czech, and Serbian. A variety of writing was produced in these languages over the years that followed the great migration, some in the private sphere, such as correspondence, memoirs, and the internal reports of various associations, while other items were written for newspapers, periodicals, church bulletins, and publications specifically for new arrivals. Immigrant languages were also used sporadically in flyers and pamphlets produced by trade unions, mutual benefit organizations, and political associations. Although diverse, this material, which has yet to be fully explored, is an excellent documentary source that allows for a better understanding of the experiences, emotions, hopes, and plans of the newcomers as they adjusted to Canadian society. At the forefront of these literary odds and ends that began to appear after 1900 are the beginnings of Yiddish literature in Canada. The dominant place of Yiddish in relation to other languages is due to the fact that of all the communities that settled in this country, the level of literacy among Eastern European immigrant Jews was the highest.[119] The volume of literary production in Yiddish was also the by-product of the fierce ideological struggles in Russia, as well as an unequalled capacity for diasporic community organization. However, this was not just a response to the new demands of modernity. Yiddish literacy had its roots in the Jewish religion that requires the ability to read the Torah from the age of thirteen.

The continuous and unmistakable growth of the Jewish population between the years 1905 and 1914 led to the appearance in Montreal of a phenomenon that at first glance is difficult to measure: a substantial Yiddish readership. Of course, as journalist Medres explains in his memoirs, many of the early immigrants had no spare time to devote to weighty tomes or long hours of reading. A certain number, however, were eager to read Yiddish newspapers and books in Yiddish. They also gave their attention to the ideological manifestos and pamphlets published by the unions in the clothing trades or by the various political factions.[120] Moreover, during the early years of the twentieth century, many workers took a keen interest in Yiddish-language public libraries, schools, and theatre companies. The same enthusiasm was to be found within the newly formed intellectual circles, worker organizations, and political groupings. The desire to participate in the development of Yiddish artistic creativity was shared by many activists and Montreal left-wing Zionists, for whom it foreshadowed genuine Jewish cultural autonomy in the city, and provided evidence of the vitality of their community. Few people at the time, however, suspected that Yiddish literature would evolve so rapidly in the Montreal context, or that a young poet by the name of J. I. Segal would reveal his talent so brilliantly at the end of the 1910s. This paradigm shift during a still tentative dawn was a good indication that modern Yiddish literature had sailed across the Atlantic together with the early immigrants. In Montreal, it became the continuation of a cultural tradition rooted in Eastern Europe for decades. And it was in Montreal that J. I. Segal, propelled by a literary movement that had become widespread by beginning of the twentieth century, as well as a Jewish nationalism that borrowed the daily language of the Jews in Imperial Russia for revolutionary ends, took up a torch that had burned with blinding intensity in his birthplace.

Notes

1 Interview in the home of Sylvia Angell, in Westmount, November 30, 2009. Sylvia Angell is the daughter of Pearl Segal, youngest sister of J. I. Segal. A short biography of Pearl Segal was written in 1978, as a school assignment, by her grandson, David J. R. Angell, entitled "A Montreal Life" (five pages). This document is in the possession of Sylvia Angell.
2. Born in Piotrków, Poland, he was 18 years old at the time.
3. This account is from Novak's memoirs, entitled *Fun mayn yunge yorn* (From my childhood), published posthumously in New York by the Workmen's Circle, in 1957. See pages 141–147. This book is available in French with the title *La première école Yiddish de Montréal, 1911–1914* (Sillery: Éditions du Septentrion, 2009), 145–153.
4. Ibid., *Fun mayn yunge yorn*, 142, and *La première école Yiddish de Montréal, 1911–1914*, 147.
5. This was the last European port at which the steamship made a stop.
6. This is what Pearl Segal intimates in her account entitled "A Montreal Life," op. cit., Note 2.
7. Undated letter from the I. L. Peretz Yiddish Writers' Association, New York, in the J. I. Segal Archive of Montreal Jewish Public Library. Also called Jewish Writers' Association, the Yiddish Writers' Association was founded in New York in 1915 as an association of Yiddish journalists. http://www.yivoarchives.org/index.php?p=collections/controlcard&id=33053
8. On this theme of the Jewish working class in Montreal at the beginning of the 20th century, see Harry (Hirsch) Hershman, "*25 yor idish arbiter bavegung in Montreal*," *Unzer Vort*, Montreal, December 23, 1927 – March 2, 1928; published in French translation as "À l'occcasion des vingt-cinq ans du movement ouvrier juif à Montréal," in *Bulletin du Regroupement des chercheurs en histoire des travailleurs du Québec* vol. 26, no. 1, (Spring 2000): 42–60; Israel Medres, "*Di idishe arbeter bavegung in kanade*," in the *Keneder Adler*, Montreal, July 8, 1932, special 25th jubilee edition, 79–80; published in French translation as "Le movement ouvrier juif canadien," in *Canadian Jewish Studies* vol. IX, (2001): 170–189.
9. Ch. L. Fox, *100 Years of Yiddish and Hebrew Literature in Canada* (Montreal: Adler Printing Reg., 1980), 184 (Yiddish). Translated into French by Pierre Anctil as Haim-Leib Fuks, *Cent ans de littérature Yiddish et hébraïque au Canada* (Sillery: Éditions du Septentrion, 2005).
10. In Montreal at that time the legal age for work was fourteen.
11. Esther Segal published only one collection of poetry entitled *Lider* [Poems] (Montreal, 1928). However, throughout the 1920s and 1930s she contributed to several Montreal Yiddish-language literary journals.
12. Mirl Erdberg-Shatan, *Esther Segal Shkolnikov tsu ir fertn yorstayt* [Esther Segal, on the fourth anniversary of her death, (a short biographical note)], undated manuscript, c.1978, Canadian Jewish Congress Archives, Montreal.
13. Haim-Leib Fuks, op. cit., 250; Ch. L. Fox, op. cit., 181.
14. Dufferin School was on Saint Urbain Street, between Saint-Antoine and René-Lévesque Boulevard.
15. This is probably Saint-Maurice Street in Old Montreal.

16. David J. R. Angell [English document], op. cit., 3.
17. Undated, untitled, unsigned document handwritten by H. M. Caiserman, Segal Archive, Montreal Jewish Public Library, Montreal. The original text is in transliterated in Yiddish as follows: *"hot er varlozen di koretser svive und arain-gekumen kmat direct in a montrealer shneider shop."* The first line of the manuscript begins: "He studied in a Russian-Hebrew Talmud Torah."
18. Haim Leib Fuks, op. cit., 251; Ch. L. Fox, op. cit., 181.
19. *Keneder Adler (Jewish Daily Eagle)*, Montreal, April 23, 1917, 4.
20. Interview with Sylvia Lustgarten, daughter of J. I. Segal, Toronto, December 15, 1988.
21. Undated, untitled, unsigned, handwritten document by H. M. Caiserman, Segal Archive, Montreal Jewish Public Library, op. cit. The document is in transliterated Yiddish as follows: *"Biz shpet bei nacht, bei a kerosin lempel, flegt er fleissig dichten – sehr oft iz di mame oifgeshtanen 2 -3 a zeiger nuch halbe nacht, un ihm gefinen schreiben – fleg sie oisleschen dus lempl – kdei er soll huben koich (koyakh) ofshtehen zie der arbet."*
22. Haim Leib Fuks, op. cit., 254. Ch. L. Fox, op. cit., 184.
23. Undated, untitled, unsigned document handwritten by H. M. Caiserman, Segal Archive, Montreal Jewish Public Library, 6 pages, op. cit. [Transliterated Yiddish].
24. This was a book by Moshe Elimelekh Levin entitled *Kinder ertsyung bay yidn (a historishe nakhforshung)* Montreal, 1910. The book advocates the application of modern educational methods to the study of religious texts. See Ch. L. Fox, op. cit., 152.
25. Yiddish language printing in North America was technologically complicated, necessitating linotype machines calibrated from right to left and capable of using the Hebrew alphabet.
26. On this subject, see H. Wolofsky, *Journey of My Life (A Book of Memories)* (Yiddish title: *Mayn lebns rayze. Zikhroynes fun iber a halbn yorhundert idish lebn in der alter un nayer velt*) (Montreal: The Eagle Publishing Co. Ltd., 1946). Translated into French by Pierre Anctil as *Hirsch Wolofsky: Mayn lebns rayze. Un demi-siècle de vie yiddish à Montréal et ailleurs dans le monde* (Sillery: Éditions du Septentrion, 2000), 391; English version: *H. Wolofsky, The Journey of My Life* (Montreal: The Eagle Publishing Co.), 1945. Translated by A. M. Klein.
27. In the Russian Empire, which included Congress Poland, the Yiddish daily press first made its appearance in St. Petersburg in 1903 with the newspaper *Fraynt* [Friend]. During the 1905 Revolution, some semi-clandestine newspapers belonging to the various Jewish political parties were also in circulation.
28. Short biographies of these writers can be found in the book by Haim Leib Fuks (Yiddish original Chaim Leib Fox) cited above.
29. Adherents of the Jewish Enlightenment of the late 18th and 19th centuries. Singular is *maskil*.
30. Israel Medres, *Montreal of Yesterday: Jewish life in Montreal, 1900–1920*, translated from the Yiddish by Vivian Felsen (Montreal: Véhicule Press, 2000), 85.
31. David Rome, *The Canadian Story of Reuben Brainin*, part 2, in *Canadian Jewish Archives*, New Series no. 48, Montreal: Canadian Jewish Congress, 1996, 7. In the citation, the names of the authors are spelled according to current usage.
32. Fuks, op. cit., 254. Fox, op. cit., 184.
33. Caiserman, op. cit. Original Yiddish transliteration:" *"Nur shabes fleg er mit grois shemevdigkeit kumen oyf Main Street, einhandlen a pur heftn, und in farloif vun der woch unpaken mit lieder."*
34. Caiserman, ibid.

35. J. I. Segal, *"Helft,"* *Keneder Adler*, October 3, 1915.

36. Ch. L. Fox, op. cit., 90; Haim-Leib Fuks, op. cit., 136.

37. *Hundert tropn tint* [One hundred drops of ink] Toronto, 1915, 100 pages; and *Fablen* [Fables] Montreal, 1918, 31 pages.

38. The pogroms of 1648, which claimed thousands of victims, took place within the context of a revolt by the Cossack army and Ukrainian peasants against the Polish landowners.

39. On this subject, see David G. Roskies, "The Pogrom Poems and the Literature of Destruction," *Notre Dame English Journal*, vol. 11, no. 2, "Judaic Literature, Critical Perspective" (April 1979), 89–113. See also, *The Literature of Destruction: Jewish Responses to Catastrophe* (Philadelphia: Jewish Publication Society, 1989).

40. In Hebrew *B'ir haHaregah*, in Yiddish *In shkhite-shtot.*

41. Medres, op. cit., 156.

42. J. I. Segal, *"In mayn shtetl," Der Keneder Adler*, November 22, 1916. See Appendix 4.

43. Joseph Leiser Kaluschiner is the author of *Sonetn*, published in New York in 1932, A. Biderman.

44. Caiserman, undated and unsigned document, op. cit.

45. Having immigrated to the United States in 1893, Shmuelsohn began publishing in various Yiddish periodicals in American beginning around 1903. In 1908, his literary reputation had been established, and his work generally favorably received by the critics. Shmuelsohn lived in Montreal until 1932 when he moved to a small agricultural village near Albany, New York. See Zalman Reisin, *Leksikon fun der yidisher literatur, prese un filologye.* Biographical Dictionary of Yiddish Literature, Press and Philology; 4 vols. 1926–1929 (Vilna: Vilner Ferlag fun B. Kletskin, 1927), vol. 2, columns 739–741.

46. Undated, untitled handwritten English manuscript by H. M. Caiserman about the life of Moshe Shmuelsohn, Segal Archive, Montreal Jewish Public Library.

47. Today boulevard René-Lévesque.

48. H. M. Caiserman, ibid.

49. H. M. Caiserman, ibid.

50. *"Di escursye zu gefinen dem dichter Segal* [the efforts to find Segal]," H. M. Caiserman, handwritten, undated and untitled manuscript about the life of J. I. Segal, Segal Archive, Montreal Jewish Public Library Archives, 6 pages, op. cit.

51. Simon Belkin, *Le mouvement ouvrier juif au Canada, 1904–1920* (Sillery: Éditions du Septentrion, 1999), 174–175, the French version of *Di Poale Zion bavegung in kanade, 1904–1920* (Montreal, 1956), 91–92.

52. Ibid., 176; Yiddish, page 93.

53. Simon Belkin, *"H. M. Caiserman hot ongefangen zayn gezelshaftlikhe tetigkayt in der treyd-union bavegung* [H. M. Caiserman began his community activities in the trade union movement]," *Keneder Adler*, December 27, 1950.

54. Ibid.

55. Israel Rabinovitch, *"Gut morgn* [Good morning]," *Keneder Adler*, March 9, 1954, 1. This was an obituary for Segal.

56. H. M. Caiserman, handwritten, undated, untitled manuscript about the life of J. I. Segal, Segal Archive, Montreal Jewish Public Library Archives, op. cit.

57. Ibid.

58. Ibid. Caiserman's spelling here is derived from German. Henceforth this book will be cited as *Fun mayn velt*, the spelling that conforms to the rules of transliteration of the YIVO Institute for Jewish Research.

59. The collection itself is not dated, and there is no reference inside to its having been published in the Montreal Yiddish press at that time.

60. This address is on the northwest corner of the intersection of St. Lawrence Boulevard and Milton Street. The printing establishment that printed this poetry collection was called City Printing Company. There is nothing to indicate that this was a publishing company.

61. It is important to note that in 1917 Ezekiel Brownstone (Bronstein) published a poetry collection entitled *Blitsn* [Lightning] in Winnipeg. Also in Winnipeg the following year, 1918, Mordecai Miller, Ezekiel Brownstone, and Hershl Galski-Gayel together published a poetry collection of 31 pages entitled *Milkhome veyen: dertseylungen un lider* [The pain of war, stories and poems]. These books and a few others during the 1920s appeared within the context of another branch of Canadian Yiddish literature, and had no immediate influence in Montreal at the time that they were published.

62. H. M. Caiserman, *"Yud Yud Segal als poet, a kurtse retsenzye"* [J. I. Segal as poet, a short review], *Der Yidisher Arbeter*, Montreal, February 1919, 3.

63. H. M. Caiserman, handwritten undated, untitled manuscript about the life of J. I. Segal, Segal Archive, Montreal Jewish Public Library Archives, 6 pages, op. cit.

64. Moshe Shmuelsohn, *Veltn un tsaytn, ertseylungen un skitsn*, 1903–1917, New York: Max N. Meizel, 1918.

65. He is referring to Hershl Novak, mentioned earlier in this chapter. Novak was one of the founders of the first Yiddish school in Montreal, in 1911 in Mile End.

66. Cited in Bernard Figler, *The H. M. Caiserman Book* (Montreal: Northern Printing and Lithographing Co., 1962), 193.

67. Unfortunately, there is no documentary evidence of his stay in Paris or his activities there.

68. Caiserman had two sisters and four brothers. He was the oldest boy, with a sister four years his senior.

69. H. M. Caiserman, *Ershte trit fun organizirm di idishe arbiter bavegung in Montreal, erinerungen fun H. M. Caiserman* [First steps in organizing the Jewish labour movement in Montreal, memoirs of H. M. Caiserman], undated document, Caiserman Archive, Canadian Jewish Congress Archives, Montreal.

70. See on this subject the description by Israel Medres in *Montreal of Yesterday*, op. cit., 58–63.

71. Hershman, op. cit., Essentially this meant acquiring electric sewing machines.

72. The Jewish Public Library was actually founded in 1914.

73. Louis Rosenberg, "By the Way," *The Israelite Press* (Winnipeg, April 21, 1944), vol. 34, no. 32.

74. On this subject see Hershl Novak, op. cit. The Mile End School lasted only a few months.

75. In 1918, the National Radical School was renamed the Peretz School after the great Eastern European Yiddish writer. When it was founded, it was situated on Prince Arthur Street, just east of St. Lawrence Boulevard.

76. Simon Belkin, *Le movement ouvrier juif au Canada, 1904–1920*, op. cit., 1999, 310. Translation of Simon Belkin, *Di Poale Zion bavegung in kanade*, op. cit., 203–204.

77. Ibid., 335. Also *Di Poale Zion bavegung in kanade*, op. cit., 224. This school was on Saint Urbain, between Ontario and Sherbrooke.

78. On this subject, see the Reuben Brainin, "First Annual Report of the Jewish Public Library and People's University, opened in May 1, 1914" (Montreal, 1915), 44 pages.

79. Simon Belkin, op. cit. 217; Yiddish version, 127.

80. On this subject, see Stefani Hoffman and Ezra Mendelsohn, *The Revolution of 1905 and Russia's Jews* (Philadelphia: University of Pennsylvania Press, 2008), 320.

81. On Ber Borochov, see Jonathan Frankl, *Prophesy and Politics: Socialism, Nationalism and the Russian Jews, 1862–1917* (New York: Cambridge University Press, 1981), chapter 7.

82. Simon Belkin, op. cit., 104; Yiddish version, op. cit., 35.

83. Flyer in French for the Montreal municipal election of April 3, 1916, Caiserman Archive, Jewish Public Library, Montreal.

84. This provincial district was essentially the Montreal neighbourhood where Caiserman was a candidate in April 1916.

85. Ibid.

86. Election material prepared in three languages (Yiddish, French and English) for the Montreal municipal election of April 3, 1916, Caiserman Archive, Montreal Jewish Public Library Archives.

87. This did not happen until a by-election in August of 1943 when the population of the electoral district of Cartier elected the Labour-Progressive Party (Communist Party) candidate Fred Rose.

88. See H. M. Caiserman, "The History of the First Canadian Jewish Congress," 465–482, Arthur Daniel Hart, *The Jew in Canada*. The Jew in Canada: A Complete Record of Canadian Jewry from the Days of the French Regime *to the Present Time* (Toronto and Montreal, Jewish Publication Limited, 1926). See also Belkin, op. cit. 15.

89. "It was a historic day, a blessed day, when Canadian Jewry founded its Congress and gave it the following goals" in an undated, unsigned report, Caiserman Archive, Canadian Jewish Congress Archives, Montreal.

90. "Montreal Bids Farewell to Prominent Worker," The Canadian Jewish Chronical, Montreal, Vol. VIII, no. 8, July 15, 1921, 1,4.

91. This manuscript is in the Caiserman Archive, Canadian Jewish Congress Archives, Montreal. *"In yene teg hob ikh zikh bagegent, nokh oifn halb-grinem veg mit H. M. Caiserman. Vi nokh haynt, hot er demolt avade un avade geshprudelt mit leben un mit kholem. Er iz ingantsen geven andersh fun ale tetige mentshn vos hoben zikh arumgedreyt oyf unzer yidish-sotsialistisher aveniu [. . .] hot Caiserman kayn eyn minut in tog nisht oyfgehert trakhtn vegn a gutn bukh, a nayem frishn gedank un ideye in der velt fun der literatur."*

92. J. I. Segal, "H. M. Caiserman," the Jewish Daily Eagle, March 24, 1944.

93. Educated in the United States in liberal arts and social philosophy, Sarah Wittal met H. M. Caiserman in Montreal Labour Zionist circles sometime after 1910. After their marriage in 1914, Sarah Caiserman was active along with her husband in various socialist Zionist organizations such as the Poale Zion, the Pioneer Women's Organization of Canada, the Canadian Association for Labor Palestine and the Habonim Youth Movement. Thanks to her talent in business, she made it possible for her husband to work for many years within the Jewish community with practically no remuneration.

94. On this subject, see H. M. Caiserman-Wittal, *A Trip to Palestine*, manuscript dated August 1925, 8 pages, Caiserman Archive, Canadian Jewish Congress Archives, Montreal.

95. Letter from H. M. Caiserman to an unknown correspondent, March 23, 1922, Caiserman Archive, Canadian Jewihs Congress Archives, Montreal. This description of Tel Aviv can be compared to the one in *Only Yesterday* by S. Y. Agnon, a novel first published in 1945 in Hebrew as *Tmol Shilshom*.

96. Telegram from Sarah Wittal-Caiserman cited in Caiserman's letter of resignation to the Palestine Corporation Ltd., November 30, 1923, Caiserman Archive, Canadian Jewish Congress Archives, Montreal. Bernard Sigler's biography

claims that Caiserman lived for several months in Palestine with his wife Sarah and that his return to Montreal was precipitated by the health of their daughter Nina. These facts are not, however, confirmed by the earliest documents filed in the Canadian Jewish Congress Archives, Montreal.

97. Letter from H. M. Caiserman to Sir Herbert Samuel, dated October 14, 1921. Caiserman Archive, Canadian Jewish Congress Archives, Montreal.

98. Pierre Anctil, "H.M. Caiserman: Yiddish as a Passion," 69–100, in Ira Robinson, Pierre Anctil and Mervin Butovsky, eds., *An Everyday Miracle, Yiddish Culture in Montreal* (Véhicule Press, 1990), 69–100. Reprinted under the title "H. M. Caiserman or the cult of Yiddish," in *Tur Malka, Flâneries sur les cimes de l'histoire juive montréalais* (Sillery: Éditions Septentrion, 1997), 75–107.

99. One page undated, unsigned document containing a biography of Caiserman which he personally prepared, Canadian Jewish Congress Archives, Montreal.

100. A small Moldavian town that included several hundred Jews on the eve of World War I. This region belonged to the "old kingdom" of Rumania created in 1881, and therefore historically the majority of the population spoke Rumanian. In Moldavia Jews were less emancipated socially and politically than in the neighbouring Austro-Hungarian Empire.

101. *Autobiography of H. M. Caiserman*, document dactylographié, non daté et non signé, fonds Caiserman, archives du Congrès juif canadien, Montréal, 26 pages. Il semble qu'une partie du texte ait été perdue.

102. On this subject, see Carol Iancu, *Les Juifs en Roumanie, 1866–1919: de l'exclusion à l'émancipation* (Aix-en-Provence: Éditions de l'Université de Provence, 1978), 150; *Permanence et ruptures dans l'histoire des Juifs de roumanie, xxixe et xixe siècles: actes du congrès international du Centre de recherche Juifs, arméniens et chrétiens d'Orient* (Montpellier, Université de Paul-Valéry-Montpellier III), 2004.

103. This is the spelling used by Caiserman in his autobiography.

104. Autobiography of H. M. Caiserman, ibid., 24.

105. Ibid.

106. Bernard Figler, op. cit., 27.

107. Jonathan Frankel, op. cit., 1.

108. Reuben Brainin, First Annual Report of the Jewish Public Library, op. cit. 7.

109. Louis Rosenberg, Canada's Jews, a Social and Economic Study of the Jews in Canada, Montreal, Canadian Jewish Archives, 1939, Table 101, page 150.

110. Haim-Leib Fuks, op. cit., see figures 1 and 2, 435.

111. Abraham Ascher, "Interpreting 1905", in Stefani Hoffman and Ezra Mendelsohn, *The Revolution of 1905 and Russia's Jews*, Philadelphia, University of Pennsylvania Press, 2008, 27.

112. Rebecca Kobrin, "The 1905 Revolution Abroad: Mass Migration, Russian Jewish Liberalism, and American Jewry, 1903–1914," in Stefani Hoffman et Ezra Mendelsohn, *The Revolution of 1905 and Russia's Jews*, Philadelphia: University of Pennsylvania Press, 2008, 229.

113. Ibid., 227–228.

114. Medres, Israel, op. cit., 45–46.

115. Hershman, op. cit., 54.

116. John Higham, *Strangers in the Land: Patterns of American Nativism, 1860–1925*, New Brunswick, N.J.: Rutgers University Press, 1988; *Send These to Me: Jews and Other Immigrants in Urban America*, New York: Atheneum, 1975.

117. See Irving Howe, *World of Our Fathers*, New York: New York University Press, 2005; Irving Howe and Kenneth Libo, *How We Lived: A Documentary History of Immigrant Jews in America, 1880–1930*, New York: Richard Marek Publishers, 1979.

118. Jean R. Burnet and Howard Palmer, *Coming Canadians: An Introduction to a History of Canada's Peoples*, Toronto, McClelland and Stewart, 1988; Valerie Knowles, *Strangers at Our Gates: Canadian Immigration and Immigration Policy, 1540–2007*, Toronto: Dundurn, 2007.
119. Louis Rosenberg, op. cit., 254–262.
120. Medres, op. cit., 76–78.

Chapter 2

Leaving Korets

When J. I. Segal began to reveal his literary talent, Montreal had only a limited number of readers who were even aware of literary work in Yiddish. His unexpected leap into the limelight, after having been read by a small group around Moshe Shmuelsohn, indicates that a literary contribution of such quality had been anticipated and desired by a few activists passionately interested in Canadian Yiddish literature. As we have seen, this momentous encounter between Segal and his admirers took place in 1917. It happened when the young poet was invited to the home of Shmuelsohn, an anarchist and worker whose long hours in the factory "did not prevent him from reading manuscripts from writers all over Canada, giving them advice, and correcting their work to ensure its publication."[1] On that occasion, surrounded by a group of Yiddish journalists and cultural activists, including H. M. Caiserman, Shmuelsohn realized that Segal's packets contained many unpublished poems. The real surprise was their length, because the poems which Segal had occasionally published in the *Der Keneder Adler* (*The Jewish Daily Eagle*) were short, and most of them on traditional Jewish themes. Even more astonishing was that the fact that poet wrote in complete isolation, without the benefit of any institutional support or interaction with colleagues. According to Caiserman, "when Shmuelsohn asked whether the young prodigy had brought any of his poems with him, Segal shyly took out a whole packet of poems, which were read all evening long. Shmuelsohn was beaming like a proud father."[2]

Segal's introduction to Montreal's Yiddish literary milieu highlighted the fact that since arriving in Canada, he had acquired a remarkable ability to write independently. Over the past seven years, he had pursued his creative activity without much concern about reaching an audience. By the time he met the members of the Montreal Writers' Association (*shrayber farayn*) in 1917, Segal already had enough material for his first volume of poetry. Shmuelsohn, twenty-five years his senior, found his writing surprisingly mature, considering the circumstances. The poems read during the course of that memorable evening, described by Caiserman, had been written by a young immigrant who had barely adjusted to his new country, whose living conditions were difficult, and who was subjected to the exhausting ten-hour-day schedule of a garment factory worker. His poems, collected in a single volume entitled *Fun mayn velt* (1918), would become the first Yiddish-language poetry book to be published in Montreal. In all likelihood funded by his new mentors, and typeset by a small printing company thanks to their support, *Fun mayn velt* signalled the launch of a new literary movement in the city. It had been less than fifteen years since the first attempts at Hebrew printing had been made in Montreal, mostly leaflets and flyers, for distribution among immigrant Jews. In 1905 Harry (Hirsch) Hershman had founded the first Yiddish-language newspaper, *Der Telegraf* (The telegraph), which lasted only four months, according to the biographical lexicon of Ch. L. Fox.[3] The first Yiddish-language journalists also had to contend with the problem of finding typographic equipment with Hebrew characters, as well as typesetters capable of producing text to be read from right to left instead of left to right. Before he could print the first page of his daily newspaper, entitled *Der Keneder Adler* (*The Jewish Daily Eagle*) in 1907, Hirsch Wolofsky needed to find skilled workers from as far away as New York, and acquire costly machinery:

> When we finally brought the plates to the *Herald* to have them printed, I soon pictured my dreams going up in smoke. Seeing the enormous machinery required to print a newspaper and knowing that even our small amount of capital had already been exhausted, I found myself in complete despair. But a comical incident made me forget the gravity of the situation. After the machine operators had put the pages in the press and it began printing, a monstrous mix-up occurred: the newspaper came out upside down and backwards—with the first page last and the last page first.[4]

Bearing in mind that for Yiddish writers there were no publishing companies in Montreal in 1918, printing a book of poetry was no easy feat from a technical as well as a commercial standpoint. At the end of the 1910s, there were only two or three bookstores owned by immigrant Jews, including Harry Hershman's, which had opened its doors in 1902, and Elstein's, established somewhat later. The appearance of a talented author like Segal demonstrated that modern Yiddish literature, which had first emerged in Eastern Europe at the end of the nineteenth century, had finally crossed the Atlantic in embryonic form and, after having taken root in New York, was now ready to take flight in Montreal. Since 1910, the impulse to write and the desire to create a new Yiddish literature had already become important elements in the development of the Eastern European Jewish community, which was now making its appearance on the banks of the St. Lawrence River. Nevertheless, it was not until the establishment of a Yiddish-language press in Montreal and the development of Yiddish-language intellectual and artistic circles, however modest in size, that this literature gradually became a reality. Another set of circumstances also had an impact on the birth of Canadian Yiddish literature during this decade. The suffering endured by the Jews of Eastern Europe during World War I, followed by political strife in Russia, injected a burst of vitality into the recently established Jewish communities of Montreal, Toronto and Winnipeg. In response to a catastrophe unprecedented in its scope, campaigns were organized to provide refuge and material assistance for displaced Jews, which galvanized the immigrants and motivated them to expand their community network. The publication of the Balfour Declaration in 1917 and the capture of Jerusalem by the British Army in December of that same year also greatly accelerated the building of a Jewish identity in a country like Canada whose fate was so closely linked to that of the British Empire. New community efforts to place the Jewish population of Montreal on the Canadian political stage indirectly gave a boost to budding artists.

Segal was "discovered" at a time when all of Montreal Jewry was completely caught up in the events taking place in Eastern Europe, but also encouraged by the news coming from the Middle East. On the heels of these two key international developments came the Russian Revolution of October 1917 and the ensuing Civil War. During this exceptionally bloody conflict between the Red Army and the reactionary Whites forces, the Jews of Poland and the Ukraine suffered severe devastation, particularly in the regions where murderous pogroms had decimated entire communities. In this climate of catastrophe coupled with intense cultural affirmation in the Yiddish language, the emergence in Montreal of a literary movement was greeted with great enthusiasm. Many local activists saw it as a spectacular manifestation of the desire to carve out a place for autonomous Jewish cultural expression in the city. In 1916 and 1917 the deadly fighting in areas where the majority of the population was Jewish, affected Segal's poetic expression. Many of his first poems reflect his profound anxiety. In a way, the writer was reacting to the threat hovering over the Yiddish-speaking Jews of Imperial Russia and indirectly over the entire diaspora. Indeed, the Montreal Jewish community was profoundly affected by the magnitude of the massacres perpetrated in Eastern Europe during the First World War. Segal's early writing also reveals the poet attempting to come to terms with his exile in Canada. These events undoubtedly signalled a more complete rupture with his birthplace and his childhood. Yet, despite being separated by geography and immigration, the content of his poetry and the maturity of his early work show that the poet had retained an unalterable organic relationship with the culture of his birthplace. The creative tension between the memory of his Eastern European childhood and his adult life in Montreal could help explain, according to David Rome, the precipitous blossoming of his poetry:

> In one sense none of the Canadian Yiddish writers are indigenous to Canada, any more than the first Canadian writers in English or French were. The Jewish writers all came to Canada completely formed as very adult human beings, shaped by their ancient European Jewish tradition. More than other immigrants on the same boats, they were dedicated to the preservation, appreciation and the centrality of the culture of the old world. Most of these creators of the Jewish literature of Canada for half a century had begun their creative writing in Europe and some of the later Canadian Yiddish authors had acquired the highest repute there.[5]

The Dawn of 1918

Before exploring the first thirteen years of Segal's life, his first book of poetry entitled *Fun mayn velt* (From my world) should be closely analysed, because its publication would radically alter the outlook of Montreal's Yiddish cultural circles. Today it is difficult to form an accurate idea of the situation in which Yiddish-speaking immigrants found themselves at that point in time. Within the span of a few short years, a great number of young men and women of Eastern European Jewish origin settled helter-skelter in Montreal. Although to outside observers it seemed to exist *de facto*, the Yiddish-speaking population was comprised of a mass of people recently uprooted from their place of birth, and still incapable of imagining a long-term future for themselves in their adopted country. Most of these immigrants made a concerted effort to learn English, Canada's dominant language, and tried to adjust to working in an industry known for its brutal exploitation. Those not directed to find work in factories, tried to open small businesses or peddle consumer goods in the French neighbourhoods as well as in the countryside. In an environment such as this, activists tried to organize their co-religionists into trade unions or get them involved in the educational, cultural and charitable institutions that were being founded at this time. The Montreal Jewish population was thus assailed by various ideologically based groups competing for the attention of the working masses, each trying in its own way to build a Canadian Jewish identity. It is difficult to imagine that in these circumstances a Yiddish culture of the highest quality would manifest itself, especially when the majority of the newcomers were preoccupied with making a living and navigating the maze of a society they barely understood. Hershl Novak, one of the founders of the National Radical School in 1913, among the first Yiddish-language schools in Montreal, described in his memoirs prevailing mood of the community:

> I lived in Montreal for twelve years—from 1909 until 1921. Montreal is where I married and began a family. Over the course of those twelve years I personally—and Jewish Montreal even more so—changed and grew [. . .]. At that time, every young person who seriously and honestly wished to serve the interests of his people could become an important component in the building of a Jewish community here in Canada. Everything was new. The cultural life of the community was just taking shape, and everyone's contribution was apparent and important.[6]

Nowhere in the *Eagle* is the publication of *Fun mayn velt* mentioned. The book itself bears no date, nor does it contain any other information that could assist in determining the exact date of publication. The many handwritten notes and subsequent references to the book, including those of Caiserman, are inconsistent in this regard, suggesting either 1919 or 1920 without providing further details. A small hard-covered book printed on good quality paper, *Fun mayn velt* undoubtedly had a small print run, and was probably never sold commercially, except, perhaps, for a short time in one or two of Montreal's Yiddish bookstores. Essentially, the book was passed around within the city's literary and intellectual circles, and a few copies found their way outside of Canada to New York, Vienna, Warsaw, Kiev, and Vilna. The fragility and novelty of Yiddish publishing in Montreal is evident in the archaic orthography employed in *Fun mayn velt* and the overuse of the vowel signs[7] customary in literary Hebrew but less so in Eastern European Yiddish. When Segal's manuscript went to press in 1918, Yiddish orthography had not yet been standardized,[8] and several variants can sometimes be found within a single poem. It is also possible that the first Yiddish lino-typists in Montreal reproduced in Segal's book regional dialects or forms little used at the time, without being aware of it. As for the date of its publication, it is important to note the existence in the Montreal Jewish Public Library of a list in Yiddish[9] of all of Segal's poetry collections, written by hand after the poet's death, giving 1918 as the date of publication of *Fun mayn velt* (see Appendix 9). A lengthy article in the form of an obituary published in the *Eagle* on March 8, 1954, also gives 1918 as the publication date.[10] We also know that H. M. Caiserman wrote a review of Segal's first book in February of 1919 in the *Der Yidisher Arbeter*,[11] a Montreal monthly published by Shlomo Wiseman and Leyzer Meltzer, two Yiddish education activists and members in good standing of the Poale Zion. In view of the date of this first review, it is probable that *Fun mayn velt* was printed before 1919. Also, as opposed to the two previous years, in 1918 Segal published only three poems in the *Eagle*, all in July. This could be explained by the fact that the young poet, busy preparing his first poetry collection, had decided to save his best work for *Fun mayn velt* rather than have it printed in Montreal's Yiddish daily.

Today it is difficult to assess the significance of the publication of *Fun mayn velt* in 1918. At that time, no one had yet published a collection of Yiddish poetry in Montreal, and most of the readers did not have sophisticated literary tastes or even a very clear idea of what creative writing in Yiddish could be like. The author only presented a small sampling of his talent in the *Adler*, so that no one really knew how it would develop in the long run. There is no reason to believe that the publication of Segal's book was a resounding success in the Yiddish-speaking community of Montreal. An extensive community structure to promote the work and its author did not yet exist. In 1918, the Jewish Public Library, for example, had been functioning for only four years, all of them devoted to keeping the institution financially afloat.[12] Nevertheless, *Fun mayn velt* represented a great step forward for the poet because the book had given him the opportunity of having a readership for his longer poems, as well as a series of poems on the theme of winter conceived in the same spirit. This would have been impossible to achieve in the Yiddish daily newspaper, given its space limitations. In the book he had the freedom to adopt a more personal tone which up until then he could not have done in the *Eagle*, where he had to comply with the aesthetic criteria and adhere to the traditional religious themes favoured by Hershl Hirsch. On the other hand, the shy and naïve personality of the author, who had recently turned twenty-four, emerges clearly in this first published volume. In 1918 Segal had not yet earned the fame he would later enjoy in the Yiddish-speaking community of Montreal. Nor had he yet been forced to confront the adverse effects of the fierce competition often encountered in immigrant literary circles. *Fun mayn velt* leaves the impression of meeting a sensitive and vulnerable human inspired by his tremendous optimism about writing, and in complete surrender to his muse. Segal's poems also reflect his solitude and the impact of an exile experienced at a very young age, from which he never seemed to recover, despite his years in Montreal. One senses that the author is in search of an emotional equilibrium where his dreams and profound artistic desires could be further realized within his immediate surroundings. The reader is also struck by the precision of his observations and the delicacy of his feelings. A difficult existence darkened and disturbed the life of the young poet, as evidenced by this poem placed near the beginning of the book:

> I am a happy child.
> Yes, a happy child,
> Aloft on a happy and playful wind.
> Happily I sing
> And rejoice in my happy song.
> You in the darkened valley
> Stare at me in wonder;
> And in your eyes I see
> A man long years confined
> In pitch darkness and in night,
> Who suddenly in his prison
> Sees the brightest light.

A miracle has happened!
And all at once
above a thousand tearful choirs
My clear voice rises high
Into the sky.
I sing aloud my song of great joy,
I sing aloud my great song of joy.
You look at me in wonder
You look at me and wonder.

* * *

Childlike am I
All is a game for me.
I laugh at your desires,
I poke fun at your solemnity
It's an amusing game for me.

Childlike am I.
Your joy and your sadness
Just another game for me.
I laugh out loud and smile silently.

Childlike am I
And I play . . . [13]

The confidential and self-revelatory tone found in *Fun mayn velt* would characterize Segal's poetry for almost forty years, making his work unique in North American Yiddish literature. The author was also distancing himself from the ideological stance that characterized the earliest examples of this literature, the aim of which was usually to engage the Jewish working masses in the social and political struggle.

Intimist Writing

From the very start, introspective writing came naturally to Segal. It is strikingly manifest in *Fun mayn velt*, all the more so considering the fact that the book was published before the poet had had any formal contact with the American modernist groups known as *Di Yunge* (the Young Ones) and *In Zikh* (the Introspectivists). By avoiding political clichés and opportunities to sermonize, especially on behalf of the workers and the oppressed, Segal gave free rein to his imagination in conveying an emotion, a sudden image, or a solitary thought. The poet listened to his inner voice and surrendered to his deepest feelings. In *Fun mayn velt*, there was no filter to block the flow of words, no obstacle to stop the spontaneous expression of his feelings or to prevent him from communicating his fears, his joys, and his disappointments. Segal's temperament led him to observe incessantly, to focus on his "child's soul." He never stopped exposing and echoing his inner angst. The seasons, as well as celestial phenomena, captured the poet's attention, especially the rippling reflections which he studied attentively because they seemed to convey the spiralling of his emotions. Nature's fury inspired Segal's writing, but from an urban perspective, where the landscape is composed of structures aligned in immovable rows, humming with constant human activity. Through attentive listening and silent transposition, Segal revealed his inner sensitivities and frailties:

> So happy with my life am I!
> The good moments forever in my mind.
> The beautiful play of dreamlike fantasies
> My beautious dream of striving heavenward
> Fill me with joy.
> My heart delights
> And laughs like spring, budding and green.
>
> So happy with my life am I!
> Beautiful too my miseries!
> Time gave me not one single day
> Without new heavens bright to climb
> Without daydreams young and new
> Free as a bird am I
> My joy as pure and boundless as the sky.[14]

How does one determine what Segal felt in his heart of hearts and to what extent his preferred form of literary expression was dictated by his times? In the beginning, the poet throbbed with a unique emotionality, listening closely to the voices within. Yet he was usually incapable of exposing his feelings. Modernity provided an opportunity to actually write about himself as someone grappling with his own inner tensions and conflicting emotions. In 1918 Segal was publishing his first collection of introspective poetry at a time when writers all over the world were struggling with their feelings, their passions and their weaknesses. Segal was plagued by a painful inner life that found an outlet in his poetry and ensured its steady flow. Whether consumed by suffering or bursting with joy, Segal placed himself at the centre of his work. His poetry reflects the intensity of the emotions he experienced on a specific day, at a specific event, or during a specific encounter. Tossed about by a winter storm or cradled by spring breezes, the poet describes the places he visited on a daily basis, at times sweltering, at times scorched, at times encrusted with frost. In *Fun mayn velt* his introspective tendency of expressing an inner excitement impossible to contain was openly exposed, and helped to propel Segal into an era when all of Yiddish literature was turning toward individualism and art for art's sake. While other poets may have carefully and deliberately chosen this direction to keep in step with the times, Segal threw himself, body and soul, into a search for self, responding from the very outset to the urgent call of his inner life.

Fun mayn velt is divided into three parts which become progressively more intense emotionally. The book opens with a section entitled "With Sun and with Spring" (*Mit der zun un mitn friling*), followed by a section called "Urban Joy" (*Shtot freyd*), and closes with "Winter" (*vinter*), a recurrent theme in Segal's work. In the "sunny" first section, the poet emerges as an unbridled optimist, in sharp contrast to the tone he adopted later in his life, in the wake of a number of personal tragedies. Anticipating these more sombre moments, the poet feels within him the same force as that of nature transforming itself with the advent of the sun after the interminable sluggishness of winter. That section also contains "erotic" poems about adolescent girls on the brink of womanhood, confused by the first stirrings of love in their bodies. This can be seen as a metaphor for the burgeoning creative impulse that sweeps away everything in its path and propels the poet to artistic heights. These pages project the poet's desire to overcome the limitations imposed on him by his immediate surroundings, by social constraints, and by traditional ideas. The sun that caresses fleeting dreams, its first rays moving across the female bodies still drowsy with sleep, and the light which pulls them out of their nocturnal torpor, evoke a powerful awakening in which the poet, who has barely emerged from his childhood, is a participant. This is particularly discernable in a long poem of sixteen stanzas entitled "Summer Gold" (*Zumergold*), where Segal for the first time displays the full measure of his poetry. In series of poems, he develops a very personal imagery, frequently based on the passing of the seasons, and the intensity of celestial phenomena:

Summer Gold (excerpt)

Who laughs so sweetly from the heart?
Who laughs so unrestrained?
The world, the world has burst out laughing!
The world laughs as she greet the guests
Standing on her threshold,
here to enjoy her riches.
She cheers and refreshes them
after their long cold winter journey…

Who laughs so sweetly from the heart?
Who laughs so unrestrained?
The world, the world has burst out laughing!
The month of May covertly kissed her;
Carefree, blushingly she laughed
Like a young maiden for the first time
slipping on a woman's evening gown.

Who laughs so sweetly from the heart?
Who laughs so unrestrained?[15]

The Urban Aesthetic

The great originality of *Fun mayn velt,* and indeed all of Segal's work, resides in his poems about winter, which were published at a time when this theme was almost non-existent in French Quebec.[16] Segal, who was so responsive to the nature's charms and large-scale climatic phenomena, had rarely left Montreal since immigrating to Canada. In fact, the poet had not actually seen much of Canada other than the urban neighbourhoods of his adopted city. Like tens of thousands of other recently arrived Yiddish-speaking immigrants to America, the city was his only experience of the New World. Working six days a week in a sweatshop and existing on the meagre earnings of a tailor, Segal only knew the area of Montreal where he lived and from which he could sometimes escape to spend a few hours, on St. Helen's Island, or a park in a distant suburb. For the poet, the city contained all the beauties of the universe, and he looked upon it as an immense fresco which he desired to know better and explore. Segal also carried with him the vivid and painful memory of being uprooted from the place he had spent his childhood, Korets. He was continually making comparisons between the old and new worlds, separated by an abyss of oceanic proportions, and so different in their emotional nuances. On one side was his idealized childhood, and on the exhausting routine of working in a noisy factory. Somewhere between the two extremes, a new city materialized for the poet to explore and discover, a city that appeared to him so complex and puzzling that he was unable to absorb it all. Like so many of his co-religionists, every day Segal suffered the consequences of his fateful departure to which he had been compelled to resign himself a few years earlier. Once he moved to Montreal, the poet understood that nothing would ever be the same, that going back was now impossible. He was assailed by doubt, nostalgia, and the pain of abandonment, and these emotions became the driving force behind his poetry at the start of his career. Like so many young Yiddish-speaking Jews who had been uprooted, he sought with all his might to begin a new life in Canada. While he tried to focus on his present life in Montreal, sometimes joyful and sometimes painful, the memory of his formative years and his Eastern European Jewish sensibility came back to haunt him. *Fun mayn velt* contains several poems that feature the transposition of Segal's poetic imagination from his Volhynian *shtetl* of Korets to the big city that would become his for most of his life as a writer. His poetry was the first in all of Quebec literature to refer to immigration and, implicitly, the throbbing pain of exile:

> The young field laughs, and adorns herself
> In a little green frock.
> Tenderly the sky sings her praises:
> "What a pretty girl you are".
>
> Brazenly the giant city laughs
> Her brown eyes wild,
> Painted and perfumed
> Like a pretty whore.
>
> From afar I yearn
> For the young field maiden;
> but to the painted harlot
> I give away my soul.[17]

Thanks to Segal, the seductiveness of big cities, the allure of a more economically secure urban existence, and the dizzying rhythm of North American life became, for the first time, themes that could stir the poetic imagination. In *Fun mayn velt*, the difficult reconciliation of humble European origins with the hope for a better life on a new continent, paved the way for the first poems about Montreal in Canadian Yiddish literature. Nothing in the old country had prepared Segal to consider his adopted city as a source of transcendent imagery. He had not even known of its existence. The poet who while very young had left for an America that was both vast and indeterminate, projected onto the Montreal landscape his profound attachment to the port city which had welcomed him and offered his family a refuge from arbitrary politics and economic oppression. Despite his status of an exploited proletarian as well as the poverty in which he found himself here in Canada, and the dislocation of exile, Segal internalized and forged a quasi-idyllic vision of Montreal. In his first poems, Montreal is endowed with a power and vitality which, in many respects, conjure up the German cinema of the early 1900s. A city that appears out of nowhere, bursting with prosperity and perfectly modern, Montreal in *Fun mayn velt* triggers in the poet a barely contained amazement. Here the young Eastern European Jew, just uprooted from his *shtetl*, contemplates the irrepressible spirit of North American society transformed by accelerated economic development. Before his very eyes, Montreal was evolving in an explosion of light and smoke, in a kind of maelstrom where the incompressible energy of scientific progress was propelling all of society toward new accomplishments, as in the following poem, which in Yiddish begins with the words *O, vundersthot!*:

O, City of Wonders!

O, city of wonders! You are ablaze
from early dawn,
fuelling and fomenting
your eternal worries.

Gigantic, lumbering
you twist and turn
wrapping yourself in light and fire
and spit out iron!

O city of wonders! Magical city!
O dazzling flame,
Over coals you burn the days
And toss them carelessly away!

O city of wonders,
O dazzling flame![18]

In all likelihood, in 1918 the poet had not yet seen New York, nor had he experienced any North American city other than Mile End, where he lived, which was then a new industrial suburb where the large clothing factories on Main Street were located. From Segal's perspective, Montreal was also a place of political freedom and cultural autonomy which, in that era, had no equivalent in Eastern Europe. Not only was the city bustling with economic activity, but it offered Jewish immigrants an extraordinary opportunity to build a community network to their own specifications. In the newly formed cultural institutions activities increased without the least government censorship, no matter what language was used. Like many other Jews, Segal was in shock over a situation that was without precedent in Eastern Europe, and he was at pains to comprehend it. Despite the uncertainties of immigration, the long hours toiling in the factory, the difficulties of adjusting to a new country, and his inability to fully understand the English and French spoken around him, Segal marvelled at the new environment in which he found himself. Having left his *shtetl* with a burning desire to access the modern world and participate in the cultural revolution engulfing the Jewish world, he found himself thrust into a radically new society in Montreal. Moreover, this new world had emerged without having had to overthrow a privileged aristocracy or an all-powerful oligarchy. The window displays containing the most modern consumer goods, the lights that adorned the city's commercial thoroughfares, the glittery movie theatres on the Main, the rapid means of transportation, the pervading sense of optimism, all this conspired to buoy up the young Segal who, as we shall soon see, had hardly experienced any signs of economic and social liberalization prior to emigrating. His poem about Montreal bears witness to this unexpected discovery, and projects onto the city the astonishment coupled with silent fear experienced by many new arrivals. In this poem are novel images intimately bound up with the imaginary exile to distant lands which was the fate of so many Eastern European Jews all over the world.

All of you in far-off villages
nestled in green forests,
All of you by one thousand
tortuous and winding ways,
From remote stretches
and distant edges,
All of you will yet come to me.
You will bring your purest hearts
to burn upon my altar.

In my labyrinth
Of passion and splendid-golden sin,
Where one thousand mighty bugles sound,
I shall reveal to you the sources
of my deepest joy!
And one thousand lights will shine upon you.

All of you in open fields,
You will all yet come
to my kingdom of stone.
Your rivers and your forests
you will leave behind
in silent peace.[19]

These poems about Montreal also reveal to what extent Segal had been seduced by the call of modernity, and how far he had had to travel emotionally and socially before tasting its fruits in America. The emotional impact of this perilous journey can be gauged by the power of his poems about the city, and their poetic exultation. Caught up in the powerful currents which in the early twentieth century had reached the most remote regions of the Russian Empire, Segal was literally on fire in his description of his adopted city that throbbed with hope and profound satisfaction. Montreal's physical attributes—its boulevards, its location at the confluence of several waterways, and its historic monuments—triggered in him a process of inner emancipation and growth of exceptional intensity. It was as though the city's geography, climate, rockiness, and Nordic orientation were continuously bursting with energy. An inveterate and observant walker, Segal traversed Montreal day after day, absorbing in great detail every façade, every cobblestone, every branch of the urban landscape spread out before him. Scrutinizing streets, intersections and public parks, Segal went in search of their poetic soul. In this respect, *Fun mayn velt* should be seen as the point of departure of a lengthy exploration by the poet of his immediate environment, a quest he pursued his entire life, infusing much of his writing with a vibrant sensitivity. Minstrel of "Montrealness," Segal saw the city as a transposition of his journey from his humble *shtetl* to the incandescent shimmering of the New World. Yet he always found a neglected street in the large metropolis that would remind him of the Korets of his childhood, or a snow-covered park at night that whispered into his ear the sounds of his native Volhynia. Montreal, the last stop on his quest and the final stage of his exile, was the anchor of his poetic introspection. It radiated majesty and symbolism. In Montreal, the pain of leaving his childhood home, the loss of a vanished world, and the hardship of the trans-Atlantic crossing, found expression worthy of great literature.

The Canadian Winter

The last part of *Fun mayn velt* is devoted to a season that the poet considered the most appropriate for expressing his inner life, a season that was the most similar in its hardships to the torments he suffered on a daily basis. Having personally experienced winter storms, snow squalls, and abrupt changes of temperature, Segal enjoyed observing and describing sudden snowfalls, freezing temperatures, and unexpected thaws. He loved to see Montreal paralysed for hours by the mighty Canadian winter. The paroxysm of the elements and the thundering of the heavens provided the poet with the opportunity to excel in his writing. This is where his collection of poems reaches its creative heights. If it were necessary to find confirmation of Segal's talent as a poet in this first book, it would be in the stanzas that the reader is about to discover. In describing winter in his adopted homeland, Segal displayed the full scope of his literary capabilities, and convincingly justified the admiration of a small circle of writers who, during one of their evening sessions, gave him pride of place. More than one hundred years later, it makes the same impact. The strength and originality of the poet's voice can be heard in the whistling of the Nordic winds:

> O great wintry storm, friend of my tempestuous spirit!
> In your feverish frenzy you hold the soul of my song.
> You carry its wild tones, you sing them flawlessly.

Who else can fathom the storm songs as deeply as I?
In my ears they rage and roar.
Great songs, which for people must stay mute,
Grand songs, giant songs, songs endless songs,
Wild songs that boil in my blood,
O great wintry storm, I'll sing them all for you!
You alone can grasp them,
To you they're all familiar.
You are my blood-brother who compels my blood to sing.[20]

The theme of winter, sombre and at times sorrowful, did not stop Segal from delighting like a toddler at the first snowfall. In the above excerpt, it is not a tormented being that the poet presents, but a young man discovering his own affinity with nature, which so suddenly and furiously invades the city's protected space. In a single night Montreal is overpowered and the regular routine of its inhabitants interrupted. For a few hours, the child poet is able to track the great atmospheric forces that encircle the continent and dictate the changing of the seasons. The unleashing of these heavenly forces undoubtedly reminded him of how his coming to America had freed him from the weight of an age-old tradition, and made possible the fulfilment of his long-suppressed desire to write. Released from his moorings, Segal could sail where he pleased, and find in the tempest raging in Montreal an allusion to his own dramatic emancipation in this new world. This tremendous opportunity did not prevent him from presenting himself in *Fun mayn velt* as a timid and vulnerable person, ignorant of the ways of the world, whose exceptional talent had so precipitously pushed him into the literary limelight in his adopted country:

Many a wind has blown my way,
Tossed me about and flung me wildly.
Yet I am a boy, a boy have I remained.[21]

Composed in Yiddish on Canadian soil, Segal's first volume of poetry contains no explicit references to Judaism, the Jewish people, or to the actual situation of the Jews in Montreal. Everything in *Fun mayn velt* revolves around the poet's inner life and his feelings as he walks around the city, surrendering himself to its climate, its streets, and its inhabitants. Translated into French, the poems are devoid of any religious or cultural allusions. One could think they were produced by a talented young poet whom Quebec literary historians have over-looked. Segal, however, was writing in a Jewish language understood only by Eastern European Jewish immigrants, a language that uses the same Hebrew alphabet as the biblical prophets and the rabbis of the Talmud. He was part of the great cultural renaissance of the Yiddish language which had its roots in Eastern Europe and reached across the continents to the entire Ashkenazi diaspora through the "teachings" of Chaim Zhitlowsky (1865–1943), I. L. Peretz, and Sholem Aleichem. To his first readers in Montreal, who were already dreaming of transplanting a Yiddish culture at the foot of Mount Royal, Segal's poetry was evidence of the vitality of modern Jewish nationalism. It was also a testimony to the capacity of immigrant Jews to adjust to the New World and take advantage of America's great social and economic achievements. For his admirers, born and edu-cated in the unique environment of the *shtetl*, Segal's writing signified the end of the isolation of Yiddish culture and its entry into the early twentieth century literary world of Leo Tolstoy, Rainer Maria Rilke, Romain Rolland, Knut Hamsun, and Alain-Fournier. In this context, encumbering Yiddish poetry with references to either recent Jewish history or religious tradition seemed superfluous to Segal. This con-stituted a thematic rupture with his first poems which had appeared in the *Eagle*. Smitten by universalism and literary modernism, Segal compiled his first book of poems without exposing those aspects of his sensibility that had their origins in his Jewish education and reflected the situation of Eastern European Jewry. Similarly, his men-tors Moshe Shmuelsohn, H. M. Caiserman, and Reuben Brainin had turned their attention to the future. They looked forward to the cre-ation of a Jewish national homeland in Palestine, and the rise of a large Yiddish-speaking urban proletariat in North America. It seemed that Jews, wherever they were living, had no choice but to finally enter the vast and perplexing modern world. Modestly, even timidly, *Fun mayn velt* paved the way in Montreal for developments that could no longer be avoided. That was the decisive contribution made by Segal in 1918 to the advancement of Yiddish letters.

The poet's declared determination to approach Yiddish poetry from a fresh perspective also manifested itself in the way he used his mother tongue. In *Fun mayn velt*, in poem after poem, he made a con-scious choice to use an almost exclusively Germanic vocabulary that closely reflects the roots of Yiddish in medieval German. In so doing, the poet was favouring a language closer to the universal references of

European culture and distancing himself from biblical imagery filled with descriptions of the vast desert expanses of the Middle East. He also made the decision to create imagery free of any obvious reference to traditional Jewish culture. For Yiddish speakers reading *Fun mayn velt* in 1918, this abrupt change seemed completely novel, to the point of inventing a new mode of literary expression out of an everyday language, cobbled together from Hebraisms, Talmudic expressions, and references to Orthodox Jewish practice. Numerous Yiddish books and articles published during this era in Montreal, in the *Keneder Adler* (*The Jewish Daily Eagle*)[22] and elsewhere, show that Yiddish journalists and authors, as a general rule, did not shy away from the everyday language of the Eastern European Jewish immigrants. It was not unusual for immigrants to include in spoken Yiddish a hodgepodge of foreign words recently acquired from Russian, Polish, maskilic Hebrew, or North American English. Segal's linguistic choices in *Fun mayn velt* correspond to his desire to develop a distilled language removed from its medieval roots and ancient religious heritage in order to serve his objective of a universal modernist form of literary expression. In choosing this direction, utopian at that time, to say the very least, the poet was seeking to create a language which, in terms of its power and impact, was on a par with the great European languages that had benefitted, since the Renaissance, from the contributions of grammarians, literary critics, and connoisseurs determined to fashion superior forms of literary expression in contrast to the language spoken by the masses. Segal's approach to poetry was also in keeping with attempts by Europe's minorities to create modern literature in languages such as Danish, Polish, and Rumanian, by extracting elements from rural folklore that could further their national aspirations. The skillful and sometimes ideological manipulation of Yiddish in Segal's writing in1918, also found in several other places in the Eastern European diaspora at that time, contributed to the novel tone of *Fun mayn velt*. That is why the poet's innovative and carefully polished language elicited enthusiasm in Montreal's small literary circles, which were also passionately committed to modernity. Segal's book heralded not only a break with the laborious writing methods employed until then by Montreal's Yiddish journalists, but also a much more significant change in the spirit and style of the language. Even a present-day reader can grasp the great difference between Segal and his predecessors by reading the transliterated version of a poem about Montreal translated above as "O, City of Wonders." The use of bold and modern images, all associated with a sprawling industrial city, is echoed by the jerky rhythm of the verses, and the sequence of sharp sounds grouped in short and repetitive phrases:

O! Vundershtot! Du flakerst oyf
fun friyen morgn,
fartumelst un farshturemst
dayn eybige zorgn.

Tsudreyst zikh azoy rizig-shver
in dayne krayzn,
du varfst zikh um mit flam un likht,
un shpayst mit ayzn!

O vundershtot! O tsoybershtot!
Du flam, du bunter,
farbrenst di teg oyf koyl un varfst
zey rosh arunter!

O vundershtot! O tsoybershtot!
Du flam, du bunter![23]

Segal could not purge the language of every trace of its Judaic origins, nor could he erase the thousand years that Yiddish was used alongside Hebrew in the practice of the Mosaic faith. For example, on page 13 of *Fun mayn velt* there is a poem entitled "*Yontef,*" meaning holiday, which opens with the following words: "*Haynt iz yontef bay dem himel* (Today is a holiday in heaven)." The title, "*Yontef,*" is composed of two Hebrew words, "*yom tov,*" which together literally mean "good day," referring to a day devoted to God and the study of His revealed word. Since the Yiddish word for holiday in a secular sense is also "*yontef,*" Segal could allow himself to introduce it into his poetry without undermining his modernist approach. The same can be said of the poem about immigration cited earlier, which begins: "*Ir ale, ale in di derfer vayt!* (All of you in far-off villages)." In the first verse, Segal uses the word *misbeyakh*, which in biblical Hebrew means "altar," the type of sacrificial altar used by Abraham when he offered his son Isaac to God. In the poem, *mizbeyakh* alludes to the furnaces in the large factories that took in immigrants by the thousands, and forced them to work long hours in a noxious environment. Just as the ancient rituals of animal sacrifices and harvest offerings were performed to find favour in the eyes of God, so the city feeds upon the blood and energy of its defenceless inhabitants to hasten the advance of capitalism and increase the profits of the propertied classes. This allusion was clear to the readers of *Fun mayn velt* who were familiar with the Bible and had no need for an explanation. The word *mizbeyakh* is not generally used in this "industrial" sense. Hence, when Segal in 1918 employed religious terminology, it was for the purpose of giving it new and unexpected meanings. This device of updating and universalizing the Judaic component of Yiddish was a major part of the young Segal's originality, and considered very creative at that time.

Another aspect of Segal's shift to modernity in *Fun mayn velt* is the utilization of free verse, and the fact that he chose to include poems of various lengths. The poems that were printed in the *Eagle* before 1917 were consistently structured in rhyming quatrains. The following year, in his published book, he broke all conventions by offering a variety of forms. Segal achieved this result without sacrificing the aesthetics of language and the established criteria of poetic sonority. The result was the redesigning of the formal and structural aspect of his writing and the displacement of the usual meanings of Yiddish words, two directions that propelled the author far along the road to the radical refurbishing of Yiddish poetry. This is evidenced by the segment of the poem found on page 10 of *Fun mayn velt*, earlier presented in translation that begins with "Childlke am I." The simplicity of the words, the irregularity of the form, and the introspective nature of the text make it a good example of what Segal was trying to accomplish in his first volume of poetry that captured the imagination of his Montreal colleagues:

> Kindish bin ikh:
> ales iz bay mir a shpil!
> K'lakh zikh oys fun ayer tsil!
> Kh'shpil zikh um mit ayer ernst,
> er iz mir a shener shpil.

> Kindish bin ikh :
> ayer freyd un ayer umet
> iz far mir a bunter shpil;
> lakh ikh hoykh un shmeykhl shtil!

> Kindish bin ikh,
> un ikh shpil zikh…[24]

This approach, already present in Segal's youthful writing, would be his for the duration of his career, with the addition of new elements already introduced in 1918 in *Fun mayn velt*, although not yet fully developed. The vivacity of his writing, the exuberance of his creativity, and the powerful flow of his words would be among the elements that in time would assert themselves to the point where he would become incontestably the most prolific and recognized of the Canadian Yiddish writers. Having arrived in the country very early, he was seen by many less experienced poets as a trailblazer whose advice and assistance they sometimes sought.[25] The poem about Montreal, among others, sealed his reputation as a great literary innovator, and an important source of inspiration for Jewish Anglophone writers in Canada. Over the ensuing decades, Segal would interweave the same complex biblical vocabulary and imagery in describing the city from the vantage point of a solitary pedestrian.[26] To his theme of "Montrealness" would later be added subjects such as exile and the loss of one's birthplace that remained a source of suffering, but also of nostalgia, for a poet who tended to idealize his early years in the Pale of Settlement.

An Exemplary Influence

Despite its limited circulation and the small size of Montreal's literary circles, *Fun mayn velt* contributed enormously to Segal's artistic and literary influence, both in Canada and abroad. Indeed, the book made its way well beyond Montreal, as Melekh Ravitch pointed out in the *Eagle* in 1945.[27] This was notably the case in Vienna, where Ravitch found himself in 1919, and where newly arrived Yiddish poets discovered the work of Segal for the first time, thanks to H. M. Caiserman. As for Shmuelsohn, he decided to send some poems written by his protégé to Saul Joseph Janovsky (1864–1939), editor-in-chief of the anarchist New York weekly *Di Freie Arbeiter Stimme*, known in English as the *Free Voice of Labour*, where they made a strong impression when they were published: "Janovsky was known as an extremely severe editor, particularly to beginners. But Segal's first serial [*sic*] of poems he published prominently."[28] According to Caiserman, who reported this information in the Toronto Yiddish newspaper *Der Yidisher Zhurnal*,[29] known in English as the *Hebrew Journal*, Janovsky himself published a critique of Segal in the *Di Freie Arbeiter Stimme* in which he praised him highly. In addition to Melekh Ravitch, Caiserman recalled having contacted the Viennese poets Alexander and Esther Kashin,[30] Moshe Zilberg, A. M. Fuchs, Melekh Chmelnitzki, David Fogel and Tukhatchevsky about Segal. Kashin apparently declared at that time: "Everything the Young Jewish Poets' Group (*Di Yunge* in New York) looked for in their poetry—J. I. Segal had already revealed in his first book of 67 pages (*Fun mayn velt*)."[31] Later, in 1922, when Caiserman visited Vienna on his way to Palestine, he discovered that Segal was already known to the editors of the Yiddish literary journal *Kritik*.

However, at this point in his young career, the most interesting information about Segal comes from Melekh Ravitch, a native of Galicia, who lived in Vienna from 1912 to 1921, where he published in first book of poetry in 1921 entitled *Nakete lider* (Naked poems). The members of the modernist literary group called *Khalyastre* [the gang], which included Ravitch, had assumed that J. I. Segal, in addition to his exceptional talent, would have a clearly identifiable handwriting. They had expected his handwriting to be uneven and full of erasures, as befitted a poet charting a new course in literature. How surprised they were to discover that "on the contrary, his handwriting was smooth and graceful, without a trace of tension, as fluid and sparkling as a little forest stream, babbling in the sunlight and singing when it encounters stones and little chasms along its way, but most of all it continues onward—never looking back, always onward, onward . . ."[32] Except for Ravitch's resort to poetic license, his description corresponds exactly to the literary manuscripts donated by Segal's heirs to the Jewish Public Library. On these pages, the letters and words are perfectly aligned by a sure and patient hand befitting the son of a scribe, without almost no corrections or changes in rhythm.. In his description, Ravitch also alludes to the fluidity of Segal's early poems. The Viennese poets' emphasis on Segal's handwriting is understandable because in 1919 it was the only physical manifestation of the man from distant Canada with whom they had corresponded. This situation changed the day a picture of Segal arrived in Vienna. Melekh Ravitch, also a poet, who moved to Montreal in 1941, penned a striking account in 1945 of the impression made on him twenty-five years earlier by Segal's photograph. His text merits attention because it is one of the rare descriptions of Segal's physical appearance at the time that *Fun mayn velt* was published:

> [His face] had an intensity, a clarity. Even his eyeglasses—we noticed—were also plain, shiny, not horn-rimmed but frameless. His lips were disproportionately large for his face, passionate and

tragic, and not—as is the case with most poets, especially gentle, lyric wordsmiths—pleasant and affable, just as his poems suggested. That Segal was only of medium height, we did not know. We thought he was tall—both because of his poems and the face in the photograph. Why? I don't know.[33]

In February of 1919, a few weeks after the publication of *Fun mayn velt*, Caiserman announced the publication of Segal's book in a left-wing Montreal monthly journal.[34] This was an event of paramount significance, because it was the first time in its history that Canadian Yiddish literature had found someone capable of analysing and judging the quality of work published in Yiddish in Canada. Caiserman's review of 1919 also reaffirmed the friendship shared by the two men, a relationship that endured, except for minor interruptions, for over thirty years. A bond was also created that would play a crucial role in Montreal Yiddish literature when it came to literary criticism. Evidently at this time, Caiserman already had a long-term vision for Jewish creativity in Montreal and its artistic potential. A community activist and journalist, as well as entrepreneur, Caiserman also sought to play the role of fatherly mentor to young Jewish writers. He did not hesitate to become their patron, giving them material support as well as promoting their work outside of immigrant circles, as evidenced by the numerous references in the archives to the literary and cultural soirées he hosted in his home. Furthermore, in his first review of 1919, the critic stressed the need for a venue for cultural exchange between authors and readers, to alleviate the isolation suffered by Montreal's Yiddish writers. Caiserman's care and concern would prove to be crucial in accelerating the broader dissemination of their work. In Caiserman's view, the community was not doing enough to enter into a dialogue with its most promising writers: "O modesty, modesty! If we were not so modest with regard to our young talents, perhaps they would, at the very least, develop a better sense for evaluating the most brilliant as well as the less successful aspects of their writing."[35] Nonetheless, in his 1919 critique, Caiserman had no qualms about pointing out that Segal lacked literary judgment in publishing his weaker poems in the first section of his book. According to Caiserman, the author should have begun with some of his strongest poems, which unfortunately were relegated to the back, in particular the poem cited above, which begins with the line "O great wintry storm, friend of my tempestuous spirit!"[36]

On the other hand, Caiserman stated that the poems in the second and third sections of *Fun mayn velt* compared favourably with the best Yiddish poetry in Europe or even America. What a pity, he maintained, that a young talent like Segal sometimes allowed banalities to creep into his writing, whereas he deserved comparison with the Hebrew poet Chaim Nachman Bialik,[37] above all with regard to his poems about Montreal. Such effusive praise, of which Segal was perhaps more deserving later in his career, was indicative of the high regard Caiserman had for the author of *Fun mayn velt*, and how promising he considered his literary talent. In the critic's opinion, the inner world that the poet revealed to his readers was "huge, immense and limitless, full of storms and fantasies and secret wonders." The critic was immediately struck by the forceful energy of the poems. Segal's talent was real, palpable, and capable of producing an enduring body of work. More than that, Caiserman wanted to convey to the young and inexperienced writer that his language was "brilliant and marvellously beautiful," capable of growing and reaching the summit of Yiddish literature. Having in its midst such a Heaven-blessed poet[38] required an awareness on the part of the Montreal Jewish community that it was duty-bound, in the interests of Yiddish high culture, to give Segal financial support, and provide him with long-term creative space. At stake was also Montreal's reputation as the main Jewish centre in Canada and the hub of Yiddish creativity. It is clear from his 1919 critique that Caiserman already understood that writers, artists, and intellectuals living on the Mount Royal Plateau would instil in their fellow Jews a sense of cultural achievement unimaginable in Canada thus far, especially for such a small immigrant group. This was undoubtedly the reason he ended his review with the most encouraging words about Segal:

> His winter poems are new and original, both in their ideas and their form. I can't imagine that any serious critic would have the least hesitation in welcoming J. I. Segal into the small family of our best writers.
> Except for the first section, this book is a brilliant beginning. And if the various city and winter poems are the offspring of Segal's world, then that world is rich, robust, and fantastic, and Yiddish literature can expect many discoveries from this magical world.[39]

The Genesis of a Yiddish Poet

The previous remarks help explain how J. I. Segal's literary talent manifested itself for the first time in Montreal, as well as the manner in which he was welcomed in 1917 by the small group of Yiddish cultural activists. Modern in spirit and innovative in form, his poetry caused a sensation among those dedicated to the development of a body of Canadian Yiddish literature. By 1919, Segal was being read and appreciated as much in Europe as in America, and at least one well-known New York periodical had given him rave reviews. This unexpected success, however, should not overshadow the circumstances of his childhood in the Russian Pale. The year 1910, the year he moved to Montreal, marked a time of profound dislocation in Segal's emotional life, especially because of the way he would henceforth internalize his traditional Jewish upbringing. Abruptly separated by an impassible distance from the environment where he was born, and immediately thrust into a totally unfamiliar factory setting, almost overnight Segal had had to sever his ties with the world of his early childhood, the world of the *shtetl*. Nonetheless, this rupture, which appeared permanent and irreversible to the young immigrant, did not prevent traditional imagery from resurfacing later in his writing, and inspiring his poetic imagination in the long run. The physical separation, the loss of extended family references, and the abandonment of religious practice—three factors that might have been a significant encumbrance for the Montreal poet in search of a new identity, and all clearly detectible in *Fun mayn velt*—would ultimately have only a fleeting influence on Segal and his work. For that reason, we must now go back and examine the first thirteen years of his life in the empire of the Russian tsars to better grasp the cultural and religious ideas to which the author was exposed at an impressionable age, as well as events of a more personal nature that he had had to confront at a very young age. As much as Segal claimed to be a modernist, and rightly so, deep inside he carried the enduring fragments of a prior epoch of which no concrete trace remained in America, including Montreal.

A return to the years from 1896 to 1910 presents unique difficulties because that world was swept away by the October Revolution of 1917. For most Montreal Jews it brought back memories of pogroms and widespread anti-Semitic persecution, as well as tremendous deprivation and destitution. Two successive world wars and the horrors of the Holocaust have created an almost unbridgeable divide between our era and the conditions in which Eastern European Jews found themselves at the turn of the previous century. Segal himself, as we shall soon see, was really not interested in describing his childhood in great detail, and he left behind very little that could shed light on his family life. First and foremost a poet, Segal evidently was not convinced that an objective autobiography would contribute much to the advancement of his career. Instead, one must search the emotional component of his poetry to find the necessary material for even a partial reconstruction of his Russian childhood. However, were it not for the biographical efforts of his friend and literary critic H. M. Caiserman, the oblique references in Segal's poetry would most likely be insufficient to provide us with an accurate picture of his early upbringing and education in Europe.

Caiserman, who immediately understood that his friend's artistic and cultural contribution was unparalleled in the world of Montreal Yiddish literature, at some point decided to interview Segal about noteworthy aspects of his years in Volhynia. In so doing, Caiserman was most certainly aware of the importance of paving the way for future researchers who would one day try to assess the significance of Segal's poetry from a global perspective. Caiserman's desire to prepare the groundwork and bequeath to posterity the history of Canadian Yiddish literature in its infancy, continued to motivate him for the rest of his working life, and led him to become a literary critic. However, nothing had really prepared this man, who was an accountant by profession, to play this crucial role in Yiddish literature. The desire to chronicle and perpetuate Yiddish culture was not exclusive to literary critics. It can be found throughout Montreal Yiddish culture and politics, and especially among journalists and political activists closely associated with the construction of an institutional community framework.[40] No one, however, did as much as Caiserman in describing the literary and artistic circles that were launched many decades earlier at the foot of Mount Royal:

> I have always wondered in what milieu Segal was born, how he developed, and from whom and how he inherited such great talents, and often when I questioned Segal, and seeked [sic] information, I retired in silence, and with extreme attention listened to him, whose words seemed to flow from his innermost being, and then many things became clear, about his personality and about his creative work, and he thus became nearest to me.[41]

These precious autobiographical fragments, most written in English and some in Yiddish, obviously dictated by Segal during personal encounters between the two men, have been gathered together in an undated twenty-page manuscript. They can be dated roughly with reference to a handwritten marginal note in Caiserman's handwriting in a similar document.[42] In an attempt to ascertain Segal's exact age during one such interview, the literary critic hastily subtracted 1896, the poet's year of birth, from the year 1939. This spontaneous mathematical calculation is a reasonable indication of when Caiserman began collecting material for a book about Segal's life, which he never formally completed. "Segal's mother resided for a time in the garret of his grand-father's [sic] residence. These chapters Segal will reveal in a planned auto-biography. My intention is only a short narated [sic] biography of the poet,"[43] he declares in one of these surviving documents. Elsewhere, in the same manuscript, Caiserman provides another chronological clue by writing "I enjoy [sic] J. I. Segal's friendship soon after his arrival to Canada about thirty years ago. During all these years, I recall the constant literary conversations in my home and on the silent streets of Montreal."[44] The information Caiserman collected a long time after the fact, at a time when the poet was revered by the Montreal cultural elite, contains enough reliable information to merit our attention. Moreover, it was obtained in a situation of mutual trust, as emphasized by the biographer from the outset: "I met Segall [sic] soon after his arrival to Canada, when a friendship developed, which today retains mutual confidence and loving quality. This friendship was and is based on this great literary creativeness, and on his rare intelligence, sparkling humour and devotion."[45] As opposed to the document addressed to the I. L. Peretz Writers' Association in 1923, cited in Chapter 1, the poet tells Caiserman that he was born on August 3, 1896, in Solobkovtsy (*Slobkovitz* in Yiddish), a village situated near Proskurov,[46] a large town in the province of Podolia in the Russian Pale of Settlement. As already mentioned, J. I. Segal was born to an extremely pious family that already included five children.

In 1927 Zalman Rejzen, an eminent lexicographer and literary historian who lived in Vilna during the interwar period, tried to present a more formal description of Segal's family background. According to Rejzen, on his father's side, Segal was a descendant of Rabbi Yom Tov Lippman Heller (1579–1654),[47] a Talmudic scholar from Moravia and revered commentator on the Mishnah.[48] Rejzen also claims that Segal's mother belonged to the family of Rabbi Jacob of Anopol who was a student of the Baal Shem Tov (1700–1770), the founder of Hassidism. As the poet's genealogy would indicate, within the context of Eastern European traditional Judaism, the poet was of illustrious descent. That Segal's contemporaries sought to emphasize the poet's pious pedigree (*yikhes* in Yiddish) and link him with his venerable and saintly ancestors is indicative of the high esteem they had for his work. This search for the rabbinical pedigree of famous people persisted among modern Jews, even in the case of someone whose accomplishments were completely in the secular sphere and who during his lifetime was not a practising Jew. In addition, the poet's father, Aaron Ber, the cantor at the Proskurov synagogue and known for his musical talent, was also a scribe, an occupation requiring fine calligraphy and generally practised by people known for their piety. In a 1934 poem Segal painted a picture of his father and the milieu in which he had lived for most of his life. His father appears on the day of his death when a heavenly messenger has arrived to take him away from the world of the living. Outside his home the profound spirituality of his world is apparent.

Winter

(Translated by Grace Schulman)

My father woke at dawn
and found death at the table
in an empty grey house.

Death rose from the bench,
cane in hand,
came to his bed,
and said, like a Jewish stranger:

Reb Aron Ber,
you're not well;
it's still and white;
the road is easy and silent.
Look: just hold on to me
and off we'll go.

And off they went.
They passed the synagogue.
The first *minyen** was at prayer,

candles and and lamps in the window,
and goodness lay
over the high snow.[49]

* *minyen* (in Hebrew *minyan*): a minimum of ten Jews who may
form a communal prayer quorum

Aaron Ber, described by Caiserman as "a scribe, an intellectual,
prominent in the community," died at the age of forty-eight, when his
youngest son was only three years old. This tragic event forced Segal's
mother to return with her seven children to the home of her father,
an established merchant in the small town of Korets,[50] located about
100 km north of Proskurov. Segal's grandfather, David Perlmuter, is
described by Caiserman, presumably according to information given
him by Segal, as follows: "[A] cultured man and God-fearing and a
warm adept of the Trisk rabbi. He was in addition an aesthetic person, clean and well dressed, with a measured proud walk and good
appearance."[51] This seemingly straightforward portrait identifies
Segal's grandfather as part of the Hasidic movement, and a follower
of Rabbi Abraham Twersky (1806–1889) of the town of Trisk (Turisyk),
and known as the Trisker *magid*. David Perlmuter's personality also
fits the profile generally ascribed to his followers, namely, well-edu-
cated, well-to-do, and distinguished-looking. Twersky was an ener-
getic leader. His religious teachings were on based on the *Kabbalah*,
and on *gematria*, a system according to which words in the Torah were
interpreted according to the numeric value of their Hebrew letters.

The above details conclusively confirm that Segal grew up in a
strictly religious household, surrounded by relatives who were highly
regarded in their community. In Korets, which was a *shtetl* according
to the classic definition of this term, the poet lived in proximity to his
maternal grandfather, a Hasid who followed to the letter the teachings of his Hasidic *rebbe*. Perlmuter's strict adherence to the precepts
and customs of the Trisk Hasidim did not prevent him from being
open to the modern secular world. This is reflected, for example, in
the fact that Segal as a child learned so-called secular subjects such as
non-Jewish languages, geography, history, and the natural sciences.
In fact, in response to the scientific advances of their century, many
great Orthodox Jewish scholars advised their disciples not to turn
their backs on the advantages of a more general education, on condition, however, that they subordinate their new knowledge to belief in

God and obedience to His laws. This balance of religious conviction and objective knowledge helped the young poet to gradually become aware of the outside world and the great social and economic transformations which would radically affect the life of Eastern European Jewry at the turn of the century.

The Korets *Talmud Torah* and Its *Nigun*

While Segal was awaiting the day when he could escape the confines of his *shtetl*, from a very young age he attended a traditional school for young boys run by a certain Reb Shmuel. According to Caiserman's account, he attended this *heder* for two years where he was taught the basic concepts of his religion by the proven method that consisted of tirelessly repeating verses from the *Torah* and the prayer book of the Ashkenazi Jews called the *siddur*. This pedagogical approach, based exclusively on memorization, familiarized the poet from an early age with the traditional rhythmical chanting of the Masoretic text according to markings indicating vocalization and accentuation, markings contained in the biblical text passed down among Eastern European Jews for thousands of years. The result is a melody called a *nigun*, a term that includes both the phonetic pronunciation of the text letter by letter, and the musicality of the recitation. A child in *heder* is introduced to a kind of traditional leitmotif sung repeatedly, which, instead of allowing for an immediate understanding of the profound meaning of the text, opens his senses to its melodic and symbolic significance. Caiserman believed that this environment was where the poet first absorbed the musicality and rhythm of traditional Hebrew, which he later tried to reproduce in his Yiddish writing. According to him, Segal's earliest *heder* with its *nigun* repeated a thousand times played a crucial role in the poet's future literary sensibility. The melody endlessly repeated became a rhythm that embedded itself deep in the poet's memory. "I have heard Segal say how much poetic joy results from the sublime years of childhood. It was in fact one of the most joyous remembrances of Segal's childhood."[52]

The same fascination occurred when Segal, at the age of eight, was enrolled in the more progressive *heder* of Rabbi Nukhem. The poet had a similar experience two years later when he began his studies at the Korets Talmud Torah, a modern religious institution (*heder metukan* or *heder mesukan*) where secular subjects were taught, although still within the context of rigorous religious observance. Financed by the Korets Jewish community it was intended for boys whose families could not otherwise afford a Jewish education. Its director, Aaron Hershenhorn, was a practising Jew and author of scientific books. There was a vast difference between the traditional *heder* of Segal's early childhood and the Talmud Torah, which Caiserman described as follows:

> An entirely new world opened up for Segal in the Talmud Thora compared; with the previous narrow cheder, with permanent children-noise, with narrow benches near the ground, around the walls, on which children moved from one place to another, the present Talmud Thora, with large classes, well-lit large windows, benches arranged in a perfect order.[53]

In the Talmud Torah the young student was initiated into the Jewish tradition by reading the Book of Isaiah and a Hebrew poem by the Spanish poet Judah Halevy (1075–1141) *Tsion ha-lo tishali* ("Zion, will you not ask about the welfare of your prisoners?"). He also studied the famous commentaries on the Bible and the Babylonian Talmud by Rashi (1020–1105), one of the bases of Jewish rabbinic interpretation. Once again, the specific melody of the Hebrew text roused Segal's imagination, as he confided to Caiserman: "This particular *nigun* has sparkled and glittered somewhere in the distances and depths of my poems."[54] These words, which were not those of a young poet at the beginning of his career, but of a mature man at the apex of his artistic achievement, underscore the existence of a strong link between his Yiddish writing and traditional Hebrew texts. In another biographical account in English interspersed with Yiddish, Caiserman recalls the influence of a certain Reb Mordecai Eisig on the young student. A teacher of Jewish studies and the Yiddish language in the *Korets* Talmud Torah, Eisig was a *maskil*, an adherent of the Jewish Enlightenment. He called himself a member of the *Chovevei Zion* (lovers of Zion), who fervently hoped for the creation of a national Jewish homeland in Palestine. It was mainly thanks to him that Segal was introduced to a deeper understanding of the *nigun* of the Hebrew prayers and the Bible. About this authority figure Segal confided to his biographer:

> In a later class, Mordechai Eisig studied the *Sefer Ishaya* with his students with a *nigun* that Segal partially remembers, but is sure

that he carries within and thinks that a moment will come when it will come back to him completely, and it seems that in speaking to me about Mordechai Eisig, Segal remarked that this particular melody was glowing somewhere deep down within his songs, and he thinks that if one of Eisig's pupils should ever be destined to read his poems, they would remind the reader of that melody.[55]

In a later version of Segal's biography, Caiserman enlarges upon the influence of Mordechai Eisig on the poet's work. Once again the centrality of the biblical text in Segal's education is evident, as well as the attachment of the poet to this literary tradition as it was taught in the Korets Talmud Torah. According to the interviews that took place at the end of the 1930s, Eisig personally kindled in his young student the desire to become a teacher in a Jewish school, which is what actually happened in Montreal several years later but in a very different secular context. It should also be noted that Eisig shared many personality traits with Segal, including his gentleness, his patience, and his charisma:

> Segal carries in his soul the picture of his dear teacher, who taught *Tanakh* (Bible) with many commentaries, but the most important *perush*[56] was Mordechai Eisig himself, his own personality, his Voice, his fatherly mild eyes: His teacher has become a part in the world of his Memories. This world in Segal's eyes is a great book, and how many pages he may write today into it, he feels that an unseen hand which stems from the near past, re-writes them again.[57]

These personal aspects of Segal's early life highlight the Yiddish-Hebrew linguistic duality in the literary education of the generation of writers who were born and schooled in Europe but later immigrated to Montreal at the beginning of the twentieth century, a duality which sometimes makes it difficult to distinguish between the religious and secular influences in their work. Despite subsequent denials by some, and their often total lack of interest in religious practice, it is an incontrovertible fact that among several Canadian Yiddish poets there is convincing evidence of an excellent knowledge of the Bible and the Talmud. Such familiarity with the sacred texts of Judaism, and centuries of commentary, had a great influence on the literary direction of many of them such as Sholem Shtern,[58] a colleague of Segal's and ardent communist. When, in 1960, Shtern declared that he wanted to reject certain types of traditional Jewish moralistic literature it was certainly not for lack of having studied it systematically in his youth in the old country:

> We are against hackneyed variations on the themes of *kedusha* [holiness] and *ahavas Yisroel* [love for one's fellow Jews]. It is a sign that we have no foundation, that we have separated our-selves from own world of ideas and ideals. A poet who is deeply rooted in the life of his people, in the traditional Jewish melody, and draws on our own age-old sources, does not have to declare that he is an *ohev yisroel*, a lover of the Jewish people, and has no need to justify himself day in and day out.[59]

Although in his writing Segal steered clear of Shtern's strong proletar-ian proclivities, he certainly did not escape the same inner conflict. This tension manifests itself especially in the aesthetic and ideological choices evident in his first book of poetry of 1918, where there are no obvious traces of his Jewish religious education. His affiliation with the American literary group *Di Yunge*, in the early 1920s, would do nothing to alter this situation. In fact, it was not until the 1930s, and in particular in 1940, that this Judaic component would surface explicitly and incessantly in Segal's writing. Thereafter the impact of his years spent on the benches of a Jewish community school in Korets would inform all his writing and became increasingly evident. At the end of his life the poet more discernably integrated themes from his child-hood and the world of the *shtetl*, where religious observance was an integral part of Jewish life. Caiserman is very explicit about this:

> But when Segal's mood is joyous, he can return to his Korets; he does not need to fly on the wings of his fantasy. Korets is for him a living concrete place. It is etched on the chart of his memory, with its streets and alleyways, with its hilly and lower districts, with the market place and shores, with is shul-gas, the street of synagogues and prayer houses . . .[60] It is for Segal a place of artis-tic perpetuity.[61]

Nonetheless, in Montreal Segal never led the life of a religious Jew and was indifferent to the obligations of religious observance that gave a rhythm to the days and weeks of believers. Evidence to this effect is provided by the poet Melech Ravitch, Segal's colleague and, from 1941, one of his closest friends. One day, soon after Ravitch's arrival in Montreal, as they were walking in the Jewish neighbourhood, they were accosted by a very persistent individual:

> On my first day in Montreal where I had come to settle in 1941, Segal and I, two Jewish poets, were walking along the Jewish "Main Street" when a Jew ran out of a house and grabbed both of us by our coattails: "Come in for the afternoon prayer . . ." With great difficulty we managed to refuse because we were in a hurry, and this dishevelled man was not to our liking.[62]

It is not without irony that Ravitch confesses later in the same article that among Segal's poems, which he found most touching at that time, was one that was about the afternoon prayer, *minkhe,* which Segal most certainly was not in the habit of reciting. How sad the dusk was, Ravitch continues in his account. What kept the two Yiddish poets from joining their fellow Jews in reciting the afternoon prayer? These affinities so difficult to express, and the rush to follow the road to modernity, did not prevent Segal from writing poems with religious content, indeed poems that reflected the values of Hasidism, in which he acknowledged that he was far from indifferent to the divine presence. Those poems, however, belong to a much later period in the poet's life.

First Literary Influences

The Korets Talmud Torah, because it was open to the outside world, also offered Russian language classes, taught by a man by the name of Bazinover. This teacher became a father figure for Segal and introduced him to the great non-Jewish poets Alexander Pushkin (1799–1837), Mikhail Lermontov (1814–1841), and Aleksey Koltsov (1809–1842), all considered founders of modern Russian literature, and worthy representatives of the literary canon of that time. Pushkin in particular, who tragically died young, personified the spirit of the Russian language and the true Russian temperament. A living legend, in Segal's generation, and studied with veneration in institutions of higher learning, Pushkin was presented to the students as a model of classical Russian writing. More of a romantic, Lermontov was attracted to French Romanticism and inspired by Lord Byron and

Alfred de Vigny. As for Koltsov, he was known for his descriptions of the deeds, travails, and celebrations of the Russian people. According to Caiserman, Segal spent more time in his Talmud Torah studying Russian literature than modern Yiddish literature, which resulted in his unique familiarity with the official language of the tsarist Empire. While he was expanding his knowledge of biblical Hebrew and the sacred texts of Judaism, practising traditional Judaism, and speaking Yiddish with his family, the poet was, at the same time, discovering the culture of the vast Russian world. In fact, Segal began composing poems in the language of Pushkin, one of which was discovered by Bazinover, unbeknownst to its author:

> Soon Segal began writing poems in Russian. He had already filled a few thick notebooks with Russian writing without ever show-ing them to anyone. His Russian teacher in the Talmud Torah, Bazinover, looking at Segal's work, discovered some verses which he hastened to read in class at the first opportunity.[63]

This event was not without significance for Segal's literary career, all the more so because this teacher had a great deal of influence on the young student and had served as his role model when he began writing. In a more complete version of Segal's biography, Caiserman wrote: "Segal learned from Bazinover the meaning of poetry. . . . In all of Bazinover's utterings it was as if invigorating music helped him win over the children."[64] According to the critic, the teacher was not shy about informing Segal's grandfather Perlmuter about the extent of his grandson's literary talent. Similar accounts raise the issue of the profound influence of Russian literature on Segal's work, includ-ing work composed many years later in Yiddish in Canada. It does not seem unreasonable to state that, in light of the above information shared by Segal with Caiserman, the poet was greatly inspired by the Russian culture that he learned at the Korets Talmud Torah, and that he chose poetry as his preferred form of literary expression as a direct result of the secular education he acquired in an Orthodox Jewish school. This is sometimes difficult to detect in Segal's writing. Like other Canadian Yiddish writers of his generation, he did not social-ize with other Russian-speaking immigrants or use Russian Orthodox Christian imagery. Nor did he borrow Russian vocabulary, as Sholem Aleichem (1859–1916) had done. Rather, the Russian influence is to be found in Segal's infatuation with poetry, in the form of his verse, in its

melancholy mood, and in his predilection for traditional Russian literary forms. This same tendency can be detected in the work of other
Montreal Yiddish authors who, after the 1930s, were influenced by
the Russian epic poem in their work, such as, for example, Sholem
Shtern and N. I. Gotlib,[65] or those who, after the Holocaust, wrote
long autobiographical novels in the manner of Tolstoy, like Chava
Rosenfarb and Yehuda Elberg.[66] As a result, there is a striking similar-
ity between Montreal Yiddish literature and its Russian counterpart,
in particular the way poets completely dominated the literary scene.
If, as Marcelle Ehrhard states, "Russian prose, lagging behind poetry,
did not produce a truly original work in the Romantic era,"[67] so too
poets occupied almost the entire world of Montreal Yiddish literature
before 1945. A cultural and artistic relationship between the two has
not been adequately explored by scholars, and merits more attention,
despite first impressions to the contrary.

   The traditional Jewish culture of Segal's childhood in the Russian
Pale did not produce secular writing as such. Rabbinic literature,
including Hassidic literature, entirely focussed on biblical exegesis
and ethical and moral conduct, was primarily dedicated to the interpretation and transmission of the teachings of the Torah. On the other
end of the spectrum was Russian literature where protagonists were
swept up by the inexorable course of history, by wars and suffering. In
Tolstoy's novels, for example, the fate of the main protagonist, who is
often the hero, as, for example, in *War and Peace*, inevitably takes centre
stage. In most cases, the social and political circumstances in which he
finds himself will guide the sequence of events and final outcome of
the story. In the traditional Jewish world where Segal was raised, there
was no experimentation with literary form that characterized modern
writing, where classical forms were abandoned in favour of personal
creativity, regardless of where it might lead. Of course, many of the
great Hebraists who made their appearance at the end of the nineteenth
century, during the Jewish Enlightenment, were contemporaries of
Segal. In this fertile mix at the juncture of the Yiddish world and modern Hebrew, many writers, such as Yehuda Leib Gordon (1831–1892),
Sholem Yankev Abramovitch, known as Mendele Mocher Sforim
(Mendele the Bookseller, 1835 or 1836–1917), I. L. Peretz (1852–1915),
and Chaim Nachman Bialik (1873–1934), turned to new ideas. Segal,
however, given his home environment, would probably not have had
access to this type of literature. At most, as Caiserman notes, the young
poet was briefly introduced, by the son of the director of his Talmud

Torah, to the poems of the Yiddish folklorist Mark Warshawsky (1848–1907), famous for his popular songs, including *"Oyfn pripetshik* [On the hearth]" and *"Kinder mir hobn simkhes toyre* [Children, it's *Simchat Torah*]."* Presumably the younger Hershenhorn, a medical student in Kiev and raised in a Russified Jewish family, simply wanted to brighten the days of the young Korets students, rather than to expose them to the new wave of modernist Jewish literature.

Paradoxically, it was his exposure to Russian literature as a very young student that gave Segal his first taste of modern literature, literature liberated from its organic connection to religious tradition.[68] At the *heder* and the *Talmud Torah*, Segal studied Hebrew texts in the form of liturgy, Bible stories, psalms, and rabbinic and Talmudic commentaries, but undoubtedly never from a contemporary perspective. The unsettling feeling of entering a world that is immediate, incomprehensible, inexplicable and without any particular purpose, Segal owed first and foremost to Pushkin, and then his successors, members of a brilliant Russian literary elite that burst on the scene at the beginning of the nineteenth century. Nonetheless, Segal would only come to know that world through Russian literature in all its splendour, but never in its concrete incarnation in Moscow, St. Petersburg, or Kiev. The young student from Korets would eventually draw upon three different cultural traditions for the subject matter of his future literary work, all discovered in the classroom of his Talmud Torah. From the Hebrew texts, he would retain the melodies, the biblical imagery, and the Hassidic mysticism. From Russian culture, he would acquire an irresistible attraction to poetry, modern forms, and a wistful nostalgia. As for Yiddish, which was also his mother tongue, it would become his main vehicle for sharing his literary work with all of Montreal Jewry. At this point, it is important to note that at an early age Segal began penning his poetry not only in Russian, but also apparently in modern Hebrew[69] as well. Caiserman reported, with the poet's permission, that at the age of eight Segal had composed some poems poking fun at his family: "It was during those years, as far as Segal remembers, that he began his career as a poet. One of his earliest poems was a satire about his aunt who lived under the same roof as his grandfather."[70]

On the other hand, it is almost certain that Segal only began composing poems in Yiddish once he had settled in Montreal and was living on a continent where the influence of Russian culture was negligible, and where no significant readership for modern Hebrew existed. The long writing sessions on Saint Maurice Street "until late at night by the light of a kerosene lamp"[71] could only have happened thanks to the new passion that Yiddish inspired among the Eastern European working masses. In Hassidic Korets there had been no opportunity for the everyday language to become a literary vehicle for modernity or a standard-bearer for the revolution, as least not within the poet's imme-diate family. Nothing had pointed the young Segal in that direction. Only his exile in North America, and the abrupt end to his childhood, finally compelled the aspiring poet to submit to his new literary and linguistic environment, Yiddish. In having relied upon three different literary cultures during his formative years, Segal was in fact typical of the entire Ashkenaz Jewish population from the end of the Middle Ages to the dawn of the twentieth century. The Jews of Ashkenaz used the more ancient Jewish languages of Hebrew and Aramaic mostly for prayer, the study of Jewish religious doctrine, and in rabbinic dis-course. Yiddish, the Jewish vernacular, predominated in the family context and between members of the community in non-religious and commercial exchanges. Co-territorial non-Jewish languages were used in interactions with the State, the army, local administrations, and non-Jews in general, and included German, Russian, Ukrainian, Polish, and other languages prevalent in regions with long-standing Jewish communities.[72]

Like the majority of Montreal writers of his generation, before the age of thirteen Segal had mastered biblical Hebrew, everyday Yiddish, and one of the great European languages in its classical form, in his case, Russian. When he arrived in Canada, he learned a third alphabet for English and French, although for him the latter played a secondary role in the Canadian context. Presumably the poet also had some knowledge of the Ukrainian spoken by the peasants who came to Korets on market days, and even some other Slavic languages. The fact that he wrote in his third literary language—a language favoured from the end of the nineteenth century by Sholem Aleichem (Solomon Naumovich Rabinovich), Mendele Mocher Sforim (Sholem Yankev Abramowitz), and I. L. Peretz, did not preclude a solid knowledge of both biblical and modern Hebrew. This knowledge and use of many languages was shared by other Montreal writers during the same time period, and resulted in some of them, including Jacob Zipper, to write two almost identical books in tandem, one in Yiddish and the other in modern Hebrew. With remarkable intensity, however, after 1917 Segal committed himself to Yiddish, which indicated his devotion and spe-cial attachment to the language in which he conveyed his full range of emotions. The choice of a complex and plentiful literary palette partly explains how difficult it is today to interpret and translate Segal's writing and convey its evocative power and originality in the Montreal context.

The intermingling of languages and cultures, often with very different historical origins, and the layers of meaning within one and the same image or even the same word, come together in Segal's poetry to produce the effect of amazing literary richness. In one of his poems cited above, there is a phrase that exemplifies this complexity of expression: *"in shtok gedikhtn khoyshekh un in nakht."*[73] In this phrase Segal uses the word *"khoyshekh,"* which in the Book of Genesis refers to the impenetrable darkness that preceded the creation of the world, as well as the word *"nakht,"* the German word for "night" (*Nacht*) with its usual connotation. Between these two contradictory realities flows the emotion the poet feels in confronting the profound sadness of his childhood. In this poem, Segal presents himself as a pious Jew immersed in the biblical text, while at the same time a man of the world seduced by the disorienting world of modernity. This same penchant for diverse languages and multi-layered imagery can be found in the work of Montreal poet A. M. Klein, the English-speaking heir of Segal. In *The Second Scroll*, published in 1951, Klein displays a linguistic virtuosity similar to that of his Eastern European-born colleagues, except that his work was written in English and incorporated a greater proportion of Latin languages, including French, Italian, and Church Latin, more common in Montreal than in his native Ukrainian town of Ratno.

The biography of Segal also contains other elements that were important for the work he would produce decades later, and its emotional ramifications. The death of the scribe and cantor Aaron Ber very early in the poet's life would plunge the family into an intolerable economic situation. His dependents were forced to return to Korets, where Shifke, Segal's mother, could count on the financial support of her father. She had no choice but to open a stall in the market place where she sold fruit and vegetables to eke out a meagre living for her children. These were not unusual circumstances for Jews of Eastern Europe, where men were often restricted to scholarly and prestigious occupations within the Jewish sphere, but unlikely to earn sufficient income to support a family. Invariably, it fell to their wives to take charge of the practical aspects of making a living and interact with the outside world, no matter the cost. The death of her husband also placed on Segal's mother the responsibility of educating her children. It is difficult for us today to imagine the consequences of such a situation on the daily life of her youngest son in a Volhynian *shtetl* prior to the Russian Revolution of 1917. In this regard, it might be useful to cite a passage from the biography written by Caiserman, who describes the family's living quarters in Korets, just as Segal was preparing to enter the Talmud Torah. There is no doubt that Segal retained an indelible memory of this difficult experience:

> During that time, the small Segal family, consisting of his mother, of Segal and two sisters, resided in a cellar-house of Leib the shoemaker. The room had one window into the court-yard, with very little sunshine [. . .]
> Nevertheless, Segal remembers that one wall in the room breathed with cold mouldings and during the great frost emanated from the corners a snowy frosty chillness. No matter how much the house was heated, it was cold during the night, and in the morning to step down from the bed on the floor was difficult—and when the fire beamed [*sic*] the house was full of smoke—and to open the door was impossible.[74]

Segal's Maternal Grandfather

The Segal family's dire financial straits in 1906, and the absence of the first four children, Eliezer, Nehemia, Chaya, and Edith, indicate both the short- and medium-term solutions available to its members. One can reasonably conclude that the older children had already left Korets and settled in America, probably in Montreal. Compared to the persistent poverty in the Russian Pale, Canada offered some relief and certain advantages, even for immigrants who were subject to the exhausting work schedule of the garment factories. Also, the relationship between Segal's mother and his grandfather, as recounted by Caiserman, left a great deal to be desired. When Shifke went month after month to ask her father, David Perlmuter, for financial assistance, he exploded into fits of rage and humiliated her in front of the entire household. Shifke had no choice but to move with her three children into a tiny room at the back of Perlmuter's house, where one of her sisters was already living and being supported by her father. Despite the esteem he had had for his son-in-law, Aaron Ber, David Perlmuter did not want to assume responsibility for raising his grandchildren, and refused to speak to them in public. Such a family situation had a profound impact on the young Segal, who, by his own admission, was left emotionally scarred for the rest of his life. According to Caiserman, it was at that time that Segal began to write in Russian.

> Thus, for the first time Segal was confronted by the evil in the world, and in such a way that it cast a long dark shadow over his entire psychological state [. . .]
>
> Feeling himself a stranger within his own family, he saw the entire world as alien. Although he was just a child, he understood very well the anguish of his mother when she came to his grandfather to beg him crying, to help her out with a few rubles to pay her rent for the year.[75]

The time came when Shifke had to buy her son, newly enrolled in the Talmud Torah, the books he needed for his classes. In a school funded by the local Jewish community, education was free except for school supplies and books. As the future poet lived under the same roof as one of the more affluent merchants in the town, it was difficult for his teachers to believe that this child had been reduced to abject poverty, and that only through tremendous self-sacrifice was Shifke able to cover the costs of his education. Without the determination and hard work of his mother, the young Segal would never have had access to the Jewish education that would make possible his literary career. David Perlmuter was not without some good qualities, however, and Caiserman claims that the man had "a feeling for beauty which influenced J. I. Segal."[76] A prominent figure, dressed in a long frock coat, he walked back and forth between his home and the market, where he had a business. Very devout and concerned about his place in the next world, he often studied the sacred books and knew how to create for himself an atmosphere conducive to reflection. In a poetic fashion Caiserman has provided an intimate description of Perlmuter, which the young Segal could probably only see from a distance. In every respect it is a classic portrait of an Eastern European Jew devoted to the practice of Judaism, although his relative prosperity and moderate exposure to modernity had given him an appreciation of material beauty. How, wondered Caiserman, could such a person neglect the aspirations of such a talented grandson, when he himself had such a keen sense of observation when it came to art and culture:

> At daybreak he was already seated at his little table by the kitchen window studying. The window looked out onto a garden where a large pear tree reached over the fence. This pear tree was a partner in my grandfather's studies, in springtime with its fragrant white blossoms, in the month of Tamuz with its rosy-cheeked pears, and in winter covered in snow-white stillness [. . .].
>
> In my grandfather's home, apart from three large bookcases with a wide array of holy books, from the largest set of the Talmud to the smallest, newest *musar* book (a book on moral conduct), were two cabinets with the most beautiful porcelain dishes and crystal glassware. My grandfather would travel once a year to Kiev and bring back magnificent antiques made of transparent porcelain. And as much as he delighted in the spiritual sources of his sacred books, so too he derived extraordinary pleasure from his silver, gold and crystal objets d'art and antiques.[77]

The anguish Segal suffered over his grandfather's attitude toward him, his mother's humiliation within her own family, and the biting poverty they had to secretly endure day after day no doubt greatly contributed to his vulnerability and unusual emotional sensitivity as a child. Confronted by so many inner tensions and insoluble contradictions, Segal found an escape in writing, and shut himself away. Many accounts testify to this. Caiserman, in his description of the poet's childhood, recounts David Perlmuter's reaction when he discovered that his eight-year-old grandson had written satires in Russian about members of his immediate family: "Segal from his earliest childhood was stubborn, and this time he stood his ground about his right to free speech, and put up a thousand barriers against those who wished to violate it."[78] It was the same when his classmates in the Talmud Torah discovered, thanks to their Russian teacher, that there was a poet among them. This premature exposure of his literary talent in an environment not in the least receptive to introspective writing singled Segal out from his classmates and made him feel different. His unmasking at school and within his family simultaneously was painfully upsetting to the young writer. At the same time, the budding poet must have derived both pride and satisfaction at having been able to express the feelings he had kept bottled up for so long, in particular about the injustice of his family situation and his inability to change it. Caiserman's biographical account thus offers an important perspective on what motivated the child in Korets who picked up a pen and began to write, and how this occurred at a critical moment in his emotional development. The subject matter and creative vitality of his first "poems" presage many aspects of his later work, including the poet's social and emotional isolation, his glum personality, and his desire to raise himself to an artistic universe where he would be beyond the reach of the common people. This is how Caiserman described the poet's feelings when he produced his first very personal poem in Korets.

> In that poem he expressed, in a naïve and childlike way, of course, much of the pent up bitterness that was at the root of his temperament as a child. It constituted his first protest against injustice, his first outburst against his fate. He had not yet found the kind of soothing artistic language that heals, consoles, and liberates, the kind of language that could take the poet beyond all the constrictions, constraints, and crowding into a place where the whole world was his, where he could feel at ease.[79]

Segal also confessed to Caiserman that in Korets he had experienced love for the first time with a cousin named Genia, who was twelve years old at the time, and the daughter of his uncle Aaron Perlmuter. By his own admission, Segal would meet Genia secretly whenever the opportunity presented itself. Although their friendship remained purely platonic, it further complicated the poet's family situation, and resulted in emotional setbacks that would serve to hone his artistic sensibilities. Among Segal's correspondence there are several letters and postcards, postmarked as late as May 1917, from Korets,[80] written in Russian by Genia Aaronovna, in which the young woman complains of not hearing from the poet who had left for Canada, and expresses her regret at finding herself prevented from joining him because of the war that was raging in Europe. Written prior to the Russian Revolution, stamped by the Russian censor, this correspondence reached Segal while he was living on Beaumont Street in Mile End (see Appendix B). It contains the heart-rending confession of a young woman who wants to keep alive the love they had felt for one another in Korets. This happy episode in his life in Eastern Europe contrasts sharply with the rest of his childhood, made bitter by his isolation and the loss of a father. Raised by a mother who was completely consumed by trying to provide for her family, and endowed with exceptional artistic talent, Segal through his writing was able to escape into the far reaches of his most intimate thoughts: "Segal had always been a lonely child, without friends to chum around with."[81] As if this situation were not trying and dismal enough for a sensitive child, a number of tragic events in America were to exacerbate the poet's innate melancholy and reserve. Through a lens darkened by grief, Segal saw his childhood as a long series of hindrances and hardships, as this poem from his first book indicates:

I Don't Wish!

I don't wish to recall my grey and gloomy childhood.
I don't wish to remember the years of lonely sadness
That swaddled my soul in dreary thoughts.
I shall renounce the love
that tethers me to those places
dimmed by memory-dreams.

Let my gloomy childhood rest in a lonely grave!
I don't wish to recall the dark and sickly spirits.
Clouded have become my childhood's sacred happy times.
May my youth not be squandered
in hours of recalling past suffering and hurt.

Alone I shall create serenity and solace
And my heart I shall cradle and console.[82]

Segal did not have to wait until he came to Canada to experience social situations that were distressing and incomprehensible to him. As a young boy, he also suffered physical harm in non-Jewish society. Despite the precautions taken by his mother and the privileges he enjoyed by virtue of being the grandson of an influential man, the abuse was all the more traumatic given the fact that he was generally sheltered from direct interaction with his Christian neighbours. In 1909 or 1910, at the age of thirteen, Segal suffered at least one episode of brutal treatment at the hands of the tsarist authorities. He was held in custody for several hours after being accused of stealing a purse from a Christian in the Korets market square. Segal was flogged with a piece of heavy rope by a policeman, and then thrown into a prison cell where he remained until late at night, when his mother finally arrived to find him more dead than alive. It is difficult to glean much else about this incident, reported by Zalman Rejzen in his 1927 biographical dictionary—it had probably been recounted to him by Segal himself[83]—except that it exemplifies the arbitrary violence endemic in Russian society. Was this classic anti-Semitism or the fanaticism of a desperate government in the years that followed the failed Revolution of 1905? It is hard to believe that a frail boy like Segal could have been perceived as a threat by the local authorities, especially in a small provincial town like Korets. Was it this incident that finally convinced his mother to abandon any hope she may have had for a better life in Eastern Europe? Regardless of what had triggered this brutal reaction, it was undoubtedly fresh in Segal's memory when he left for America.

The Great Crossing

In his unfinished biography of Segal, Caiserman confirmed that Segal, prior to his departure for America in 1910, had lived in a Jewish environment apparently unaffected by the great political upheavals that shook Russian society under the old regime. The terrible Russo-Japanese War of 1904–1905 fought on the border between Siberia and China for control of the port city of Port Arthur,[84] which the Russians had been forced to relinquish in battle, does not seem to have loomed large in his childhood. The same can be said about the failed revolution of 1905, which lasted for months, unleashing bloody confrontations between protesters and the authorities, and generating widespread revolutionary activity among the Empire's Jewish population. Protected by the social class to which his grandfather belonged, Segal had no memory of ever coming into contact with Labour Zionists, Yiddish-speaking union organizers, or any other opponents of the established order. While in his Talmud Torah, even during the tumultuous years of 1905 to 1907, the poet seems not to have witnessed any significant social unrest or events that might have disrupted the student routine. It is true that religious Jews were not prominent among political agitators in Russia. The Jewish elite of Korets probably opposed the overthrow of the established order, which could jeopardize their economic interests and bring to power atheists and agnostics. Segal remembered having seen various symbols of Imperial Russia, including an image of the tsar himself, displayed in the spacious school where he had studied for several years: "At the very entrance opposite the door at the Central wall, hanging in a large frame in his majestic uniform and a red mantle covered with various medals, was the tsar of Russia, Alexander III."[85] Segal's indifference to the struggles around him is further reflected in the fact that throughout his life he kept his distance from the ongoing ideological debates within the Montreal Jewish community, and almost nothing in his work betrays sympathy for any particular political cause. As an ordinary garment worker, he does not appear to have openly participated in the labour disputes or union demands that periodically shook the clothing industry in Montreal. Perhaps this can be attributed to his education in the Korets Talmud Torah, and the "aristocratic" sympathies of his mother's family.

In the Segal Archive is a Table of Contents[86] for a biography of Segal that Caiserman planned to write, which would have fleshed out the existing preliminary notes (see Appendix 10). In fact, Caiserman had written a draft in Yiddish and English of the first ten chapters, dealing with the first thirteen years of Segal's life in Korets, as well as his adolescence in Montreal. It stopped with the publication of *Fun mayn velt* in 1918. Presumably the biography was never written. No traces of it are to be found in the archives. Among his papers, Segal himself left a handwritten table of contents for a very different kind of autobiography entitled *Fun mayn mames shvel* (From my mother's threshold) (see Appendix 11). Evidently this book was intended to describe Segal's childhood in Korets and the people whom he knew as a small child. The fact that Segal left nothing about his voyage to Canada or the larger context of Jewish life prior to the Russian Revolution of 1917 in what is now the Ukraine is yet another indication of Segal's tendency toward introspection and indifference to political issues or ideological debates. His projected autobiography seems to have been abandoned, and the poet prepared no further material, except for a rather long piece about his grandfather, David Perlmuter, simply entitled "*Mayn zeyde* [My grandfather]," which appeared in the *Keneder Adler* (*The Jewish Eagle*) in the fall of 1946.[87] Published as an excerpt from a book entitled *Funvanen* [Whence?] it must have been part of the autobiography planned by Segal, but never completed.[88] It contains an unembellished description of daily life in Korets and several autobiographical details already documented by Caiserman. An undated handwritten manuscript entitled "*Variant*" has the same content with the addition of a very moving passage about Segal's paternal grandfather, Reb Sholem:

> There were times in my childhood when I very much wanted to exchange my grandfathers. I would have gladly exchanged the

grandfather who was always before my eyes in the same town, the same street, and the same house, for the other grandfather who lived somewhere else in another town and about whom I had created for myself a certain image [. . .] .

My grandfather Sholem, my father's father, was a scribe and a teacher in a small town in Podolia. [. . .] . He did not belong to the propertied class but rather to the dispossessed. Nonetheless he was faithful to the Jewish tradition, and had no other choice but to carry his burden of misery from this world to the next.[89]

The trials and tribulations endured in silence by the young Segal while living with his mother's family in Korets played a large role in forging his personality and impelling him to write. His dreary childhood was occasionally brightened by a ray of sunshine such as the attention given him by some of the teachers at the Talmud Torah, and his grandfather's love of beauty. For the most part, however, the young orphan left his *shtetl* emotionally scarred. The decision to emigrate to America was taken not by Segal, of course, but by his mother Shifke who made up her mind to join her children already living in Montreal. The strained family situation, difficult not just for her but for her two daughters and her youngest son as well, must have contributed to her decision. It was certainly influenced by the deprivation felt by all the members of the Segal family in the home of David Perlmuter. Both Caiserman and Segal are silent regarding the exact circumstances of the rupture between Shifke and her father in 1910, but one can easily surmise that it was hostile and acrimonious. Within the Korets Jewish community, Perlmuter's grandchildren would not have been the most likely candidates for emigration. The grandfather's comfortable circumstances and his adherence to Orthodox religious observance would have kept his daughter Shifke from making so difficult a decision fraught with uncertainly and risk when it came to the long-term prospect of maintaining the strict practice of Judaism. Moreover, crossing oceans and continents was potentially dangerous to the health of young children. Furthermore, it must have involved costs which Shifke could not have covered on her own. That Segal's mother would have undertaken such a radical step demonstrates how desperate she was, as well as how certain she was that her family's situation in Korets would never improve. The abject poverty of Segal's childhood appears in poems he published much later in his Montreal career:

Under a Spent Sun

At your hungry table, Mother,
In the grey impoverished markets
Where small vendors with stooped shoulders
Hunch from dawn to dusk
And over the poles of the telegraph wires
Fly the crows of early autumn.
And a winter sets in, a winter.
And it snows on the little people
And slaps them in the head with cold
and burns with storms and flames in the west
and frightens with wars and evil decrees.
And here in the corners such loneliness grows
until the first young onions appear in the market,
and a bird lands on the doorstep of a shop.
And a frightening funeral so forlorn
Passes through the market square.
And from everywhere one can see the stone wall
That encircles the cemetery.[90]

Segal reached Montreal already formed as a writer, accustomed to holding a pen in his hand, day after day, week after week. One can assume that, once he had settled in his new home, the poet continued writing and expanded his literary palette through daily contact with the Canadian and New York Yiddish press, which regularly published his high-quality pieces. In fact, Segal must have adopted Yiddish as his literary language soon after his arrival when he realized that it was the dominant language of the local Jewish community and that it offered unanticipated possibilities for poetic expression. Sailing up the St. Lawrence River and arriving in a new city must have given the Segal family, including the young poet on the cusp of adulthood, the impression of liberty and prosperity. Unlike the Perlmuter residence in Korets, here there was nothing to prevent Segal from putting down on paper his most intimate thoughts and undeclared personal aspirations. Nonetheless, several years would go by before the lowly garment worker could see any possibility of a literary or journalistic career in Montreal. For a long time the poet's age, along with his innate shyness and humble social status, interfered with such a plan. For years Segal must have written for himself alone, in the intimacy

of his own home, without being read by anyone. We already know
the rest of the journey of the author of *Fun mayn velt*, and how a small
circle of writers in 1917 brought him out of anonymity. When Segal
emerged onto the Montreal scene, he had already been writing poetry
for at least ten years, and could express himself in that genre with an
ease and spontaneity that surprised his first few admirers. Within a
short time, the young man, schooled in Russian poetry, had been able
to produce a large number of first-rate poems. According to his friend
and colleague Melekh Ravitch, he was "as prolific as a cherry tree in
summer."[91] Segal would sustain and strengthen these qualities over
the forty years that he lived in Montreal. However, his talent and the
inner tensions he expressed would remain connected to his upbringing in the Russian Pale and his family life in Korets. Above all, the
poet would never forget the moment of his departure for America and
the irreparable rupture it caused in his life:

O, Call Us Back!

O call us back to the bright beginning
to the great archway of resplendent day

Golden fire in the heavens,
In the west a holy world.

We were such quiet boys
with our dreamy eyes turned toward God

We clung to beauty
Like Levites in the Holy Temple.

We set out into the distance
Like Nazarites into the desert.

Alas, ships captured us
Alas, the sea drove us.

We wander in the greyness of weeks
without an exit on the sands of a sea.[92]

Notes

1. H. M. Caiserman, "*Baym keyver fun M. Shmuelsohn (a bletl kanader literarish geshi-
    khte vos iz forgekumen in Montreal)* [At the grave of M. Shmuelsohn (a chapter
    of Canadian literary history that took place in Montreal)]," The Daily Hebrew
    Journal, *Der Idisher Zhurnal* (Toronto, May 30, 1947), 4, 2

2. Ibid.

3. Fox, op. cit., 98–99; Haim Leib Fuks, op. cit., 144–145. See also "*H. Hershman, pioner-farshpreyter fun gedruktn idishn vort in kanade, nekhtn geshtorbn* [H. Hershman, pioneer in the dissemination of Yiddish-language printing in Canada, died yesterday]." *The Jewish Daily Eagle*, January 25, 1955.

4. H. Wolofsky, *Journey of My Life (A Book of Memoirs)* [*Mayn-lebns rayze; zikhroynes fun iber a halbn yorhundert idish lebn in der alter un nayer velt*] (The Eagle Publishing Company: Montreal, 1946), 71; Hirsch Wolofsky, *Mayn lebens rayze. Un demi-siècle de vie Yiddish à Montreal et ailleurs dans le monde*, translated into French by Pierre Anctil (Sillery: Éditions du Septentrion, 2000), 124–125.

5. Unpublished text by David Rome, obtained during an interview with him at the Canadian Jewish Congress on November 22, 1989.

6. Hershel Novak, *Fun Meine Yunge Yorn* (Educational committee of the Workmen's Circle, New York, New York, 1957), 154–155. Translated in part into French by Pierre Anctil as Hershl Novak, *La première école Yiddish de Montréal, 1911–1914* (Sillery: Éditions du Septentrion, 2009).

7. *Nekudot* were diacritical signs used to represent vowels in masoretic Hebrew for the purpose of indicating pronunciation. They were used in early Yiddish but less frequently in modern Yiddish.

8. The standardization of Yiddish orthography did not occur until after the founding in Vilna, Poland, in 1925, of the YIVO Institute for Jewish Research, the Yidisher visenshaftlikher institut which, for the first time, instituted a "scientific" philological study of the Yiddish language. Nonetheless, it was not until the 1930s that North American Yiddish publications began using a more systematized orthography.

9. "*Di verk fun yud yud Segal* [The work of J. I. Segal]," undated and unsigned article, Segal Archive, Jewish Public Library.

10. Mordecai Ginzburg, "*Plutsimdiker toyt fun yud yud segal ruft aroys troyer in shot* [The sudden death of J. I. Segal puts the city into mourning], *Keneder Adler*, March 8, 1954.

11. "*Yud Yud Segal als poet, a kurtse retsenzie* [J. I. Segal as poet, a short critique], *Der Idisher Arbeter*, Montreal, February, 1919, 3.

12. On this subject, see the *First Annual Report of the Jewish Public Library (Ershter yerlikher berikht fun der idisher folks bibliotek un folks universitet)*, 1915, 44.

13. J. I. Segal, untitled poem, *Fun mayn velt* (Montreal, 1918), 9–10.

14. Ibid., 7.

15. J. I. Segal, *Zumergold* [Summer Gold], Ibid., 21.

16. It was not until 1945, the year the novel *Bonheur d'occasion* was published by Gabrielle Roy, that the Montreal urban landscape became the subject of a French-language literary work providing a broad social panorama about ordinary people.

17. Untitled poem, *Ibid.* 37.

18. Ibid., 40.

19. Ibid., 41.

20. Ibid., 63.

21. Ibid., 60.

22. For an anthology of writing published in the *Jewish Daily Eagle* (*Der Keneder Adler*) before and after World Wor I, see David Rome and Pierre Anctil, *Through the Eyes of the Eagle: The Early Montreal Yiddish Press (1907–1916)*, Montreal: Véhicule Press, 2001.

23. J. I. Segal, op. cit., 40.

24. Ibid., 10.

25. That was the case with Sholem Shtern who states in his memoirs that he approached Segal at the end of the 1920s to help him publish his first poems in the *Tsukunft* [Future], a New York literary monthly journal. See Sholem Shtern, *Nostalgie et tristesse, Mémoires littéraires du Montréal Yiddish*, Montreal, Éditions du Noroît, 2006, 60–61. This is a partial translation of the Yiddish book entitled *Writers I Knew: Memoirs and Essays* [Shrayber vos ikh hot gekent], Montreal, 1982.

26. On this subject, see my article entitled "De Tur Malka au mont Royal, le poème yiddish montréalais" in Marie-Andrée Beaudet and Karim Larose, eds., *Le marcheur des Amériques. Mélanges offerts à Pierre Nepveu*, Montreal, *Paragraphes*, no. 29, 2010, 45–62.

27. Melekh Ravitch, *"Yud Yud Segal, An intimer portret fun a khaver* [J. I. Segal, An intimate portrait of a friend], *Keneder Adler*, November 12, 1945, 5–6.

28. H. M Caiserman, undated, untitled manuscript about the life of J. I. Segal, Segal Archive, Canadian Jewish Congress Archives, 6 pages. The first line of the manuscript states: "Gelernt in der rusish-hebreyisher Talmud Torah."

29. H. M. Caiserman, *"Forshteyer fun der idisher literatur in Kanade* [Representatives of Yiddish literature in Canada]," *Der Yidisher Zhurnal*, January 12, 1941, 52.

30. According to Ch. L. Fuks, Alexander Kashin lived in Montreal from 1915 to 1917, before Segal had achieved renown. See Fuks, op. cit., 205; Ch. L. Fox, op. cit., 145.

31. H. M Caiserman, undated untitled manuscript about the life of J. I. Segal, Segal Archive, Canadian Jewish Congress Archives, op. cit.

32. Melekh Ravitch, op. cit. 141–142.

33. Ibid., 142.

34. H. M. Caiserman, "Yud Yud Segal als poet, a kurtse retsenzie [J. I. Segal as poet, a short review]," *Der Yidisher Arbeter*, Montreal, February 1919, 3.

35. Ibid.

36. J. I. Segal, op. cit., 63.

37. Chaim Nachman Bialik, who was born in Poland and emigrated to Palestine in 1924, today considered the greatest modern Hebrew poet, in 1919 was known as a Yiddish poet as well.

38. This expression is stronger in a culture where the name of God must not be taken in vain.

39. Caiserman, op. cit.

40. The most convincing examples are the memoirs of Israel Medres, Hirsch Wolofsky, Hershl Novak, and Harry (Hirsch) Hershman.

41. Undated, untitled handwritten document entitled "Biography of J. I. Segal," by H. M. Caiserman, Segal Archive, Jewish Public Library Archive, 1–2.

42. Undated, untitled handwritten document by H. M. Caiserman, Segal Archive, Jewish Public Library Archive, 6 pages, op. cit.

43. Undated, untitled handwritten document entitled "Biography of J. I. Segal," by H. M. Caiserman, Segal Archive, Jewish Public Library Archive, 5.

44. Ibid., 1.

45. Ibid., 1.

46. The town of Proskurov in the southwestern Ukraine is today known by its Ukrainian name, Khmelnytskyi.

47. Yom Tov Lipmann Ben Nathan Halevi Heller. In the Jewish tradition, a Talmudic scholar is often named after his book. *Tosefot Yom Tov* is the title of the main work authored by Rabbi Heller, who set out to systematize the text of the Mishna. Rejzen's name is variously spelled Reyzen (YIVO), Reisen (most common).

48. Zalman Rejzen, *Leksikon fun der idisher literatur, prese un filologye* [Biographical dictionary of Yiddish literature, the press and philology], Vilna: Kletskin Farlag, 1927, vol. 2, 625–629.

49. J. I. Segal, "Vinter [Winter], Montreal, *Lirik*, 1930, 92. English translation by Grace Schulman, in Irving Howe, Ruth R. Wisse, and Khone Shmeruk, eds., *The Penguin Book of Modern Yiddish Verse*, New York: Viking Penguin Inc., 1987, 414–416.

50. In 1897, there were 4,608 Jews in Korets (in Polish Korzec) who constituted 76 per cent of the town's population. Founded in the 8th century, the Jewish community of Korets was one of the oldest in Poland. At the end of the 18th century, Korets was one of the main centres of Hassidism. When the young Segal lived there, the town had a few textile plants, tanneries, and sugar-beet factories, all owned by Jews. See Michel Berenbaum and Fred Skolnik, eds., *Encyclopaedia Judaica*, Detroit, 2007, 2nd edition, vol. 12, 307.

51. Undated, unsigned document handwritten by H. M. Caiserman in English entitled "Biography of I. J. Segal," Segal Archive, Jewish Public Library Archives, 1.

52. Ibid., 13–14.

53. Ibid., 28.

54. Ibid. 25–26.

55. TRANSLATOR'S NOTE: This paragraph was originally written in English with several Yiddish words which have here been translated into English. Ibid. 34.

56. A *perush* is commentary on a text to clarify the meaning.

57. Document entitled "Biography of I. J. Segal," op. cit., 25.

58. Sholem Shtern's father was a member of a Hasidic community. He himself received a strictly religious education during his childhood in Tyszowce (Tishevits in Yiddish), Poland.

59. Sholem Shtern, *Nostalgie et tristesse, Mémoires littéraires du Montréal yiddish,* op. cit., 262. Sholem Shtern, *Writers I Knew: Memoirs and Essays* [Shrayber vos ikh hot gekent], op. cit., 204.

60. The original paragraph was written in English interspersed with several Yiddish words, which are here translated into English. Ibid., 32.

61. Document entitled *"Biography of I. J. Segal,"* op. cit., 22–23.

62. Melech Ravitch, *My Lexicon: Pen Portraits of Jewish Writers and Artists in the Americas and other Countries, Volume 6, Book 2* (in Yiddish) (Tel Aviv: I. L. Peretz Publishing House, 1980), 143.

63. Undated, unsigned, handwritten document by H. M. Caiserman entitled "Biography of I. J. Segal," Segal Archive, Ibid., 9.

64. Ibid., 21.

65. See, for example, Sholem Shtern, *In Kanade*, 2 volumes (Montreal, 1960–1963), and N. I. Gotlib, *Montreal* (Montreal, 1968).

66. See for example Chava Rosenfarb's *The Tree of Life*, Madison Wisconsin, 2004, 3 volumes (translated from the Yiddish *Der boym fun lebn*, Tel Aviv, 1972) and Yehuda Elberg, *Kalman kalikes imperye*, Tel Aviv, 1983, translated into French as *L'empire de Kalman l'infirme*, Montreal, 2002.

67. Marcelle Ehrhard, *La littérature russe*, Paris, Presses universitaires de France, collection "Que sais-je?", no. 290, 6th edition, 1972, 30.

68. The memoirs of Hershl Novak, op. cit., clearly leave the same impression.

69. Ch. L. Fox claims that Segal left behind a notebook full of Hebrew poems in Korets before leaving for America. See Fuks, op. cit., 251; Fox, op. cit., 181.

70. A passage from the Yiddish draft version of Segal's biography written by Caiserman, Segal Archive, Montreal Jewish Public Library, Montreal, 6.

71. *"biz sphet bay nakht bay a kerosin lempl"*

72. On this subject see Bernard Spolsky and Elana Shohamy, *The Languages of Israel: Policy, Ideology and Practice* (Clevedon, Great Britain, Multilingual Matters, 1999).

73. "In pitch darkness and in night," untitled poem in *Fun mayn velt*, Montreal, 1918, 9–10.

74. Document entitled "Biography of I. J. Segal", op. cit., 12.

75. H. M. Caiserman, Draft copy in Yiddish of Segal's biography, Segal Archive, Jewish Public Library, 4–6.

76. Document entitled "Biography of I.J. Segal," op. cit., 5.

77. H. M. Caiserman, Draft copy in Yiddish of Segal's biography, Segal Archive, Jewish Public Library, 3–4.

78. Ibid., 6–7.

79. Ibid., 7.

80. Genia Aaronovna in Russian means Genia, daughter of Aaron.

81. Ibid., 9.

82. J. I. Segal, *"Ikh vil nit* [I do not wish]," *Fun mayn velt*, Montreal, 1918, 38.

83. Zalman Rejzen, op. cit. Chaim Leib Fuks repeats this episode in his biographical dictionary. See Fuks, op. cit., 351. Fox, op. cit.

84. Today the Chinese city of Lushunkou.

85. "Biography of I.J. Segal" undated, unsigned, handwritten document by H. M. Caiserman, J. I. Segal Archive, Montreal Jewish Public Library Archives, 21–22. Alexander II died in 1894, and was succeeded bty Nicolas II, the last tsar of Russia.

86. Several dates mentioned by Caiserman in this document do not correspond to the biographical data obtained from a more reliable source.

87. *"Mayn zayde,"* Der Keneder Adler, September 29, 1946, 4; October 4, 1946, 4; October 9, 1946, 4, and October 20, 1946, 4. Two other possible extracts from this autobiography appeared in a book edited by Elieser Leoni and published in Tel Aviv in 1959 as *Korets (Volyn); sefer zikaron le-kehilatenu she-ala aleha ha-koret* [The Korets Book: In memory of our community that is no more], Tel Aviv: Azari Press, 791. These are the poems *"Vinter* [Winter]," 65–71, and *"Koretser orimelayt* [The poor people of Korets]," 103–106. However, these two extracts contain no biographical details about Segal himself. Leoni received these two texts from Esther Segal and A. S. Shkolnikov, as stated on page 285 of his book.

88. In a 1951 interview in the New York newspaper *Der Tog*, Segal stated that he was working on a poem inspired by his childhood memories. See *"Barimter dikhter Yud Yud Segal git op freylikhn grus fun kanade* [The famous poet J. I. Segal sends happy regards from Canada]," *Der Tog*, May 29, 1951, 7.

89. Undated handwritten manuscript entitled *Varyant*, Segal Archive, Montreal Jewish Public Library.

90. J. I. Segal, *"Di mide zun* [Under a spent sun]," excerpt, Montreal, *Lirik*, 1910, 141.

91. Melekh Ravitch, "Yiddish culture in Canada," *Canadian Jewish Reference Book and Dictionary* (Montreal, Jewish Institute of Higher Research, Central Rabbinical Seminary of Canada, 1963), 79.

92. J. I. Segal, *"O ruf!* [O, call us back]," op. cit., 49.

Chapter 3

First Literary Success

In the summer of 1919, just as critics on two continents were beginning to debate the literary merits of *Fun mayn velt*, in Montreal, J. I. Segal married a young immigrant by the name of Elke Rosen.[1] Both were in their early 20s, and both from Eastern Europe. Since each of them were garment workers and belonged to the least privileged class in Montreal society, their wedding was not reported in the newspapers, nor can any mention of it be found in any other document from that era. Still in the Segal family's possession, however, is a single photograph of the young couple looking a little embarrassed in front of the camera. Elegantly dressed for the occasion, Jacob and Elke seem to have taken a pose that betrays their shyness and inexperience with Canadian life. The picture taken on this solemn occasion also reflects the path followed by Segal during his first few years in his adopted country. Having spent his childhood in Korets in dire poverty, he could now allow himself to sport a suit befitting his immigrant status and display his modest material success. A copy of this photograph was probably sent to relatives on the other side of the Atlantic, as was often the case among recent immigrants to North America, to deliver a strong message of success and prosperity. Like her husband, Elke Rosen had experienced a family tragedy. Her departure for Canada was also occasioned by the premature death of her father. Like Segal's mother Shifke, Elke's mother, Sara Halperin, lost her husband, Abba Steinman, in a work accident somewhere in Eastern Europe, and had no choice but to leave for America with her three young children in tow.[2] Hence, united by marriage and their Jewish cultural heritage, the young couple also had in common their painful life experiences and an acute awareness, from a very young age, of the fragility of human existence. That the Segals' wedding took place in 1919 is a reasonable assumption, given the fact that their first daughter, Tsharna, was born the following year.[3]

Like her husband, Elke was not a strictly observant Jew. The couple spoke Yiddish to one another both at home and with their friends. According to their two surviving children, Sylvia and Annette, Elke was quiet and reserved, and did not participate in the literary or social life of her husband. While the poet became a celebrity in Yiddish cultural circles both in Montreal and abroad, his wife was content to accompany him and provide emotional support. Elke was rarely involved in J. I. Segal's public life. She is not mentioned in the numerous documents relating to him as a Yiddish writer. Among the few photographs in which she appears, none was ever published in the Yiddish press during her lifetime. On the other hand, all the information provided by her family confirms the fact that the poet was completely dependent on her emotionally and practically. Had it not been for his wife, Segal would not have been able to devote himself with such tenacity to his writing and his literary career. Not only did Elke assume responsibility for the pressing demands of daily life, but she also supported her husband by constantly welcoming his visiting New York colleagues and his Montreal friends into her home. At the time of Elke's marriage and the birth her first child, her mother, Sara Halperin, lived in Mile End at 40 Mozart Street West[4] (see Appendix B). Segal and his young family lived with her at that address for a few months in the middle of 1922, and then again at the end of 1928 and the beginning of 1929, when they returned from New York. This would seem to suggest that Elke's family played a large role in the poet's life, and that he and his wife were bound by shared sentiments.

Over the years Elke also played an important economic role in the Segal household by taking in piecework, as well as working on a sub-contract basis for clothing manufacturers. Prior to World War II, this type of work was commonplace among Montreal's immigrant Jews, allowing mothers to earn a few extra dollars to supplement the family income, while leaving them free to attend to the immediate needs of their families. Elke also rented out one of the two bedrooms in their apartment at 4540 Clark Street, either to another family or to a pensioner, to further augment the family income.[5] This usually meant providing meals and other services for strangers, in addition to her own household chores. All this would seem to indicate that the Segals' income was at times either insufficient or too unstable to meet their ongoing needs. Without his wife's modest but steady contribution, the poet would have been forced to take a full-time job in a sweatshop or find some other type of factory work. Elke also received work on a regular basis from her husband's mentor, H. M. Caiserman, or rather from his wife, Sarah Wittal Caiserman, who owned factories that produced children's wear under the brand names Belle Maid and Goosey Gander. One of the factories was located at 5505 St. Lawrence Boulevard, close to the Segals' home. The substantial size of these commercial enterprises[6] can be inferred from a letter that Caiserman wrote to one of his cousins in 1947: "Sarah is very well. She is conducting a large factory in Montreal where more than 150 people work and also operates two branches, one in Quebec City and one in a smaller community. These were necessary because of the difficulty of getting workers in Montreal, so she has her hands full."[7]

Thus, at the beginning of the 1920s a dual relationship was established between the Segals and the Caisermans that would endure for thirty years, until the death of the two husbands. On the one hand, Caiserman, the literary critic and activist, guaranteed the poet and his family a decent standard of living by providing them with as much steady piecework as they were capable of accepting. On the other hand, he spent time and energy promoting his protégé's career, sometimes by covering the cost of printing and distributing his books. By all accounts Caiserman's boundless enthusiasm was not in the least affected by this double role. Neither was the high regard the two men had for one another. On the contrary, documents from that time reveal their deep bond and mutual respect. The odds are that without his mentor, the poet would not have been able to take the steps required to achieve international renown, nor would he have overcome the obstacles that initially must have seemed insurmountable to a young man who, from the moment he landed in Canada, was forced to work long hours in a sweatshop. To pursue a successful literary career, it was absolutely necessary, for Segal had to have a book of his poetry published, and then have that book distributed beyond the limited circle of his Montreal admirers. He also had to have his books reviewed by serious critics, such as Sh. Niger or Zalman Rejzen, to be favourably received by the great Yiddish poets of Eastern Europe and America, and to participate in important literary events in Montreal and abroad. Above all, he had to gain access to a milieu where art was considered to be, in the words of Caiserman, "a sublime reflection of the soul." None of this was easy at first for the tailor-poet predisposed to melancholy and solitude. In fact, from the time he was a child, Segal was hesitant to enter the wider world, to venture beyond the orbit of his immediate family. There is no doubt that without Caiserman by his side from the very beginning, Segal would have retreated to a more private type of writing and stayed in a world with which he was familiar. Caiserman, by opening his home to Segal and introducing him to a more affluent Montreal milieu, changed the poet's prospects:

> In those years the Caiserman home was the sole refuge for the serious intellectual, a home with an open heart and an open ear, open for every man who did not always confide to the open street which was somewhat deaf to the more refined word. In that home, huddled the family of intellectuals who have since become the spiritual creators of our life and gave Montreal the title of great Jewish centre.
> [. . .] We are living witnesses to attest that the first seeds of thought for the cultural institutions and movements founded here were sown in the Caiserman home.
> In all propriety I dare affirm that there I found shelter, even protective shelter for my first writing in a world full of passive indifference, when I so needed a warm, comradely eye, the world of sincere, understanding men like Caiserman's or H. Novek's,[8] friends who could bring third parties close.[9]

Caiserman's care and concern for the poet and his work manifested itself in countless ways. There are many examples in his personal papers deposited in the Canadian Jewish Congress Archives after his death. For example, in February of 1937, Caiserman took the initiative of writing to some of his acquaintances to invite them to his home at 4223 Esplanade Avenue. The purpose of this gathering was to support and promote the imminent publication of Segal's eighth poetry collection, *Di drite sude* [The third meal]: "You are hereby invited to a short informal meeting in my house [. . .] We shall complete the final preparations so this book can to go to print."[10] Clearly this meant that Caiserman was organizing a fundraising event to cover the printing costs, without which Segal's book would never have seen the light of day, in addition to ensuring the author some publicity by arranging a book launch and local readings. Segal's various poetry collections printed in Montreal, although neither expensively bound nor printed on the best quality paper, nonetheless were attractively produced at a cost the poet would never have been able to afford on his own. Caiserman was not the only one who performed this service for Segal. Segal was often invited to read excerpts from his work in private homes, and make himself available to his hosts, just as he did on the evening of February 20, 1937: "J. I. Segal will recite a few poems from his manuscript."[11] At one such occasion that took place on November 30, 1946, Caiserman invited Segal to an elegant and exclusive party at his home to celebrate the poet's fiftieth birthday with prominent personalities from the Montreal Yiddish world. That evening the well-known actor Chaim Brisman recited a poem by Segal, the artist Olga Liber played the piano, and the poet himself performed before the assembled guests. At the end of the evening, Sarah Caiserman, on behalf of those in attendance, presented Segal with a cheque for $500 toward the publication of his next poetry book. The journalist from the *Eagle* who reported on this event emphasized that: "This splendid affair ended in a warm atmosphere and a note of thanks to the Caisermans for their support of writers and artists."[12] The mutual affection shared by these two men was captured in a moving article that Segal wrote in his literary column in the *Eagle* a few days after his friend's death, where he paid tribute to Caiserman for having been his confidant and a selfless friend of literature:

> He had high esteem for artists, poets, and writers, and would not have been able to live without always having a book in his hands. He didn't just read at work or at home. I often bumped into him in the street walking slowly and quietly reading a book. At such times he reacted as though he didn't want to be discovered in the middle of committing such an outrage—reading while walking— and poetry to boot. I used to tease him. "Caiserman, be careful you don't get caught behaving like this. You won't be forgiven for such folly."
>
> Caiserman responded with a smile, "Now that I have the poet in front of me, what do I need his poetry book for . . . "[13]

Bazunder lider (1921)

Caiserman's kindness could not completely dispel the tensions in the Segal household, where Segal spent long hours writing and not always succeeding in meeting his financial obligations. There is an obvious parallel here between the situation of the Montreal Yiddish poet who lacked a stable income, and that of the Eastern European scholars preoccupied with their "learning," who left their wives in charge of somehow finding the means to attend to the material needs of the family. It was only gradually that Segal succeeded, after 1940, in improving his social situation and become less dependent on the largesse of his mentor. Throughout the 1920s, however, the poet had to resort to finding employment in Montreal's newly formed Jewish community institutions, as did most of the other writers and intellectuals of his generation. Libraries, part-time schools, and Yiddish periodicals, especially the daily newspaper, the *Keneder Adler*—in English known as the *Jewish Daily Eagle*—founded in 1907 by Hirsch Wololfsky, offered Yiddish writers opportunities to earn a modest salary or a little money on a contract basis. A certain number of activists had taken advantage of the dizzying rate of growth of the Yiddish-speaking population of Canada, especially in Montreal, Toronto, and Winnipeg, to create centres for the dissemination of Eastern European Jewish culture. At the outbreak of World War I, these centres were still in their infancy. That was particularly true of Montreal where a network of Yiddish secular schools was founded in 1913 and 1914, offering afternoon classes for Jewish children enrolled in Montreal's Protestant School Board. In 1920, the Segal was hired by the Peretz[14] School as a part-time teacher. Thus, the poet joined a small team of about a dozen clothing workers who wanted to instil in the new generation the Eastern European cultural heritage and the socialist Zionist ideals of the Poale Zion[15] party. For Segal, it was a way of augmenting his income. The Peretz School also provided the poet with the opportunity to come into contact with community activists who could give him moral support and help disseminate his work. Dr. Shlomo Gold, one of the poet's closest friends in Montreal, whom Segal met around this time, painted the following portrait of him as a young teacher working in an institution where activists competed in their zeal to inculcate the children with their own ideologies:

> J. I. Segal never really got used to this environment.[16] His poetic demon stalked him every minute of the day. On his way to class he thought about poems, at teachers' meetings he wrote poems, and in class he dictated or wrote on the blackboard verses which he had actually composed on the spot.[17]

It is safe to say that that this was the time when Segal left his job in the factory and stopped working as a full-time tailor. From then on the poet and his wife worked in the clothing industry on a contract basis exclusively. They could do their work at home without too much

National Radical (Peretz) School, probably on Cadieux Street (today de Bullion, near Roy Street), Montreal, 1920. Last row, from left to right, J. I. Segal and Hershel Novak. (Montreal Jewish Public Library)

disruption to the family. At the end of the 1920s, after a break that lasted a few years, Segal continued his career as a teacher at the Jewish People's School (*Yidishe Folk Shule*), where he made the acquaintance of the director, Shlomo Wiseman, a fine writer and Labour Zionist who had been won over to modern teaching methods. The poet remained connected to this educational institution until the end of his career, while maintaining a positive relationship with the Peretz School and its director Jacob Zipper, who was to become his next-door neighbour on Clark Street in the early thirties. The poet also gave private Yiddish lessons to young students who were struggling to meet the expectations of the Jewish school board. Occasionally he also worked in the Jewish schools, called *heders*, where Hebrew was taught for religious purposes or in preparation for the Bar Mitzvah. The available evidence corroborates that Segal was not a very good teacher, and that he found it difficult to be in front of a large class. Despite his vast knowledge of Jewish tradition and modern Yiddish literature, Segal found it hard to communicate the rudiments of the Yiddish language to beginners.

On the other hand, the poet excelled as a tutor where the relationship with the student was more personal and engaged, such as when he went to a student's home to give private classes.[18] At the end of his career, Segal joined, on a part-time basis, the faculty of the Montreal Jewish Teacher's Seminar, a community institution charged with the task of training teachers for Montreal's Jewish parochial schools.

During the 1920s, Segal made some extra money by submitting poems and short book reviews to the *Keneder Adler*, probably on an *ad hoc* basis. At this time, Segal was regularly publishing poetry in the well-known American leftist literary review, *Di Tsukunft* (The future), was well as several European Yiddish-language cultural periodicals. This is confirmed in a 1929 review by Caiserman in which he mentions that the poet regularly had short pieces for children, in addition to his literary articles, published in the Montreal daily: "We read his interesting, original and insightful literary reviews in the *Keneder Adler*. His form of literary criticism, traditional yet modern, demands of all Yiddish wordsmiths the highest artistic standards."[19] In his more in-depth biography, Leib Wasserman also emphasizes Segal's participation in the *Keneder Adler* (*The Jewish Daily Eagle*). The poet is described as being a "full-time staff writer"[20] at the Montreal daily in the 1920s. "He wrote about contemporary issues and mostly about literature."[21] However, this arrangement ended abruptly in the fall of 1931, a development that evidently had nothing to do with the poet's talent or personality. Rather, it was due to the impact of the Great Depression on the fortunes of the *Adler's* owner, the Wolofsky family. Nonetheless, the decision to reduce the number of full-time journalists and authors put an end to a productive collaboration that had lasted for quite some time. It also left the poet vulnerable during the sudden economic downturn. The result was that Segal occasionally worked as a proofreader for Yiddish writers about to publish their work. This is what happened, for example, in the case of Sheindl Franzus-Garfinkle who turned to Segal during the 1940s to help her with the final preparation of her novels that were published in Montreal.

Leaving aside for a moment the subject of the Segal family's financial situation, let us return to 1918, when Segal launched his literary career with the publication of his first volume of poetry, *Fun mayn velt*. Backed by a few individuals committed to supporting the creation of a new literary and artistic movement within the Montreal Jewish community, Segal unexpectedly made his literary debut. In less than three years, he had published a second volume of poetry entitled *Bazunder lider* [Separate poems] in 1921. It was 199 pages long and printed by the Artistish Drukeray [Artistic printing] company of Montreal.[22] In this second poetry collection the same themes appear as in *Fun mayn velt*, but in a more assured and expansive form. In *Bazunder lider* Segal had gained confidence, and enhanced his writing by putting more emphasis on the metrical structure and graphic aspects of his poems, on their appearance and placement on the page. Whereas his first book contained obvious instances of awkwardness in presentation and form—which Caiserman did not fail to notice—the second enjoyed a more professional and artistic presentation. In effect, *Bazunder lider* is the first complete realization of the poet's artistic expression. Unlike Segal's first, his second book was conceived as a unit and presented as a coherent whole. Some new themes make their appearance, including a few poems dedicated to his young wife Elke, usually entitled, "To My Wife." There are also poems about God, most of them deploring His absence and powerlessness in coming to the aid of mankind. *Bazunder lider* also reflects an intensification of the poet's writing on the theme of the city. In this volume, Segal extols the attraction that Montreal holds for immigrants arriving at the city's gates to partake of its pleasures and delights. Nevertheless, it is not without nostalgia and longing for the lost world of childhood, for a pristine natural world, which, alas, has become a distant memory. Disturbed to the core of his being by the humiliations suffered in his family environment in Korets, the poet now suffers from the strangeness of the big city, from the coldness and detachment of the urban landscape. He deplores the state of anonymity in which its inhabitants find themselves, especially when they work in a factory from dawn until dusk and speak a foreign language. These observations are reflected in several poems, including one in which the poet discloses his inner turmoil and social isolation (see Appendix 12):

The City Is My Village

Long ago the city became my village —
My heart is now content with the city.
As content as with fields
As content as with rivers and mountains.
And with the stillness of buzzing insects
Humming for gold and for faraway vistas.
And echoes of crystal . . .

Oh, how many luminous fields and forests
Stand guard day and night round the city!
A delight for the fields,
A delight for the forests,
the dancing glittering city!
And flies and bees come looking for gold and faraway vistas.
Gold and vistas and echoes of crystal,
in the city —

Long ago the city became my village.
And the girls, naive from work and fatigue,
Walk home like goats every evening.
Long ago the city became my village.
I have stifled its grating voices inside me,
I am deaf to its banging and clanging:
through the wildest noise its stillness speaks to me . . .
for me its deadness stays silent . . . .[23]

Reading *Bazunder lider* confirms the impression that Segal had distilled and simplified his writing to be able to better express the flow of his emotions. In this collection, he exposes his feelings about everything around him, without inhibitions. Segal's poetic imagery, his capacity to convey in a few words, or a few short lines, a flash of inspiration or a contemplative moment, is realized without artifice or rhetorical detours. Above all, the poet is now focussed on his inner life, on his feelings during the day or at night, while out for a walk, or happening upon a fortuitous event, or in the privacy of his own home. He himself has become the landscape to be painted, the object to be portrayed, or the moment to be seized. The chaos of his sometimes contradictory feelings, the profusion of inner doubts, the creative impulse pulled in opposite directions by two cities on either side of an ocean of unresolved pain—all of this is poured into his poetry in creative disarray. In his writing, Segal did not seek to explain his suffering, to order his afflictions, or to find the root causes of his problems, as the "proletarian" poets were doing at that very moment. Rather, he navigated alone into the unknown and committed to paper his painful individuality without a filter, without appealing to a grand idea that would unite mankind, without adhering to any particular school of thought. He followed his whims like the child in Korets who wrote satirical poems, and like the young factory worker in Montreal who, fresh off the boat, wrote late into the night in perfect solitude. In *Bazunder lider* this type of writing, free of any constraints, was further reinforced. It emerged into broad daylight and found an outlet in a vast universe as yet undefined. Segal followed his penchant for introspection, where external reality was merely the reflection of his own thoughts and actions, and not vice versa. Shy, reserved and secretive by nature, he looked at the world with apprehension and distrust. In his poetry, he powerfully projected his inner voice onto this backdrop, sensitive to the smallest variation in temperature, on the lookout for the least hint of a threat. And his "I" was not so much egoism or a rejection of others, but a search for authenticity, for personal truth, and a place for himself in the world (See Appendix 13)

I

The rail-long hours run from the now estranged world,
Pulling everything with them and discarding it in the dirt.
I gather what's left of me and go into my night.
I sit down in the smoke of their vapours and smells.
And weigh my heaviness on spiderweb scales:
Waves smile around my eyes:
I am as weightless as the quiet of my lost light
that still lies hidden.
I am as light as the distant places that have still not seen my
    shadow,
and do not call me . . .
Smooth heavens still soar above my head —
Under smooth heavens a few hairs on my head turn grey.
A few precious grey hairs . . .

I have scattered crooked paths on the harmony of the world.
No birds fly over them, no shadow lies across them.
In the meantime no one will miss them or long for them.
Even snow will not come to whiten them.
I shall call no sun to them,
No moon, no stars.
By night I see moon-dust fall on them like sand.
They straighten out and stretch toward sunny apparitions . . .
Somewhere great cities lie sprawling and naked
and turn to my crooked paths that I scattered
over the harmony of the harmony of the world . . .[24]

The New York Modernist Movement

Segal wrote in order to alleviate his insuperable inner suffering and a family situation he was powerless to change, both in the old world and in the new. He most certainly wished to someday make his work known and attract a readership aware of his talent. The moment finally arrived when his poetry travelled across borders and was read by other Jewish writers, most of whom were committed to a literary approach driven by a specific ideological aesthetic. Of the myriad possibilities available to Segal in 1919, once he had achieved some fame in the world of Yiddish literature, one in particular caught his attention: the New York modernist school, better known today as *Di Yunge*. Or rather, the Montreal intimist poet was noticed and courted by the leading figures of American Yiddish cultural life, among them Moshe Leib Halpern, Mani Leib, Zishe Landau, Reuben Iceland, Joseph Rolnick, and a few others, all of them older and more established than Segal. The key organizers of *Di Yunge* were young Eastern European immigrants who began publishing poetry in New York at the turn of the century. In 1907, on their own initiative, they founded a movement which claimed to have initiated a new direction in Yiddish literature. Until then Yiddish literature in the United States was dominated by a didactic and moralistic vision, where propaganda and political militancy eclipsed any aesthetic considerations. Turning their backs on authors like Morris Winchevsky (1856–1932), David Edelstadt (1866–1892), and Morris Rosenfeld, who were their predecessors in the late nineteenth century, the members of *Di Yunge* sought to introduce the idea of "poetry for poetry's sake,"[25] of literature as an end in itself, and poetry as the expression of the inner voice and mood of each individual poet. In the universe of North American Yiddish letters, this was a complete reversal of the viewpoint that had predominated in the previous century:

> What soon made them a revolutionary force within Yiddish literature was that they refused political commitment and denied any obligation to speak for national ideals. Never at home with either America or the English language, these young men turned to world literature and, most of all, ideas of aesthetic autonomy and symbolist refinement.[26]

Segal, who in Montreal had already embraced the ideas of *Di Yunge*, had much in common with his New York colleagues. Nevertheless, unlike Moshe Leib Halpern, Mani Leib, and Zishe Landau, who had to contend with long established literary norms and influential newspapers in America, Canadian Yiddish writers did not have to free themselves from a populist trend or to overthrow an already existing establishment. In fact, Segal had been the first to publish high quality Yiddish poetry in Canada. No one before him had occupied this ground, either directly or indirectly, and hence the the title of one of the first Montreal Yiddish literary journals, *Royerd* [literally "raw earth," virgin soil]. Operating in a previously unoccupied space and addressing a relatively large audience, Segal never had to "liberate" himself from the weight of his predecessors or the tyranny of a preexisting cultural establishment. Thus, he quickly gravitated to *Di Yunge*, and soon became known as one of its principal spokesmen. The majority of letters received by Segal during the course of his career in the Jewish Public Library's collection of his correspondence, most of them saved by the poet himself, were often from New York Yiddish writers. Most of the letters are very personal. Segal began a correspondence with Zishe Landau in the early 1920s, with poets H. Leivick and Baruch Glassman in 1921, with poets Aaron Glanz Leyeles and Abraham Reisen in 1922, and with critic Sh. Niger almost at the same time. Some of the more significant and lengthy epistolary relationships lasted more than thirty-five years. In 1926, for example, Leivik wrote to Segal from Moscow about a variety of issues, including his complaints against his New York colleagues connected with the modernist journal *Indzl* [Island]. He ended his letter by declaring:

> At least you are not one of those who choke at the very mention of my name. Of that I am convinced. I trust you because I believe in your integrity and your magnificent talent, which can only be pure and noble.
> Still, I would like to hear from you. I thank you for your short letter and those few words which prove that my heart was not mistaken about you.[27]

Segal began exchanging letters with the Viennese Yiddish poets Melekh Chmielnitzki and Melekh Ravitch[28] in 1919, with Nachman Meisel and Ezra Korman of the *Kultur Lige* (Culture League) in Warsaw, in 1921–1922, with the Vilna philologist and literary critic Zalman Rejzen and the Berlin poet Daniel Charney in 1926. However, the correspondence with Eastern European personalities generally did not last, often because the correspondents themselves moved to America, usually to New York. Also, Segal's contact with Yiddish writers in the Old Country was mostly limited to the period between 1933 and 1939. In this connection, the Segal Archive at the Jewish Public Library contains a list, although probably incomplete, of the articles published about him in the Yiddish press internationally between 1919 and 1937 (see Appendix 14). Thanks to this document by an unknown author, it can be stated with a fair degree of certainty that Segal was read in modernist circles in the United States beginning in the 1920s, and it was there that the poet received the most attention from literary critics. Around 1922, Zishe Landau[29] in New York confirmed in a letter that he had received from Segal a copy of the literary journal *Royerd*, and expressed his desire to obtain a copy of *Bazunder lider*. On another occasion Landau requested the three issues of *Nyuansn* (Nuances), a journal published in Montreal under Segal's editorship. "What a pity that your literary journal is so little known in New York. I don't even know whether our people have read it. I heard from Leivick that when he was in the office of *Di Tsayt* he saw one issue."[30] It is no surprise that the New York Yiddish poets were so anxious to read Segal. To begin with, the American metropolis was only a day's journey by train from Montreal. Secondly, Yiddish writers living in the United States often came to visit their relatives living on the Canadian side of the border. This travelling back and forth, very significant for Canadian Yiddish literature, began in the early 1920s, and increased during the interwar period. Often Montreal cultural institutions invited well-known American Yiddish writers to participate in their activities, as evidenced by the memoirs of Sholem Shtern.[31]

The Journal *Nyuansn*

Montreal Yiddish literature entered a new phase in January of 1921 when the first issue of the literary journal *Nyuansn* (Nuances)[32] went to press. Self-described as a monthly journal for poems, "miniatures"[33] and essays, *Nyusansn* had only a short run of three issues. However, its contributors were the authors who would go on to make a name for themselves in Canadian Yiddish literature over the following two decades, namely J. I Segal, A. S. Shkolnikov,[34] H. M. Caiserman, Asher Royzn,[35] and Israel Rabinovitch who, in 1924, became the editor-in-chief of the *Keneder Adler*. Among those who regularly wrote for *Nyuansn* were Leib Bercovitch,[36] Efraim Fishl Perlmuter,[37] Simon

Nepom of Toronto, Mordechai Miller of Winnipeg, Leiser Mendel Benjamin, and Vladimir Grossman. The address of *Nyuansn* was 619a Colonial Avenue,[38] the home address of its editor-in-chief at the time, J. I. Segal. This journal was actually the first attempt to create a Montreal Yiddish literary school composed of aspiring Eastern European immigrant writers in Canada. Thus, *Nyuansn* functioned less as an organ for young modernists opposed to the existing literary establishment, as was the case in New York, than as a vehicle for a creating a new synergy in a city where the first seeds of Yiddish culture had barely begun to sprout. In this sense *Nyuansn* was like a torch lighting the way to new talent. The journal appeared with neither an introduction by its founders nor any polemical articles announcing a particular ideological or aesthetic stance. On the other hand, *Nuansn* deliberately aligned itself with the modern movement in its January 1921 issue by publishing three essays on great personalities who had contributed to the artistic revival internationally: Leo Ornstein (1893–2002), then a world-renowned pianist and brilliant interpreter of Claude Debussy and Arnold Schoenberg; Georg Brandes (1842–1927), a Danish writer, literary critic, and founder of the Scandinavian school of naturalism; and Moshe Broderson (1890–1956), a Russian-born Yiddish poet and actor. The title of the journal, *Nyuansn,* appeared in French on the cover page to signal the attachment of its founders to European high culture and universal modes of artistic expression.

The first issue of *Nyuansn* began with nineteen poems by Segal, followed by fourteen rather short poems by Shkonikov, five by Sh. Shnayder,[39] three by Asher Royzn, and one by Simon Nepom, indicating the editor's dominant role in Canadian Yiddish letters, and his desire to set the bar high. In the two issues that followed, the proportional amount of space assigned to each of the writers remained more or less the same, as did the order in which they appeared. Segal's contribution was mostly introspective free verse, written in much the same spirit as *Bazunder lider*. It should be noted that *Nyuansn* did not attain the level of its New York equivalents such as *Yugnt, Literatur, Ist Brodvey* or *Shriftn*. Born ten years earlier, these American literary journals reached a much larger readership and could draw upon a large pool of diverse writers. However, the connection between the Canadian and American modernist movements was evident in the pages of *Nyuansn*, especially in the second issue where Segal wrote a six-page article about Mani Leib, Moshe Leib Halpern, Zishe Landau, and H. Leivick entitled "*Durkh di ershte fir*[40] [Through the first four]." In this essay, Segal introduced a model for literary criticism that he use for the rest of his career. He favoured an in-depth analysis of the text and its meaning. Unlike the writers who were his contemporaries, Segal avoided biographical details and political considerations, unless they had some genuine relevance to the work's artistic value. The following year, in *Epokhe*,[41] he wrote an article about the young poet Melekh Ravitch, who, along with Uri Zvi Greenberg and Peretz Markish, in 1921 had formed the Warsaw literary group known as the *Khalyastre*. In *Royerd*, in 1922, Segal discussed the literary contribution of the *In Zikh* movement, composed of Aaron Glanz Leyeles, Jacob Glatstein, and N. B. Minkov. This approach earned Segal a reputation throughout the Yiddish world as an astute observer of the literary scene and its major writers. Dozens more articles of this type, penned in literary language, are to be found in various Canadian Yiddish newspapers of the 1930s, 1940s, and 1950s, but have never been assembled as a collection. In them, Segal addressed important issues in a highly poetic style. He was interested in the sources of the writers' creativity as well as their influence on Yiddish literature, before going on to describe the sentiments a work evoked in him as a literary critic. It is not an exaggeration to say that using this method, Segal reviewed all the Yiddish literature produced during his lifetime, and that he made himself its interpreter for a Canadian public with little awareness of the newest contemporary literary trends. In a single volume, these articles would form a complete history of Yiddish literature in the twentieth century in all its diversity, in particular in North America. With regard to Mani Leib, Segal wrote in the *Nyuansn* in 1921:

> Mani Leib's sorrow is profound, but not without compassion [. . .] Rather, his sorrow is bathed in the warm springs of mysterious kindness, and therefore at times filled with regret. It seems as though Mani Leib were hiding a treasure—magnificent colourful birds which he will not let out of their dark cage. Perhaps he is afraid that we will be blinded by their brilliant colours.[42]

The momentum behind *Nyuansn* could not be sustained beyond three months. However, a few months later, this journal was succeeded by a new literary monthly called *Royerd*, also edited by J. I. Segal and A. S. Shkolnikov. Three issues appeared in Montreal in 1922, and three in Toronto under the auspices of the Toronto Jewish Cultural League (*kulturlige*). *Royerd* enjoyed two more short runs in Montreal, in 1927

Cover page of the literary journal *Epokhe*, Montreal, 1922.
(Canadian Jewish Congress Archives).

and 1929. Before disappearing, *Nyuansn* made the following impression on a commentator whose name has not survived: "Thanks to its novelty and freshness, this literary journal has attracted a great deal of attention in Yiddish literary centres on both sides of the Atlantic."[43]

Royerd was followed in 1922 by a three-hundred-page literary anthology entitled *Epokhe* [Epoch] under the editorship of J. I. Segal, A. Almi,[44] and A. S. Shkolnikov. Although conceived as a trimonthly, *Epokhe* was no more commercially successful than its predecessors, and its founders had to be content with a single issue. In 1922, however, this periodical was welcomed enthusiastically by the impressionist poet Melekh Chmelnitzki, who wrote to Segal from Vienna: "I read your poems in *Epokhe*. It's unnecessary for me to describe to you the powerful effect that many of them had on me."[45] At the same time, on another continent, Moshe (Moissaye) J. Olgin reviewed *Epokhe* for the New York Communist newspaper *Di Frayhayt* (*Morgen Freiheit*). According to Olgin, it was important to note that Yiddish periodicals of superior quality were appearing in smaller centres like Montreal, while in New York literary journals of recent origin were gradually disappearing. This literary critic then singled out two writers in the Canadian literary anthology who, he believed, would not remain unknown for much longer in the world of Yiddish letters, Segal and Shkolnikov. With regard to the author of *Bazunder lider*, Olgin wrote:

> Judging by the thirty or so poems which Segal published in *Epokhe*, he is a talented and imaginative writer capable of powerful expression, demonstrating from the outset a classic mastery of the language and gifted with a personality that makes the reader feel compelled to stay and listen to him.[46]

Olgin also noted Segal's disenchantment with society and man in general, and a dark predisposition to suffering in his poetry. His only reservation was that Segal occasionally produced work which was monotonous and dull, although not to the point of boring the reader. From Vilna, a veritable bastion of Eastern European Yiddish culture at the time, Zalman Rejzen made the following comments in 1927 about the literary achievements and publications in Montreal:

> Segal was one of the first to put all his energy into creating a Yiddish cultural milieu in faraway Canada with its small Jewish population, thus rendering the greatest service to serious Yiddish literature in that country. Around the publications of which he was editor, were gathered together the best creative talents in Canada. Even after he left for New York in the summer of 1923, he maintained contact with these talented writers, and contributed to their periodicals [. . .] [47]

A few other literary journals were published in Montreal in the 1920s, including *Der Kval* [The source] in December of 1922, under the direction of A. Almi. In 1925, on the initiative of Israel Rabinovitch and A.S. Shkolnikov, a magazine entitled *Kanade* appeared, lasting only three months. Unlike New York, where the literary journal *Shriftn*[48] was published from 1912 until 1927, Montreal could not provide a readership large and diverse enough to sustain literary publications over long periods of time. The disappointment at such lack of interest was all the more acute among literary enthusiasts because, from an artistic standpoint, Montreal's literary production left nothing to be desired, as Segal's poem in the second issue of *Nyuansn* demonstrates (see Appendix 15). In the poem "Mount Royal," the force of his imagery and scope of his poetic ability are readily apparent. Beginning at the top of the "mountain" and descending along its gentle slope to his neighbourhood, Segal imagines a winter scene that his pen transforms into a furious battlefield, paralysed by the cold and harshness of the elements.

Mount Royal

At twilight a proud mountain stood
and from the city moved away, arrogant, head high.
No trees descend from him as in the light.
Frozen is heaven's purity and full and full of cold.

The cold is the grieving sunshine that remains from the day
and when no eye can see, dies of darkness and falls away;
and sometimes from that falling great miracles can happen in
     the stillness;
And no one must know, it must stay dead, forever closed.

A row of frozen trees, steadfast, brave and strong
Face the city from the mountaintop, armed with spear and sword ---
A fearless army sunk knee-deep in earth that cannot take a step,
Paralysed at the edge if the black mountain. [49]

Segal was evidently hit very hard by the financial difficulties that thwarted his many literary projects in Montreal. At some point in 1922, he decided to join his modernist colleagues in *Di Yunge* in New York.[50] It was not that he had failed to publish first-rate work. On the contrary, several decades later, his biographer Leib Wasserman stated in the *Leksikon fun de nayer yiddisher literatur* [Biographical Dictionary of Modern Yiddish Literature] that *Fun mayn velt* had "had an impact"[51] and that *Nyuansn* "was of a high literary calibre."[52] Quite simply, Segal had not been able to obtain the financial support required to realize his artistic ambitions. The short-lived publications of the 1920s also proved how difficult it could be to create a literary movement, especially in a city that had only 45,000 Yiddish speakers in 1921, most of them poor factory workers and small shopkeepers who had recently immigrated. Although during the 1920s and 1930s there were a certain number of Yiddish literary careers that flourished in Montreal,[53] the city lacked a large enough Jewish population to sustain a literary school with well-defined artistic goals capable of attracting a more general readership, like *Di Yunge* in New York. Instead, the writers who lived in the Jewish neighbourhood at the foot of Mount Royal were not alike in their affiliations, with some espousing modernist tenets, while others found inspiration in proletarian ideologies, or were simply content to describe their personal and family lives, not to mention those writers who were Orthodox Jews. The Jewish parochial schools, the Jewish Public Library, and the garment workers' unions were also divided at that time and too often plagued by internal conflict to impose some form of order on Montreal's literary scene.

Montreal's literary circles were somewhat like the newspaper founded in 1907 by Hirsch Wolofsky, the *Keneder Adler*. Under intense pressure to attract as many readers as possible, Wolofsky conceived of his newspaper as a forum for debate and the exchange of ideas within the community, and not as the mouthpiece for any particular group, political or otherwise. This was the price the *Keneder Adler* had to pay to survive in a relatively limited market. Few and far between, Yiddish writers also ended up sharing a large building, where divergent ideas and words were tolerated up to a certain point. This attitude of openness and tolerance, which developed over time, did not prevent Segal from leaving Montreal embittered and determined to pursue his career elsewhere, specifically in New York, where the members of the modernist school *Di Yunge* awaited him. The feeling of powerlessness comes through very clearly in a letter addressed to him by H. M. Caiserman in April of 1924:

> [Yiddish] I thank you with all my heart for your letter, and I regret very much that I inadvertently provoked painful memories of terrible experiences. Yes, yes! Unfortunately you are right that Montreal has brought upon itself the most horrible of all afflictions, the curse of vulgarity. But these vulgar people are sometimes capable of devotion and spontaneous discernment. Be patient with the Jews of Montreal, my great beloved poet.[54]

Under the Wing of Mani Leib

When he left for New York in 1923, Segal undoubtedly wanted to feel the intoxication of being surrounded by a circle of writers and friends who shared his aesthetic choices in every respect, and who had formed a school based on some powerful ideas. This desire, which he had expressed on numerous occasions, finally convinced him to move to the undisputed capital of Yiddish culture in North America. Some of the key figures in *Di Yunge* had already developed a close friendship with Segal, especially H. Leivick and Mani Leib. The idea of his moving to New York had previously been raised in a letter from Zishe Landau to Segal in the early 1920s. At the same time, this correspondence provides a glimpse of the difficult living conditions of the modernist Yiddish poets in America's largest city, and how hard they had to work in order to be able to devote a few moments to their art.

> [Yiddish] Don't come to New York. Certainly it would be better if you were a New Yorker. But it's no use. You are more or less settled in Montreal and what can you do in New York? You'll be torn to shreds. I mean economically. It's very hard to make ends meet here, although I imagine that it's not so great there either. In any case, it's better than in New York.[55]

In the aftermath of World War I, all the luminaries of New York Yiddish literature, almost without exception, earned their living by the sweat of their brow, either working in the garment industry or doing seasonal work. What was true for the Montreal poets was doubly so in New York. The writers' social isolation, their lack of viable work opportunities in the publishing field, the absence of a readership familiar with avant-garde poetry, and the fact that they were obliged to produce work in a language known only by immigrants, shook the most resolute of intentions, and affected the most promising careers. Although the poets of *Di Yunge* were glorified in the Yiddish literary world at the beginning of the century and lived in an international city that was the home of important artistic movements, most of them, at the end of a hard day in the factory or sweatshop, met only among themselves and essentially lived on the margins of mainstream America. This is the portrait presented by historian Irving Howe in *World of Our Fathers*:

Most were shopworkers, few had an extended secular education, almost all were cut off from writers in other languages. As
they hurried to and from the shops, they read with eagerness the
modern European poets, and in the evening, nursing a glass of
tea in Goodman and Levine's café, they would discuss impressionism, expressionism, symbolism. Sharing the lot of millions
of Jewish immigrants and never able, in their writings, to detach
themselves from the preoccupations of the immigrant world . . .[56]

The enthusiasm with which Segal set out for New York was of short
duration. More than that is difficult to ascertain because there is little
documentation pertaining to that period in the poet's life. For a long
time Segal kept silent about his stay in the American metropolis, a
stay marked by great material deprivation and a particularly tragic
event. Already in March of 1922 there is evidence of Segal's financial difficulties in his correspondence with Chmelnitzki cited above:
"From your letter and what you've written to other friends, it seems
that your life there is very hard. It pains me that I can't be of any
help to you . . ."[57] From an official letter dated 1923, in the archives
of the Montreal Jewish Public Library, we know that the poet was
the official representative in New York of the Hebrew Sheltering and
Immigrant Aid society. It is also possible that he taught part-time
in the city's Yiddish schools, perhaps, as Caiserman suggests, in the
Sholem Aleichem Shule. These activities do not seem to have been of
long duration, and Segal joined other poets in a cooperative shoe factory that had been founded in the early 1920s.[58] In addition to being
a respected Yiddish writer, Mani Leib was, according to his biographer, "an excellent craftsman."[59] There is also the testimony of Aaron
Rappoport who visited the factory founded and directed by Mani
Leib: "It was astounding to see how he worked, such sensitive hands,
flooded with light. He held the pieces of brown leather in his hands as
though they were alive and he was stitching together a living thing."[60]
Given his manual dexterity and technical skills as a shoemaker, Mani
Leib decided to set up a factory where the poets of Di Yunge could
work side by side without feeling that they were being exploited, and
develop a sense that they were contributing to a shared artistic cause.
The idea was very simple. In exchange for their work, and after a certain number of months of learning the trade, the poets would receive,
instead of a weekly salary, an equal share in the profits generated by
the business. This idea was influenced by the anarchists who rejected

private property and exclusive control by the dominant classes over the productivity of the workers. Among the workers Rappoport met in the shoe factory managed by Mani Leib was a young Montrealer freshly arrived in New York:

> Four shoemakers were sitting at their machines and J. I. Segal among them. He had just moved to New York and Mani Leib "took him on" and tried to teach him the trade . . . I said hello to Mani Leib as well as the newly arrived proletarian who looked so irritated sitting at his machine, angry at the world . . . I could not even elicit a smile from him.
> [. . .] Mani Leib gestured with his hand: "He's in a huff, like me sometimes, in his poems also . . ." [61]

In the long run, however, Mani Leib's business did not cover his expenses, with the result that those poets who had invested their time and effort in it found their situation deteriorating rapidly. During slack periods, or when business was slow, the workers of the Safran and Brahinsky Company [62] were simply not paid and were forced to resort to stopgap measures.

It is also quite possible that the factory set up by Mani Leib, given its size, could not generate the profit required to compete in the New York footwear industry. Furthermore, some of the workers had poorly mastered the tricks of the trade and could not pull their weight during the busy periods. Indeed, Mani Leib had hired the members of his cooperative more on the basis of their writing ability and poetic talent than their competence as workers. Driven by his idealism and his desire to promote modern Yiddish literature, Mani Leib had deliberately neglected to take into consideration the manual dexterity of his protégés. This was certainly true in the case of Segal, who never learned how to handle leather or to use the machinery required for the production of footwear. The following is what Rappoport had to say about him:

> To his left sat Segal at his machine, brooding . . . His fingers approached the machine as though he were trying to stave off some kind of small animal that was trying to bite his finger. He held the pieces of leather with the tips of his fingers as though they were abominable things—perhaps some kind of creepy, crawly creatures? . . . Mani Leib seeing my reaction, interjected: "He's just clumsy! He'll never catch on . . ." [63]

In the end, the cooperative organized by Mani Leib finally went under, leaving penniless the worker poets as well as its founder, who in the meantime had become one of the leading lights of the new American Yiddish literature. In an obituary published in 1954, Serlin states that Segal lived in New York from 1923 to 1928, no doubt with a few relatively short interruptions during which the poet returned to Montreal to see his family.[64] In the absence of precise reference points, this information is helpful.

According to Segal's two daughters in a recent interview, this period was one of the darkest in the life of their father who rarely spoke about it. In addition to the physical stress involved in making shoes, as well as the privations resulting from an uncertain livelihood, Segal was devastated by the unexpected loss of his daughter Tsharna.[65] This tragedy apparently occurred toward the end of 1925. Melekh Ravitch alluded to it in a postcard dated November 29, 1925: "My dear friend, I had already heard about your misfortune. Can words convey what feels when one receives such terrible news?"[66] The death would also leave a gaping wound that would haunt the poet for the rest of his life. Apparently his six-year-old daughter died very suddenly because family photos taken in New York show her happy and in perfect health. According to David Rome, the loss of little Tsharna had an impact on the poet's career and left an indelible imprint on his writing: "This pain-truth deepened his work as the loss of his unforgettable child came to stamp its dark grey on the rest of his life."[67] There is no doubt that the chronic poverty and insecurity with which the Segals struggled in New York played a significant role in this tragic event. How could anyone fail to make the connection between the sudden loss of the child and the father's inability, despite tremendous sacrifice, to provide a decent standard of living for his family? For a long time the death of his child would cast a pall over the poet's life. He would associate her death with the death of his father half a century earlier, further irrefutable proof of the dominion of the kingdom of death over the living, and an inexhaustible source of anguish. The memory of this painful loss in 1925 would inspire verses charged with emotion.[68] In a poem published in 1930, entitled "*Likhtik* [Bright]," Segal meets God in his nocturnal garden on a quiet summer evening. He imagines confessing his anguish to Him and exclaiming in a heart-rending voice: "And I shall beg you: open for me the alcove where my child has been sleeping since I lost her."[69] It is difficult to find a more excruciating testament to the impact of this death on the poet's emotional stability and his career.

Notwithstanding the irreparable loss of his daughter Tsharna, not everything about Segal's stay in New York was negative. He had rubbed shoulders with some of the pre-eminent poets of his day, often establishing personal friendships and sharing their hopes for their literary movement, most notably in the cafés frequented by Yiddish-speaking artists on Second Avenue and the Lower East Side. Many of them recognized in this shy young Montrealer one of the most important talents of the new generation of writers, if not their peer. Also, Segal had published his work in the literary journals of *Di Yunge* and the *Inzikhistn*, notably in *Shriftn*, from 1925 to 1926, and in *In Zikh* and *Feder*, and even the socialist literary monthly *Tsukunft*.[70] Upon his return to Montreal, Segal would continue to nurture these precious relationships for almost thirty years, as evidenced by his copious correspondence. Although exiled to Canada's glacial expanses and separated from New York's literary circles by an international border, for the rest of his writing life Segal continued to see himself as the heir of the first American Yiddish-language modernists. Whenever Leivick, Joseph Rolnick, Aaron Glanz-Leyeles or Jacob Glatstein came to take part in cultural events at the Montreal Jewish Public Library, or to visit the literary salon of Ida Maze on Esplanade, invariably they would find in Segal an enthusiastic reader and loyal friend. During those years, Segal used his literary column in the *Keneder Adler* to keep the Montreal public informed about the New York literary scene as well as the publications of its key representatives. These sustained contacts during the interwar period gave Segal great influence in the Canadian Yiddish world, and conferred upon him the status of the dominant figure on Montreal's art scene. In anthologies and literary journals published in Montreal, Segal's poems almost always occupied a prominent place at the beginning of the volume. Similarly, young poets wishing to enter the pantheon of Montreal Yiddish literature often came to Segal with their writing to seek his support. Such was the case with Sholem Shtern[71] who had arrived from Poland penniless in 1927, burning with ambition to become a recognized Yiddish writer in America. In his memoirs published in 1982, Shtern recounts how, as a young novice, he met Segal in the late 1920s, hoping that with his encouragement he could break into the New York Yiddish literary circles, to his mind the only ones that counted:

> Thus I went to meet J. I. Segal, who was the poet laureate of Montreal, and also considered himself the *"poysek akhren"*, the

Tsharna and her mother, Elke; New York, 1925.
(Private collection of Sylvia and Annette Segal.)

final authority. [. . .] Because I did not have the courage to submit my poems anywhere directly, I went to recite them to Segal.
He was very taken with my first sanatorium poems and told that
me he would send them along with his recommendation to the
Tsukunft.[. . .]
Segal's stamp of approval and his promise to find a place for my
poetry gave me a great deal of encouragement [. . .]. J. I Segal took
a bunch of my poems and put them his vest pocket. Right there
in front of me he wrote the address on a large envelope, and said
that as soon as he had completed his own unfinished poem, he
would send away my poems as well.[72]

Fun mayn shtub un mayn velt (1923)

Segal's primary achievement in New York was the 1923 publication of
his third poetry collection entitled *Fun mayn shtub un mayn velt* [From
my house and my world], a title that echoed in part the title of his

first book of 1918. Published in New York by the Vilner Farlag fun B. Kletskin, printed in Vienna by Halpern and Company, and distributed in Europe by the Warsaw Culture League, probably thanks to Melekh Ravitch, this slim sixty-two page volume is indisputably one of the most accomplished of the poet's career, in terms of its graphic elements and physical qualities. The fine lettering of the book's title that leaps out from the front cover is in the Art Nouveau style then in vogue in Eastern Europe. Inside, elegant Hebrew characters march across pages printed on paper of the finest quality.[73] This was the remarkable work of the Vilna-based Kletskin publishing house, which specialized in modern Yiddish-language publications, notably the periodical *Literarishe Bleter*. In and of itself, this 1923 book is impressive evidence of the international character of Yiddish literature in the twentieth century where an author born in the Ukraine, but living in New York, after having first immigrated to Montreal, was published by a Russian Jewish publishing company that printed some of its books in Vienna, but was based in Vilna, which in 1923, was to become part of an independent Poland. Between the two world wars in all these cities, scattered over two continents and beyond, there emerged Yiddish cultural groups closely linked to one another, whose leading figures had crossed paths in various places in the Jewish diaspora. The title of Segal's new book also highlighted his decidedly intimist approach, in keeping with the introspectivist ideas of *Di Yunge* and the *Inzikhistn* in the United States, and similar to the expressionist notions espoused by Melekh Ravitch and the *Khalyastre* group in Poland. Indeed, *Fun mayn shtub un mayn velt* opened wide the door to the poet's inner world—his doubts, his joys, his family life, and what he observed around him in the streets of his neighbourhood. It also revealed the author's personal journey, especially his nostalgia for the traditional way of life he led in Korets, which he still carried within himself all those years later. Many of the poems in this volume have titles suggesting they are autobiographical, such as "We . . . three . . . ," "My Face," "Twenty-Six Years,"[74] and "I." Among them is the eponymous poem "*In mayn shtub* [In my Room][75] that sums up Segal's poetic process at the time (see Appendix 16).

In My Room

In the dust of my impoverished room
My meek and modest life creeps on.

And my wife and my child are always with me,
In the dust of my impoverished room.

By the window of my impoverished room
The dust of the eternal world turns grey.
Even though there's sun in the eternal world,
Even though it's blue in the eternal heights!
Yet dust falls through the sun and light,
from the eternal heights and from afar.
Greyness, the ash of time.

In the dust of my impoverished room
The green of my eye withers
A spider creeps into my eye
And in my eye a spider spins his web.

And my wife and my child in the greyness of my eye
In the dust of my impoverished room.

Although published in New York, most of the poems included in *Fun mayn shtub un mayn velt* were presumably written in Montreal in the months preceding his move to the American metropolis, when Segal was travelling back and forth regularly between the two cities. Essentially, they have the same rhythm as in his two previous books of poetry, as well as the small town atmosphere that was characteristic of his poetry thus far. Several poems published for the first time in *Fun mayn shtub un mayn velt* refer to a mountain near the poet's home, where he lived surrounded by his immediate family, notably his mother, which was not the case when Segal lived in New York. Once Segal had left Canada, he stayed in close contact with Montreal, where he had lived for over ten years. In particular, he continued publishing his writing in the various Yiddish literary journals which appeared in Montreal from time to time. One example is a long article entitled *"Briv fun New York* [Letter from New York],"[76] which was published in two consecutive issues of the journal *Kanade* at the end of 1925, about the New York modernist literary movement. In this dense text the poet revealed his personal thoughts on the appearance of *Di Yunge* on the Yiddish literary scene, describing it as "a light in the surrounding coarseness and greyness."[77] There followed some astute remarks about the influence of the Introspectivists on contemporary cultural circles. As was often the case in his articles about North American

Yiddish literature, Segal divulged nothing about his own experiences in the great city at the mouth of the Hudson. Throughout his life he remained consistently reticent about disclosing in prose the least bit of biographical information, including events that had shaped his career, except for his early childhood in Korets. The rule that Segal applied to himself, he applied to all those with whom he came into contact during this period and subsequently. Just as a narrative that is elliptical and distanced from reality can both illuminate and obscure, so too the poet's work elucidates only indirectly certain aspects of his life. That was the case with the circumstances surrounding his departure from Montreal, which Segal revealed in a unique way in the last poem of his 1923 collection (see Appendix 17).

O Montreal!

Short winter days, snow on the ground below
And a cold-warm sun above–
Like doves are they, these short winter days
Standing in the clear air wings spread.
And beautiful are they, as beautiful as kindness,
as playfulness for little children.

And on those high and lovely winter days
On the white expanse of snow
Stands a city, a lighted city.
And the city is playful against the bitter-red cold.
Her walls of watercolour green
Can barely stand . . . barely withstand
the enchantment of the short white lovely days.

That city's name is Montreal. O, Montreal!
From your short white winter days I do not wish to go away
to New York.
Yet to New York I must go
for my livelihood, and for her greatness,
and because it seems to me that in New York
some days are even shorter than in Montreal.
O, Montreal![78]

Lider (1926)

Segal published a second poetry collection while in New York entitled simply *Lider* [Poems], the fourth volume to be published in his brief career, and, at 204 pages, his longest. It appeared in 1926 at a time when the poet's life was unstable and his pain intense. It was printed on paper of obviously inferior quality, probably in Montreal, judging by the typeface, and hastily assembled, considering the misprints in the table of contents. The poems in *Lider* are all very short—rarely more than one page. They revisit the themes and language favoured by Segal in his previous books, specifically the author's personal and family life, simply expressed, without hyperbole or allegorical allusions. They convey the impression of confinement, of incapacitation, of the poet fighting for his emotional and economic survival in the midst of seemingly insurmountable obstacles. By all indications, these poems were penned prior to the sudden death of his little daughter Tsharna. None of them allude to it, nor do they suggest that it was imminent. However, *Lider* does contain a dedication, obviously written at the last minute, that does provide some inkling of the tremendous suffering that Segal and his wife experienced at the loss of their first child (see Appendix 18):

In your memory, my little Tsharna

Under the cold sky,
so alone, so alone, a white bird flew by.
As in a dream you vanished from my sight.
O, my extinguished light.
Trembling overtook me, bitterness consumed me.
The quiet beauty of your purity
turns blue through my tears.
O, my extinguished light.
I count and count my troubled years.
With frozen lips, with silent eyes.
I shall come, shall come
to lie down, ailing, next to you,
O my extinguished light.[79]

In fact, the dedication opened up a deep crater in *Lider* which the poet, in his subsequent writing, was never able to fill. The tragic death of his child accentuated the poet's rootlessness, and intensified his feelings of being adrift between two North American cities. Having recently left Montreal and his Canadian milieu, Segal included several poems in this volume that described his first adopted city. This is particularly true of the poem entitled "Windsor Park," in which the poet returns from New York in a state of deep despondency and wanders around the park near the train station: "Failed and forlorn on my return from New York/ I lean against the monument in winter's dead cold light in the park."[80] Also in *Lider* is the magnificent poem entitled "*Vinter* [winter]," that captures Mount Royal in transition between autumn and winter. Among the bare trees on its abandoned summit, "the imposing form of a cross shimmers in the golden rays of twilight . . . "[81] Further on in the book is a poem entitled "Sainte-Sophie,"[82] in which the poet ambles through fields and forests, silently discovering the vastness of a Quebec countryside buried beneath the weight of nature and the stars. Essentially, however, *Lider* presents a kind of everyday life filled with dreariness and *demi-mots*, silences and sadness. In this uncertain world beings are absorbed by innumerable tasks, dominated by a feeling of solitude, thrust into an urban environment disrupted every now and then by a remnant of a rural landscape, an inlet, or a riverbank. In this mournful existence there occasionally appears a memory of the *shtetl* with its narrow streets that lead to the synagogue, and the father who died when Segal was only a small child. Even while he was living in the largest city in America, the poet continued to inhabit a space regulated by the languid rhythm of Korets and the study of sacred texts in the comforting and familiar confines of the *heder*. If Montreal at first had seemed strange and impenetrable, New York, with its interminable neighbourhoods, its swarming masses of people, and the frenetic pace of its factories, crammed with labourers and loud machinery, was even more so. Overwhelmed by the painful circumstances of his second exile, in *Lider* Segal conveys his confusion and helplessness through his profoundly sad poetry, where his wife and child appear in the background, prisoners, like him, of the yoke imposed by the city on its most vulnerable inhabitants (see Appendix 19).

In My New Home (excerpt)

You remained all alone.
In the evening I came home.
You sat at the table and waited

Submerged between the walls.
You looked at me
And said nothing.

It's been two weeks now since we moved.
Directly in front of our wide window
is a small slice of ocean.
By day it's silver bright
and flows away to ten countries.
At night it's blue
and stays home by the shore.

I take your hand,
Sit down beside you, and stay silent.

Which road should I take to make peace with God?
Along which path shall I lead your cried-out heart
To see once more
in the distant blue of the river's shore
that little head with silky hair?
That light blue voice.[83]

Lider represents a major departure in Segal's work. The book is the last of his youthful period. It bears the after-effects of the passing folly that led the author, full of hope and promise, to move to New York to participate in the literary adventure of the group *Di Yunge*. For that reason it is weighted down by a painful sense of incompletion and an agonizing admission of failure, the failure of Segal's plan to become an accomplished poet in the larger and more prestigious American Yiddish literary arena. Exhausted by factory work and overwhelmed by the conditions of extreme poverty plaguing some of the dominant figures of New York Yiddish literature, Segal produced what is probably a less successful and less lyrical book, indicative of the doubts that were dogging him about his own literary career. The loss of his daughter was the last straw. After Tsharna's death, the poet succumbed to despair, and began calculating the cost of his sojourn in America. He went through a period of grief and terrible suffering that gradually caused him to withdraw from the New York milieu and exacerbated his emotional instability. The death of his daughter eventually unleashed a period of intense questioning and a reversal in his attitude toward Judaism. Like all his previous books, *Lider* does not provide any indication of the poet's strong attachment to his Jewish origins, nor any desire to reclaim the biblical imagery in which he had been immersed body and soul during his Eastern European childhood. For some time, it had been enough for Segal to use the Hebrew alphabet to feel attached to contemporary Jewish culture. *Lider* thus ended what could be called the secular period in Segal's literary journey. After *Lider* and the painful shocks that accompanied its publication, the poet began to explore a direction more in tune with his traditional religious upbringing. In this sense, at least, he broke with the basic premises of *Di Yunge* and the *Inzikhistn*, who insisted on rejecting cultural norms. For them, the individualistic and intro-spective approach was the prerequisite for all artistic creativity. After 1929, without ceasing to be a modernist, according to the generally accepted definition, Segal set out to revisit his past and reacquaint himself with the *nigun* of his early childhood. That was the decisive turning point which Caiserman noted years later in his biography of the poet, written in Montreal.

Throughout the years that Segal spent in the United States, he remained in close enough contact with the *Keneder Adler* to submit his work, including two poems that were published in a special edition celebrating the twentieth anniversary of the newspaper in 1927[84] — "*Tsu Montreal* [To Montreal] and "*Foygldiker friling oyf der velt* [A fine spring in the world], the latter about New York. This would seem to be the moment that Segal started to plan his return to Montreal. His second daughter, Sylvia, born in Montreal in June 1926, did not come to live in New York. Instead, she was left in the care of her mother's family, who lived in Mile End, a sign of a persisting malaise. As early as November 1926, Segal had begun receiving his mail at 1355 Cadieux Street[85] in the Plateau Mont-Royal. Two years later, in the fall of 1928, the poet and his family apparently moved in with his mother-in-law on Mozart Street West, in the north of Mile End. In March of 1929, the Segals welcomed a third daughter, Annette, necessitating a move to a larger apartment in the heart of Montreal's Jewish neighbourhood. In the spring of 1931, the Segal family moved to 4540 Clark Avenue,[86] which would remain the poet's address until his death in March 1954.

In the meantime, in the late 1920s, Segal obtained a part-time teaching position at the Jewish People's School, a secular school run by the Labour Zionists. This job in the parochial Yiddish school sys-tem assured him, in the short term, of some income in Montreal. His return to Canada and the beginning of his teaching career must have

J. I. Segal and his wife Elke, with their two daughters Annette (left) and Sylvia (right). Studio Geo. Charlab, Montreal, circa 1935. (Courtesy of Sylvia and Annette Segal.)

occurred around the same time. In the absence of reliable sources, it is difficult to know much more than that. Segal had suffered such great emotional trauma at the end of 1925, and was doing so poorly economically that he could not envisage raising his young children in New York. Hence, he came back to Canada on the eve of an economic crisis that would have made his life extremely difficult, if not impossible, on the other side of the border. His American adventure over, Segal reintegrated himself into the Montreal literary milieu, which was now more extensive and more efficiently organized. Already, the city seemed to offer better opportunities for the poet to use his talents and distribute his work. In addition, he now enjoyed the prestige of having a personal relationship with some of the greatest American modernists, which worked to his benefit in the more provincial Montreal atmosphere. On the eve of Segal's return, the literary critic Zalman Rejzen, confirming the reputation earned by the poet throughout the Yiddish-speaking world, offered the following assessment of his work:

> Segal is one of the most gifted representatives of the new Yiddish poetry. Although too abstract and cold in his lyricism, too preoccupied with expressing his moods, he has, nonetheless, an

authentic and powerful vitality, as well as a deep understanding
of the innermost world of the human soul, its darkest mysteries,
its loneliness and concomitant sadness, and its stationary calm.
And all of this is conveyed in simple, intentionally prosaic and
unadorned, yet refined and disciplined, language, which is rich
in symbolism, imagery, and pithy direct words.[87]

Caiserman, the First Yiddish Literary Critic

During the years that his friend Segal lived in New York, Caiserman's
life had also taken some difficult turns. He won a victory when the
Canadian Jewish Congress was officially founded in Montreal in
March of 1919, and he was elected its secretary general on a Board of
Directors that was increased to thirty-six members. Once the founding ceremonies and celebrations were over, Caiserman chaired a committee whose task it was to ensure the permanence of the Congress.[88]
In his book published in 1956, Belkin stated that the man "devoted
all his energies to his responsibilities without remuneration."[89] In the
aftermath of World War I, the desire of Canadian Jews to rise above
the divisions within the Jewish community manifested itself at a time
of heightened international tension. Several significant challenges
loomed on the horizon, including the Versailles peace conference
that was convened that same year, 1919. At this summit meeting of
the Allies, the question of the rights of the Jewish people and other
European minority groups was on the agenda. At this same time
Canadian Jews were also preoccupied with the unresolved issue of
Jewish Palestine, highlighted by the Balfour Declaration of November,
1917and the fall of the Ottoman Empire. In addition, a large migratory
wave was expected to touch land very soon in Canada. These harbingers of momentous change convinced uptowners and downtown-
ers to sit down together at the same community table. Furthermore,
the suffering inflicted by World War I (1914–1918) upon the Jews
of the Russian Empire, especially the well-orchestrated pogroms in
the Ukraine in the wake of the Russian Civil War, rallied Canadian
Jews for the purpose of effectively rendering aid to their Eastern
European co-religionists. In no time at all this exceptional opportunity evaporated, despite the successful aid missions of Simon Belkin
on Soviet territory, and the repatriation in 1921, under the leadership
of Harry Hershman, of almost 150 orphans from the Ukraine, victims
of anti-Semitic violence. Once these events were over, the collapse of

the Congress helped to convince Caiserman to set sail for Palestine, possibly for good. In 1920 Caiserman confided in a speech he gave to a group of workers:

> A year ago, the Canadian Jewish Congress thrilled Canadian Jewry—one year after, the standing committees all over the country have actually achieved everything that was expected of them. Logically speaking, the enthusiasm should have multiplied accordingly; actually it subsides into whispering forgetfulness and indifference. For a worker who dedicates his life to this great movement, which we call "Canadian Jewish Congress," this luke-warmness is at times depressing and painful.[90]

For its secretary general, the Canadian Jewish Congress was the culmination of many years of community activism and unwavering efforts. He had attempted to unify the Jewish population dispersed over a vast geographic expanse and fractured by multiple ideologies. In 1919, a large proportion of Canadian Jewry was composed of Eastern European immigrants who had only been in the country for a few years, trying by all possible means to stake out a respectable place in their adopted country. The existence of a central organization dedicated to the welfare of all Canadian Jews, in particular on the economic and political fronts, could only make it easier to have their needs and aspirations taken into account. What is more, these Yiddish speakers lived in large urban centers next to more prosperous and socially integrated Jews, whose mother tongue was English, with little awareness of the numerous difficulties besetting their more recently arrived co-religionists. In 1919, much work remained to be done just to mobilize and coordinate the Canadian Jewish community [, not to mention the ongoing struggles on behalf of Zionism, social justice, and human rights. In a Yiddish language report, probably written some time during the 1940s, Caiserman expressed his excitement over the creation of the Congress by declaring, "It was a lucky day, a blessed day, the day when Canadian Jewry founded its Congress."[91]

For all of the above reasons, Caiserman was dismayed by Montreal Jewry's indifference to the Congress. He seems to have made the decision to go to Palestine without much hesitation, even though it would mean grappling with difficult economic conditions and ethnic conflict. However, in letters to Hirsch Wolofsky regarding various joint commercial projects, Caiserman, in Eretz Israel, still

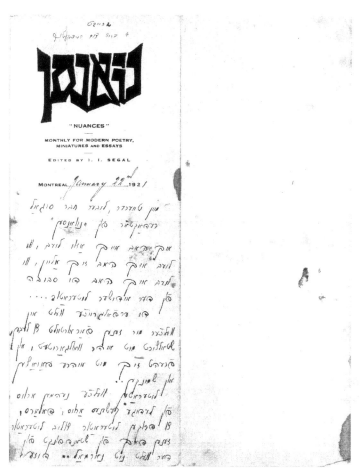

Letter from H. M. Caiserman to J. I. Segal, Montreal, January 22, 1921.
(Jewish Public Library.)

found time to worry about the fate of the Congress. His preoccupation with the unity of Canadian Jewry is evident in a letter he sent
in January of 1922: "I have been thrilled by the news that you are
calling a session of the Congress, of my dear beloved Congress and
I assure you if I would be rich enough, I would rush back just for
one week, to do my part on that Congress and then rush back to the
Holy land."[92] His rejoicing would be of short duration, for Wolofsky
replied a few weeks later to inform him that in Montreal the time for
sustaining a united organization had passed, and that nothing further could be expected. According to Wolofsky, Canadian Jews were

concerned only with those matters that affected them personally, and were no longer interested in the long-term challenges for which Caiserman had fought in 1919. "The Congress meeting was a failure, as very few attended, and only the executive was called but the resolution adopted was in connection with immigration, for which we have good prospects now."[93] Before leaving Canada in the summer of 1921, Caiserman had also been privileged to witness the flowering of Yiddish literature in Montreal. He had followed with keen interest the blossoming careers of several talented writers, the most remarkable of whom was his friend J. I. Segal. He was also so excited by the appearance in Montreal of a first-rate literary periodical, *Nyuansn*, that in January 1921, he sent Segal this spontaneous testimonial on paper with the letterhead of *Nyuansn*:

> My dear and precious friend Segal, editor of *Nyuansn*,
> I love you as much as I love myself, as much as I love the Yiddish literary milieu . . . The business-oriented world in which we were condemned to live, brags about its success, and rejoices over its clowns and buffoons . . . In the eyes of the world, writers who take dollars out of their empty pockets to print literature for literature's sake are not normal . . . I love this abnormality with all my heart.
> Your true friend and admirer,
> H. M. Caiserman.[94]

But Caiserman had not left Montreal without leaving his mark on its cultural scene, most notably at the beginning of 1921, by publishing a two-part essay entitled "Kanade [*Canada*]"[95] in the literary journal *Nyuansn*. The fact is that Caiserman had done his utmost to provide every possible means of support to J. I. Segal as well as the small group of other writers who followed in his footsteps. In the early 1920s Caiserman regularly picked up his pen to urge the creation of a body of Canadian Yiddish literature, and to pave the way for international recognition. While the editors of *Nyuansn* disseminated the work of the Yiddish writers all over the world, Caiserman pondered its significance and how to interpret it. His was a landmark essay because for the first time it provided criteria for evaluating this recent body of literature, placing it within the context of Canadian literature, and more broadly within an Eastern European Jewish context. Yiddish writers in Canada, the majority of whom were recent immigrants and fledgling authors, could not exist on the sidelines of their adopted homeland's cultural life indefinitely. Nor could they rely on the example of their colleagues living in Poland, the Ukraine, or Lithuania for whom Yiddish was a national language. In this sense, Caiserman was the first in Canada to write literary criticism in Yiddish, and try to account for the profusion of writing by Yiddish-speaking Jews in Canada. In the aftermath of World War I, there was so much to be done in this emerging field! No one had yet observed, let alone assessed, the development of a literature in Montreal in a third language that was being built on a very different foundation than that of French or English literature, and whose future at this point in history still seemed uncertain. And who better than Caiserman to undertake such a task? Was he not driven by a boundless enthusiasm for Yiddish culture? Had he not been present when Segal had first revealed the full extent of his talent? Some thirty years later, the poet had not hesitated to acknowledge the debt he owed to his friend Caiserman, recognizing him as one of the voices which had supported Canadian Yiddish literature from its very beginnings:

> Caiserman was one of the first to lay the groundwork for a modern Yiddish cultural life in Montreal. In those early years that type of work was much more difficult than today. Now there is a network within which all those who are sincerely and actively involved in intellectual and cultural activities can find a place.[96]

The Canadian Landscape

The first point made by Caiserman in his review of 1921 was that Canada's geographic terrain and natural beauty should become a source of inspiration for Yiddish-language writers, just as they had been, over several decades, for authors writing in English and French. That would be the price, wrote Caiserman, that Yiddish literature would have to pay for admission into the world of Canadian arts and letters, as well as the opportunity to prove its worth. For Eastern European immigrants arriving in Montreal, Toronto and Winnipeg at the beginning of the twentieth century and trying to adjust to life on a new continent, Canada's gigantic size was one of its most striking aspects. Nothing in Eastern Europe was comparable to the extremes of Canada's often inhospitable climate, expansive views, and unexplored vastness. In Canada every trace of human activity seemed to disappear into the landscape and be swallowed up by its apparently immutable geological features. How could Yiddish writers remain indifferent to these truly overwhelming and inescapable elements that had shaped the perceptions of the country's earlier inhabitants for so long? Immigrants from small hamlets nestled in verdant landscapes in the heart of age-old countries now had to relocate themselves in a country where agricultural development was in its infancy, where cities were literally springing up before their very eyes, and all of society seemed to be in constant flux. Very well, then, but where to start? Yiddish writers found themselves in the paradoxical position of not yet having toured the country where they had recently settled. The majority, forced to earn their daily bread in factories that occupied not more than a few city blocks in three large Canadian cities, were completely unfamiliar with the natural frontiers of their new country. When would they ever have the luxury of observing firsthand Canada's natural splendours and regional diversity?

Of course, Caiserman had been able to form this vision of Canada precisely because he had been among the first Yiddish-speaking Jews

Sewing room in the Biltmore Shirt Company, Montreal, 1930.
(Rubinstein Bros. Private Collection).

to traverse its length and breadth. Ever since the founding of the Canadian Jewish Congress in 1919, and even prior to that, Caiserman had criss-crossed the country for the purpose of rallying support, raising funds, and spreading the word in those locations where Jews were to be found in sufficient numbers. A few months after returning from Palestine at the end of 1923, Caiserman set out again to raise money on behalf of the Canadian Zionist movement. In May of 1925 he became the official representative of the Canadian Zionist Organization, reporting directly to its president, Ottawa businessman A. J. Frieman. This job required him to campaign in every region of the country. In November of 1925 he wrote from Regina, "I have just returned from a fourteen-week stay in the West where I have succeeded to organize [sic] National Funds Committees, practically in every city [. . .] and to collect and stimulate the collection of thousands of dollars."[97] The following year Caiserman confided to a friend in Jerusalem, "I have just returned from a spectacular five months [sic] trip from Montreal to Vancouver, Los Angeles and back, or about 16,000 miles, in the interests of the Zionist Organization."[98]

The fact is that few Jews of his generation would ever have the opportunity to be as aware of the regional and cultural diversity of Canada as Caiserman. Segal, at this time, had most probably never been away from what is now called the Plateau Mont-Royal, or from the Mile End district, for more than a few hours at a time before moving to New York in 1923 to join his modernist poet friends where all he did was exchange his tailor's needle for the heavy machines required for the manufacture of footwear. Either way, the poet spent long hours chained to the infernal schedule of a shoe factory. However, in New York as in Montreal, Segal continued to live his life to the rhythm of his birthplace, and dreamt of the Eastern European landscapes of his early childhood. Surrounded by high walls of brick and stone, thrust into an intense and exhausting industrial universe, the poet nonetheless continued to wander at will through his early memories and emotions, as the following poem demonstrates so well (see Appendix 20):

New York – Korets (excerpt)

There's a little town by the name of Korets
And a big city they call New York.
In each I was the quietest inhabitant
with my strange conduct and concern.

Inside me Korets is a twilight
And around me New York is wide and high.
A little tree with golden leaves,
a little Korets tree – my entire summer.

And this little tree stands
behind the gate by the old Christian cemetery –
In the silken snow a sapling,
a little Korets tree – my entire winter.

Into my flesh and bones like a cure
Trickles the peace of a Korets evening.
New York turns a thousand wheels of stone
and to me does not come near.[99]

Caiserman was not simply an admirer of the vast Canadian landscape. He also understood that the ideological preoccupations of the Yiddish writers in Eastern Europe could not be maintained in Montreal where, by every indication, Yiddish speakers would never be subject to exclusionary legislation, nor marginalized to a greater extent than any other immigrants. In a liberal democracy on a continent where the imprint of Western Europe was still fresh, the entire country seemed accessible to the Jewish newcomers. It was therefore of the utmost importance for Yiddish poets to make its acquaintance and sing its praises. Moreover, each day new masses of immigrants of various origins were entering Canada and forging the future of this new country through their toil and cultural contributions. Between the established population groups, the French Catholic and the British, no consensus seemed to have been reached on what form the country was to take, nor how it was to be governed. As opposed to Imperial Russia, where Jews were forced to live in one particular area, in Canada they were free to set down roots wherever they wished. Although limited by the fact of their recent arrival and consequent unfamiliarity with Canada's customs and traditions, they would soon gain access to the liberal professions and the means to improve their economic situation. Above all, Caiserman believed that the Jews had everything to gain by allowing themselves to be swept up by the optimistic spirit that pervaded Canadian economic and political life. Far from the Old World and its oppressive political constraints, Yiddish-speaking Jews discovered a freedom of action and movement heretofore inconceivable and deserving of their complete participation. In fact, it was with an impassioned appeal that Caiserman began his 1921 essay in *Nyuansn*. In Canada for barely ten years, this activist delivered an extremely positive message as well as an invitation to Yiddish writers to participate wholeheartedly in the cultural life of their new country in their own language:

> Canada, young Canada, with its remarkable industrial economic activity, its social and political unrest, its fantastically poetic geography, its variety of natural wonders and climates, this cosmopolitan country with acute national problems, this vast, wild yet mild Canada, which holds so much promise for the creation of a rich literature.[100]

This call to "Canadianize" Yiddish literature, to give it the flavour of the geography and history of the country to which immigrant writers now belonged, would ultimately be heard by those involved, but only after a long cultural and artistic journey. First for Segal, and later on for writers who arrived during the 1920s, nostalgia for their home town and regret for the loss of a birthplace remained central to their art. For a long time Montreal Yiddish writers, especially those who came from the newly independent Poland, maintained strong and lasting ties with family members who remained across the ocean, institutions and cultural movements with which they had been affiliated in their youth, and the way of life they had left behind. In the end, however, these ties began to weaken and unravel, especially when the Montreal authors, one by one, discovered the potent impact of New York Yiddish writing, practically within earshot of Montreal and infused with a modernism that had no obvious European connections. The feelings of closeness that time and distance could not erode were finally annihilated by the war years, especially by the terrible consequences of the Holocaust. In the meantime, Segal had found the strength and courage to inject a new theme into Canadian Yiddish literature, one adopted by his New York colleagues in the same situation, namely, poetry devoted to the North American city, in his case, Montreal. This innovation was all the more radical given that neither French nor English Canadian authors, for reasons often diametrically opposed, had never shown any interest in the life of Canada's cities. Crowded into immigrant neighbourhoods, relegated to jobs involving manual labour, or teaching in Jewish schools, what the majority of Yiddish writers knew about Canada were the streets, parks and monuments of its major cities, and the harbour or the train station where they had disembarked at the end of a long journey. For them, Canadian life meant a densely populated cityscape. Nonetheless, in the hodgepodge of buildings and intersecting streets, Montreal Yiddish writers found subjects for their poetry and the opportunity for a certain spiritual elevation. This manifested itself primarily in the work of Segal, who, at the time, was the most "Montreal" of Yiddish poets, and the most attuned to his own place within the city. In "Late Autumn in Montreal," for example, Segal gives the impression of travelling through the city far beyond the places densely populated by Jewish immigrants groups. What makes this poem so powerful are his strongly expressed Yiddish observations of the new Catholic and Francophone influences he encounters on his way, which he welcomes with without hesitation or reservation. It conveys the impression of complete surrender and quiet contentment, which may surprise the reader, and which Segal transposes into language laden with Hebrew signifiers.

Late Autumn Montreal

(Translated by Miriam Waddington)

The worm goes back to the earth
the wind glitters and sharpens his sword;
where did all the colored leaves fly
to, anyway? The branches are all locked
in a vise of sleep; the skies aspire
to climb higher, their clear-blue
washes over the roof tops and stillness
assures us that all is well.
Our churchy city becomes even more pious
on Sundays, the golden crosses shine and gleam
while the big bells ring with loud
hallelujahs and the little bells answer
their low amens; the tidy peaceful streets
lie dreaming in broad daylight murmuring
endearments to me who am such a Yiddish Jew
that even in my footsteps they must hear
how the music of my Yiddish song sounds
through the rhythm of my Hebrew prayer.[101]

Local subject matter had already appeared in some of the stories written during the first two decades of the twentieth century by Hirsch Hershman,[102] depicting French Canadian rural communities and their inhabitants,[103] including one entitled "Armand Cartier,"[104] in July of 1925 in the literary journal *Kanade*. Belatedly perhaps, but with unusual intensity and in their own unique way, Yiddish poets after World War II took up the challenge of depicting the specific realities of life in Montreal (*montréalité*) and Quebec (*québécitude*). It was at that time that Segal became the very first writer to turn his attention to his first adopted city, creating emotional descriptions of its physical appearance, its neighbourhoods, and the general atmosphere. Shut away for so long in a sorrowful inner world, observing the outer world only from afar, the poet finally crossed the threshold of his dwelling to create an intimate portrait of those parts of the city with which he now shared a mysterious, indefinable kinship.

As for Sholem Shtern, he subsequently began recounting his 1927 stay in the Mount Sinai Sanatorium in Saint Agathe, including the relationships he formed with the Francophone population in that part of the Laurentians. This Quebec theme would provide the subject matter for two novels in verse form, *In Kanade*[105] [In Canada], published in two volumes, in 1960 and 1963 respectively; and *Dos vayse hoyz*[106] (The White House) in 1967. N. I. Gotlib, who came to Montreal in 1930 from Lithuania, dedicated a long epic poem to his land of refuge which was printed posthumously in 1968 with the title *Montreal*.[107] Some writers who immigrated to Montreal after the Holocaust, such as Chava Rosenfarb, wrote short stories, some of which were published in the Yiddish-language Israeli literary journal *Di Goldene Keyt*,[108] about survivors of Nazi concentration camps living in Montreal. After 1945, Jewish poets writing in English, who were either born in Canada or had arrived here at a very young age, exhibited the same predilection for Montreal themes as their Yiddish-language predecessors. This was particularly true of A. M. Klein whose 1948 book *The Rocking Chair and Other Poems*, a volume dedicated to Montreal and French Canadian traditions, included this engaging poem about Mount Royal:

The Mountain (excerpt)

Who knows it only by the famous cross which bleeds
into the fifty miles of night its light
knows a night-scene;

and who upon a postcard knows its shape —
the buffalo straggled of the Laurentian herd, —
holds in his hand a postcard.

In layers of mountains the history of mankind,
and in Mount Royal
which daily in a streetcar I surround
my youth, my childhood — [109]
the pissabed dandelion, the coolie acorn,
green prickly husk of chestnut beneath mat of grass—
O all the amber afternoons
are still to be found.

Following the Lead of the French-Canadian Poets

But that was only part of the agenda set by Caiserman in his 1921 article. Not only was it appropriate for Yiddish writers to tailor their writing to their new homeland, but it was also important for all Jewish writers to become well acquainted with the accomplishments of their Francophone and Anglophone forerunners in order to situate themselves among the great authors of Canadian literature. Caiserman shared this conviction, because he himself had read most of the works of Canada's great poets in the original, and had quite a clear sense of their artistic contributions. In fact, his 1921 article was undoubtedly the first time that someone had written about the evolution of French-Canadian literature in a non-official language, in this case Yiddish. By crossing this divide as early as the 1910s and becoming the first Yiddish speaker to delve into the literature of French Canada, Caiserman opened up a whole new area in the cultural discourse of his community. Exploring this imaginary space, he had effectively discovered "an entire gallery of French Canadian poets whose poetry exudes the intimate, wild, and unpredictable Canadian atmosphere, the personal aspirations of the typical Canadian, and the dreams, cloaked in mist, of this national, religious, and mystical community."[110] For that reason, his analysis and interpretation have exceptional value, and his attempts at intercultural understanding are truly monumental for that era. Through his efforts, Caiserman made Yiddish-speaking Jews aware of the importance of French-Canadian literature in Canada. Moreover, he would pursue this objective in the years to come with astonishing energy, especially considering his other professional responsibilities. Indeed, it is quite moving for a contemporary researcher reading this literary critique in the 1921 issue of *Nyuansn* to find the names of French-Canadian writers transliterated into the Hebrew alphabet and floating in a sea of Yiddish signifiers:

> This definitely explains why the French Canadians can point to so many poets from a variety of literary movements who wrote poems about the aspirations of their people. Thus, for example, in the period from 1860 to 1879 they already had three important poets who wrote mainly about the national ambitions of their people, namely, F[rançois-Xavier] Garneau, Joseph Lenoir, and the closest of all to the common folk, Octave Crémazie, followed a short time later by lyric poets like [Pamphile] Le May and Adolphe Poisson, as well as Romantic mystics like [Apollinaire] Gingras and Émile Nelligan.[111]

Caiserman got to know French-Canadian literature because he was convinced that the French-Canadian poets could point the way for their Yiddish-speaking counterparts in Canada. In resisting the British conquest by defying attempts to establish English cultural hegemony in the colony, and by remaining receptive to the voices of the working masses, these writers had become the symbols of their nation. Naturally the situation in nineteenth century French Canada differed in many respects from that of the Yiddish-speaking Jews who arrived decades later. This is best exemplified by the fact that the Francophone writers usually wrote about rural life, whereas Jews in Canada were mostly city dwellers and frequently factory workers. However, in Caiserman's mind, the two peoples were motivated by a common desire for liberation, and sought to propagate a national language under threat. What better way to support the promotion of French or Yiddish than to create a literature that would become the favoured vehicle for ensuring a national future? Less influential in the economic and political spheres than the English, the French Canadians had nevertheless generated many literary movements in the country. They had ventured off the beaten track by fostering their distinct cultural identity. "It is sufficient to note the fact that here in Canada the general rule also applies that wherever a minority is actively struggling for self-preservation, it must create new forms of literature."[112] The development of a literary tradition in French Canada led Caiserman to note that Francophones, more so than Anglophones, had projected their national aspirations into a higher sphere, that of art, literature, and ideas. In this way they would assure the continuity of their culture in the North American context, and create the ties that in times of crises would unite the common people with the political and religious elites. How could it be otherwise, Caiserman wondered, when "the French Canadians, the true proprietors of this gigantic Canada, had fought and suffered here for centuries, and left the stamp of their ethnic individuality on all of Canadian life?"[113]

In the archives of the Canadian Jewish Congress there is a 140-page[114] handwritten Yiddish manuscript by Caiserman on the theme of Canadian poetry in French and English as well as Yiddish, as if all these cultural currents had converged on common ground. It is difficult to date this document, which was never published, because it seems to have been written in instalments over a long period of time, as evidenced by the various sizes and colours of the paper used.[115] The first part of the manuscript, which is thirty pages long, is almost identical, with slight variations, to the essay published in *Nyuansn* in January and February of 1921, with the addition of a series of more detailed studies of the English Canadian writers E. Pauline Johnson, Archibald Lampman, Bliss Carmen, Duncan Campbell Scott, and Marjorie Pickthall, followed by reflections on the writers Pamphile Le May, Louis Fréchette, Alphonse Beauregard, and Paul Morin, with explicit reference to the École littéraire de Montréal (Montreal Literary School).[116] Presumably Caiserman had completed the groundwork for his essay before his hasty departure for Palestine in the summer of 1921, and it had remained on hold for several years.[117] Had this manuscript been published in its entirety in a more polished form, it would certainly have altered how the Yiddish cultural milieu perceived French Canadian literature. Read today, it is an eloquent testimony to Caiserman's sensitivity to his new cultural environment, and his extraordinary ability to familiarize himself with new languages and cultures. Whether authors wrote in English or French, Caiserman always quoted them in their mother tongue. When he cited verses by Francophone poets, he never made mistakes in spelling, not even with accents and diacritical marks. So enchanted was he with Pamphile Le May that he went so far as to translate some of his verses into Yiddish, unquestionably the first attempt ever made to provide an opportunity for Yiddish-speaking Montrealers to read French-Canadian literature (see Appendix 21). This infatuation with Le May is better understood when Caiserman explains that for him

Le May was the best example of a poet who found his inspiration in the Canadian landscape and its FrenchCanadian inhabitants. Caiserman believed that Le May had opened the door, inadvertently, of course, to Jewish writers freshly arrived in Canada in search of a deeper connection to their new land:

> Pamphile Le May is an important French Canadian poet, a lyric folk poet through and through, in love with Canada's natural beauty and its people. In his most heartfelt national and religious aspirations, he sings most of all about Canada's earth, sky, mountains, forests, and rivers, often crossing over into national religious interpretations.[118]

By all indications Caiserman maintained his interest in French-Canadian literature at least until the mid-1930s, because in 1936 journalist Bernard Figler declared in an article about him: "This Yiddishist is now working on a study of French-Canadian poetry!"[119] The second part of the manuscript,[120] which addresses Yiddish-language poetry in Canada, was written subsequent to his 1921 article in *Nyuansn*, and after Caiserman had returned from his exploratory stay in Palestine. There, among other issues, he discusses Segal's book *Fun mayn shtub un fun mayn velt*, published in 1923, and the literary journals *Epokhe* and *Royerd*, dating from the same period. The author's intention in the second part of his manuscript was very different. After providing an overview of poetry in the two official languages, Caiserman wished to demonstrate that Canadian Yiddish literature, although without historical roots in that country, had nonetheless begun to bear fruit. This appraisal may appear premature in an era when Yiddish letters had only existed in Canada for a few years, but it was of prime importance to Caiserman. Indeed, this entire undertaking was based on the premise that Canadian literary activity in the Yiddish language had to be logically organized and structured and its authors subjected to careful and rigorous analysis. In a country with neither a Yiddish publishing company nor a large Yiddish readership, as in New York, Warsaw, Vilna, or Kiev, it was vital that a serious observer follow the often disorderly and unpredictable evolution of Canadian Yiddish literature even if it meant chastising poets for being too complacent. The authors themselves were incapable of assuming such a role, including the most talented amongst them, J. I. Segal, whose career had barely begun when, in 1923, he went into self-imposed exile in New York to have the benefit of a more active and established literary environment. Nonetheless, despite the distance, the two men remained in close contact. In a letter dated April 1924, Caiserman revealed to his friend the criteria that guided him in his work as a literary critic and historian. After having reproached Segal for the simplicity of some of his poems in *Nyuansn*, deeming their subject matter to be too prosaic and banal, Caiserman confided to Segal:

> ... literature must be an idealization of life, larger than life. Poetry in particular, with its unmediated beauty, must elevate peoples' spirits and their souls, and ennoble and influence all their aspirations. It makes no difference to me whether a poet sings about his personal life, nature, society, the past, or the future. His writing must be interesting intelligent, and beautiful to lift me out of my banal, humdrum, grimy, repetitive, day-to-day existence.[121]

An Emerging Literature

Nonetheless, Yiddish writing remained Jewish in terms of its historical legacy, its unique sensibility, and the cultural identity of its practitioners and readers. For that reason, a Yiddish writer also had a responsibility to his people, to the future of his literary language, and for introducing modernity to his community. He also had to join the great movement toward the decompartmentalization of cultures, and in addition, to contribute to the renewal of prevailing attitudes within the Jewish art world. Here is what Caiserman proposed to his friend Segal with regard to Jewish poets in particular:

> The modern Yiddish poet has a specific task: not—heaven forbid—to produce proclamations or to preach, but a much more interesting task, namely to universalize Yiddish literature through Jewish types and aspirations which will permit Jewish life to strive for excellence and embrace the finest cultural nuances of mankind.[122]

These were the three essential components of Caiserman's agenda: the aspiration toward idealfulfilment, faithfulness to the Jewish heritage, and openness to the great innovations of modern art worldwide. These three criteria would define his approach to literary criticism as it related to Yiddish literature in Canada.

What was most extraordinary of all about Caiserman's ideas about the direction to be taken by modern Yiddish poetry was the fact that they were coming from a man who had never actually mastered literary Yiddish,[123] whose writing in Yiddish was often clumsy, and who, given his often laborious writing style, could never hope to personally "pursue a career" in poetry. While Segal, thanks to the formal Jewish education he had received in Korets and the marvellous fluidity of his writing, found himself thrust into the heart of the Yiddish cultural scene, his friend Caiserman was at pains to navigate the subtleties of Hebrew grammar and spelling. Yet he was able to recognize exceptional writing. He also held the strong conviction that Canadian Yiddish poetry would be the salvation of Jewish identity in Canada, that it would provide an unanticipated perspective on the local cultural scene that could perhaps succeed in inspiring other Jewish creators. If Yiddish writers could reach the heights of artistic expression in their new homeland, surely, they would pave the way for their fellow Jews in other more prosaic fields of excellence where recognition was often slow in coming. Montreal Yiddish poets also had the opportunity to enhance the reputation of their community within the Eastern European Jewish diaspora and throughout the Yiddish world, in New York and in Buenos Aires, and, of course, in places like Poland, Russia, Lithuania, and the Ukraine, where major Jewish modernist movements had sprung into existence, notably under the Soviet regime.

Paradoxically, Caiserman's remarks to Segal in 1924 about Yiddish literature were written on paper with the following letterhead: "H. M. Caiserman, Accountancy, Collections, Commission, Import and Export, 2081c St. Urbain Street, Montreal." After his Palestinian adventure, Caiserman had great difficulty in reintegrating into the Montreal community, and he had to return to his business affairs and accounting. That same month he wrote to Segal:

> I returned from sunny Israel with a heavy heart, and began the most difficult period of my life in Canada. I was financially ruined, my courage depleted, and all those people who could and should have helped me, left me disappointed and alone . . . But in the last little while everything is improving. I've paid my creditors, I'm earning a living, and I've sent the whole world packing. Once again, I'm working for the community, and I helped the first Labour Party alderman on City Council (Joseph Schubert) to get elected.[124]

Furthermore, in the mid-1920s there was very little left to say about Canadian Yiddish poetry. In his unpublished manuscript Caiserman simply noted that it was born in 1915, the year that Hershl Hirsch had published in Toronto a collection entitled *Hundert tropn tint* [One hundred drops of ink] whose main virtue was its humour. He placed in the same category the works of Ezekiel Bronstein and Mordecai Miller, published in Winnipeg in 1919 with identical titles, *Tsvey veltn* [Two worlds], which, in his opinion, were simply rough drafts. According to Caiserman, the literary periodical *Kanade*, launched in Toronto in 1919 by Leibush Rosenberg, was the first attempt to bring together a group of poets who had made a name for themselves in Canadian Yiddish dailies. Among them were J. I. Segal, Simon Nepom, Shlomo Halperin, Pesakh Matenko, Leib Bercovitch, and Leibush Rosenberg himself. Of this entire group, deemed "primitive" by Caiserman, only Segal found favour.[125] The next decisive step, according to Caiserman, was the appearance in 1921 of *Nyuansn*, under the direction of J. I. Segal, the first authentic Canadian Yiddish literary journal, and he critiqued it at length. It was soon to be followed by *Epokhe* in 1922, and *Royerd* in 1922–1923. Caiserman also attached some importance to both A. S. Shkolnikov and Shin Shnayder, whom he called budding talents. However, Caiserman reserved the lion's share of his unpublished manuscript for Segal, whose first three poetry collections, those of 1918, 1921, and 1923, he critiqued in great detail. He singled out *Bazunder Lider*, a volume which distinguished its author from the other poets active during this period, for special tribute as follows: "The principle themes in this collection are sadness, doubt, disappointment, and, at times, resignation. He achieves a rare refinement, particularly when dealing with intimate and personal subject matter."[126] This praise did not prevent Caiserman from scolding Segal at times for his formal laxity and overly simplistic treatment of erotic subject matter.

Throughout the 1920s, this undated manuscript would serve as a point of departure for Caiserman for other, more in-depth, studies, including a review of the last issue of *Royerd* that came out in Montreal in 1929.[127] Meanwhile, other talented observers of the Yiddish literary scene were also beginning to examine the literary experiments taking place in Montreal. In 1927 Israel Rabinovitch published a lengthy article in the *Keneder Adler* in which he attempted to provide the first history of Jewish writing in Canada.[128] He even went so far as to acknowledge that Jewish literature in the English language dated back at least to the mid-nineteenth century. His main purpose, however, was to provide a systematic survey of the entire body of Yiddish literature in Canada, and he emphatically stated that literary creativity in the Yiddish language was off to a dynamic start.[129] He continued by noting that Canadian Yiddish literature was essentially a branch of world Yiddish literature that had been transplanted onto North American soil, rather than a body of literature inspired by and about life in Canada.[130] In sum, according to Rabinovitch, Yiddish writers in the 1920s had not yet established themselves sufficiently in their new home to be able to treat more local subject matter. They were still looking back to the continent where they were born and bred. All the same, considering that the first Yiddish literary circle worthy of that name, centered around Reuben Brainin and the *Keneder Adler*, had come into existence in Montreal only in 1912, its production within such a short time had been prodigious. The 1927 article mentioned no fewer than twenty-seven authors,[131] including many poets, as well as several literary journals and a few volumes of poetry, without counting the activities of Yiddish writers residing in Toronto and Winnipeg. This was the most detailed and well-documented analysis so far of Yiddish literature in Canada, and to this day provides a solid basis for its study. It is true that several of these writers stayed in Canada only a few years before leaving for greener pastures, but they were replaced by writers who arrived from Eastern Europe during the 1920s, or had been raised in Yiddish in Montreal. During this same period there emerged a group of writers interested in Jewish history that included authors such as Abraham Reinvein of Toronto and B.G. Sack, a journalist who wrote for the *Keneder Adler*. In his 1927 article Rabinovitch even noted the existence of a group of talented translators, such as Rabbi Yudel Rosenberg, who translated the Zohar[132] into modern Hebrew, and L. M. Benjamin, who translated the novel *Jean-Christophe* by Romain Rolland into Yiddish.[133]

By the end of the 1920s everything was in place for Canadian Yiddish literature to soar artistically and creatively, and to be recognized worldwide. After having produced so much work in so short a time, wrote Rabinovitch, the writers who had come from Eastern Europe were poised to reach new heights. With the Montreal Jewish community becoming more stable economically and the Yiddish poets, for the first time, having the leisure time to intensify their efforts, that moment seemed imminent. What is more, after a long period of wandering and wavering, Segal and Caiserman were again reunited in Montreal. During the following decade, the poet and literary critic, each in his own way, would play a major role on the Canadian literary scene. At least that was the prediction made by Caiserman with complete confidence in his 1929 review:

> Since J. I. Segal's return to Montreal, the city has become a Yiddish literary centre, referred to by people all over the Jewish world connected to Yiddish literature [. . .] J. I. Segal is now a recognized poet whose work is attentively read and widely discussed. And when he settles in a city, it does not take long before that city becomes an important place of literary creativity.[134]

Notes

1. See the obituary written by Mordecai Ginzburg in the *Keneder Adler*, March 18, 1954, entitled *"Plutsimdiker toyt fun Yud Yud Segal ruft aroys troyer in shto*t [Sudden death of J. I. Segal mourned in the city]."
2. From an interview with Annette Zakuta and Sylvia Lustgarten, the two daughters of J. I. Segal, Toronto, October 17, 2009.
3. *Tsharna* means "black" in Russian.
4. 40 Mozart Street West was at the corner of Clark Street.
5. The Segal family moved to Clark Street just north of Mount Royal Avenue in the early 1930s, and kept this apartment at least until Segal's death in 1954. The Segals lived in Apartment 2, on the ground floor, beside the laneway.
6. That Sarah Wittal-Caiserman had already made her fortune by the 1920s can be inferred from the following statement in an article that appeared in the *Gazette* on August 22, 1924, entitled "23 Transfers in Realty Market": "Of the twenty-three realty transfers reported yesterday, the largest was for $35,000 in which was recorded the sale by Avila Saint-Aubin to H. M. Caiserman et al of part of a lot no. 474, Ahuntsic Ward. . ." It can be assumed that Caiserman was acting on behalf of his wife.
7. Letter in English from H. M. Caiserman to Adolfe Kaiserman of New York, Montreal, March 18, 1947, Caiserman Archive, Canadian Jewish Congress Archives, Montreal.
8. This reference is to cultural activist Hershl Novak whose *Memoirs* are mentioned above.
9. J. I. Segal, "H. M. Caiserman (*tsu zayn 60-yorikn yubiley*) [H. M. Caiserman, on his 60th birthday," *Keneder Adler*, Montreal, March 24, 1944, s. 4, 3. Translated into English by David Rome in an unpublished manuscript, Rome Archive, Canadian Jewish Congress Archive, Montreal.
10. Letter from H.M. Caiserman, Montreal, February 17, 1937, Jewish Culture in Canada Archive, Jewish Public Library, Montreal.
11. Ibid.
12. *"Yud Yud Segal geern bay intimen tsuzamenkunft tsu zayn fuftstik yorikn yubiley* [J. I. Segal honoured at a private gathering on the occasion of his 50th birthday]," *Keneder Adler*, December 3, 1946.

13. J. I. Segal, *"H. M. Caiserman – der mentsh vos hot lib gehat* [*H. M. Caiserman* – the man who loved]," *Der Keneder Adler*, January 1, 1951, 5–6.

14. Segal wrote about his experience at the Peretz Shule in a piece entitled *"A yidish kind* [A Jewish child]" published in the *Peretz Shul bukh* [The Peretz School Book], 1938, 41–43.

15. For a history of the Yiddish-language schools see my introduction to the French translation of the memoirs of Hershl Novak, op. cit.

16. Gold meant by this that Segal was never really at ease among union militants or political activists. His temperament was more that of a yeshiva student studying the Talmud with a revered rabbinic scholar.

17. Dr. Shlomo Gold, *"Fun di ershte yorn* [From the early years]," *Peretz shul bukh*, Montreal 1938, 38.

18. Interview with Judge Allan B. Gold, April 19, 1989. Gold, who was a student at the Jewish People's School, took private Yiddish classes with Segal beginning in 1926.

19. On this subject, see the review of H. M. Caiserman: *"Royerd*, a literary review," *Keneder Adler*, August 19, 1929.

20. *"shtendiker mitarbeter."* See Leib Wasserman, "Segal, Yankev Yitskhok," in Sh. Niger and Jacob Shatzky, eds., *Leksikon fun der nayer yiddisher literatur* (*Biographical Dictionary of Modern Yiddish Literature*) (New York: Congress for Jewish Culture, 1965), 8:397–403.

21. Ibid.

22. The book mentions *"Farlag Royerd* (Royerd Publications)," Montreal, a publishing company named after a small Yiddish literary journal created by Segal and some other poets, is also mentioned.

23. J. I. Segal, *Di shtot is mayn dorf. . .* [The city is my village. . .], in *Bazunder lider* (Montreal, 1921), 131.

24. J. I. Segal, *Ikh* ["I"], Montreal, *Bazunder lider,* 1921, 18.

25. In Yiddish, *"lider leshem lider."*

26. Irving Howe, *World of Our Fathers. The Journey of East European Jews to America and the Life They Found and Made* (New York, Harcourt Brace Jovanovich, 1976), 429.

27. Letter from H. Leivick to J. I. Segal, Moscow, January 10, 1936, Segal Archive, Montreal Jewish Public Library Archives.

28. According to Melekh Ravitch, Chmelnitzki met Segal on a trip to Canada. See Melekh Ravitch, *Mayn Leksikon*, op. cit., 141.

29. Undated letter from Zishe Landau, New York, Segal Archive, Montreal Jewish Public Library Archives, 1 page.

30. Undated letter from Zishe Landau, New York, Segal Archive, Montreal Jewish Public Library Archives, 3 pages, page 1. *Di Tsayt* [Time] was a publication affiliated with the Poale Zion.

31. Sholem Shtern, *Nostalgie et tristesse. Mémoires littéraires du Montréal yiddish*, Montreal: Éditions du Noroît, 2006.; Sholem Stern, *Shrayber vos ikh hob gekent, memuarn un esayn* [Writers I Knew], op. cit., Montreal, 1982.

32. *Nyuansn* was not the first Canadian Yiddish literary journal. Leibush Rosenberg published a journal entitled *Kanade* [Canada] in Toronto for a short time in 1919.

33. Short fiction.

34. Shkolnikov had immigrated to Montreal in 1919 and married Esther Segal, sister of J. I. Segal.

35. Moved to New York in 1925.

36. Left for New York in 1927.

37. Immigrated to California in 1939.

38. This was on the corner of Marie-Anne Street.
39. Shnayder left Montreal in 1924 for New York. See Rebecca Margolis, *Jewish Roots, Canadian Soil: Yiddish Cultural Life in Montreal, 1905–1945*. Montreal, McGill-Queen's Press, 2011, 59, 68, 78, 105. There he is referred to as Shloyme Shneider. It is possible that his family name was spelled Schneider.
40. J. I. Segal, *Nyuansn* (Montreal, January 1921, no. 1), 55–60.
41. J. I. Segal, *Vegn Melekh Ravitch* [about Melekh Ravitch], *Epokhe* (Montreal, 1922), 3–7.
42. J. I. Segal, *Durkh di ershte fir*, *Nyuansn* (Montreal, no. 1, January 1921), 57.
43. Undated, unsigned document entitled *Literarishe oysgabes in Montreal* [Montreal literary publications], Caiserman Archive, Canadian Jewish Congres Archives.
44. Pen-name of Eliyahu Haim Sheps. According to the Lexicon of Chaim Leib Fox, Almi only lived in Montreal from 1918 to 1922.
45. Letter from Melekh Chmelnitzki to J. I. Segal, Vienna, March 30, 1922, Segal Archive, Montreal Public Library Archives.
46. M. J. Ogin, *"Idishe dikhter in Kanade* [Yiddish poets in Canada]," *Di Frayhayt*, New York, 29 July 1922, 5–6.
47. Entry for J. I. Segal in Zalman Rejzen, *Leksikon fun der idisher literatur, prese un filologye*, Vilna, Kletskin farlag, Vilna, 1927, vol. 2, 625–629.
48. The journal *Shriftn* championed the tenets of *Di Yunge*.
49. J. I. Segal, "Mount Royal," *Nyuansn* (Montreal, no. 2, February 1921), 65.
50. From May of 1923, Segal received his mail at 1017 Trinity Avenue, Bronx, New York. He remained at that address until the beginning of 1924. In August of 1924 he lived in Crown Heights, Brooklyn, at which time he received his mail at *Feder*, a New York literary journal. The following year, in November of 1925, his mail was delivered to a certain Yong who also lived in Brooklyn (see Appendix B).
51. Wasserman, *Leksikon fun de nayer idisher literatur* (Biographical Dictionary of Modern Yiddish Literature), op. cit.
52. Wasserman, op. cit.
53. The most important writers of the 1920s and 1930s are, in alphabetical order according to the Hebrew alphabet: N. I. Gotlib, Shlomo Wiseman, Benjamin Gutl Sack, Jacob Zipper, Yudika, Ida Maze, Esther Segal, J. I. Nehemia Segal, H. M. Caiserman, Israel Rabinovitch, Yudl Rosenberg, Sholem Shtern, and A. S. Shkolnikov.
54. Letter from H. M. Caiserman to J. I. Segal, Montreal, April 29, 1924, Caiserman Archive, Canadian Jewish Congress Archives.
55. Undated letter from Zishe Landau, New York, Segal Archive, Montreal Jewish Public Library, 3 pages.
56. Howe, op. cit., 429.
57. Letter from Melekh Chmelnitzki to J. I. Segal, Vienna, March 30, 1922, Segal Archive, Montreal Jewish Public Library, Montreal. Chmelnitzki does not specify whether Segal was already living in New York or just visting.
58. On this subject see Ruth R. Wisse, *A Little Love in Big Manhattan* (Harvard University Press, Cambridge, Mass. 1988), 147.
59. See the entry on Mani Leib by Mordecaie Jaffe in Shmuel Niger and Jacob Shatzky, op. cit., vol. 5, 450–457.
60. Aaron Rappoport, *"Mit Mani Leib in shop* [in Mani Leib's shop] *Di Tsukunft* (New York, vol. 62, no. 4, April 1957), 167–169.
61. Ibid., 167.
62. Brahinsky Mani Leib's family name. Mani Leib Brahinsky (1883–1953).
63. Aaron Rappoport, ibid. 168.

64. Serlin, *"Der Umfargeslekher Yud Yud Sega*l [the unforgettable I.J. Segal]," *Keneder Adler*, Montreal, March 1954.

65. Sometimes spelled "Tsherna."

66. Postcard from Melekh Ravitch to J. I. Segal, Warsaw, November 29, 1925, Segal Archive, Jewish Public Library Archive, Montreal.

67. Unpublished interview in English with David Rome at the Canadian Jewish Congress, November 22, 1989.

68. The fact that the Montreal writer Ida Maze lost a young child around the same time brought her closer to Segal.

69. J. I. Segal, excerpt from "Likhtik," *Lirik* (Montreal, 1930), 166.

70. Zalman Rejzen, op. cit.

71. Younger brother of Jacob Zipper, principal of the Peretz School.

72. Shtern, *Nostalgie et Tristesse*, op. cit., 60–61. Shtern, *Writers I Knew*, op. cit., 46–47. Shtern, *Writers I Knew* [Yiddish], op. cit., 46–47.

73. The only available copy of this book is in the Fishstein Collection, in the rare book section of the McLennan Library, McGill University.

74. The poet's age in 1923 when *Fun mayn shtub un mayn velt* was published.

75. J. I. Segal, *"In mayn shtub," Fun mayn shtub un mayn velt* (New York, 1923, Vilner Farlag fun B. Kletskin), 51. Note that in Yiddish the word *shtub* can mean either "house" or "room."

76. J. I. Segal, *"Briv fun New York,"* in *Kanade, Montreal*, vol. 1, no. 3, December 1925, 25.

77. Ibid., *"a likhter punkt in der arumiker megushemdikayt un groykayt"*

78. J. I. Segal, "O Montreal!" *Fun mayn shtub un mayn velt*, op. cit., 62.

79. J. I. Segal, Dedication which begins: *"Dayn ondenkn, mayn tsarnele," Lider*, Montreal, 1926, 3.

80. *"gefalener, farfalener, in opfal fun New York/kegn monument, un toytn kaltn likht in vinterdikn park,"* J. I. Segal, "Windsor Park," *Lider* (Montreal, 1926), 84.

81. J. I. Segal, ibid., 190.

82. Ibid., 184. Sainte-Sophie is a little village just east of Saint-Jérôme, where a few Jewish farmers settled at the beginning of the 20th century.

83. Ibid., 87.

84. *Keneder Adler*, August 20, 1927, 23.

85. Today rue de Bullion. This address is just north of Rachel Street.

86. The apartment is just north of Mont Royal Avenue.

87. Zalman Rejzen, op. cit., 627–628.

88. With regard to the Congress in 1919, see H. M. Caiserman in "The History of the First Canadian Jewish Congress," in Arthur Daniel Hart, *The Jew in Canada, A Complete Record of Canadian Jewry From the Days of the French Regime to the Present Day* (Toronto and Montreal, Jewish Publications Limited, 1926), 575.

89. Simon Belkin, op. cit., 291.

90. Undated English manuscript entitled "Rally of Workers. Talk for February 6th," Caiserman Archive, Canadian Jewish Congress Archives, Montreal.

91. H. M. Caiserman, undated and unsigned report in English, Caiserman Archive, Canadian Jewish Congress Archives, Montreal.

92. Letter from H. M. Caiserman to Hirsch Wolofsky in English, Petah Tikva, January 20, 1922, Caiserman Archive, Canadian Jewish Congress Archives, Montreal.

93. Letter from Hirsch Wolofsky to H. M. Caiserman in English, Montreal, March 6, 1922, Caiserman Archive, Canadian Jewish Congress Archives, Montreal.

94. Letter from H. M. Caiserman to J. I. Segal (translated from the Yiddish), Montreal, January 22, 1921, Segal Archive, Jewish Public Library.

95. *"Kanade," Nyuansn* (Montreal January 1921, 15–17 and February 1921), 36–38.

96.   J. I. Segal, "*H. M. Caiserman tsu zayn 65 yorign yuvl* [On his 65th birthday]," *Keneder Adler*, March 18, 1949.

97.   Letter from H. M. Caiserman to Elias Epstein in English, Jewish National Fund, Jerusalem, sent from Regina, Saskatchewan on November 1925. Caiserman Archive, Canadian Jewish Congress Archives, Montreal. At that time, all travel was by train.

98.   Letter from H. M. Caiserman to Miss Anna Caplan in English, Hadassah Medical Organization, Jerusalem, January 28, 1926. Caiserman Archive, Canadian Jewish Congress Archives, Montreal.

99.   J. I. Segal, undated manuscript, Segal Archive, Jewish Public Library Archives, Montreal.

100. H. M. Caiserman, "*Kanade*," *Nyuansn* (January 1921, no. 1), 15.

101. Translation by Miriam Waddington in Irving Howe and Eliezer Greenberg, eds., *A Treasury of Yiddish Poetry*. (Schocken, 1987), 153 of J. I. Segal, "*Shpet harbst in Montreal*," *Letste lider* [Last poems] (Montreal: J. I., Segal Committee and Canadian Jewish Congress, 1955), 106.

102. Hershman had immigrated to Montreal in 1902, the year he opened the first bookstore exclusively for Yiddish newspapers and books. His literary work can be found in the *Keneder Adler* shortly after it began publication in 1907.

103. One of his stories, translated into English by David Rome, was published with the title "A Quebec Story" in *Through the Eyes of the Eagle, the Early Montreal Yiddish Press, 1907–1917* (Montreal, Vehicule Press, 2001), 196–204.

104. Hirsch Hershman, "Armand Cartier," *Kanade* (Montreal, July 1921), 11–21.

105. *In Kanade* (2 vols.) (Montreal: Sholem Shtern Bukh-komitet, 1960–1963). *In Kanade* was published in English as *In Canada: A Novel in Verse* (Translated by Judith Rotstein. Montreal, 1984) and *Au Canada: un roman en vers* (Translated by Tatania Hais. Montréal: S. Shtern, 1984). The second volume of *In Kanade*, Montreal, 1963, appeared in French translation as *Au Canada, un roman en vers*, translated by Guy Maheux, Montreal, 1984.

106. *Dos vayse hoyz* (New York: YKUF), 1967, was translated into French by Guy Maheux as *Velvl: roman*, Montreal: Société de belles-lettres, 1977. It had earlier been translated into Hebrew with the title *Ha-Bayit ha-lavan be-harim* (Translated by Shimshon Meltzer, Tel Aviv: ha-Menorah), 1972, and in English as *The White House* (Translated by Max Rosenfeld. New York: Warbrooke Publishers, 1974).

107. N. I. Gotlib, *Montreal*, Montreal, 1968.

108. Some of the short stories by Chava Rosenfarb have been translated by her daughter Goldie Morgenthaler, and published under the title *Survivors*, Toronto, Cormorant Books, 2004.

109. A. M. Klein, "The Mountain," *The Rocking Chair and Other Poems* (Toronto, The Ryerson Press, 1951), 35.

110. Caiserman, op. cit., 16.

111. Caiserman, op. cit., 17.

112. Caiserman, op. cit., 17.

113. Caiserman, op. cit., 16.

114. Unsigned, undated, untitled manuscript beginning with the line: "*O, Kanada! O, Kanada!...*" Caiserman archive, Canadian Jewish Congress Archive, Montreal.

115. Nothing indicates that Caiserman had any personal contact at this time with the writers or literary critics of French Canada. All his knowledge of this subject seems to have been purely from books.

116. Caiserman actually named over twenty more French-Canadian authors in this manuscript, divided into four historical periods, without, however, specifically

commenting on their work. The following list of names, in the order in which they appear, sheds light on how Caiserman approached his subject: Jacques Viger, Michel Bibaud, Joseph-Édouard Turcotte; Pierre-Joseph-Olivier Chauveau, Octave Crémazie, Gonzalve Desaulniers, Adolphe Poisson, Eudore Évanturel, Nérée Beauchemin; Émile Nelligan, Albert Lozeau, Charles Gill, Engelbert Gallèze, Jean Charbonneau, Alonzo Cinq-Mars, Émile Vézina, Albert Ferland, Charles Daoust, Germain Beaulieu; René Chopin, Benjamin Michaud, Édouard Chauvin, Jean Nolin, Roger Maillet, Émile Venne, Blanche Lamontagne-Beauregard and Alfred Garneau. Also mentioned are Madeleine de Verchères, Dollard des Ormeaux, and Louis-Joseph Papineau as "national heroes" of French Canada.

117.   It would seem that Caiserman remained very attached to this project for a long time because he mentioned it in the introduction to his 1934 anthology *Idishe dikhter in kanade* [Jewish Poets in Canada], Montreal, Farlag Nyuansn.
118.   Caiserman Archive, Canadian Jewish Congress Archives, Montreal, 21.
119.   Bernard Figler, "Meet the Canadian Jewish Congress," *The Jewish Standard* (April 1936), 21.
120.   In the manuscript, there are 11 pages (7–18) devoted to Canadian poetry in the English language, 12 pages to Canadian poetry in French (18–30), and 110 pages (30–140) to Canadian poetry in Yiddish.
121.   Letter from H. M. Caiserman to J. I. Segal, Montreal, April 29, 1924, 2–3. Caiserman Archive, Canadian Jewish Congress Archives, Montreal.
122.   Ibid.
123.   See Pierre Anctil, *"H. M. Caiserman ou la passion du Yiddish," Tur Malka, flâneries sur les cimes de l'histoire juive montrélaise* (Sillery, éditions du Septentrion, 1977), 75–107.
124.   Letter from Caiserman to J. I. Segal, Montreal, April 10, 1924, Caiserman Archive, Canadian Jewish Congress Archives, Montreal.
125.   Untitled, undated manuscript on Canadian poetry beginning with the line "*O, Kanada! O, Kanada! . . .*", Caiserman Archive, Canadian Jewish Congress Archive, Montreal, 34.
126.   Ibid., 77.
127.   H. M. Caiserman, "*Royerd*, retsentsye [*Royerd*, a review]," *Der Keneder Adler*, August 19, 1929.
128.   I. Rabinovitch, "*Idishe literarishe tetigkayt in kanade, kronologisher iberblik* [Yiddish Literary Activity in Canada, a chronological overview]," *Der Keneder Adler* (September 2, 1927), 5, 2.
129.   Ibid.
130.   Ibid.
131.   Those authors are: Reuben Brainin, Leon Khazanovitch, Konrad Bercovici, Moishe Leib Halpern, Hershl Hirsch, Moshe Shmuelsohn, Baruch J. Goldstein, J. I. Segal, Yehuda Kaufman, Nahum Perlman, Hirsch Wolofsky, A. S. Shkolnikov, Esther Segal, A. Almi (Eliahu Chaim Sheps], Yehuda Elzet (Yehuda Leib Zlotnik), Leiser Meltzer, Benjamin Gutl Sack, Chaim Talmatch, Hirsch Hershman, Rivke Rosenblatt, Agnes Cohen, Ida Maze, Leiser Mendl Benjamin, Yudel Rosenberg, H. M. Caiserman, Aron Barsky and Jacob Zipper.
132.   The Zohar, the foundational work of the kabbalistic tradition, written in Aramaic in the late 18th century, is considered to have been written by Spanish kabbalist and Rabbi Moses de Leon.
133.   Benjamin's translation was published in New York between 1918 and 1922, probably first in instalments in the Yiddish press. Benjamin came from Rumania.
134.   H. M. Caiserman, August 19, 1929, op. cit.

Chapter 4

Toward a Golden Age

O ften, and sometimes even with a certain nostalgia, the 1930s are referred to as the "Golden Age" of Yiddish literature in Montreal. This designation is not without an element of truth in terms of the sheer number of writers who found a haven in Montreal during that decade, and the diversity of their literary output. While Montreal Yiddish literature was undergoing a period of both con-solidation and growth, it seemed to have reached a level of creativity never attained again. First of all, the early writers, who had previ-ously worked in isolation, were able to benefit from an expanding institutional network where they found support and encouragement. Secondly, during the 1920s new talented writers arrived from the dis-tant countries of Eastern Europe. These newcomers would be respon-sible for the second largest peak on the curve of Jewish immigration to Montreal, after the one resulting from the Sifton Plan instituted by Prime Minister Wilfrid Laurier. The biographical data in the book by Ch. L. Fox would suggest that the first two waves of Yiddish-speaking immigrants, that of 1905–1914 and that 1920–1925, brought an almost equal number of writers and scholars to Canadian ports, approxi-mately 150 in each instance.[1] Whereas Yiddish writers in Canada in the early twentieth century at first found themselves preaching in the wilderness and up against the indifference of their co-religionists, by the 1930s a more loyal, better educated, and, most importantly, more numerous readership awaited those who picked up their pens. In 1931, the Yiddish-speaking population of Montreal numbered almost 60,000, compared to only 30,000 in 1911. Essentially, over the two decades the immigrants' standard of living had clearly improved, as had their knowledge of Canadian society. Journalist Israel Medres, who personally witnessed the second influx of Jews in the 1920s, described the situation as follows:

> In 1920 Jewish immigrants from Europe once more began to
> arrive in Canada. They were quite different from those who had
> immigrated prior to the war. [. . .]
> The new immigrants of the post-war period adapted more quickly
> to the life of the community. As a matter of fact, they found a
> much better organized Jewish community in Montreal. [. . .]
> Among the new immigrants were Jewish writers, poets, artists,
> rabbis, teachers and even Hassidic rabbis. An entirely different
> atmosphere prevailed, unlike that before 1914.[2]

The magnitude of the political events taking place in Eastern Europe
during and after World War I rocked the very foundations of Jewish
life, and the context in which Yiddish writers had evolved on that
continent. During the Russian Civil War of 1918–1920, the revolutionary groups which had emerged victorious in October of 1917
proved able to resist attacks by the forces of reaction and the troops
financed by foreign governments. The period of post-war reconstruction in the Soviet Union was also a time of widespread artistic activity in the Yiddish language dedicated to international leftist ideals,
and freed of the shackles of tsarist censorship. In the 1920s, sparked
by the radical reformist fervour affecting all classes of Russian society, an extraordinary Jewish cultural renaissance manifested itself in
every branch of knowledge, beginning with literature and the visual
arts. New voices were heard, voices inspired by the great European
modernist movements that no longer professed the same attachment
to traditional Jewish forms. Among them were David Bergelson,
David Hofstein, Peretz Markish, Moshe Kulbak, and Der Nister, the
penname of Pinkhes Kahanovich. This paradigm shift temporarily
halted the exodus of Russian Jews to America, and gave rise to the
creation of trade unions and Yiddish cultural organizations in New
York and Montreal closely affiliated with the Soviet Union.[3] At a
time that Russian borders were becoming less porous than they had
been prior to the war and the West was becoming increasingly suspi-
cious of everything coming out of the Soviet Union, an independent
Poland was rising from the ashes thanks to the Versailles peace nego-
tiations.[4] While Russian Jews had joined the ranks of the revolution in
droves and were enjoying full political and civil liberties for the first
time, Jews in Poland in 1919 suddenly found themselves governed
by a conservative nationalist regime that would prove to be viciously
anti-Semitic.

Whereas Soviet doctrine dominated Jewish life in Russia in the early 1920s, nationalist sentiment in Poland was conducive to the appearance of a wide assortment of ideas and ideologies, ranging from traditional Judaism to left-wing Zionism, and including assimilationism, revolutionary Bundism, radical modernism, and Yiddishism. Several of the Jewish institutions and organizations that appeared in post-war Poland organized very successful educational and cultural networks, all politically affiliated and promoting, to varying degrees, the use of either Hebrew, Yiddish, Polish, or Russian, according to the expectations of their members. The hostility of the Polish regime to national minorities attained such intensity that after 1919 Poland replaced pre-Soviet Russia as the principal source of Eastern Jewish immigration to Canada. In addition to Polish Jews, who accounted for the majority of Jewish immigrants during the interwar period, Jewish immigrants also came from the newly independent Lithuania, and the new Soviet Republics of Ukraine and Byelorussia. The first generation of Yiddish writers and intellectuals who settled in Montreal at the beginning of the twentieth century, arriving in the wake of the failed Russian Revolution of 1905, was followed by a second influx after the Bolshevik Revolution of 1917, mostly from Poland. Whereas immigrants who landed in Canada between 1900 and 1910 were from a vast undifferentiated Russian reservoir, those of the 1920s reflected conditions specific to the various parts of the now-dismembered Russian Empire in the grips of various forms of virulent anti-Russian nationalism. Born in a Jewish world to a large extent untouched by modernity, schooled in traditional Judaism, and having entered Canada, for the most part at a very young age, the pioneers of Montreal Yiddish literature found themselves some twenty years later in the company of newcomers from a very different cultural milieu. More likely to be attracted to political activism, and mainly on the left of the political spectrum, the writers who came in the 1920s viewed Yiddish cultural affirmation through a filter of militancy and Jewish nationalism to which their predecessors of an earlier generation had not been exposed.

New Waves of Immigration

Among the authors and intellectuals arriving in Montreal as part of the second migratory wave were several people who would have a lasting influence on Yiddish literature, as well as on Jewish community life in the city. In 1922 Montreal welcomed Shimshon Dunsky and, in 1925, Jacob (Ya'akov) Zipper. Both were from Poland, and both would go on to make a name for themselves in the field of Yiddish education. The former became the assistant principal of the Jewish People's School (*Yidishe folkshule*) and the second, the principal of the Peretz School. Both schools had been founded ten years earlier and pursued the same goals of left-wing Zionism. The pedagogical careers of both Dunsky and Zipper extended over a span of forty years in Montreal, and both men wrote numerous essays on modern teaching methods applied to Yiddish language and culture. Although committed to transmitting Jewish culture to new generations and active in the Yiddish-language institutional network, both these men found time to publish their writing. Besides producing several historically important personal accounts, Zipper was known for his many contributions to the Yiddish press in Canada and abroad. His literary work included stories and novellas in Yiddish and Hebrew, some of which were collected and published as books in Montreal after the World War II, including *Oyf yener zayt Bug* (The Other Side of the River) in 1946, *Tsvishn taykhn un vasern* (Between Lakes and Waters) in 1961, and *Fun Nekhtn un haynt* (Of Yesterday and Today) in 1978. Dunsky took a slightly different path, publishing Yiddish children's books and writing opinion pieces about the Jewish community in Canada. We are indebted to him for his monumental and carefully annotated translations into Yiddish of the biblical books of Lamentations, Esther, Ruth, Ecclesiastes, and Song of Songs, all published during the 1950s and 1960s. At the Peoples' School, Dunsky became the right-hand man of Shlomo Wiseman, who had immigrated to Montreal in 1913 and was the author of a vast body of pedagogical material in three languages, namely Yiddish, Hebrew and English. Literary critic and editor of a literary anthology designed for teaching Yiddish, first published in 1931 as *Dos vort* (The word), Wiseman was also acclaimed for his translation of the work of Epictetus into modern Hebrew.

Zipper, whose real name was Jacob Isaac Shtern, had been forced to leave Poland because of his political activities as a member of Labour Zionist and Jewish workers' parties. Having already taught Yiddish in the land of his birth, he naturally gravitated to the Canadian Jewish school system, first in Winnipeg and then in Montreal. His immigration to Canada convinced other members of his family to leave for America, including his younger brother Sholem Joseph, also a militant leftist, who disembarked in Halifax in 1927.

Once in Montreal, Sholem Shtern followed in his brother's footsteps, and in 1938 became the principal of the Winchevsky School, a Yiddish-language school affiliated with the Communist party. Very attached to the Yiddish language, Sholem Shtern, as we have seen, had ambitions of becoming a poet. As early as 1928 he began publishing his poems in various American and Canadian periodicals. In 1929 he published his first poetry collection entitled *Noentkayt* (Nearness), in Toronto, followed by a second in Montreal, in 1941, called *Es likhtikt* (It Grows Light), both with a proletarian perspective. After the war, and for over thirty years, Shtern pursued a literary career in Yiddish featuring autobiographical stories and essays about contemporary Jewish literature. In 1933, Shifra Shtern[5] reached Montreal, followed by Yechiel Shtern in 1936, and finally Yisroel Hersh Shtern in 1937.[6] Shifra made a name for herself in the Montreal Yiddish-language school system as a writer of books, including textbooks, for children, while her brothers also joined the ranks of the teaching profession while publishing their poetry in a great many newspapers and periodicals. The entire family was finally reunited in 1938 when Abraham Shtern[7]— father of Jacob, Sholem, Shifre, Yechiel, and Yisroel—joined his family in Montreal only a few months before the outbreak of World War II. A Hasidic Jew,

From left to right, the poets J. I. Segal, Mani-Leib and Sholem Shtern, along with writer Joseph Dimentstein, Studio Geo. Charlab, Park Avenue, Montreal, around 1930. (Private collection of Sylvia and Annette Segal.)

educated in a *beys medresh* in Tishivits near Lublin, Abraham Shtern published several books in Montreal, in Yiddish and in Hebrew, about traditional Judaism. Most were scholarly commentaries on the Torah, the Kabbalah, and rabbinic literature. The Shtern family is a good example of just how profound and potent the combination of a strictly religious universe and Jewish proletarian militancy could be in interwar Montreal. Within a span of twenty years, the ideological abyss between the father and his sons had widened without, however, severing the historical and cultural continuum that made it possible for them to share the same linguistic and cultural space.

In 1930 Canada also opened its doors to a young poet from Kaunas, Lithuania, by the name of Noah Isaac Gotlib who published his first volume of poetry entitled *Zeglen in zun* (Sails in the Sun) in Montreal in 1932. Active until the end of the 1960s, Gotlib became a key figure in Montreal's Yiddish cultural life, in particular after 1950 as the president of the of the Canadian Jewish Writers' Association. The crowning achievement of Gotlib's career was the posthumous publication of a poetry book entitled *Montreal* about the Canadian landscape and his adopted city. Another young man named Moses Mordecai Shaffir arrived in 1930 from Bukovina and soon afterward began submitting Yiddish poems to Canadian newspapers and periodicals. Shaffir also wrote countless literary critiques and several articles on the philology of Yiddish. His first book of poetry entitled *A stezhke* [A path], published in 1940, was followed over the next four decades by several others written in a lyrical style rooted in the Jewish folk tradition. Many talented women also converged upon Montreal during that same era, contributing to the diversity of Yiddish literary forms. In 1922, Miriam Krant and Sheindl Franzus Garfinkle settled in Montreal, each embarking on her own very interesting literary career. Both began to write in the 1930s, with the former publishing poems, essays, short stories, and stories for children in various newspapers and periodicals, and the latter completing two novels about life in Russia at the time of the Bolshevik Revolution of 1917: *Rokhl* [Rachel] in 1942 and *Erev Oktober* [On the eve of October]in 1947. Their arrival in Canada preceded by a few years that of a writer known as Yudika,[8] who settled in Montreal in 1927 and devoted her career exclusively to poetry. Her first publication in 1934 was *Vandervegn* [Migrant roads] soon followed by *Shpliters* [Splinters] in 1943, and *Tsar un freyd* [Sorrow and joy] in 1949. All three books demonstrated her rare and superior literary ability in describing the urban working class milieu. This

Cover of the magazine *Montreal*, December 1932.
(Canadian Jewish Congress Archives.)

overview would be incomplete without mentioning Rokhl Ravitch Eisenberg[9] and Mirl Erdberg Shatan, who immigrated to Montreal in 1923 and 1926 respectively. Both became extremely active in the literary scene, the former as librarian at the Jewish Public Library, translator, and editor of anthologies; the latter as poet, literary critic, novelist, and essayist.

The 1930s also witnessed the birth of two literary monthlies in Montreal, *Montreal* and *Heften* [Notebooks], which attempted to pick up the torch that had been dropped a decade earlier by *Nyuansn*, *Epokhe*, *Kanade*, and *Royerd* for lack of readers. Founded in 1932 by

N. I. Gotlib and A. S. Shkonikov, twelve issues of *Montreal* appeared before its demise in June of 1935. They featured proletarian writing closely aligned with Soviet ideology. One fact worthy of note is that in its fourth issue, this magazine, instead of using the conventional spelling of Yiddish words in general use at the time, including in Canada,[10] adopted the orthography then in force in the Soviet Union, in particular with regard to Yiddish words of Hebrew origin. In *Montreal* were published the poetry of N. I. Gotlib, A.S. Shkolnikov, Ida Maze, Yudika, Hanna Steinberg, Simon Nepom, Hirsch Hershman and Esther Segal, as well as some stories and essays, including one by Gotlib on the poetry of Itsik Manger, and another, also by Gotlib, about the publication of the book *Mesholim* (Fables) by Eliezer Steinbarg. *Montreal* was followed by *Heftn*, a magazine published simultaneously in Montreal and Detroit by Gotlib and Ezra Korman,[11] of which only four issues appeared between January of 1936 and June of 1937. It should be noted that *Heftn* offered a curious coupling of a North American aesthetic with sympathy for the Soviet regime, then considered to be the hub of an important modernist Yiddish literary and artistic movement. The entire third issue of *Heftn* was dedicated to the American writer Moishe Leib Halpern, a member of *Di Yunge*. Also in *Heftn* were translations into Yiddish of the poetry of Carl Sandburg, an essay by Korman about the Soviet poet Izi Kharik, and an article by Gotlib about the Byelorussian-born Kadya Molodowsky, who sometimes attended Yiddish literary gatherings in Montreal.

The wave of immigration of the 1920s and the beginning of the 1930s was the last before the Holocaust, meaning that for almost two decades, until 1948 to be exact, very few Yiddish speakers were admitted into Canada. After 1929, and for the entire duration of the Second World War, the government of Canada, despite significant political pressure by several community organizations, essentially shut its doors to immigrant Jews with the result that the migratory flow of Jews from Eastern Europe came to an almost complete standstill.[12] Yiddish writers, as well as Yiddish-speaking artists and intellectuals, who had benefitted from the relative economic prosperity of the 1920s in making Montreal their home, began to command centre stage over the following decade. Arriving young, they were able to take advantage of the expansion of the Yiddish-language cultural network to establish their reputations and find the means to publish their work. Like their predecessors in the first migratory wave, they launched their careers in Canada without any prior experience in

Esther Segal, sister of J. I. Segal, with her husband,
A. S. Shkolnikov, Chicago, 1923.
(Private collection of Sylvia and Annette Segal.)

Yiddish literature, and without having earned any prior recognition
in the Eastern European literary milieu. Jewish demographic growth
in Montreal opened new opportunities for newcomers that had not
been available to the immigrants arriving between 1905–1914, opportunities created in particular by the consolidation of the Yiddish press
and the Yiddish-language parochial school system. At the beginning
of the 1920s, all the Jewish community institutions moved north of
Sherbrooke Street and set up shop along St. Lawrence Boulevard,
between the neighbourhoods today known as Plateau Mont-Royal
and Mile End. The same was true for many of the clothing factories,

upon which a large part of Montreal's Yiddish-speaking population depended for their livelihood. In this recently developed area flats were larger and airier, urban infrastructure of better quality, and sanitary conditions significantly enhanced. It should also be noted that these improvements were also the result of bitter struggles during World War I between competing garment workers' unions, whose members were mainly Yiddish-speaking.[13] It was the dawn of a new era, full of hope but overshadowed by the growing economic difficulties worldwide. In the midst of the general uncertainty, Montreal Yiddish literature had made remarkable progress, as Gotlib noted in the first issue of *Montreal*, which appeared in 1932:

> In recent years Montreal has been home to an artistic flowering in the field of Yiddish literature, among others. Montreal, the great Canadian metropolis, is also a major centre of Yiddish literature and poetry. Montreal has produced excellent literary periodicals, including *Nyuansn, Epokhe, Royerd, Kanade*, etc. Montreal has inspired, supported and encouraged the development of its young talents.[14]

The Crash of 1929

The economic downturn unleashed by the crash of the New York stock exchange in October of 1929 dealt a heavy blow to Montreal's Yiddish cultural institutions without, however, actually diminishing their verve and vitality of the previous decade. The principal reason for their resilience was the fact that they essentially depended on volunteers to promote their cause, and on the ideological fervour of a membership long since committed to activism. Several Yiddish-language institutions were founded in Montreal in the 1910s by Jewish political parties that came into existence during the failed Revolution of 1905 in Russia, and nurtured by a deep-rooted militancy among the masses. Modern Jewish nationalism, the defence of Yiddish language and culture, and the attraction of progressive ideas sparked widespread interest among the immigrants, which often took the form of passionate engagement. That was the case, for example, at the Jewish Public Library, which had been founded by members of the Poale Zion and profited from the immense organizational resources enjoyed by the Labour Zionists. When the library was founded in 1914, the head of that organization, Reuben Brainin, did not hesitate to promote the Library's global mission and revolutionary objectives among its stakeholders: "The pride of our public library lies in the fact that it was created by the people and for the people, as well as the fact that it's only objective is to spread enlightenment and knowledge among the people".[15] The same was true of the *Peretz shule* and the *Yidishe Folkshule*, the Peretz and Peoples' Schools, both of which, at the end of the 1920s and the beginning of the 1930s, offered full-time educational programs in relatively spacious buildings.[16] When it was founded, the *Folkshule* included in the publicity material it prepared for recruitment purposes, those ideological goals which were likely to arouse enthusiasm and attract enrolment among the large number of nationalists on the left.

> The *Yidishe Folkshule* considers its first task to be the education of the Jewish child in a healthy national spirit, connecting him with his brother Jews of every era and every country in the world, acquainting him with the main fundamentals of Jewish culture. We hope to reach this objective through a national education in Yiddish and Hebrew [. . .].
> The second task will be to instil in the Jewish child a love of freedom, self-reliance and social justice, uniting him with all who suffered and struggled in every era and in every country.[17]

As opposed to Jewish community institutions, which, thanks to their increasing reliance on volunteers and political activism, were in a position to absorb the chronic loss of revenue in the 1930s, industrial enterprises were forced to slow their pace of production after 1929 and to reduce hours of employment, driving all social classes into a downward spiral. In 1931, almost 35 per cent of Montreal Jews depended on work in the garment factories for their livelihood.[18] That would seem to imply that almost half of all Jewish families were severely impacted by the decline in production in the clothing sector. An entire Jewish economic sub-sector was affected by these losses, including retailers and peddlers, and in the long term so were synagogues and the various Jewish schools. While teachers, community leaders, rabbis, and other people who worked for the Jewish community could compensate to a certain extent for their reduced cash flow thanks to increased voluntary contributions by parents, activists, and the recipients of services, it was different for a news organization like the *Keneder Adler*, which depended on profits and earned its revenue from advertising. Everyone employed by the larger community, especially in the parochial school system, knew that part of their work would remain unpaid, and that they could not expect to receive the same salary as their counterparts in the public sector. Usually, the Yiddish schools' budgetary deficits were covered at the year's end by a few large donors who considered it their duty to fund an educational institution open to all, including pupils whose parents were not able to pay the general tuition. The *Keneder Adler*, however, was the property of the Wolofsky family, and its owners could not allow themselves to deplete their assets, nor to require their workers to contribute to the newspaper without financial remuneration.

On September 25, 1931, Daniel Wolofsky,[19] the chief administrator of the *Adler* at the time, sent J. I. Segal a letter stating that he was unilaterally cancelling the latter's contract with the daily paper. Segal was not a regular employee of the *Adler*, and he probably was not receiving a weekly salary, but the articles he wrote every week ensured him of extra income as well as visibility in the Yiddish literary milieu. In his letter, Wolofsky asked Segal to stop submitting articles after October 3, 1931: "We are very sorry that we have to notify you that due to the fact that we are forced to curtail expenses in order to continue to do business, we shall be obliged to dispense with your services."[20] Another letter sent that same day to full-time employees of the *Adler* explained that the newspaper's revenues had been steadily decreasing over the past six months, and that a deficit of $6,000 had accumulated: "Besides this, we find it extremely difficult to collect accounts from many of those who advertise. From present indications, we can see no improvement in the coming months."[21] People who worked at the newspaper had their salaries cut by 10 per cent, while some were let go. The newspaper's financial situation was so precarious that even these draconian measures could not ensure that it could pursue its two-fold mission as spokesperson for the community and independent commercial enterprise: "These deductions will not be enough to cover our losses, but at the present time we hope to be able to carry on on this basis. [. . .] It is in your interest to help us economize, as otherwise we are very doubtful if we can continue to operate for any length of time."[22] In view of this evidence, it is easy to imagine how profoundly the Depression of 1929 affected the entire Yiddish-language organizational structure in Montreal, forcing its leaders to make very difficult choices. On a much broader scale, the Depression forced community leaders to postpone several large projects, such as the construction of a new building on Saint Joseph Boulevard for the United Talmud Torah as well as a new Jewish hospital in the Côte-des-Neiges district.[23]

Literary Salons and Book Committees

Like the majority of his freelance colleagues, Segal stopped publishing in the *Keneder Adler* for a number of years. One of the few reliable opportunities available to Yiddish writers in the 1920s to publish their work and gain exposure in the Eastern European Jewish diaspora outside of Montreal and Canada had disappeared. The articles and poems published in the local press had often been reprinted in Yiddish newspapers abroad, and could be read just as easily in Warsaw, Kiev, Buenos Aires, Johannesburg, and New York. The *Adler* travelled surprising distances and was available in the many libraries and reading rooms maintained by immigrant Eastern European Jews on several continents.[24] While the daily paper slowed production and threatened to go under completely, the Jewish People's School kept Segal in its employ throughout the 1930s, and, by tapping community resources, found the means to provide him with the necessities of daily life. In a certain sense, the Yiddish schools, less well funded and more exposed in normal times than capitalist enterprises, had unique means of survival that kept them relatively sheltered from fluctuations in the stock market. The same was true of the Jewish Public Library, the Yiddish-language garment unions, and several small charitable organizations. This form of stubborn resistance could also be found in political associations, such as the Arbeiter Ring (Workmen's Circle) or the Poale Zion, which depended almost entirely on the voluntary contributions of their members. The economic crisis of the 1930s, which paralysed the Jewish middle class in Montreal and endangered the fortunes recently amassed by a few of the immigrants, neither dampened the creative spirit nor halted the momentum of the city's Yiddish literary endeavours. The very serious problems experienced by the population as a whole paled in comparison with the suffering and persecution which the immigrant Jews had endured in Eastern Europe before departing for North America. Although in Canada there were several manifestations of anti-Semitism on the political front,[25] official censorship of Yiddish publications and institutions, as well as laws specifically targeting Jewish citizens, did not exist. Nothing in this country even closely resembled the repression of Jewish writers by the tsarist police prior to 1917, nor that instituted at the beginning of the 1930s in the Soviet Union under Stalin.

That global financial failures and market turbulence did not become an insurmountable obstacle to the publication of Yiddish books, even in Montreal, is proven by the fact that Segal published three volumes of his poetry during the 1930s: *Lirik* [Lyric] in 1930, *Mayn nigun* [My melody] in 1934, and *Di drite sude* [The third meal] in 1937. In other words, within a span of seven years, he had produced over a thousand pages of printed text. The greatest hurdle for Montreal poets was collecting enough money through individual contributions to take their manuscripts directly to the printer. To raise the amount required, it was necessary for the author to enjoy an outstanding reputation and be available for numerous social events likely to result in financial contributions toward the book project. Above all, an author had to earn the unconditional esteem of a few community leaders and literary colleagues, who would become his spokesmen and gain him access to Montreal social circles with more plentiful material resources. To rally greater support in the Jewish community, the author and his book had to transcend the ideological and political divisions that could obstruct a successful fundraising process. Having returned to Montreal at the end of the 1920s, Segal remained one of those rare Yiddish authors who possessed both the personal charisma and superior artistic ability needed to publish poetry during a serious economic depression — a remarkable tour de force. So great was his ascendancy among the various Yiddish-language cultural factions and his writing so popular, that a committee was struck in May of 1932 to prepare an event in honour of the fifteenth anniversary of his literary career.[26] This is what the organizers unreservedly declared about Segal:

> When Segal made his debut as a poet fifteen years ago, no one imagined that he would have such creative power. However, it only took a few years for the news to spread throughout the Yiddish literary world that in Montreal there lived and wrote a renowned Yiddish poet of with God-given talent.
>
> Up until now, Segal has published five poetry collections, each of which has brought us a breath of fresh air. We can expect much of Segal in future because he is still young and full of creative energy. We wish him years and years of productive activity that will continue to enrich Yiddish literature.[27]

In addition to organizing a grand celebration in the large hall of the YMHA (Young Men's Hebrew Association) on Mount Royal Avenue, the committee found the energy to publish a 25-page brochure containing fifteen poems from his forthcoming collection.[28] The following year, in 1933, a group of the writer's loyal friends formed the "J. I. Segal Committee" with the aim of "publishing the newest work of our poet."[29] This informal group seems to have had two distinct sections representing two different parts of the community. There was a list of members in English, and another, somewhat different list, in Yiddish. In a notice sent out in December of 1933, the members of the J. I. Segal Committee made known their intentions in the following way:

> There are but few of our race in Canada to whom we appeal to cooperate with us, materially and morally, in this task of bringing forth the poetical works of this greatest of Jewish poets in Canada. In doing so, we will enhance the prestige of our literature as well as that of our people.[30]

Among the people who lent their support to this initiative were unionist and Poale Zion activists such as Moshe Dickstein, Shmuel Kaplan, and H. M. Caiserman. Also among Segal's admirers were the principals of the Peretz and People's Schools, Jacob Zipper and Shlomo Wiseman, as well as some of Montreal's senior cultural activists. In addition, Yiddish journalists, the owner of the *Keneder Adler*, Hirch Wolosky, as well as the Communist poet and educator Sholem Shtern were part of this group. On the English list were Rabbi Yehuda Zlotnik, who was an Orthodox Jew, Israel Rabinovitch, the editor-in-chief of the *Keneder Adler*, and translator and journalist Louis Benjamin. To achieve its ends, the committee was perfectly explicit:

> Knowing you as we do to be a friend of Jewish literature and a fervent adherent of Jewish renascence [sic], we trust you will help us carry through this undertaking by joining the J. I. Segal Committee and by contributing generously to its funds for the publication of the works of this eminent Jewish Canadian Poet.[31]

In the archives there are several other examples of this type of community mobilization on behalf J. I. Segal, always with the objective of making it possible for him to reach a broad public in Canada and throughout the Yiddish-speaking world. It is not difficult to believe that most of the Montreal Yiddish authors were also supported in a comparable way, often by the same admirers and activists. That was certainly true of Esther Segal, sister of J. I. Segal, who published a small poetry collection in 1928 entitled *Lider* [Poems], mostly thanks to the financial assistance of the Toronto section of the Poale Zion.[32] This form of small-scale sponsorship, unique to the Yiddish-speaking world, explains to a large extent how Yiddish literature came into its own during a dark economic chapter thanks to very strong financial support. For the contributors, to support the publication of a volume of poetry by defraying the cost of only one copy was the equivalent of participating in the moral and spiritual preservation of an entire people. That is what the letter from the J. I. Segal Committee in 1933 reminded its recipients: "We will also deepen the national conscious-ness of our race and fortify it, morally and spiritually, in our strug-gle for self-preservation at this critical juncture of our history."[33] The noble nature of their contributions, however small, combined with the quasi-prophetic aura ascribed to poets in modern Yiddish culture, suf-ficed to ensure a substantial audience to the better writers. Once the book had been printed in Montreal by a printer specialized in Hebrew printing, most often the Eagle Publishing Company, it was then dis-tributed to private subscribers and the various Yiddish periodicals worldwide to announce its appearance. During the months that fol-lowed, many reviews discussed the book's literary value, thus paving the way for a future publication, if the poet was prolific and if the reviews were favourable. Thus, the book was assembled, printed, and publicized without a publishing house as intermediary, in the usual sense of the word, and without bookstores. Often the poet would keep for himself a certain number of copies which he could sell at various venues in the city where there were Yiddish speakers, or during orga-nized readings at Jewish cultural institutions. The following is the scene described repeatedly by Sholem Shtern in his memoirs about the 1930s:

> The entire week that I. J. Schwartz was busy distributing his books, I leafed through and read his *Kentoki* [Kentucky].[34] One evening I was walking home from school. A white winter wind was blowing. Suddenly I saw I. J. Schwartz coming toward me carrying a satchel full of books. Bundled up in his overcoat, he was making his way through the snowy, frosty night.[35]

Apart from the Yiddish press and other Jewish organizations, there was yet another way to publicize a newly published book and pay for its printing in Montreal. Several people opened their homes to artists and poets, including those who were visiting the city and whose reputation had preceded them. Sometimes these gatherings were organized by cultural organizations for the purpose of collecting money on the spot, such as when the *Ikuf*[36] invited the New York poet Zishe Weinper to Montreal to recite or speak spontaneously to small groups during the 1930s. Sholem Shtern, who often participated, described the atmosphere during these private events as follows:

> When Weinper visited, however, the real Ikuf celebration took place in the home of cultural activist Sarah Mindes, where the atmosphere was more comfortable and warmer. Naturally Weinper spoke. We helped ourselves to the delicacies already laid out on the table. We all sang, and Weinper himself used to sing his own songs *Toybn* [Doves] and *A Pastukhl* [A little shepherd].[37]

In certain cases, these events happened with such frequency that, over the years, actual literary salons came into existence. They were gladly attended by all those who aspired to become a Yiddish writer of any type, even if it meant putting their ideological differences aside. Ida Maze, who had come to Montreal in 1908 from her native Lithuania, received local writers as well as visiting authors in her home on Esplanade over several decades, thus becoming a figure of renown within the Yiddish literary milieu.[38] The author of three poetry collections—*A mame* [A mother] (1931), *Naye lider* [New poems] (1941), and *Vaksn mayne kinderlekh* [My children are growing] (1954)—Maze was the confidante of budding poets, and her house became a refuge for numerous writers who arrived in Montreal penniless and without organized support. There is no doubt that many books were brought to completion and published thanks to her efforts.[39]

The Montreal Yiddish literary salons served not only as social venues but sometimes also as temporary residences for artists who unexpectedly arrived from Europe unannounced with no means of support, generally after a rough journey or fleeing an inextricable political situation. At the end of the 1930s, during World War II, and especially after the Holocaust, many immigrants reached Montreal in a state of profound disorientation. They were welcomed into literary and intellectual circles where they could find comfort and support.

The same was true for New York Yiddish writers who regularly visited Montreal to deliver lectures, sell their books, or simply to see
their relatives and close friends. Contact with New York colleagues
became so frequent that when the leading figures in *Di Yunge* and *In
Zikh* came to Montreal during the interwar period, they were often
received very informally in private homes. On the other hand, some of
the salons were very elitist, reserved for only the most accomplished
artists. Such were the more formal events held at the home of Sara
and H. M. Caiserman, where concerts of the highest quality, as well
as poetry readings, were held regularly. In other instances, the salon's
hostess was a women of modest means who opened her doors to offer
simple snacks and accommodate informal meetings, like Ida Maze,
who lived in an apartment on Esplanade, just south of Mount Royal,
only steps away from the Jewish Public Library and Segal's home.[40]
Thanks to such intermediaries, Yiddish books travelled far distances
and reached diverse social circles. In fact, most of the leading lights of
Yiddish literature passed through Maze's salon, as evidenced by photos and personal accounts of that era, including that of Sholem Shtern:

> Rolnick was also very close to Ida Maze. They often wrote letters
> to one another. He felt completely at home in her house, not just
> because his poetry was highly esteemed there, but also because
> her motherly qualities attracted most of the young poets.[41]

The Sinister Echoes of Nazism

Coping with the serious economic problems of the 1930s could not
mask another more troubling development, this time in the international political arena. The dizzying decline of industrial production
in Germany accompanied by widespread social discontent strongly
contributed to the seizure of power by the National Socialist party
and its leader, Adolf Hitler. As soon as he was appointed chancellor in
January of 1933, Hitler quickly proceeded to Nazify German society,
including its cultural and intellectual sectors, and impose his party's
doctrine. Within a matter of weeks all the fundamental rights guaranteed by the Weimar Republic pursuant to the Treaty of Versailles
were abolished. The beginning of March 1933 saw the first organized
boycotts of Jews, who constituted less than one per cent of Germany's
total population. In April of that year, all Jews were dismissed from the
federal civil service, except for veterans of the First World War. In the

months that followed, this measure was extended to the professions and universities, targeting both professors and students. Soon press organizations were subjected to similar treatment. A climate of terror and racial oppression very quickly settled over Germany, accompanied by frequent physical attacks on individuals and businesses identified by the authorities as being Jewish, not to mention violent demonstrations and the burning of books by forbidden authors, such as the much-publicized book burnings of May 10, 1933. Although Hitler had made his intentions known with the publication of his book *Mein Kampf* in 1925, his ascent to the highest office in Germany opened an extremely painful chapter for Canadian Jewry, who were forced to helplessly observe the rise of radical and violent anti-Semitism in Germany:

> The takeover of power by the arch-anti-Semite Hitler had at one fell swoop removed constraints on violence toward Jews. Without any order from above and without any coordination, assaults on Jewish businesses and the beating-up of Jews by Nazi thugs became commonplace.[42]

After a lull that lasted only a few months, partly due to the threat of economic reprisals by the American Jewish community and the fear of attracting bad publicity, the tensions in Germany soon resurfaced. At the end of March 1935, a new round of boycotts took place in various cities targeting the most visible Jewish businesses. In September of that same year, the Nazi Party promulgated the Nuremberg Laws, which stripped German Jews of all their civil rights and prohibited marriages and sexual relations with so-called Aryans. These terrible events ignited profound anxiety on this side of the Atlantic because they presaged the long-term intensification of anti-Semitism throughout Europe, particularly in the countries whose democratic fabric had begun to unravel in the Depression. The rise of Nazism coincided with the appearance and consolidation of power of authoritarian regimes hostile to Jews, for example, in Poland, Austria, Rumania, and Hungary. In Germany, the escalation of the murderous attitude toward Jews was confirmed during *Kristallnacht*—the Night of Broken Glass—when pogroms were perpetrated during the night of November 9, 1938, in the majority of German cities. Synagogues were set on fire, and thousands of Jewish businesses were destroyed. Over the next few days, as a consequence of this state-supported violence, nearly 30,000 Jews were taken to concentrations camps.

Although Yiddish-speaking Jews in Canada had come from Eastern European countries where their families were as yet unscathed by Nazi atrocities, when *Kristallnacht* was reported, a collective feeling of despair and helplessness gripped all of Jewish Montreal. Many people feared that in the event of an actual military conflagration these persecutions would spread eastward. The Night of Broken Glass marked the end of the legal emigration of Jews from Germany to Palestine, which the Nazi regime had deviously encouraged for propaganda purposes, making it possible for thousands to narrowly escape certain death. These developments definitively confirmed that the most extreme anti-Semitism had finally become government policy in Germany, waiting to be exported to other vulnerable regions in Europe.

> By now, even though still not centrally coordinated, the "Jewish Question" pervaded all key areas of government; party pressure at headquarters and in the localities for new forms of discrimination was unceasing [. . .] Anti-Semitism had come by now to suffuse all walks of life [in Germany].[43]

The persecutions in Germany cast a dark shadow over the literary and cultural Golden Age in Montreal where Yiddish, for the first time, had found a wide range of opportunities for expression. In September of 1934 Segal, far from indifferent to these events, commented in the *Eagle* that the creation of the Canadian Jewish Congress had finally provided a means for Montreal Jews to defend themselves in frightening circumstances. In the same article the poet described the atmosphere worldwide as "the extremely bitter times in which we are being called upon as a people"[44] and "the strident and savage undercurrents of our brutal times."[45]

The sense of isolation felt by Canadian Jews was aggravated by the presence of imitators of European fascist movements. The members of Adrien Arcand's National Social Christian Party, as well as other groups, claimed that once in power they could immediately implement with impunity the anti-Semitic measures of the Nazi Party in Germany.[46] On this subject, there are numerous authoritative eyewitness accounts by Jewish personalities, including journalist Israel Medres, who wrote: "As the Nazis gained momentum in Germany, the anti-Semitic gangs in Montreal, and in the Province of Quebec as a whole, became more aggressive and militant."[47] Caiserman's observations are equally eloquent: "The Anti-Jewish pogroms in Germany during 1932/33 and the [Jewish] refugees from Germany in various parts of the world made a deep impression in Canada."[48] The fear aroused by anti-Semitic acts and discourse escalated in the late 1930s due to the Canadian government's refusal to admit practically all German and Austrian Jews desperately trying to flee Europe. The discriminatory immigration practices of the Canadian government were perceived by the Jewish community as a denial of justice, a measure intended to keep people out of the country solely because they were Jewish. These developments caused Montreal's Yiddish-speaking writers and artists, whose attention was focussed on their countries of origin where they still had family and friends, to fear the worst. Several of them had come to believe that an ever-increasing danger was threatening to engulf the world they had left behind, and to which they remained attached with their entire being. How would it be possible to work for the development of Yiddish culture in Montreal, which was still only a modest twig uprooted from the vast Eastern European soil, if the living source of this recently transplanted and still fragile culture was running dry? And if misfortune were to strike the Jewish communities of Europe, which for centuries had constituted the bedrock of Yiddish life, would the writers who had settled in the New World find the necessary inspiration and energy for their literary pursuits?

As an attentive observer of Montreal Jewish cultural life, Caiserman surely had sensed what the change of pace in the 1930s had meant for Canadian Yiddish writers. Free of any immediate responsibilities within the Jewish community at that time, Caiserman was able to divide his energies between pursuing more lucrative occupations and reading work by the new talented writers on the Canadian Yiddish cultural scene. Curiously, almost no written evidence of the business dealings of this Zionist activist exists today. In this regard, I found only a brief mention in an obituary in the *The Gazette* in December of 1950: "For a time Mr. Caiserman was engaged in business in Montreal. Several large office buildings downtown were erected on his initiative at that time."[49] It is feasible that Caiserman may have been an agent for these real estate companies, using his skills in accountancy and asset management. By contrast, there is a great deal of information about his cultural and community work in Montreal. The Canadian Jewish Congress Archives houses almost all of the many documents he produced during the 1930s relating to his literary activities, as well as countless examples of his personal correspondence. As Montreal's downtown was being built up and a new commercial centre emerged along Saint Catherine Street West, Caiserman used his free time to assess the surge of recent Canadian poetry in Yiddish. At the same time, he was also interested in identifying the work of Eastern European immigrant writers who wrote in the language of Shakespeare. Change was in the air in the early 1930s in the realm of Anglo-Jewish poetry that presaged a watershed in Montreal literature in the long term. His efforts as a literary critic are detailed in the transcription of a presentation made by Caiserman to an unknown Jewish audience:

> During 1931–32–33, I spent a great deal of time discovering Jewish poets in Canada who had written either in Jewish[50] or English, and who had had their works published, or had merely accumulated unpublished manuscripts. Of 150 such manuscripts, which I received from every part of the country, I selected not less than 43 manuscripts . . . 34 in Jewish, and 9 in English, from 43 poets . . . and published them, in 1934, in one volume, entitled "Jewish Poets in Canada" . . . 221 pages. It was an attempt to appraise the work of these Canadian Jewish poets. The field of Jewish-English prose by Canadian authors had not even been touched.[51]

When it was published in Yiddish in 1934, *Idishe dikhter in kanade* (Jewish Poets in Canada)[52] was the first literary anthology of Canadian poetry by Jewish authors.[53] It was an attempt by Caiserman to give exposure to a new body of literature which, up until then, had been buried in short-lived periodicals or scattered in a variety of collections. After having explored all of Canadian poetry in the 1920s in an unpublished manuscript[54] devoted mainly to Yiddish, Caiserman had finally gathered together all his ideas into one volume and published it in Montreal. In *Idishe dikhter in kanade* he improved upon his previous study by organizing and updating it with excerpts of work by the newest authors. In this sense, Caiserman's anthology reflected the new conditions in which Canadian Jewish literature was evolving in the new decade that had resulted in a greater diversity of style, subject matter, and sources of inspiration. Yiddish literature no longer depended on a handful of literati who were recent immigrants stranded in a cold and immense wilderness but sheltering under a canopy brilliantly lit by new constellations hitherto absent or invisible

ת. מ. קייזערמאן־וויטאל

אידישע דיכטער
אין קאנאדע

געצייכנט פון אלעקסאנדער בערקאוויטש

אַרויסגעגעבן פון פֿאריאג "ניואנסו"
מאָנטרעאל, 1934

Cover page of *Idishe dikhter in kanade*, published in Montreal in 1934
by H. M. Caiserman. (Canadian Jewish Congress Archives.)

to the naked eye. Suddenly, in a few short years, a literary movement
had appeared that seemed to anticipate a true Yiddish cultural renaissance, and the revitalization of Jewish culture as a whole, in Canada.
In 1934, the critic, who stood at the confluence of the persistent stream
of Jewish writing in Canada, did not use the term "Golden Age" or
any other similar expression. As previously observed, such an optimistic characterization was not appropriate for an era of economic
and political uncertainty. This is demonstrated by Caiserman's cau-
tionary language in a speech he made to an audience interested in
Canadian Jewish literature at the time:

> Dealing first with literature in the broader sense . . . poetry, prose,
> journalism, literary criticism, history, etc., there are serious differ-
> ences of opinion regarding the existence of a Canadian Jewish lit-
> erature, although all agree that we have a large and varied group
> of Jewish poets, novelists, publicists and critics who have written
> and published books for many years, both in English and Jewish,
> and who have definitely enriched Canadian-Jewish literature.[55]

The deteriorating situation in 1933 for the Jews of Germany had a galvanizing effect on Caiserman, as on the majority of Jews in Canada,
resulting in a renewed determination to become actively engaged in
the community. Politically isolated, unable to influence government
policy with regard to admitting Jews fleeing Nazi persecution into
Canada, and themselves the object of verbal attacks by notorious
anti-Semites in Montreal, Canadian Jewish leaders wanted to openly
protest against the fate of the Jews of Germany.[56] To this end, they res-
urrected an organization that had proven itself capable of an unprecedented mobilization of community resources in a previous time of
crisis during World War I, namely the Canadian Jewish Congress
of 1919. It was proposed that a large demonstration take place in
Montreal to protest the treatment of Jews in Germany. To respond
appropriately to the magnitude of the Nazi atrocities, a conference of
the various Montreal Jewish organizations was convened in March of
1933, whose secretary was none other than H. M. Caiserman. A committee of twenty-five influential people, many of whom were Yiddish
speakers, was elected at this conference with the task of renting the
Mount Royal arena on Mount Royal Avenue,[57] in heart of the immigrant neighbourhood. These individuals also ensured that high level
political representatives would speak at the event, scheduled for April
6, 1933. On that day, 15,000 people came to hear the mayor of Montreal,
Fernand Rinfret, as well as Senator Raoul Dandurand, then president
of the League of Nations, denounce the terror unleashed against the
Jews by the Hitler regime. They were followed by Francophone representatives of the federal and provincial governments, Rabbi Harry J.
Stern of the Temple Emanu-El, H. M. Caiserman, and a dignitary from
the Protestant Church. When the Yiddish-speaking activists realized
that their mobilization against the Nazi persecutions had attained its
full objective, and so quickly, they decided to consolidate the gains
made by the protest meeting by setting up a committee to revive the
Canadian Jewish Congress. Over the next few months, Caiserman

played such a key role in the numerous efforts to raise awareness about the world situation that at the end of 1933 he was once more elected General Secretary of the Canadian Jewish Congress, a position he held until his death in 1950.

Despite the very onerous administrative duties this post must have entailed, the archives of the Canadian Jewish Congress offer up countless references to Caiserman's efforts during the 1930s on behalf of people aspiring to careers in the cultural sphere. They also contain many literary manuscripts, mostly unpublished but signed by him, among them poems in several languages. For example, in December of 1936 Caiserman wrote to a Toronto impresario for help in organizing a Canadian tour by Chayele Grober from Bialystok, Poland, an actress famous in the Yiddish world as one of the founders of the Hebrew-language Habimah theatre troupe in Moscow.[58] During the Spanish Civil War, Caiserman also kept up a lively correspondence with the flamboyant Emma Goldman. Goldman, with whom he shared an intense aversion for Communist ideology, had most likely visited him in his home on Esplanade. Several Jewish community leaders would no doubt have been astonished by the tone of the General Secretary's letters to Goldman. In a letter of March 16, 1936, Caiserman wrote: "A loving impulse makes me detach myself from my superhuman endeavours to dictate a few lines to you."[59] Caiserman's ongoing commitment to artists was often coupled with boundless admiration for young women endowed with musical talent, which sometimes led him to construct imaginary romances. At the end of 1931, for instance, the Caisermans hosted in their home an impromptu classical concert by three Eastern European musicians passing through Montreal, including a violinist by the name of Ibolyka. So enchanted was Caiserman by this event that he sent her a poem with the following note: "Please accept this little token as a compliment of the season, and the little poem as a salutation and very deepest admiration, that my mind and heart hold in store for you, dearest person and blessed artist."[60] Other artistic performances in the same intimate venue prompted Caiserman to send three young women increasingly engaging letters, among them this poem in English which, despite the occasional awkwardness, conveys his ardent admiration:

> Days run like rivers
> Into the tomorrow of eternity,
> And my mind invents your presence

Continuously in my heart
Like the perpetual march of time.
Let my modest rhyme
Sing my adoration
Into your musical souls,
The way my mind invents
Your presence in my heart . . .[61]

Idishe dikhter in kanade (1934)

During this turbulent period, Caiserman continued to pay close attention to Yiddish literature and Yiddish writers in Montreal, as demonstrated by the 1934 publication of the anthology entitled *Idishe dikhter
in kanade* (Jewish Poets in Canada). Until then it had been impossible
to have a clear idea regarding Yiddish literary activity in Canada
without expending considerable effort. Apart from a few small books
published at the author's expense with limited distribution, including
those of Segal, Yiddish writing could only reach a wider readership
by means of the *Jewish Daily Eagle* and the few short-lived periodicals published from time to time by the Montreal or Toronto intelligentsia. Occasionally, the most talented Canadian authors acquired
a following abroad, especially in the United States and Poland, but it
was difficult to regularly monitor fleeting praise from afar. To attain
his goal of compiling an anthology of Canadian Yiddish writing,
Caiserman decided to include only those authors who had published
in Canadian literary journals and anthologies. He personally corresponded with scores of poets, asking them to send him their recent
manuscripts. As Caiserman could not claim to know everything there
was to know about Yiddish writing in Canada, he had to conduct thor-
ough research before writing his book. He also consulted with writers
who were knowledgeable about Yiddish writing in three Canadian
cities, namely, Ida Maze, who had immigrated to Montreal in 1908,
Benjamin Katz, who had come to Toronto in 1921, and Jacob Zipper
who had lived in Winnipeg in the mid-1920s. Because he was dealing
with literature produced during a time of mass migration and relative
economic instability, Caiserman acknowledged in the introduction to
his book that it had taken him two years just to collect the texts from
which he made his final choice. In his opinion, the time had finally
come in 1934 to bring "under one roof"[62] all the poets who had made
a name for themselves in Canadian Yiddish-language publications, as

well as the still small number of newer poets who had chosen to veer off into English, without, however, abandoning their Jewish roots. Paradoxically, time was now of the essence because the earliest traces of Canadian Yiddish writing, in existence for barely a single generation, were gradually disappearing.

> I have the feeling that the time has now come to bring together the various poets who laid the foundation for Canadian Yiddish poetry, and to compile a partial list of their work to prevent it from getting lost.[63]

Nevertheless, in *Idishe dikhter in kanade*, Caiserman had not wanted to formally classify the poets according to the merit of their work or the extent of their talent. He believed that a nascent body of literature ought to include more modestly successful work that reflected the fact that the general course of its development was still uncertain. To deny less accomplished authors entry to the pantheon of Yiddish literary creativity was like trying to keep a forest of only giant age-old trees while excluding young seedlings. Although Yiddish literature had occasionally produced outstanding work, most often it consisted of less successful attempts. "A [national] literature does not consist only of the most gifted writers, but of average and less talented writers as well."[64] For Caiserman it was essential to depict the cultural environment that had made possible the appearance of such intense literary activity during a time when the Yiddish-speaking community was still recovering from the trauma of immigration, and struggling to find a place for itself in Canadian society. The real achievement of the Montreal Jewish community over the previous twenty years was to have succeeded in creating a space for artistic expression where all writers, ranging from the most promising to the least distinguished, would be welcomed and recognized. "To do so it was necessary to cultivate an environment that would stimulate creativity, struggle, and more creativity, within a large and creatively active collectivity."[65] Nonetheless, Caiserman chose to showcase nine Yiddish authors, namely Simon Nepom, Jacob Isaac Segal, Abraham Shlomo Shkolnikov, Esther Segal, Ida Maze, Rabbi Yehuda Leib Zlotnik, Yudika, Noah Isaac Gotlib, and Sholem Shtern, as well as four poets who wrote in English.[66] He also decided to present Canadian Yiddish literature chronologically in order to show the steady increase in the number of writers and readers in Canada since 1905. This might have been unnecessary in the case of well-established national literatures in countries that were fully developed culturally, explained Caiserman, but it was a different matter for a body of literature born less than twenty years earlier, and transplanted onto foreign soil.

Since the poems in *Idishe dikhter in kanade* either had appeared in literary journals with limited print runs, or had never been published at all, Caiserman chose to include a large number of excerpts in his anthology, without providing much commentary. He believed that readers would otherwise never have access to these poems, and that in this way he was helping to publicize literature which, in 1934, did not yet enjoy the benefits of independent publishing houses or objective literary criticism. Caiserman also elected not to pass judgment on the artistic or literary merit of the work he had gathered into a single volume. In a letter to David Rome, dated July 1935, he acknowledged: "You're right when you say that my intention and approach are not artistic but cultural. The forward [*sic*] to the book makes it perfectly clear."[67] The Introduction to *Idishe dikhter in kanade* made no secret of Caiserman's intention to announce the continual progress of Canadian Yiddish literature and to clearly define its contours: "I make no claims that [this work] has purely artistic significance. I am presenting my book to Jewish readers with the modesty of a man who did his work with honesty and love."[68] Who but a very few would have suspected that Yiddish poetry in Canada at the time boasted twenty-five noteworthy representatives, that it had generated four high-quality literary magazines, and that it was essentially being perpetuated in the work of fourteen Anglophone authors? Although Caiserman does not refer to this fact in his book, poetry was the most developed and successful form of Yiddish literature in Canada, where there were few Yiddish novelists, playwrights or essayists. In the year 1934, a survey of Yiddish poetry alone would attest to the vitality of Yiddish writing in Canada and underscore its finest achievements aesthetically and formally. It should be noted that Caiserman compiled *Idishe dikhter in kanade* at a time when the international situation had brought Eastern European immigration to a standstill. Meanwhile, the generation which had begun arriving in 1905 had made great strides artistically and welcomed a new group of younger authors. In a sense, this anthology marked an important stage in the production of Canadian Jewish literature. After 1934, the state of Yiddish literature would change very little, and its main practitioners would stay the course until 1948, when the last group of Yiddish writers, all Holocaust survivors of one kind or another, reached the shores of Canada.

The process of compiling *Idishe dikhter in kanade* had also exposed a fundamental difference of opinion between Caiserman and the poet Segal, to which the latter clearly refers in his preface. In fact, the debate between critic and poet sheds light in a unique way on the emergence Yiddish literature in Montreal in the wake of World War I, and the direction it would take during the 1940s and 1950s. As Caiserman admits in his introduction, he had been encouraged in his compilation efforts by the novelist Moshe Shmuelsohn, an eye-witness to the earliest beginnings of Yiddish writing in Montreal. Caiserman had also received moral support from the actor Chayale Grober, and in particular from his friend Segal. The poet was at Caiserman's side throughout the entire process. The extent of their collaboration can be measured by the following passage written by Segal: "Where else, in what other Jewish home in this city, have I seen the Jewish book shine like the most exquisite jewel? Nowhere else, in no other house, have I felt so at home [. . .].[69] Segal, one of the original creators of that literature, conceived of his fellow writers as a cultural elite aspiring to the highest summits of art and beauty, in a spirit of intimate communion with the greatest Jewish artists scattered throughout the Eastern European Jewish diaspora. Welcomed to New York by the modernist school, appreciated in Warsaw by the Khalyastre group, and revered in Buenos Aires, Segal was addressing himself to a select audience and publishing his work in literary journals of superior quality. It would never have occurred to him to associate himself with writers who would never have more than local significance, and whose creativity never took them beyond conventional themes, particularly in a cultural milieu like that of Montreal, which was still in its infancy. Aware of the magnitude of his own talent, and striving for recognition on the international scene, Segal found it difficult to accept the idea that Caiserman was giving his attention to every word ever published in Yiddish in Canada. What good did it do, thought Segal, to place all Montreal poets on an equal footing.

> When I first leafed through parts of your book and saw how much space you gave to the many people involved in the local cultural and literary life, it was quite difficult for me to accept the inclusiveness of your approach. Over and over again we discussed this, and argued about it. Again and again we debated the issue without reaching an agreement.[70]

Caiserman, who did not share Segal's views on literary creation, had understood that a broader movement was evolving in Montreal's Yiddish cultural life that urgently needed to be taken it into account. He wanted to reconcile the type of writing dictated by an individual-istic impulse with the goal of reaching artistic heights, with another, more pragmatic, cultural development that served the more pressing objectives of the various educational institutions, labour organiza-tions, and Yiddish-speaking community groups. Was it so regrettable that certain writers did not exemplify the highest spheres of modernist art but wrote instead about the more immediate realities of Canadian Jewish life? Did all poets have to be endowed with exceptional talent and strive for international glory? In a truly national literature was there no room for more modest aspirations and successes on a smaller scale, inspired by family life, the slow passage of time, and day-to-day hardships? Caiserman believed that the time had come for Montreal Yiddish literature to cease being a unqiue phenomenon, born unex-pectedly in a faraway country not particularly hospitable to culture. What harm did it do if Yiddish literature occasionally embodied the hopes for social advancement of a rapidly growing community in a new country? Between these two irreconcilable poles, was there no place for the compromise envisioned by *Idishe dikhter in kanade*, which traced the development of Yiddish literature in its social context, and included all forms of creativity, from the most sublime to the most spontaneous and mundane? Segal, who for a generation had been generally accepted as the preeminent representative of Yiddish *belles lettres*, conceded to Caiserman that a divide had recently been bridged in this regard.

I also understood that you were able to objectively grasp more quickly than I, the present moment in historical perspective. You saw literary creation, and not only here [in Canada], through a cultural lens, and therefore you would be able to create a more complete and comprehensive overview, and gather together everything that has a certain intrinsic value. You simply cherish anything that has made the slightest ripple in our local cultural atmosphere. You hold it dear, not allowing it to be swept away by the wind. I also understand very well the humanism of your approach. You go about your task with the trepidation of someone who must, and rightly so, preserve whatever has the slightest cultural or literary value for the masses, who barely give it heed.[71]

Caiserman as Literary Historian

What historical and cultural conclusions did Caiserman draw from assembling the material for *Idishe dikhter in kanade*? His first finding was that there were two main directions in Canadian Yiddish literature, which appeared at the same time, both profoundly influenced by the example set by earlier American Yiddish literature. To begin with, Caiserman noted the rise of the New York literary movement at the end of the nineteenth century, represented by Morris Rosenfeld, David Edelstadt, Morris Winchevsky, and Joseph Bovshover (1873–1915) that focussed on the working class and the clothing factories. Proletarian writers, militant socialists, and the bards of productive labour, these poets echoed the call for social justice and the coming of a world free of the political, national and cultural oppression of capitalism. The realistic style of their work sometimes resembled that of a pamphlet, slogan, or manifesto because it was often composed for the sole purpose of rallying the masses to the ideological struggle. One example of this type of poet is Moishe Leib Halpern, an American Yiddish poet who was living in Montreal from April to October of 1912, during the first general strike in the garment sector led by the Tailors' Union.[72] In June, in the midst of this confrontation, Halpern, with the aim of galvanizing the workers published a poem in the Montreal newspaper *Di Folkstsaytung* entitled *"Tsum strayk"* (To the strike) (see Appendix 23), still famous today.[73]

To the Strike

Arise, arise, you've slogged enough!
Enough you've suffered hunger, want,
and sold your blood for bread.
Let stand the wheel, thrust out your chest
And come with us and fight!
Leave the shop, the cage of slaves.
Arise and join the strike.[74]

Among the principal representatives of proletarian literature in Canada were Simon Nepom, who published a book entitled *In gerangl* [In struggle] in Toronto in 1926, and Sholem Shtern, whose collection *Noentkayt* [Closeness] appeared in Toronto in 1929. This literary approach was, at various times, adopted by A. S. Shkolnikov, his wife

Esther Segal, Nehemia Segal, Hannah Steinberg, and N. I. Gotlib, all
of whom were only average poets in Caiserman's estimation, nothing
more. As a general rule, Caiserman believed that proletarian writers
had descended into shallowness, and that the majority of their poems
lacked true literary value, especially those of Benjamin Katz, whose
book *Baginen: lider* [At dawn: poems] came out in 1928. The same went
for Shimon Perl, the author of *Fun khaver tsu khaver* [From one com-
rade to another], and Israel Trut. The only one to find favour with
Caiserman was Sholem Shtern, as the following excerpt from a 1942
article demonstrates:

> Another talented poet is the ambulant bookseller, Sholem Shtern.
> The son of a *shoyket*, a Talmudic scholar, Shulem Shtern's first
> poems were based on themes of Jewish Lore. Later came his
> "Sanatorium Songs" which were received favourably. It became
> evident that Shtern was talented. His proletarian songs are the
> only artistic ones of that category to have appeared in Canadian
> Jewish literature.[75]

In Canada, the relative failure of proletarian poetry paved the way
for more personal and expressive writing inspired by the American
literary schools *Di Yunge* and *In Zikh*. These later schools became
known in Montreal when their members began accepting invitations from the Yiddish institutions of the Plateau Mont-Royal, where
they received a warm welcome. Among them were Mani Leib, Isaac
Raboy, Menachem Boraisha, Zishe Weinper, H. Leivick, Aaron Glanz-
Leyeles, and Jacob Glatstein. In 1934 Caiserman, who had a particular
affection for lyric poetry, believed that this type of poetry represented
the pinnacle of Montreal Yiddish literature, and would prove to be
the most promising in the long term. Modernist in form, subjective in
approach, and strongly influenced by the bold new literary trends in
Europe, it appeared to be forward-looking and on the verge of intense
literary creativity. Among those attracted to this movement, first and
foremost, was J. I. Segal, but also lesser luminaries like Ida Maze and
Yudika, who both used the themes of family life and domestic labour
to express their most intimate thoughts. In Caiserman's view, Segal
had distinguished himself by being the first of the earlier generation
of poets to enjoy a long and fruitful career. The critic also believed
that Pesach Matenko, who had published *Lider* [Poems] in Toronto in
1917, had made the right choice when he gave up writing altogether,

as had Ezekiel Bronstein, Mordecai Miller, and Hershl Galski-Gayel, whose work had first appeared all at the same time in Winnipeg. After fifteen years, Caiserman came to the conclusion that the publication in Montreal of the poetry collection *Fun mayn velt* in 1918, and the launching of the journal *Kanade* in March of 1919 in Toronto, had constituted the true inception of Canadian Yiddish literature.

> Almost at that same time J. I. Segal published first book *Fun mayn velt*, which was immediately recognized by critics both here and in Europe, as an important poetic achievement. [. . .] I should also point out that his poems, which appeared in the journal *Kanade*, heralded the arrival of a new poet in Yiddish literature. [. . .] Segal's participation in *Kanade* was an important literary event, and promised great accomplishments in the field of poetry.[76]

While Segal had pride of place in *Idishe dikhter in kanade* by virtue of his international reputation and the breadth of his accomplishments as a poet (twenty-five pages are devoted to him), Caiserman also gave prominence to Ida Maze, even though the modesty and simplicity of her writing were on a different scale. In a cultural milieu that was limited in its size and influence, the role played by activists and literary salons was of prime importance. By virtue of her personality alone, and the warmth with which she welcomed aspiring writers into her home on Esplanade Avenue, Maze herself became a kind of institution, providing a space where Yiddish literature could find expression, develop, and reach its readers. Indeed, the fact that poetry collections were printed, that reviews had appeared, and that writers could occasionally read their work in a public place, was not enough. It was still necessary for the most talented authors to exchange ideas, receive critical feedback, and feel that they belonged to a generational cohort united by a common artistic journey. As Caiserman recognized from the outset, within the Yiddish-speaking community in Montreal this vital function was assumed by a few individuals who generously gave of their time and energy. "Even if all these years Ida Maze had not written a single one of her many poems, or supported, influenced, served, helped, encouraged, elevated and inspired everything that had to do with humanity and art, her interesting personality alone would have been a wondrous poetic phenomenon."[77] Caiserman was well-situated to appreciate the importance of literary salons, since he and his wife frequently opened their home to artists of every description.

What is more, his activities as a literary critic were most certainly honed thanks to his personal contact with some of Montreal's foremost Yiddish poets, primarily J. I. Segal. Without this ongoing and constant contact between writers and critics, Yiddish literature would never have enjoyed such resounding success over the course of the 1930s.

Caiserman's work as a critic also introduced the public to a certain number of fresh, young, talented writers who had published during the 1920s and 1930s in Canadian literary journals, and highlighted the pivotal role played by Yiddish periodicals dedicated to poetry, as well as the occasional novella or short story. Some of these newcomers, such as Shlomo Halperin and Leibush Rosenberg, made their debut in the Toronto periodical *Kanade*, while others like Leib Bercovitch, Shlomo Schneider, and Asher Royzn, contributed in various ways to *Royerd, Nyuansn, Epokhe, Baginen, Heftn* and *In Gevirbl*. On the same subject, Caiserman also mentioned poets Abraham L. Seltser, Gershon Pomerantz, Meyer Segal, and Mirl Erdberg-Shatan. Several of these writers had written and published their work in Eastern European Yiddish literary periodicals before immigrating to America. However, the majority were very young when they arrived in Canada and, like their predecessors who settled in Montreal prior to World War I, began to write only after they had settled in the New World. A certain percentage, including Myer Segal and Leib Bercovitch, were drawn to proletarian themes and tried to promote socialism in their poetry, while others belonged more generally to the Introspectivist and Modernist movements popular in New York. Although these young poets early in their careers became part of Canadian Yiddish literature , their place in the long term was not yet assured because, as Caiserman remarked in his public lecture in 1942, "Not all writers during the last quarter century have shown progress and those who have received universal recognition are few."[78] Nonetheless, Yiddish literature in several Canadian cities produced worthy representatives whose work elicited the critical acclaim of Caiserman. Already there were many more Yiddish poets than ten years earlier when there were only a few talented but isolated poets appreciated by only a very small audience.

Idishe dikhter in kanade was the first attempt to write a history of Canadian Yiddish literature by concentrating mainly on poetry, which at the time was the most developed literary form. Segal was not mistaken when he stated in his Introduction that Caiserman was doing pioneering work: "What a debt of gratitude will be owed to you by historians of general Yiddish literature for having presented them with such a large collection of documents. I know that you will have truly earned their great appreciation and thanks."[79] The book also introduces quite a significant number of young writers from modest social origins, including those who were barely Canadianized, and still focussing their efforts on Eastern Europe. It also brought to light their tight-knit milieu comprised of individuals deeply rooted in Judaism, who were essentially developing their poetic skills without exposure to the two main Canadian literary traditions. In this sense, Yiddish literature seemed to be a third way, an alternative option that had the benefit of strong international connections while finding expression in a literary landscape dominated since the nineteenth century by Canada's two official languages. Despite its recent emergence in Canada, Yiddish poetry often opted for modernist forms and favoured subject matter inspired by a variety of progressive social ideologies, such as socialism, communism, and trade unionism. Most of all, Yiddish literature differed from the two other literatures that had earlier taken root in the country, English and French, in that all its authors had been born abroad. Canadian Yiddish poetry, having surfaced during a great migratory wave, provided a fresh and detached view of Canadian society, free of any particular historical or conceptual constraints.

In 1934 Caiserman had provided a snapshot of Yiddish literature in its early stages of development, when it was still difficult to foresee its ultimate creative progress. Essentially, Canadian poets writing in Yiddish, without having had the time to reach a certain level of artistic maturity, formed a universe still strongly influenced by the continent where they were born. Nonetheless, a new phenomenon appeared in the early 1930s that seemed to predict a major reorientation in Canadian Jewish literature. A new generation born and educated in Canada was turning to the language of Shakespeare to express its feelings, to fulfil its literary ambitions, and to deepen its relationship with the host society. Caiserman could not ignore these new voices. He chose to make room for them alongside the Yiddish poets in *Idishe dikhter in kanade*. Still barely perceptible during this era, the transition to English signalled a radical shift in Canadian Jewish writing in the long term. For the first time, poets of Eastern European Jewish origin were choosing to make a career for themselves in a non-Jewish language, which meant addressing Jewish life within the context of a Christian society. The transition was not without complex and even painful problems. Having left a comparatively closed Yiddish world, in the broader society Anglophone Jewish authors ran the risk of incurring contempt or marginalization based on their cultural origins. Even so, the extremely strong attraction of English quickly quelled any misgivings, especially when it became clear that the English language would open the door to more advantageous career prospects. All the same, Caiserman noted that several Anglophone Jewish poets remained attached to their religious heritage, and were able to distinguish themselves from their Anglo-Saxon colleagues, as in the case of a very promising newcomer by the name of Abraham M. Klein:

> Not only are many of his poems, such as Portraits of a Minyan, The Kaddish, Koheleth, The Words of Plauni-Ben-Plauni *to Job*, Gestures Hebraic, Dance Chassidic, Nehemiah, and dozens of others, on themes derived from the wealth of Jewish sources, but he is also Jewish in outlook and temperament [. . .] .[80]

However, the hour when English would come to dominate Canadian Jewish literature had not yet sounded in 1934. Aware of the fact that Canadian Jewish literature was still primarily Yiddish and inspired by the Eastern European tradition, Caiserman undertook to translate into Yiddish the verses of Klein and Miron, although in the book he presented them first in the original English, followed by his Yiddish version.[81] *Idishe dikhter in kanade* was to be the first of at least four studies of the various literary genres explored by Canadian Yiddish writers. At least that is what Caiserman stated in June of 1935 when he applied for a travel pass from the Canadian National Railway, in order to conduct interviews for this purpose in other Canadian cities: "I am now engaged in collecting material for a second and third book, namely, *Jewish Prose in Canada* and *The History of the Jewish Press of this Dominion*, this in connection with another work on *Social & Economic Research*."[82] His books on Jewish prose and the Jewish press never materialized, most likely due to external circumstances, which forced him to abandon his literary research. After 1934, the critic and historian of Yiddish literature was obliged to spend the bulk of his time contending with growing anti-Jewish sentiment in Canada, and establishing a Canadian Jewish Congress capable of combatting fascist ideologies. Given these developments, Caiserman's anthology of poetry would remain his last major effort to compile and study Yiddish literature in Canada. In addition to the unfinished biography of his friend Segal, mentioned earlier, and some studies that appeared in both Yiddish and English in the Canadian Jewish press, Caiserman made a final attempt toward the end of the 1940s to gather into a single volume the work of several Canadian Yiddish poets. At least that is what is suggested by the large amount of correspondence dated 1947 and 1948 in the Caiserman Archive of the Canadian Jewish Congress, which also contains a multitude of uncatalogued manuscripts belonging to Ida Maze, Mordecai Miller, Jacob Isaac Segal, Abraham Nisnevitsh, Mordecai Yoffe, Chava Rosenfarb, Mirl Erdberg-Shatan, Hanna Steinberg, Moses Mordecai Shaffir, Ruth Rubin, Mrs. G. Wiseman, Benjamin Katz, Broche Kopstein and Shlomo Zalman Schneirson. In the end, death surprised Caiserman before this project could finally come to fruition.

The Poet at His Peak

In the mid-1930s, while Caiserman was gradually stepping away from the Montreal Yiddish literary scene that he had done so much to promote and structure, Segal was reaching the peak of his ability. Caiserman, consumed by his community responsibilities and soon to be drawn into the whirlwind of World War II, could nonetheless contemplate from afar the irresistible force of Montreal Yiddish letters. Already, the achievements of the major writers, whom he had helped to emerge from the shadows, were beginning to spill over the country's borders. Some authors were even winning recognition in the world's largest centres of Yiddish creativity like Warsaw, Vilna, Kiev, and Berlin, not to mention New York, Buenos Aires and Johannesburg. At the centre of this sudden efflorescence, Segal stood out from his Montreal colleagues because of the reach of his reputation and the cogency of his writing, a fact corroborated by several eloquent testimonials from that era: "Although a resident of Montreal, with his poetry J. I. Segal crossed all the borders that divide the Jewish people into different countries, and won recognition throughout the Jewish world."[83] Segal was now being invited to publish his work in the most prestigious literary journals in both New York and Eastern Europe. In 1928 none other than Nachman Meisel wrote to him soliciting a contribution to the influential Warsaw literary weekly *Literarishe Bleter*: "At the same time, I would like to ask you to send us the occasional article on a timely subject or about a recently published book. It has been a long time since your work has appeared in our publication."[84] Meisel's offer was duplicated that same year by *Yidishe velt* [Jewish world], a monthly devoted to literature, criticism, art and culture, also based in the Polish capital.[85] In 1932 Meisel again made a request on behalf of *Literarishe Bleter* for a new contribution from Segal.[86] These contacts quickly bore fruit when an article by Segal entitled *"Der goyrl fun dem idishn dikhter"* (The fate of the Yiddish poet)[87] appeared in this prestigious journal in 1933. In 1934, Melekh Ravitch highly recommended Segal as a foreign correspondent to the *Post* of London, a Yiddish daily looking for contacts in America.[88] A few years later, in 1940, Ravitch also asked Segal to submit book reviews to the journal *Der Veg*, published in Mexico City.[89] At this same time, Segal contributed to several literary publications in Buenos Aires and Paris.

These increasingly persistent solicitations from abroad were not to change the poet's career prospects in the long run. Returning to his first adopted city at the beginning of the 1930s after a long and difficult sojourn in America's cultural capital, Segal was certain that his literary destiny would henceforth be inextricably linked with Montreal. After having attempted to join the great literary adventure of the New York group *Di Yunge*, by 1928 the poet had little choice but to return to Canada, which had witnessed the birth of his writing career, and presided over his first steps in Yiddish literature. Incapable of making ends meet in the highly competitive economic environment south of the border, Segal reintegrated himself into Montreal's much smaller Jewish community and its artistic milieu, which he deemed decidedly more provincial. Melekh Ravitch, now in Melbourne, Australia after having fled Warsaw, wrote to Segal in 1936 to try to rescue him from his pessimism, and convince him of the advantages offered by Montreal to a Yiddish writer: "You're complaining that you have to stay in Montreal, 10 hours away from New York . . . What should I say being here in Melbourne, 800 hours from New York . . . . At least I'm happy that I left Poland."[90] It is doubtful that these good-humoured reproaches could have done very much to lighten Segal's mood. His New York experience left him bitter and impatient with the narrow-mindedness of Montreal Jews. This nagging regret would manifest itself in many ways, both in his poetry and in his relationships with people in the community involved in more practical pursuits, as, for example, in this poem aptly entitled "Montreal":

Montreal

I look through the window in my wall:
the passersby –my friends once, all.
Now they are merchants in this land
and community leaders – all.

That one claims the orphan's home,
this one the cemetery grounds.
Every little man – now great –
People hold in high regard.

As for me, I have such wealth
As many treasures as the sun.
As much freedom as the sea.
Who in this town knows not thereof?

The merchants have a word of praise
for my divinely given grace,
and loud extol the golden dust
of my poetic, rhythmic pace.[91]

On the other hand, Segal's return to Montreal creates additional difficulties for a biographer because the poet abruptly stopped his regular
correspondence with all those who now lived in the same city, leaving
fewer opportunities to know his views on certain important issues.
His exchange of letters with Caiserman came to a halt, even though
the two men maintained their unwavering friendship, and often met
at Yiddish cultural events. The poet and the literary critic shared such
a lengthy personal relationship, and complemented each other so perfectly in the artistic sphere, that they would remain closely connected
to the very end. This is confirmed by a short note of 1937 in which
Caiserman described to his friend Segal his emotional reaction upon
reading one of the latter's articles: "My dear J. I. Segal, I have just read
your review of Leivick's *Lider fun gan eydn* [Poems from the Garden of
Eden], and my heart felt such joy, such beautiful singing, that I must
send you my thanks and my blessings."[92] In addition, after Segal had
moved back to Montreal, the *Yidishe Folkshule* imposed a schedule on
him which, from the early 1930s, changed very little over the next
quarter century. According to his two daughters, Sylvia and Annette,
Segal had no social life outside the Yiddish literary milieu and some
of his Montreal mentors, such as Caiserman, who formed for him

an aesthetically rich and meaningful world apart.[93] In the presence of his children and among family members, the poet maintained a discrete reserve as if he were keeping his distance from the outside world, especially when it came to his work as a school teacher and the students he taught privately. Early every morning Segal wrote at length at the kitchen table, most often in a haphazard stream of words and images that at first he did not seek to organize in any particular way, as if he were completely in the control of his poetic inspiration.[94] Presumably most of these notes remained as drafts, or later became the basis for more finished work. The writer Chava Rosenfarb, who came to Montreal in 1950, witnessed Segal's writing process during this era:

> Segal himself was so frightened of his muse, so terrified that it might, heaven forbid, play a trick on him at night while he was asleep and run away, that every morning, without waiting for so-called inspiration, he sat down at his desk and wrote two entire poems, as if to reassure himself that his muse was still faithful to him. Among them were good poems, genuine poetry. Like a master tradesman who is always cleaning and shining his tools, so Segal sharpened and polished his tool, the Yiddish word.[95]

In public, Segal had a dazzling personality. During cultural events, he assumed the role of a poet revered by all. His ascendancy was evident whenever Montreal's Yiddish artistic elite hosted a distinguished guest from New York or elsewhere. According to his daughters, the demands of Segal's literary career took precedence over all other facets of life, including his immediate family, his regular employment, or the exigencies of daily life. Starting in 1932, Segal became the central figure of Montreal's Yiddish intelligentsia and found himself constantly sought after to display his art or participate in get-togethers of a literary nature. Throughout this period, the Jewish Public Library hosted many evenings where he played the role of poet laureate, honoured by a cultural milieu eager to pay homage to his exceptional talent. This tradition was carried on even after his death at ceremonies commemorating his life and work. Not one of the six volumes of poetry he published after 1930, while he was still alive, passed unnoticed in Montreal's Jewish community. The same was true of his numerous contributions to various Canadian and American anthologies as well as his two posthumously published books. Despite the constant eagerness of the Montreal Yiddish-speaking milieu to give him recognition, Segal was also known to be intractable with those in his immediate entourage. In private, he did not hesitate to complain about the narrowness of the Jewish milieu in the neighbourhoods at the foot of Mount Royal, in which he found himself confined. Temperamental, and completely absorbed in his art, the poet often suffered from isolation, incomprehension, and the pain of not being able to regularly participate in the incomparably more exciting New York Yiddish scene. Although idolized in certain circles, Segal throbbed with an inner passion difficult to communicate, to which only a select few could have access, and which had no outlet other than his nuanced, delicate, and subtle poetry. To him, writing represented a secret interior journey that consumed all his energy and required his best efforts, day after day, year after year.

> Contradictory and powerful feelings were constantly fighting one another in his heart like on a battlefield. At the same time, practically at the very same moment, he could love and hate with passion. . . In reality he was not one of those poet hermits who find inspiration in seclusion. He sought out people, and he loved to surround himself with them. He was infatuated with Jewish life in Montreal, especially the literary milieu, and he could talk about it very lovingly. At the same time he was bitter, cynical, and sarcastic about the same milieu, and yearned to get away from it.[96]

The Great Mystical Watershed

Segal's return to Montreal also marked a definitive reorientation in his poetry, as much in form as in subject matter. This shift asserted itself in *Lirik* in 1930, described by Caiserman as "the first volume of deeply religious lyrical poetry,"[97] again in 1934 in *Mayn nigun*, and once more in 1937 in *Di drite sude*, "the third book of religious, national and social poetry in lyrical form."[98] During this stage of his career, the poet for, the first time, allowed himself to contemplate the Jewish religious tradition as his fundamental source of inspiration and the prevailing motif in his poetry. Paradoxically, it seemed as if by constantly delving deeper into modernity Segal, in fact, found a religious feeling free of emotional conflict and social dictates. For the poet, it was not a matter of returning to his childhood steeped in Hasidism and the Talmud, but rather of going beyond strict religious observance into a new and infinitely more abstract and spiritual sphere. In a universe where the God of Moses revealed himself to human beings and the great Jewish mystics made their appearance, Segal could find meaning in his own existence and was at liberty to explore his own interior landscape. By opening himself up to the poetic imagery and symbolism of sacred texts, ranging from the Bible to the teachings of the Baal Shem Tov, Segal became aware that he was entering a domain of unsurpassed poetic splendour. The fact that his exploration was taking place outside any religious framework, and without subscribing to a belief in the divine origin of the world, made him all the more receptive. A Jew by birth and the product of an Orthodox Jewish education, Segal made this transition all the more easily because he was able to tap into the vast cultural repertoire of the Yiddish language while still powerfully attached to ancient Hebrew literature. He effortlessly discovered a vision of a world that dated back to the opening verses of Genesis and had persisted over several millennia with a remarkable continuity.

In making the leap in the early 1930s to poetry with strong traditional Jewish underpinnings, Segal seemed to be rejecting a part of the avant-garde credo, proclaimed by *Di Yunge* twenty years earlier, which he had espoused during his stay in New York. For the members of this literary school, adherence to a fixed belief system seemed contrary to free personal expression, and would only stifle, little by little, the development of Yiddish belles-lettres. Certainly, among the many obstacles standing in the way of art for art's sake was the ideological stance of the various labour movements, whether anarchist, socialist, or Marxist. However, *Di Yunge* also considered the strict application of the legalistic dogma of traditional Judaism to be an impediment. Raised in the Eastern European Jewish religious tradition, but aspiring to membership in the great international fraternity of modernist writers, the new generation of North American Yiddish writers turned its back on its own Jewish heritage to pursue what it considered to be the more universal themes of introspection. For Segal, the introduction of religious content into his writing also signified a rejection of leftist ideology that demanded of its followers a scrupulous adherence to a party line, which he believed posed a threat to individual creativity and any form of Jewish cultural identity. At the dawn of the 1930s Segal opted for a rigorous modernity but did not shy away from liberally exploiting the historical and spiritual sources of traditional Judaism. This was completely in keeping with the educational philosophy of the Peretz and Jewish People's Schools, institutions upon which his career as a writer depended, and which professed to be teaching their students the Jewish tradition but from a purely cultural and historical perspective. For the poet, the more ancient forms of Jewish culture provided a complex tapestry of motifs and images of undeniable artistic value which resonated powerfully within him. Moreover, it was difficult for Segal to express his abiding attachment to his maternal home and his childhood without returning to Judaism and without embarking upon a long and sometimes perilous exploration of his Hasidic roots:

> A heart nurtured on suffering and sorrow, he longed for his childhood, for his birthplace. It seemed to him that there, in his former home, was an entirely familiar Jewish, pious, and pure life, in which he would have felt at home to this day. He revered Rabbi Pinchas of Korets, the most "innocent and pure" of the Hasidic *rebbes*.[99]

In a literary critique published in *Literarishe Bleter* in 1932, N. I. Gotlib remarked that Segal, thanks to the originality of his style and his world view, was unique in modern Yiddish poetry. Yet the book *Lirik* seemed to signal a departure in his work. According to Gotlib, it evidenced a stage of inner healing and calm in Segal's artistic journey. "Segal's concept of life has become more profound and his poetic angst has transformed. The poet's dark feelings have become lighter, his language clearer, and his words appear more restrained . . . "[100] In *Lirik* the poet also returned to earlier themes, such as his retreat from the world around him and his refusal to be drawn into the pervasive social pessimism. The book also introduced a novel thematic that included the sanctification of the past, the acknowledgment of God's presence, and recourse to an exclusively Jewish cultural imagination. More importantly, Segal now seemed more emotionally engaged in an ethereal world that no longer existed, the world of his childhood and the Eastern European environment prior to the failed Revolution of 1905. Even in the great metropolis New York, which he left just as *Lirik* was going to press, in neighbourhoods further removed from the centre, Segal recognized here and there the rhythm of his native *shtetl*. Visions came to him of Abraham in his tent speaking with God, a scene the poet described in language derived from deep within the biblical literature, often inspired by the Song of Songs. However, as Gotlib conceded, the work was strikingly modern in form and evidenced the irreversibility of the poet's personal detachment from religious practice. For over twenty years he had been exiled from the land of his childhood, wandering around without being able to settle down. He had turned his back on the religious beliefs and practices he had observed in Korets, practices which had provided a sacred rhythm to the days and hours of his Volhynian existence. His words were the result of a painful uprooting and unbearable solitude. Overcoming a reluctance embedded in a present he found oppressive, Segal in *Lirik* projected himself back into the millennia-long Jewish tradition. Gotlib observed:

> This collection is a combination of the wisdom of Ecclesiastes and modern lyricism as exemplified by Rilke. Many poems read like chapters from the marvellous book of Psalms. [. . .] This book, *Lirik*, has a radiance that derives simultaneously from a wholesome Jewish nationalism, ancient Judaic texts, and modern Jewish life.[101]

These complex and contradictory impulses are revealed in a poem that exemplifies Segal's new poetic process entitled "This Is How God Sings in My Ear." Although eminently modern in form, it is traditional in his evocation of a world that is no more. Segal introduces religious notions such as the existence of a God who gazes down benevolently upon the Jews forced into exile, yet at the same time his writing is amazingly fluid in form and tone, thus dispelling any impression of piety. Dominant in this poem are the poetic image and the poet's emotional response to the suffering of his people. Despite the fact that the poem strongly evokes an Eastern European milieu about to disappear, its rhythm and the form suggest a startling modernity.

This Is How God Sings in My Ear

And in your streets I shall light again
my noble Sabbath lanterns.
Your little Josephs in velvet hats
will walk beside you
carrying their prayer shawls in wine-red silken bags.
The large doors of the great synagogue stand open
as my great sun sets over the earth

and my sky is clear and still.
Growing by the picket fence of the synagogue garden
are slender mossy thorns,
wild weeds and nettles –
I know it very well.
It gladdens me to know it well.
I let you settle
on hill and vale
beside a gentile people.
Their little churches call to me
and the blue smoke of their prayers
rises and swirls before my eyes.
I also feel their restlessness
and the sorrow of their hard-earned, hardened
black piece of bread.[102]

The title *Lirik* also indicated that Segal had adopted a new form of writing, which, as opposed to proletarian poetry, emphasized the musicality of the language, the outpouring of noble sentiments, and the search for the ideal of perfect beauty. In this regard, at least, the poet departed radically from the ancient Hebrew texts and their intimate relationship to God to find inspiration for the formal elements of his poetry in a Hellenistic tradition redesigned by the major modern literary trends. Subjectivity, esthetic rendering, and existential themes would henceforth characterize Segal's poetry, even though it was written in a vernacular language in which, until very recently, these elements had been almost totally absent. By opting for refinement, individual destiny, and existential impressionism, the poet joined the vanguard of a Jewish literary movement that aspired to excellence and innovation, and sought a place for himself within the great European modernist currents, as had Chagall, Meer Axelrod, El Lissitzky, and Joseph Chaikov.[103] In the push for artistic renewal that shook Europe and America during an era of rapid industrialization and social change, Yiddish literature, influenced by French symbolism, German expressionism, Russian futurism and socialist realism, was also demanding an opportunity to showcase its originality and immense creative potential. Segal, in Montreal, was at the forefront of the artistic surge that rocked the capitals of Europe and caught the imagination of the American metropolis. Except that in Segal's case, this desire was often transformed into a peaceful contemplation of the world of his childhood, as in the following poem where God and the Baal Shem Tov, the founder of Hasidism, appeared to meet in a setting reminiscent of a Chagall painting.

Footprints

The world at dusk.
While the Baal Shem Tov sits
at the edge of a forest.
The red of the sunset
Fades away.

The Baal Shem Tov is silent.

All around
there is only silence.
God is silent in the forest
and God is silent in the grass.

As in the grass and in the tree
God is also silent in me.
A wind will come,
A tree will rustle,
The grass will rustle,
My heart will rustle
In praise of Him.

Still lying on the distant road
the golden footprints
of the sun that has gone,
of the day that is done,
of my mood.[104]

Lirik represented an important milestone in Segal's poetic oeuvre, and sparked a new direction that would become more pronounced in his subsequent books. *Lirik* also contained several poems about New York, especially Brooklyn, which suggests that the poet had composed some of its contents while in America when he was still in transition between the two urban centres that most influenced his literary career. Even though echoes of Korets and Hasidism reverberate through-out *Lirik*, the poet nonetheless had not abandoned the very personal introspective tone that had thus far constituted the originality of his writing. This is particularly noticeable in the titles of each of his poems which often convey the impression of strong subjectivity, such as "*Loyterkayt* [Purity]," "*Ikh bin* [I am]," "*Likhtik* [Bright]," and "*Ikh vel aykh zingn* [I will sing to you]." In these poems, Segal adopts the voice of a mourner looking back at his distant childhood. It resonates with a painful nostalgia for a universe eroded by both the passage of time and the progressive obliteration of a traditional way of life that had become unsustainable with the advent of modernity. Far from wishing to reclaim the circumstances of his Eastern European youth, the poet makes clear in *Lirik* that he has simply traded the suffering endured in an oppressive family environment for an equally painful present where he finds himself traversing an endless desert of exile and isolation. In the process of being suddenly catapulted from Korets to Montreal, and then to the mouth of the Hudson River, Segal felt the presence of the God of Abraham, Isaac, and Jacob like a shadow following his every step. His memories were of a marvellous past full of iconic holy men communing at dawn with a very personal God whose intense flame had been extinguished on the threshold of the New World. The synagogue lit by flickering candles, the comforting words of the Baal Shem Tov, and the ardour of his disciples pressing against the doors of the *beys medresh* had been replaced long ago by the sombre mass of factories, the poverty of immigrant populations, and the materialism of North American cities. This is how years later the poet N. I. Gotlib would describe the work and creative process of his colleague Segal when *Lirik* was published:

> Thus, during all those years on the Montreal scene, Segal lived in imaginary places where the sky and the land were vast and the houses small. In this land whose inhabitants surrendered to the will of God, grandfathers were only interested in the psalms, and a young husband in the dowry his wife would bring. In the middle of this very particular literary world the echo of Korets reverberated constantly. This world of the *shtetl*, which had just vanished, shone resplendently in Segal's dreary life, bringing consolation to the author in his sorrowful solitude and comfort to his miserable existence.[105]

The Agnostic Poet Before God

Lirik (1930) paved the way for the appearance a few years later of *Mayn nigun* (1934)—its title alone indicates the poet's mystical sentiments—followed by *Di drite sude* (1937), a reference to the third meal of the Sabbath before the return to the dreariness of everyday life. In both these new poetry collections, Segal continued to evoke a past infused with religious fervour. In the poet's mind, the inviolable separation between the Sabbath and the rest of the week, between the sacred and the secular, corresponded to the distance between his childhood *shtetl* and his American exile. By summoning his memories of those blessed times when the Sabbath was observed in all its splendour, he tried to ward off the implied threat posed by the present with its constant reminders of the absence of God. In *Mayn nigun* and *Di drite sude*, Segal tried with all his might to dispel the unspeakable suffering caused by a new world built without a spiritual foundation. It was not that Segal wanted to return to his earlier piety, which would have been impossible for him. Instead, he was trying to recover the innocence and tranquility so cruelly lacking in the anonymous hubbub of modern life. "So foreign to him is the large modern city, where he was destined to live, that he continues to escape into the *shtetl* that is constantly in his thoughts, and into scenes of small towns and villages."[106] The great New York literary critic Shmuel Niger, whose words were just quoted, was not fooled by this subterfuge, which consisted of looking to the past to escape the unbearable yoke of the present. Even in taking refuge among past generations, indelibly marked by the divine presence, Segal still belonged to the modernist brotherhood of *Di Yunge*, even though he maintained the illusion of a Volhynian world that had long since vanished, while his New York colleagues were turning their attention to the revolutionary unrest that they expected would put an end to national oppression and rampant materialism. Hence the Montreal poet, even when he was lending an ear to the Baal Shem Tov's mystical sermons, fundamentally remained a modern writer.

> Segal, however, is not quiet, not calm, and, of course, not old. His poetry is the poetry of a modern Yiddish poet. Simple, yet refined. The folkloric tone for him is only a sophisticated way of creating his modern "I-tone". His lines are free and loose, like the lines of today's lyrical poets. His rhymes are often assonant, as in

all of modern Yiddish poetry. He is old-fashioned only in his *long-ing* for the past, not because he *is* behind the times.[107]

This interweaving of two contradictory worlds characterized Segal's work during the 1930s, as if the modernity inside him could not flourish without a sorrowful backward glance at a recent past, as though full participation in the world of artistic creation in its most universal sense could only be accompanied by a loss of meaning and profound grief. Having been intimately acquainted with an Eastern European world with a different conception of Judaism, Segal explored new regions of contemporary poetry with a feeling of liberation, while at the same time in the grips of an unrelenting nostalgia. This constant tug of war between a tradition that had been annihilated, but nonetheless was incessantly resurfacing in his poetic repertoire, and the insatiable desire to be carried by the powerful flow of modern individualism created a tension in Segal's writing, upon which younger Yiddish poets, such as Benjamin Jacob Bialostotzki, did not fail to comment: "Your anger against the new and how you evoke past eras and ancient sources, interest me, despite the fact that I myself am very far from them!"[108] This dissonance between Segal's introspectivist aspirations and the Hasidic imagery of some of his poems injected an element of originality and Jewish authenticity into his poetry, a certain tone of voice derived from the rhythm of prayer and the reading of the scriptures, practices no longer remembered by the other members of *Di Yunge*. Despite this, the religious and mystical elements in Segal's poetry that increasingly asserted themselves after the appearance of *Lirik* won the enthusiastic support of several literary critics and modern writers, who discovered a direction rarely explored in this context, including Benjamin Jacob Bialostotzki, who made the following comments about the collection entitled *Di drite sude*:

> Your *nigun*, your rhythm, your true lyricism echo in my heart. In the literary world (which is so detestable) it is good to have a J. I. Segal, a poet who shies away from factions, from cliques and from fashions, a poet who produces prose and poetry that shines and shimmers with marvellous poetic flashes—please accept my blessings and my congratulations, my dear J. I. Segal.[109]

Chava Rosenfarb hinted at this when she suggested that like Rilke, Segal was inspired by his great predecessors in the Western pantheon

of arts and letters. He was particularly sympathetic to the writing of
Norwegian novelist Knut Hamsun (1859–1952), who at the end of
the nineteenth century had imagined a character wandering along
on the fringes of society, constantly tormented by hunger, destitution, and the intangible dream. At times, there is a marked similar-
ity between the protagonists of Hamsun's *Hunger* and *Mysteries*,
who were incapable of adapting to the demands of society, and the
young poet from Korets whom a particularly difficult childhood had
rendered closed to the sheer joys of existence. Nevertheless, Segal
carried within him the legacy of an ethical tradition which pro-
pounded an unfailing adherence to series of religious precepts and
laws dictated by God and passed down over the ages in a body of
sacred texts. To fulfil and foster these tenets, the people of Israel had
entered into communion with the Master of the Universe and submitted themselves to His unfathomable will, specifically by following a series of well-defined practices and behaviours. For the author
of poetry collections entitled *Lirik, Mayn nigun,* and *Di drite sude*, this
legacy, which had deep personal significance for him, even though
he was not a believer, provided him with a set of images that served
as a wonderful source of inspiration. Mosaic law coupled with the
biblical and Talmudic literary tradition, was further supplemented
by the commentaries of Rashi, liturgical poetry, ritual prayer, the
inspirational creativity of the Kabalah, and Hasidic chants. This
intricate maze of traditions, stories and teachings dating back to the
beginnings of Judaism, paradoxically gave Segal a framework for a
new type of modernist and impressionist poetry, as in the following poem from *Di drite sude*, loosely constructed around the theme
of the Hebrew month of Tishrei and the Feast of Tabernacles.[110] In
this text, there is a reference to the Talmudic concept of the thirty-
six hidden righteous men in every generation, who by their saintly
behaviour secretly bear the responsibility of justifying the purpose
of humankind before a vengeful God. Also making an appearance in
this poem are the weekly Torah reading in the synagogue called the
parsha—in this case about the Jews in the desert after their enslave-
ment in Egypt—and the chanting of the prayers heard through the
windows of small Eastern European synagogues amid luxuriant
fields[111] (see Appendix 26):

Tishrei

Echoes,
home and distant,
and of long ago.

A tired solitary bee,
bronze-gold,
buzzes 'round the sun by day
in the quiet garden.

The last warmth
above the cornstalks
whiffs of pungent spices –
Tishrei-saffron.

The sound of psalms
over sky and rooftops.
A window hums the weekly Torah portion:
Forty years in the desert.

Tired, flickering Tishrei candles.
Silent cornstalks.
Downhill – a river.
Saintly water carriers
Knock on early-morning doors:
Water, water.

The holy days over,
a pious sadness sings
on the tousled heads of the *sukkahs*.[112]

Thus, Segal found room in his writing for the religious tradition in which he was raised, and for the Hasidic masters, especially the three venerated miracle rabbis, the Baal Shem Tov, Rabbi Nachman of Bratslav, and the Berditchever Rebbe, Levi Isaac ben Meir. In Hasidism, which remained largely untouched by the Enlightenment and secular ideas, Segal found an inner peace and a breadth of vision that had eluded him since the time of his hurried departure from Korets. "Segal's refuge was the world of Hasidic ecstasy and mysticism, a world not reallydevoid of reality, but where the material was transformed into the spiritual, where every physical form of life on earth became a symbol, an abstract allusion cloaked in mystery."[113]

On these ethereal heights, in a universe of legends and mystical phenomena, Segal wove his poetic tapestry, while around him swirled
the everyday practicalities of life in an America consumed by its own
material progress. Conjuring up images of the divine seemed all the
more urgent to the poet for whom nothing in his present life was able
to revive his past fervour or rekindle the flame of the divine presence, apart from the memory stored deep within of a childhood long
since over. These images from the past came to haunt him while, in
complete solitude, he embarked upon the unsettling path of modernism, introspection, lyricism, and self-discovery, along roads unknown
to the *gaonim* and *tsaddikim* of old, who only listened to the rustling
whisper of the divine word. This is how, when overcome by feelings
of nostalgia and persistent sadness, Segal ended up in the fields of his
native Volhynia, on the same roads travelled by the Baal Shem Tov,
where he dreamt of God in quiets forests and on peaceful riverbanks,
carried along by immutability of the seasons and the simple gestures
of his people (see Appendix 27):

Purity

From my quiet days a road descends
Into the coolness of the shaded valley.
And having shed my heaviness and fear
I shall meet you there some day.

Dressed in white, on the grey earth
With pure, clear eyes, peacefully
you shall sit — free of all your earthly burdens,
with others as radiant as you.

I shall take your small white hand,
And warm it in the breath of my mouth.
High above us — hills of green.
Westward the sun — like a golden pillar.

Throughout the world there are specks of sickly red
But you are white and tranquil as the twilight.
I leave you sitting at the entrance to your tent
In the sun and shadow of the evening.

Notes

1. In general, half the Yiddish speakers admitted to Canada as immigrants between 1905 to 1929 settled in Montreal. See Haim-Leib Fuks, op. cit., page 437, Graphs 5 and 6.

2. Israel Medres, *Montreal of Yesterday: Jewish life in Montreal, 1900–1920* (Translated by Vivian Felsen, Véhicule Press, Montreal, 2000), 176.

3. See Merrily Weisbord, *The Strangest Dream: Canadian Communists, the Spy Trials, and the Cold War* (Toronto, Lester & Orpen Dennys, 1983).

4. See Margaret MacMillan, *Paris 1919: Six Months That Changed the World,* New York, Random House, 2002.

5. Better known as Shifra Krishtalka.

6. Yisroel Shtern published mostly under his Hebrew pseudonym Ish Yair.

7. Abraham arrived in Canada with his wife.

8. Pseudonym of Yudis (Judith) Tsik (1898–1988).

9. She would later marry poet Melekh Ravitch, originally from Poland, who arrived in Montreal in 1941.

10. As Hebrew writing and publishing were not allowed in the Soviet Union, Soviet Yiddish publications were required to spell out phonetically in Yiddish any words derived from Hebrew or Aramaic.

11. Korman had emigrated to the United States during the 1920s, relocating in Detroit, which explains the Detroit connection.

12. Harold Troper and Irving Abella, *None is Too Many: Canada and the Jews of Europe, 1933–1948,* Toronto: Lester & Orpen Denys, 1983.

13. Bernard Dansereau, "La place des travailleurs juifs dans le mouvement ouvrier québécois au début du xixᵉ siècle," in Pierre Anctil, Ira Robinson and Gérard Bouchard, eds., *Juifs et Canadiens français dans la société québécoise* (Sillery, Editions du Septentrion, 2000), 127–154; and "La contribution juive à la sphère économique et syndicale jusqu'à la Deuxième Guerre mondiale," Pierre Anctil and Ira Robinson, eds., *Les communautés juives de Montréal, histoire et enjeux contemporains* (Sillery: Editions du Septentrion, 2010), 141–164. See also: Mercedes Steedman, *Angels of the Workplace: Women and the Construction of Gender Relations in the Canadian Clothing Industry, 1890–1940,* Toronto: Oxford University Press, 1997.

14. N. I. Gotlib, in his Introduction to the first issue of *Montreal,* December 1932, 16.

15. From the First Annual Report of the Jewish Public Library, Montreal/*Ershter yerlikher barikht fun der idisher folks biblyoket un folks universitet* (Montreal, 1914), 7.

16. See the translator's preface to the book by Hershl Novak, op. cit., 11–60.

17. Manifesto of the *Idishe Folkshule* (People's School) published on July 9, 1915, in the *Keneder Adler,* and quoted by Simon Belkin, op. cit., 328; Belkin (original Yiddish), op. cit., 218.

18. For more precise statistical data on this subject see Louis Rosenberg, "Canada's Jews. A Social and Economic Study of Jews in Canada" (Montreal: Canadian Jewish Congress, 1939), 160.

19. Daniel Wolofsky was the second oldest son of Hirsch Wolofsky, founder of the newspaper in 1907.

20. Letter from Daniel Wolofsky to to J. I. Segal [in English] *The Jewish Daily Eagle/ Keneder Adler,* Montreal September 25, 1931, Segal Archive, Jewish Public Library Archives, Montreal.

21. Letter from Daniel Wolofsky to his employees [in English] The Eagle Publishing Company Limited, Montreal, September 25, 1931, Segal Archive, Jewish Public Library Archives, Montreal.

22. Ibid.

23. On this subject, see Hirsch Wolofsky, *Mayn lebns rayze. Un demi-siècle de vie Yiddish à Montréal et ailleurs dans le monde*, op. cit., Chapters 22 and 24; Original published in Yiddish as H. Wolofsky, *Mayn lebns-rayze* (Journey of My Life: A Book of Memoirs), Eagle Publishing Co. Ltd., Montreal, 1946.

24. See the comments of Wolofsky on this subject in his memoirs, op. cit., 264–265. Wolofsky, original Yiddish, pages 181–182.

25. On this subject see: Martin Robin, *Shades of Right: Nativists and Fascist Politics in Canada, 1920–1940*, Toronto: University of Toronto Press, 1992. Published in French as *Le spectre de la droite: histoire des politiques nativistes et fascistes au Canada entre 1920 et 1940*, Montréal, Balzac-Le Griot, 1995.

26. The organizers of this event decided to make the publication of his poetry in the *Keneder Adler* in 1917 the starting date of his literary career, rather than the publication of first poetry collection in 1918.

27. Taken from the Jubilee Souvenir, Montreal, 1932, page 2 published by the J. I. Segal Jubilee Committee on the 15th anniversary of J. I. Segal's career as a poet. (*Tsum 15 yorikn yubileum fun Yud Yud Segals dikhterishn shafung*).

28. This was *Mayn nigun*, did not appear until two years later.

29. Undated, unused letterhead, Segal Archive, Jewish Public Library Archives, Montreal.

30. A letter in English circulated by the J. I. Segal Committee, Montreal, December 23, 1933, Segal Archive, Jewish Public Library Archives, Montreal.

31. Ibid.

32. About the life and work of Esther Segal, see Noah-Isaac Gotlib, "Esther Segal," *Keneder Adler*, March 3, 1965, 6, 5; Miriam Krant, "Esther Segal," *Keneder Adler*, May 16, 1965, 6; and Mirl Erdberg-Shatan, "Esther Segal-Shkolnikov – in ondenk [Esther Segal-Shkolnikov – In memoriam,] *Keneder Adler*, September 17, 1976, 9.

33. Ibid. This appeal was sent out the year that the Nazi party came to power in Germany.

34. Israel Jacob Schwartz, *Kentoki* (in Yiddish), New York, N. M. Mayzl, 1925.

35. I. J. Schwartz was a New York poet who often visited Montreal in the 1930s. See Shlolem Shtern, op. cit., 190–191. Yiddish original, op. cit., 109.

36. The Ikuf (*Yidisher Kultur Farband* [Yiddish Culture Alliance]) was founded in Paris in 1937 for the diffusion of Yiddish culture throughout the world. Known by its acronym, "Ikuf," it was especially active in New York. According to Sholem Shtern, there was a branch of the Ikuf in Montreal until the 1960s.

37. Sholem Shtern, op. cit., 240–241. Yiddish original, op. cit., 225.

38. On this subject see Irving Massey, *Identity and Community: Reflections on English, Yiddish, and French Literature in Canada*, Detroit, Wayne State University Press, 1994. Irving Massey is the son of Ida Maze.

39. On this subject see Chantal Ringuet, "L'engagement littéraire et communautaire d'Ida Maze, la mère des écrivains yiddish montréalais" in *Globe, Revue internationale d'études québécoises* (vol. 12, no. 1, June 2009), 149–166.

40. Ida Maze's exact address was 4479B, Esplanade Avenue, Apt. 7.

41. Joseph Rolnick was a highly respected New York poet. See Shtern, op. cit., 132. Original Yiddish, op. cit., 36.

42. Ian Kershaw, *Hitler, 1889–1933: Hubris* (New York: Penguin Books, 1998), 471–472.

43. Ibid., 573.

44. "*Der kanader idisher kongres* [the Canadian Jewish Congress]," *Keneder Adler*, September 24, 1934.

45. Ibid.

46. See François Nadeau, *Adrien Arcand, führer canadien*, Montreal: Lux Éditeur, 2010. See also Irving Abella and Harold Troper, op. cit.

47. Israel Medres, *Tsvishn tsvey velt milkhomes* (Eagle Publishing Co. Montreal, 1964), 89. Translated into French by Pierre Anctil as *Le Montréal juif entre les deux guerres* (Sillery: Éditions du Septentrion, 2001), 159. English version published as Israel Medres, *Between Two World Wars: Canadian Jews in Transition* (Translated by Vivian Felsen. Montreal, Véhicule Press, 2003), 98.

48. Undated, untitled manuscript by H. M. Caiserman, Caiserman Archive, Jewish Public Library Archives.

49. H. M. Caiserman Dies in 68th Year, *The Gazette*, Montreal, December 25, 1950.

50. Here the speaker is referring to Yiddish.

51. Untitled, undated manuscript by H. M. Caiserman beginning with "I was graciously invited to address you to-night on Montreal Jewish literature and art," Caiserman file, Personalia Archive, Canadian Jewish Congress Archives, Montreal. This text was later published with the title "Is there a Canadian Jewish Literature?" *The Canadian Jewish Magazine* (Passover 1942), 9–12, 14.

52. See Appendix 22 for a detailed Table of Contents of this book.

53. According to a letter from Caiserman to David Rome in the Canadian Jewish Congress Archives, this book was printed in mid-1935 in 1,000 copies, financed by Caiserman himself. See Caiserman's letters to Rome dated February 25, 1935 and March 22, 1935.

54. Undated, unsigned manuscript beginning with "*O, Kanada! O, Kanada!...* ", Caiserman Archive, Canaian Jewish Congress Archives, Montreal. This text is analyzed in the previous chapter.

55. Untitled, undated manuscript by H. M. Caiserman beginning with "I was graciously invited to address you to-night on Montreal Jewish literature and art," Caiserman file, Personalia Archive, Canadian Jewish Congress Archives, Montreal.

56. See Pierre Anctil, *Le rendez-vous manqué. Les Juifs de Montréal face au Québec de l'entre-deux-guerres* (Québec, l'Institut québécois de recherche sur la culture, 1988), Chapter 5.

57. This building at the corner of St. Urbain Street was the home of the National Hockey League until 1926 when it became an auditorium.

58. Letter from H. M. Caiserman to I. J. Weinroth, Toronto, December 29, 1936, Caiserman Archive, Canadian Jewish Congress Archives, Montreal. Not long afterward, Grober would move to Canada to pursue her career here.

59. Letter from H. M. Caiserman to Emma Goldman, March 16, 1936, Caiserman Archive, Canadian Jewish Congress Archives, Montreal.

60. Letter from H. M. Caiserman to Ibolyka, December 1931, Caiserman Archive, Canadian Jewish Congress Archives, Montreal.

61. Manuscript entitled "Dedicated to artists Olga, Ibolyka and Tania, Practicing-evening, Jan 21, 1932." Montreal. Caiserman Archive, Canadian Jewish Congress Archives, Montreal. English was the official language that Caiserman knew best, and came naturally to him. However, he sometimes still made mistakes in English, and expressed himself somewhat awkwardly in his literary attempts.

62. The expression used by Caiserman in the first sentence of his preface to *Idishe dickhter in Kanade* (Montreal, Farlag Nyuansn, 1934), 9.

63. Ibid., 9–10.

64. Ibid., 9.

65. Ibid., 9.

66.   The four are Hyman Edelstein, A. M. Klein, Frida Miron, and Regina Lenore Shoolman. Jewish poets who wrote in English take up about one quarter of Caiserman's 1934 anthology.

67.   Letter in English from H. M. Caiserman to David Rome, Vancouver, July 21, 1935, Caiserman Archive, Canadian Jewish Congress Archives, Montreal.

68.   H. M. Caiserman, *Idishe dikhter in kanade*, op. cit., 10.

69.   J. I. Segal, *"A vort* [Preface]", *Idishe Dikhter in kanade*, op. cit., 5.

70.   Ibid.

71.   Ibid., 5–6.

72.   Halpern would later renounce this ideological approach and become one of the main poets in the New York modernist school *Di Yunge*.

73.   On this subject, see: Eliezer Grinberg, *Moshe-Leib Halpern in ram fun zayn dor* ([Moshe Leib Halpern in his generation], New York, M. L. Halpern Arbeter Ring Branch 450, 1942), 17–18; Ruth R. Wisse, *A Little Love in Big Manhattan* (Cambridge, Mass., Harvard University Press, 1988), 88–91.

74.   Moish Leib Halpern, *"Tsum strayk,"* *Di Folkstsaytung*, Montreal, June 7, 1912.

75.   H. M. Caiserman, "Is There a Canadian Jewish Literature?", op. cit., 9.

76.   H. M. Caiserman, op. cit., 18.

77.   H. M. Caiserman, op. cit., 76.

78.   H. M. Caiserman, "Is There a Canadian Jewish Literature?", op. cit., 9.

79.   J. I. Segal in *Idishe dikhter in kanade*, op. cit., 7.

80.   H. M. Caiserman, *Idishe dikhter in kanade*, op. cit., 167.

81.   This is one of the rare examples in Canadian Jewish letters of texts translated from English into Yiddish. The opposite was very common during this era.

82.   Letter from H. M. Caiserman to C. Apter, Passenger Traffic Representative, Canadian National Railway, Montreal, June 26, 1935, Caiserman Archive, Canadian Jewish Congress Archives, Montreal. The proposed book by the name of *Social & Economic Research* to which he refers is most likely the manuscript of the book edited by Louis Rosenberg and published by the Canadian Jewish Congress entitled *Canada's Jews. A Social and Economic Study of Jews in Canada*, Montreal: Canadian Jewish Congress,1939.

83.   A letter sent out by the I. J. Segal Jubilee Committee, Montreal, March 25, 1932, Segal Archive, Jewish Public Library, Montreal.

84.   Letter from Nachman Meisel to J. I. Segal, *Literarishe Bleter*, Warsaw, 1928, Segal Archive, Jewish Public Library, Montreal.

85.   Letter from Nachman Meisel to J. I. Segal, *Di yidishe velt*, Warsaw, April 8, 1928, Segal Archive, Jewish Public Library, Montreal.

86.   Letter from Nachman Meisel to J. I. Segal, *Literarishe Bleter*, Warsaw, February 9, 1932, Segal Archive, Jewish Public Library, Montreal.

87.   J. I. Segal, *"Der goyrl fun dem idisdhn dikhter* [The fate of the Yiddish poet]," Literarishe Bleter, Warsaw, vol. 10, no. 9, February 24, 1933, 133–134. Segal Archive, Jewish Public Library, Montreal.

88.   Letter from Ezriel Carlebach to J. I. Segal, *Di post*, London, November 29, 1934, Segal Archive, Jewish Public Library, Montreal.

89.   Letter from Melekh Ravitch to J. I. Segal, Mexico City, October 24, 1930, Segal Archive, Jewish Public Library, Montreal.

90.   Letter from Melekh Ravitch to J. I. Segal, January 9, 1936, Melbourne, Australia, Segal Archive, Jewish Public Library, Montreal.

91.   J. I. Segal, Montreal, *Di drite sude*, 1937, 173.

92.   Letter from H. M. Caiserman to J. I. Segal, Montreal, June 20, 1937, Caiserman Archive, Canadian Jewish Congress Archives, Montreal.

93. Interview with Sylvia Lustgarten, second oldest daughter of J. I. Segal, Toronto, December 15, 1988; interview with Sylvia Lustgarten and Annette Zakuta, Toronto, November 30, 2009.

94. The Segal Archive at the Montreal Jewish Public Library Archives has several hundred manuscripts written in pencil on newsprint, probably written in a hurry in the early morning. Most are from the late 1940s and the early 1950s.

95. Chava Rosenfarb, "Yud Yud Segal," unpublished manuscript dated November 13, 1988, 9–10. This document was given to me during an interview at the home of the author, in Ville Mont-Royal, January 20, 1989.

96. Ibid., 9.

97. "*Dos ersht band fun tif religyezer lirishe dikhtung*", untitled manuscript by H. M. Caiserman, 1950, Montreal Jewish Public Library Archive, Montreal. These were probably the preliminary notes for an article about Segal's book.

98. "*Dos drite groys bukh fun religyeze, natyonale un sotsyale gezangn in grishlikhenste lirik,*" ibid.

99. Sholem Shtern, *Nostalgie et Tristesse*, op. cit., 276 (French version). Original Yiddish in Sholem Shtern, *Shrayber Ikh hob gekent (Writers I Knew)*, op. cit., 262.

100. N. I. Gotlib, "Yud Yud Segal," *Literarishe Bleter* (Warsaw, vol. 9, no. 14, April 1, 1932), 218.

101. Gotlib, op. cit., 219.

102. J. I. Segal, "*Azoy zingt got mir in oyer, Lirik,*" op. cit., 259.

103. See Nathalie Hazan-Brunet and Ada Ackerman, eds., *Futur antérieur. L'avant-garde et le livre yiddish (1914–1939)* (Paris, Musée d'art et d'histoire du judaïsme and Skira Flammarion, 2009), 271.

104. J. I. Segal, "Trit [Footprints]," *Lirik*, op. cit., 254.

105. N. I. Gotlib, "Yud Yud Segal," *Der Keneder Adler*, March 9, 1959, 6. This article was published on the 5th anniversary of Segal's death.

106. Shmuel Niger, "*Altvor*t [ancient word]," *Der Tog*, New York, February 13, 1938.

107. Ibid.

108. Letter from Benjamin Jacob Bialostotski, Bronx, New York, to J. I. Segal, June 16, 1938, Segal Archived, Montreal Jewish Public Library Archive.

109. Ibid.

110. The Feast of Tabernacles (in Hebrew *Sukkot* and in Yiddish *sukkes*), literally Feast of Booths, is the third of the great festivals on which all males were required to make pilgrimages to the Temple in Jerusalem. For seven days Jews eat their meals in a temporary structure called a *sukka* to remember the temporary dwellings in which they lived for forty years in the desert after their flight from Egypt. It is also a time to celebrate the autumn harvest.

111. The Feast of Tabernacles is celebrated in early autumn, during the month of Tishrei.

112. J. I. Segal, "*Tishre,*" *Di drite sude*, Montreal, 1937, 109.

113. Rosenfarb, op. cit., 10.

Chapter 5

The "Years of Lead":
The Holocaust and Its Aftermath

T he dark forebodings at the end of the 1930s that impelled Melekh
Ravitch to leave the country of his birth, and caused Europe's Jewish
communities to fear the worst, proved justified when the German army
invaded Poland on September 1, 1939, only days after the signing of the
German-Soviet Non-Aggression Pact. These events convinced Great
Britain and France to declare war on Germany. From the very beginning, the Second World War left a trail of suffering and devastation on a
scale never before imagined. Within a matter of weeks, nearly two million Jews in Poland found themselves under Nazi rule. After Germany
invaded the Soviet Union in June of 1941, the Jewish populations in
the previously Soviet-occupied part of Poland, as well as Lithuania,
the Ukraine, and Russia proper, also found themselves living under a
Nazi reign of terror, which, in 1942, culminated in their systematic and
deliberate genocide.[1] In the fall of 1939, when war erupted in Europe,
no one could have foreseen the course of this worldwide conflict, nor
predicted the consequences for all the nations involved. Jews, dispersed in various countries on both sides of the front lines, had little
indication of the policy the Allies would adopt in their regard. In the
event of an Axis victory, how would the democracies react to the brutal
treatment of religious and national minorities by their new Nazi masters? Above all, to what extent would the Nazi rhetoric that demonized
Jews be taken seriously in the event of war, and implemented amid the
new conditions created by the outbreak of hostilities? After a decade
of helplessly witnessing the exodus of German and Austrian Jews, the
escalation of Nazi propaganda, and the dissolution of the system of
international cooperation put in place by the Treaty of Versailles, in
September of 1939 Yiddish-speaking Jews in Canada were confronted
by a completely new and unforeseeable situation.

The commencement of military hostilities had a severe impact on the Montreal Jewish community, particularly since many of its members had come from Eastern Europe not long before, having left family and friends behind. The vast majority of Jews who settled in Canada in the early twentieth century were of Eastern European origin, and maintained strong personal and cultural ties with the old country through the creation of *landsmanshaftn*, self-help organizations with specific political and ideological affiliations. In 1931, 55 per cent of Jews living in Montreal were immigrants, a percentage which does not include those who, although born in Canada, were the descendants of Eastern European Jews and lived in daily contact with that culture. Of those born abroad, 51 per cent had come from the former Russian Empire, 21.4 per cent from Poland, and 13.7 per cent from Romania.[2] They all retained a deep and abiding interest in Jewish life in Central and Eastern Europe, even more so during the 1930s when the situation of the Jewish populations there was markedly deteriorating. That was especially true of Poland, where an authoritarian nationalist government enacted an ever-increasing number of exclusionary measures against Jewish merchants and professionals. The *Jewish Daily Eagle*, whose journalists had grown up in the former Russian Empire, faithfully reported, on a daily basis, the condition of Jewish minorities in the various European countries, especially those with large Yiddish-speaking populations. Because he wanted to witness firsthand the situation in the newly independent Poland, which had been established pursuant to the Treaty of Versailles, the owner of the *Eagle*, Hirsch Wolofsky, had visited the land of his birth in 1921, 1929, and 1935. His three trips were the subject of dozens of articles which appeared in the *Eagle* over the years, as well as two books published in 1922 and 1946 respectively.[3]

During the 1930s, Wolofsky's readers had been well aware of the precarious position of Eastern European Jewry. Many were expecting the pogroms, which had taken place in Germany during Kristallnacht in November of 1938 to repeat themselves, but on an even larger scale in Poland, and eventually in occupied Russia. However, at this point in time, no one suspected the enormity of the suffering that would befall the Jews who found themselves at the mercy of Nazi troops. Although Hitler, in his speeches and publications, most notably in *Mein Kampf*, published in 1925–1926, had clearly alluded to his determination to annihilate the Jews of Europe, no specific plan in this regard had yet surfaced in Germany immediately after the 1939.

For a short time, it seemed that the humiliations being inflicted on Jewish populations would be limited to restrictions on their freedom of movement, severe food rationing, and forced labour brigades. However, in the summer of 1941, reports reached the North American Jewish media of mass executions of Jews in various parts of the Soviet Union now under German control, including the Baltic states, most often by shooting or gassing with carbon monoxide in vans specifically designed for this purpose. These systematic killings, the work of small teams called *Einsatzgruppen*, had been observed by members of underground groups who transmitted the information to the Allies and the Polish government in exile in London and Moscow. In early 1942, underground Jewish organizations based in Poland had succeeded in piercing the veil of secrecy surrounding these massacres and had assembled a more complete picture of the treatment of Jewish populations by German authorities. This information, although piecemeal, finally reached Allied governments, thanks to a network of intermediaries:

> Sometime that same May [1942], the Jewish Labor Bund in Poland compiled a summary of verified massacres and succeeded in transmitting it, along with an anguished plea for action, to the Polish government in London. The persistence of the two Jewish members of the Polish National Council in London — Szmul Zygielbojm, of the Bund, and Dr. Ignacy Schwarzbart, of the Zionist group — forced British and American government officials and news media to take notice. The Bund report became the decisive factor in the first breakthrough of extermination news.[4]

In the beginning, these reports were received with scepticism by non-Jews. At first glance they often seemed more like military propaganda and were hard to believe, given the magnitude of the numbers cited. Other documents from the same source outlined the systematic resettlement of Western European Jews in the east, mainly Poland. Several witnesses reported that thousands of French Jews arrested during the largescale round-ups in the summer of 1942 had been deported to an unknown destination beyond the German border. In August of 1942, the American diplomatic service in Switzerland was made aware, for the first time, of the Nazi plan for the organized extermination of European Jewry. It was Dr. Gerhart Riegner, the representative of the World Jewish Congress in Geneva, who, having obtained a document from a German industrialist, divulged the plan to concentrate Jews from all over Europe in Poland, and then exterminate them using new methods specifically devised for this purpose. In September of that same year, Isaac Sternbuch, a representative of the Agudath Israel World Organization in Switzerland, sent a telegram to the American members of his organization containing information about the recent deportation and extermination of part of the population of the Warsaw ghetto. According to historian David S. Wyman, after that it was virtually impossible for North American Jews not to know that the Nazi occupation forces were poised to perpetrate a genocide on a scale never before recorded in the history of Europe.

> German documents seized after the war reveal that almost 1.5 million Polish Jews had been deported to killing centers by December 31, 1942. In addition, hundreds of thousands of Polish Jews had perished either through starvation and ghetto conditions or at the hands of the Einsatzgruppen in what had been pre-war eastern Poland. It turns out that the statistics dispatched by Polish underground sources were cautiously compiled indeed. It is also apparent that [rabbi Stephen S.] Wise's estimate of two million Jewish dead in all of Europe was long out of date by November 1942.[5]

First Indications of Genocide

At the same time that this disturbing news was reaching Western governments and Allied military officials, leaders of the various Canadian Jewish communities were being inundated by eye-witness accounts from fellow Jews. While various governments were attempting to find out the actual situation of the Jews in continental Europe, Montreal Yiddish-speaking Jews, through other channels, were receiving horrifying descriptions of what had happened to their relatives. These troubling reports were sometimes transmitted by Jews who were active in underground organizations, or by partisans operating in the immediate vicinity of large Eastern European urban centres. Beginning in 1940, the *Jewish Daily Eagle*, written in a colloquial Yiddish and widely distributed throughout Montreal's Jewish community, started publishing detailed accounts about Polish Jewry. Early in 1942, when the first death camps went into operation in Poland, these reports intensified. Few readers of the *Eagle* questioned the reliability of these descriptions of conditions in the ghettos and concentration camps. The repetitive nature of this information detailing the intolerable suffering endured by Polish Jews, beginning in the summer of 1942, gave Yiddish-speaking Montrealers a very clear idea of what was happening in Eastern Europe under the Nazis. In July of 1942, the Jewish Labour Committee,[6] housed in the Workmen's Circle Building on St. Lawrence Boulevard, informed Canadian Jewish Congress officials about specific information which had been circulating for several weeks through the network of left-wing Jewish organizations:

> The reports which have been gradually coming through to us of the terrible toll which the Jewish people is paying in Nazi occupied territory, is indescribable. Many of us, though hardened already to the Nazi blows, still refuse to believe that these reports could be true. Figures recently obtained directly from Poland, and presented to the Polish national council in London by the Jewish Deputy, Arthur Zigolboim [sic], reveal that between 700,000 and 1,000,000 Jews have perished at the Nazi hands, in Poland alone. The mass executions continue daily and increase in ferocity and in number of its victims.[7]

The still fragmentary news reports that reached Canadian Jews had a devastating effect on the morale of the Montreal community's leadership, which found itself powerless vis-à-vis the mechanized inferno being put into place in countries under Nazi control. Military operations had cast a shroud of silence over all of European Jewry that obscured the ultimate aim of the executioners and prevented an understanding of the events unfolding. Under these circumstances, it was extremely difficult to come to the aid of the victims or try to alleviate their suffering. The worldwide military conflict had mobilized all the energies of the Allied governments, leaving no prospect of diverting strategic resources for humanitarian purposes, such as destroying the railroad tracks leading to the death camps. This profound discouragement is apparent in Hirsch Wolofsky's account of his childhood in the Polish town of Szydlowiec (Shidlovtse Yiddish), which he wrote between 1942 and 1943. At one point, the author interrupts the story of his arrival in Warsaw in 1900 to comment on how painful it was for him to write knowing that, at that very moment, Polish Jews were under attack by the Nazis and dying in huge numbers under frightful conditions:

Now, as I begin to describe my memories of Warsaw, I am in
Montreal for the winter
[. . .] and I have no desire to go back to Florida. How can one
travel to a warm place at a time when millions of our brothers are
being murdered, simply slaughtered like sheep
[. . .]? Just thinking about it can drive one insane.[8]

In the wake of the Holocaust, the writer Sholem Shtern, also born in
Poland, went through a very dark period, deeply depressed over the
deliberate massacre of his people. In his description of the Montreal
Yiddish literary milieu in his book entitled *Shrayber vos ikh hob gekent*,
a sense of helplessness and irreparable loss invariably emerges whenever this subject is mentioned:

Rolnick often came to Montreal. Once, just before Passover, he
brought his dear wife Feygl who had always been in love with

Yiddish writers and activists at a meeting in 1942 at the Montreal Jewish Public
Library during the visit of writer Sholem Asch. Segal is the first on the right
in the second row. Asch is seated in the first row, to the left of his wife, Madja.
(Montreal Jewish Public Library.)

him. They came with their cousin, Feygl Kuper. She was also in love with Rolnick. He, however, was in love with the other Feygl, who became his wife. [. . .] When they came to visit us, we discussed literature, but everything we said was permeated by the pain of our great catastrophe – the death of over six million Jews.[9]

Jewish Montrealers' worst fears were confirmed when two important Soviet Jewish figures, the poet Itsik Fefer and the actor Solomon Mikhoels, came to address the Canadian people on behalf of the Soviet Union's Jewish Anti-Fascist Committee. When they arrived in Montreal at the beginning of September of 1943, they were accompanied by the great American Yiddish writer Sholem Asch, who was also from Eastern Europe. The latter delivered an impassioned speech in the Mount Royal Arena about the suffering of Jews at the hands of the Nazis, at a time when the Red Army seemed to be gaining the upper hand. Sholem Asch's delivery, as described by Shtern, left no doubt about the gravity of the situation:

It was a broken Jew who was speaking. His tearful voice quivered with fear. Then Asch took his seat. I was sitting near him. He was wringing his hands, tears were running down his cheeks, and he was muttering, "Oh my God! What will happen to our Jews?"[10]

The distress of Yiddish-speaking community activists and writers over the carnage in Europe was amplified by the fact that they could not talk about it outside their own narrow circle because non-Jews were likely to find it preposterous. How could anyone believe that a military power, locked in mortal combat with the Soviet Union, would divert a part of its vital resources for an undertaking that would provide no strategic advantage on the ground, and even deprive its occupying armies of needed manpower in a time of war? More than that, why would they give credence to evidence that seemed pure exaggeration, given the alleged number of victims and the degree of the cruelty being inflicted on them? Caiserman, whose task it was to appeal to the media and politicians on behalf of Jewish causes, was forced to admit that the Holocaust, in terms of its scope and horror, exceeded anything the Canadian public in general could imagine. Confronted in 1942–1943 by the first news of the Holocaust, the Secretary of the Canadian Jewish Congress for a long time sought to find a way to convince his interlocutors of the exceptional nature, and the veracity, of the reported facts:

We have read your editorial in your issue of Dec. 25, 1942 entitled: "Fantastic Fallacy" with a great deal of interest.

We feel that your reaction towards the reports of the massacres of Jews in Europe is a very natural one; decent men are inclined to dismiss as incredible reports from however responsible sources that any organised society of mankind can perpetrate such tremendous crimes on an incredibly large scale.

The logical thought, however, is that if the atrocities against the Jews of Europe as reported by such diverse authorities as the government of the United States, the World Jewish Congress and the government in exile in Poland are even partially true, even if they are only half true or one quarter true or one tenth true, they are nevertheless so unprecedented and so terrifying that no reaction of peoples still free can be too strong.[11]

The End of a World

For Montreal Yiddish writers, the news from Europe was both a catastrophe and an unprecedented violation of their realm of meaning. Within a matter of months, the world in which they had been raised, the world which was the source of inspiration for most of their creative work, was on the brink of destruction. The language in which was embedded many centuries of Ashkenaz culture, which had provided a vehicle for their most intimate thoughts, was itself now in danger of disappearing as an increasing number of it speakers fell victim to Nazi atrocities. In view of these events, the themes most favoured by the Yiddish writers seemed to lose their relevance. How could one continue recalling and describing Eastern European Jewish civilization with its unique institutions and traditions, when the places that exemplified this way of life lay in ruins, reduced to fields of rubble as far as the eye could see? Even large Polish urban centres like Warsaw, once the home of a dynamic and important Jewish community, had literally been wiped off the map, without a trace of a Jewish presence. In the wake of this irreparable damage Canadian Yiddish literature, which had only recently emerged on the banks of the St. Lawrence River thanks to a set of unexpected circumstances, suddenly found itself cut off from its very foundation, from its deep historic roots. The major writers, who had enjoyed the reassurance and encouragement of their Eastern European colleagues, now had to confront a scorched land, a desert without the slightest trace of what had just been obliterated.

After having struggled so hard to create a Yiddish-language artistic milieu worthy of its name in Canada, Montreal writers would henceforth feel the pain of a double exile, the first when they crossed the Atlantic, and the second—perhaps the more significant—only one generation later, when they were robbed of their homeland.

Forced into a new, symbolic exile, even more agonizing than the one they had experienced in their youth, Montreal Yiddish poets were now suffering a loss that would be impossible to mitigate or repair. Although many were now at the peak of their abilities—some with an international following—their future looked bleak. The extent of the anger and distress experienced by Canadian Yiddish writers as a result of the genocide of European Jewry can be measured by the profound change in their work that occurred after 1945. Many felt like the only survivors of a vanished culture, well aware that they owed their lives to a series of fortuitous events which had situated them far from the mass killings. Whereas before the war they had written eagerly and objectively about the Jewish communities where they were born, unreservedly describing their childhood and upbringing, after Auschwitz such themes acquired dark and disturbing overtones. How could one even conceive of a work of literature that would ultimately be nothing more than a mournful evocation of a world that was gone forever? What was there to gain by dwelling on the incomprehensible suffering inflicted on an entire people? A large number of Montrealers of Eastern European origin had lost family members in the death camps, and sometimes they had no news of their loved ones at all. In the immediate post-war period, as more precise information about the fate of the victims of genocide was becoming available, the world of the Montreal Yiddish poets kept on shrinking, and their creativity withered in the face of such horror. Sholem Shtern, who, thanks to his Communist sympathies, in 1949 was able to witness firsthand the disastrous consequences of the Holocaust, returned home shaken by his experience:

> I have seen firsthand the great catastrophe, how small Jewish towns, as well as large cities whose Jewish neighbourhoods teemed with Jewish life, have disappeared forever. The Nazis destroyed all of Jewish life and Jewish culture in Poland, the traditional as well as the modern. A Jewish world has been reduced to ashes. The famous Jewish cities of Poland, such as Lublin, Lemberg, Krakow, Zamosc, Vilna and Warsaw, centres of Torah

> scholarship and generations of Jewish creativity, will never be
> resurrected [. . .] I saw the Holocaust in all its horror and it struck
> me that we must turn our attention elsewhere.[12]

At the same time, beginning with the murder of Solomon Mikhoels
in 1948, the Stalin regime began sentencing the majority of the great
Soviet Yiddish writers to death, life imprisonment, or other inhuman
forms of incarceration. With the execution, in August 1952, of Itsik
Fefer, David Hofstein, Peretz Markish, David Bergelson, Lieb Kvitko,
and others, the last great modern Yiddish literary centre in Europe,
which during the interwar period had produced remarkable work and
carried the torch of Yiddish creativity to unsurpassed heights, had
been brutally eradicated. The Soviet Union's Yiddish cultural elite,
which was targeted not because of its Jewish race, as in Nazi ideology,
but because of its ongoing contact with the West and thus deemed a
threat to the political monopoly of the Communist Party, had suddenly
disappeared without a trace. Within a few short years, the loss of the
Yiddish cultural centres, which had given birth to bold new Yiddish
art forms at end of the nineteenth century, dramatically shook the very
foundations of the various cultural and linguistic components of world
Jewry. First in Poland, Lithuania, the Ukraine, and Romania, and then,
a few years later in Soviet Russia proper, the Yiddish-speaking population was almost annihilated, and its survivors dispersed throughout
the globe. After 1945, the prime responsibility for fostering and perpetuating the Yiddish language fell to Jews living on the North American
continent, with the United States taking the lead. However, on this new
continent, the Yiddish presence was less than a century old. Moreover,
the language had taken root in countries radically different from those
of Eastern Europe, countries where democratic freedoms and social
and economic mobility meant that Jewish populations could break
down barriers and quickly begin speaking the predominant language,
English. How could anyone believe that North American Yiddish literature, still in its infancy, such as the poetry of *Di Yunge* and *In Zikh*,
would not be affected by the sudden and brutal obliteration of not only
the majority of Eastern European Jewish intellectuals and artists, but
also greater part of its readership? What was true for Yiddish speakers
living in New York, Boston, Philadelphia, and Baltimore was true to
even a greater extent for those in Montreal, Toronto, and Winnipeg. At
the end of the 1940s, a devastating feeling of impotence and grief had
descended upon Yiddish cultural life throughout the New World.

For J. I. Segal, as for most of the Yiddish poets who had been living in North America for several decades, the calamitous events of the Holocaust would henceforth pervade his very being. He, who was living in the glorified atmosphere of traditional Jewish life as it had existed in Korets prior to his departure for Canada, now realized that his memories of Volhynia were henceforth the only tangible remnants of a universe that had first been undermined by the ideological transformations that occurred in the aftermath of the Russian Revolution of 1917, and then physically eradicated and annihilated by the Nazis. While Segal in his books *Lirik, Mayn nigun,* and *Di drite sude* had been extolling the ardent faith of the Hasidim and the fervour of their great rabbis, and describing the market place, the narrow streets, and the synagogues of the town where he spent his childhood, other forces were at work effacing the last remnants. Unwittingly, the poet had become the single remaining repository of the Jewish life he had shared in his early years with his family in Korets, whose voices had been silenced for all eternity in the mass graves of Babi Yar and behind the barbed wire of Auschwitz, Treblinka, Maidanek, and Sobibor. The genocide perpetrated during World War II had made Segal a living witness of a world twice trampled, battered, and bled, a witness whose exile to a distant continent had spared him the same fate. Unlike many other Yiddish writers who were consumed by anger, Segal chose not to introduce into his work the images of death and destruction which hovered over the beloved faces of his childhood. Unlike Leib Kvitko, Peretz Markish, and David Hofstein, who denounced the pogroms perpetrated during the Russian Civil War, that raged from 1919 to 1921, by resorting to gory and gruesome imagery, Segal emphasized the idyllic and saintly character of a place forever lost, yet continuously recreated in his poetic imagination. Henceforth, for him, the Yiddish language, reduced to tatters, was as important, if not more so, than the flow of images and impressions it allowed him to channel.

> Segal sanctified the word of the survivors and the language of the martyrs, the Yiddish word. [. . .] For Segal, the Yiddish language was holy. Yiddish for him was not just a language. Yiddish was everything associated with being a Jew. Yiddish now became his country and his kingdom. It was the light of a way of life that burned inside him with the bloody-fiery letters of the Hebrew alphabet. It was the generations-old path of pain and redemption. Yiddish was both his house of prayer and the prayer itself.[13]

The terrible consequences of the Holocaust reinforced Segal's shift in the 1930s toward the traditional Eastern European way of life and its mode of Orthodox Jewish observance. At the same time that this world was vanishing forever, the poet became ever more engaged in describing it and carefully preserving it for future generations. Confronted by the frightful reality of the genocide, he also made every effort to highlight the myriad nuances of the Yiddish language and illustrate its multiple layers of meaning as living testimonies to his thoroughly secular devotion to Judaism, Ashkenazic history and culture, and the Eastern European diaspora. As his pain and suffering increased, he grew more determined to write. Similarly, his desire to remain a Yiddish poet to the very end was strengthened. Segal undertook this commitment without leaving the Mount Royal Plateau and his adopted country Canada, and, as opposed to other writers and activists, he never returned to the places where his people had been murdered or to the continent where he was born. It was in Montreal in 1948 that he first met people who had survived the death camps. or had somehow or other escaped the destruction of European Jewry. The encounter in Montreal between the generation of immigrants who had arrived before World War I and Holocaust survivors was intensely emotional. Everyone was aware that these Yiddish speakers would be the last to enter the country, and that never again would people come to Montreal who were raised in the Yiddish culture which, for all intents and purposes, had perished during the Nazi upheaval. The significance of this face-to-face encounter is captured in the following poem, in which Segal symbolically welcomes victims of the Nazi atrocities to his city. Despite their unspeakable suffering and profound sorrow, the poet does not abandon the lyrical quality so characteristic of his writing (see Appendix 28):

White World

I shall remove from you your wounded body
and you will feel lighter.
I shall carry you, a sleeping dove,
away from here to another star.

After a day, a night or two
I shall kiss away from your frail mouth
the black bitterness of your silent pain,
and take away your pillow of stone.

Very early, so no one will see
I shall slip out with you like a weightless shadow.
On the streets glows the stillness
Of the first untouched untrodden snow.

And with the blue breath of early dawn we shall depart
On a light, white sled
With no gasp of fear, no trace, no fleck
Of the anguish you've endured.

In just one day, one hour, one moment
All your wounds will have fallen asleep.
Blessed be the whiteness of the earth,
Blessed be the blueness of the sky.[14]

New Sources of Inspiration

When the Second World War ended, Segal had lived in Montreal for almost thirty years, with the exception of the few years he spent in New York. In contrast to the immigrant Jews who began arriving after 1948 from the displaced persons camps situated mainly in West Germany or Austria, the earlier generation of Yiddish speakers who had entered Canada before 1914 had only distant memories of Europe, and had long ago discovered Canada's virtues. Over the course of their literary careers, as they became better acquainted with their adopted country, Segal and his contemporaries had gradually incorporated more Canadian subject matter, a shift that was accelerated by the Holocaust, which had made any return impossible. Sholem Shtern, who changed his literary direction after 1945, explained in the early 1960s that the destruction of Polish Jewry had driven him to despair, and that he had been compelled to abandon the type of writing that he had been producing for years.

> That was what first compelled me to abandon the course I had set for myself long ago, which was to spend the greater part of my life in a new land always looking back longingly on my home *shtetl*, describing what life had been like on other side of the ocean. I am not denying the importance and artistic value of those who bring a new tone to the theme of the *shtetl* [. . .] But we who came here young with lofty ideas and high ideals, we were poor, we sweated for a piece of bread [. . .] we battled in the shops and on the Jewish

street [. . .] With each passing day, fewer of those fighters and builders remain. Therefore, the writers who participated in the struggles of those early days have an obligation to recount and describe that period here [in Montreal].[15]

The tragic turn of events led Shtern to focus his attention on the country he had discovered when, upon landing in Canada in 1927, he had been forced to spend a few months in a tuberculosis sanatorium north of Montreal, in Sainte Agathe, in the heart of the Laurentians. Among the fertile fields and pristine forests, the author made the acquaintance of small French-Canadian villages and humble, hard-working farmers. Recuperating from his illness, he gradually became aware of the geographic proportions of the New World, its harsh climate, and how recently it had been settled. Having moderated his political opinions, Shtern began showcasing this landscape in his last great books, a long epic poem published in two volumes between 1960 and 1963 entitled *In Kanade*, which appeared in English as *In Canada: A Novel in Verse* in 1984, and in French as *Au Canada: un roman en vers* in 1984. *Dos vayse hoyze* was published in English as *The White House* in 1974, and in French as *Velvl: un roman en vers*. These were followed in 1978 by *Di mishpokhe in kanade*, published in English translation as *The Family in Canada*, Montreal, 1984, and in French translation as *La Famille Au Canada: un roman en vers*, also in 1984, which, as the titles indicate, deals with Jewish immigrants trying to adapt to their new life in Canada.

Segal's writing followed the same trajectory, but in a more personal series of smaller works, more suited to a writer who wrote short poems on a daily basis rather than sweeping panoramas that would have required sustained attention over long periods of time. His reluctance can be explained by several factors, including the elusiveness of Canadian culture for Eastern European immigrants bemused by the country's immense geographic size. To Yiddish speakers, Canada seemed to dissolve into an almost infinite succession of elemental and unexplored landscapes which, for all intents and purposes, defied description.[16] Much of the writing from this era available today reveals the awe and admiration felt by Canadian Jews once they realized that they had set foot in a country as large as all of Europe: "The beauty of the Canadian landscape, the grandeur of its rugged mountainsides, the charm of its rivers, the majesty of its lakes—the quality of Canada's natural endowments radiates mystic emanations which enter the soul of the Jewish people and evoke in it the finest response of love and tenderness."[17] However, this enthusiasm for Canada's natural beauty was mostly based on reading about it from afar, or looking at pictures, including photographs taken by tourists, which at first glance were often difficult to decipher, with the result that the country seemed abstract, inaccessible, even surreal. More than one Canadian Yiddish writer seemed to have that impression, most of all Segal, who lacked the temperament of an explorer, and who, in fact, after 1930, rarely left the streets of the Mount Royal Plateau, except, perhaps, for the occasional visit to New York. In that era, everything known by Montreal Jews about Canada came from reading the local press, and what they could glean here and there on short Sunday outings or during vacations in the country. Into his quest for "Canadianness" Segal came face to face with a society divided into two separate linguistic entities, each claiming its own distinct identity. Canada apparently lacked the powerful assimilationist tendencies which very early on had led immigrants in the United States to strive for a common identity. On the contrary, Canada prior to World War II had no desire to shed its colonial ties to Great Britain and affirm its own national identity. Such a situation undoubtedly affected the treatment of Canadian life in Segal's work:

> His Canadianness is expressed less frequently in his work than their Americanness is conveyed in the work of the American Yiddish writers. Perhaps one of the reasons is the fact that Canada itself is so different culturally from America. Americanness imposes itself. Canadianness must be sought.[18]

In addition, there were no precedents in Eastern European Yiddish literature for such a radical break with the traditional Judaism and life in the *shtetl*. While professing a strong attachment to religious practice, and attempting to conserve the essence of Yiddish popular culture, Canadian Yiddish writers found themselves in a country where the prevailing liberalism, a weak sense of national identity, and the absence of political censorship made possible all types of cultural experimentation. Prior to 1905, the Eastern European Jewish world had been characterized by an ardent adherence to religious tradition, cultural exclusion fortified by its own community structures, and the constant threat of physical violence. Once in Canada, and suddenly aware of its evidently unrestricted cultural openness, Yiddish writers experienced a long period of disorientation that was hardly conducive to developing a specifically Canadian creative imagination.

At first, during the 1920s and 1930s, this tolerant atmosphere led Segal to explore his inner landscape, his own uncertain identity, and the hardships of family life, in keeping with the modernist tenets of *Di Yunge*. In this respect, the Canadian Yiddish milieu differed from its American counterpart, where Moishe Leib Halpern, as early as 1919, had published a remarkable volume of poetry entitled *In New York*, soon followed by I. J. Schwartz's book-length poem entitled *Kentoki* [Kentucky] in 1925. Hailed by the critics, the latter described a freshly arrived Jewish immigrant finding a new promised land in fertile rural America. Quite early in the twentieth century other New York Yiddish writers, like Lamed Shapiro, in his 1931 book *Nyuyorkish un andere dertsaylungen* [New York and other stories] and Isaac Raboy, in his 1944 novel *Iz gekumen a yid kayn Amerike* [A Jew came to America], were also describing life in the great American metropolis. Raboy also wrote two novels in which his protagonists take part in the opening of the American West and farming the land, *Herr Goldenbarg* in 1923 and *Der idisher kauboy* [The Jewish cowboy] in 1942. Nothing similar had appeared in Montreal before World War II, undoubtedly because the unravelling of national references and the tenuousness of Canadian cultural achievements had deprived Yiddish writers of clearly iden-tifiable points of reference in their quest for a country into which to integrate themselves. That is probably why Canadian Jews were able to remain within the boundaries of their own community longer, at the risk of lagging behind the general societal trends.

For Segal, the turning point finally came with the realization that the country of his birth and his childhood no longer existed, other than in the hidden recesses of his imagination and the lines of his poetry. He transferred to the city of Montreal his emotional attach-ment to his native land of which only a distant memory remained. The city that had welcomed him as an adolescent, that had seen him real-ize his desire to write and had nurtured his first hopes for a literary career gradually became more Jewish and filled with the sounds of a language that had originated in a radically different part of the world. In Segal's mind, Montreal, which he had viewed from a young age through the lens of an Eastern European culture transplanted onto the New World, became a substitute for the Korets of his childhood, and soon throbbed with such authentic Jewish intensity that its streets and its public parks became the objects of veneration. In his poetic enthusiasm, in the rhythm of his lyrical poetry, Montreal appeared as a daily, intangible, and inestimable presence. Segal wove his intimist aesthetic around the images he observed in a city that became inseparable from the other basic elements of his identity, namely, the Yiddish language, Hasidic Judaism, the intimacy of the *shtetl*, and the voice of God. To explore Montreal, to traverse its breadth and climb the heights of its unique rocky promontory became actions endowed with a sensibility in perfect harmony with, and almost indistinguishable from, other aspects of his literary imagination. From then on, thanks to his new-found "Montreal" approach, Segal sought to better situate himself within his adopted city, and make peace with his painful exile. Thus, he welcomed into his poems the images that populated his inner world from day to day, images that came effortlessly into his imagination and which he kept under constant observation. After a long initial period of adjustment, a second exile in New York, and a devastating personal loss, Segal turned the Montreal landscape into a symbolic presence in his work, a soothing and multi-layered space of unexpected depth, as he conveyed in this mysterious 1930 poem from his book *Lirik*:

Autumn

I shall go to the cold forest
Near the rim of the mountain
to pick golden flowers
for your little mound of earth.

God, O good God,
How you have made me old
Earlier than all the old.
I see you beside me,
I feel you beside me,
And I go to the cold forest.

Little trees are turning red
at the edge of the great mountain.
The beauty of early autumn,
Yellow footprints of death.

God, O good God,
Through the mournful red
You now look at me

With a golden eye
At the edge of the cold forest.[19]

Looking Toward Montreal

The Montrealization of Segal's poetry increased after *Lirik*, not so much in terms of the number of poems on this subject, which in fact remained stable throughout the 1930s and 1940s, but because of the profound significance the author ascribed to the landscape of his adopted city. Montreal was transformed into a symbolic place that encompassed and sustained Segal's Jewish identity, where his feelings of belonging to a Yiddish community, which had been threatened with annihilation in the Old World and irrelevance in the New World, were developed and reinforced. Everything happened as though the poet had decided that above Montreal hovered a merciful divine presence, a remnant of the fire that had guided the Jews from Egypt to the land of Canaan, and in their exile across the millennia over land and sea to the shores of a city dominated by a hill reminiscent of the lost Jerusalem. Segal did not arrive at this conclusion when he first landed in North America, but only after a long and arduous journey filled with doubt and deprivation, and after witnessing the growth, year after year, of a Yiddish-language literary and artistic community. Ironically, the poet's coming to terms with the Montreal environment happened in the wake of the Holocaust, and only after he had abandoned once and for all his plans to join the New York modernist movement. Of course, in Montreal, Jews could not pray at Jerusalem's Western Wall, or contemplate the tomb of the Maharal of Prague, or feel the spirit of the Vilna Gaon gliding through the streets. But the city had opened its doors to a new Eastern European exile which had saved it from certain destruction. Montreal's Francophones were most certainly not aware of the tragic trek the Jews had made across the centuries, but they had allowed them to settle in one of the city's neighbourhoods, and closed their eyes to the rest. French Canadians, thought Segal, were too busy in their churches proclaiming the words of the gospels and the symbols of their own nationhood to notice that at the foot of Mount Royal lived another people with the will and the strength to perpetuate its own religious tradition (see Appendix 29). This observation can be found, for example, in the following poem published after Segal's death. Here, the poet walks through the city amidst the symbols of Catholicism triumphant, without ever experiencing a sense of oppression or a threat to maintaining his own religious identity.

Late Autumn Montreal

(Translated by Miriam Waddington)

The worm goes back to the earth
the wind glitters and sharpens his sword;
where did all the colored leaves fly
to, anyway? The branches are all locked
in a vise of sleep; the skies aspire
to climb higher, their clear-blue
washes over the roof tops and stillness
assures us that all is well.
Our churchy city becomes even more pious
on Sundays, the golden crosses shine and gleam
while the big bells ring with loud
hallelujahs and the little bells answer
their low amens; the tidy peaceful streets
lie dreaming in broad daylight murmuring
endearments to me who am such a Yiddish Jew
that even in my footsteps they must hear
how the music of my Yiddish song sounds
through the rhythm of my Hebrew prayer.[20]

This Yiddish poem about Montreal contains several elements that were novel for all of Quebec literature, including the fact that Segal was serenely contemplating the urban environment during a period of intense growth accompanied by all the characteristic traits of modernity. Published at a time when the Eastern European Jewish presence in Montreal was very new, it incorporated the images of several religious traditions, especially the French Catholic, to which Segal refers with remarkable openness, taking into account the persecutions inflicted on the Jews of Eastern Europe over the centuries. Based on sights readily accessible to all residents of the Mount Royal Plateau, the Montreal poems offer views of the narrow streets that the garment workers would have seen from their modest dwellings, and the public places where they would meet one another. Also in the poems are references to the harbour and the docks of Old Montreal where the Yiddish speakers first disembarked, and therefore evoked familiar and positive feelings. Above all, the Yiddish poems about Montreal placed Mount Royal at the geographic centre of the city, and used its height as a universal benchmark for everything related to Montreal, including the illuminated cross rising from its summit and visible from every east-west street in the Jewish neighbourhood. Sheltering at its base the little island that constituted the Jewish immigrant neighbourhood, the "mountain" became a beacon for Montreal's Jews, and its impressive size made it a symbol of the divine presence, a reminder of both the earthly and the heavenly Jerusalem. From this perspective, Mount Royal appears even more as a symbol of the wildness and inaccessibility of Canada's natural forces as it towers undaunted over a city mercilessly lashed by winter, a city whose residents and homes are tormented by a harsh climate, year after year. Generally without access to the infinite expanse of Canada's hinterland and its vast northern solitudes, Yiddish speakers imagined that the entire country looked like Montreal's royal mountain—solemn, silent, and invincible:

Montreal (excerpt)

When no one is looking, I bow
Ever lower to the dust.
And yet—I love the voice of the world,
and the smile of a windowpane.

Children are playing in the street,
and grownups—in the market.
And proudly in my city stands,
Opposite the market—the mountain.

Now it stands in the cold white
and clear light of the snow.
Like tall antlered deer
The trees—row on row.

That is where winter has set
its royal throne.
The cross burns all night long.
Who knows—perhaps forever.[21]

Due to an unanticipated turn of events, the Jewish neighbourhood next to Mount Royal became a constant reminder for Segal of the town of his childhood, Korets, for which he professed an enduring attachment, and which fuelled his imagination. The greater the unbridgeable gulf created by time and distance between the poet and Korets, the closer he was drawn in his writing to that small town in Volhynia of yesteryear. The Mount Royal Plateau, bursting with incessant Jewish community activity and the familiar sounds of the Yiddish language, in Segal's writing mirrored the spirit of the Eastern European *shtetl*. Certainly, Montreal was not Korets, but the details of everyday life, the piety visible in certain synagogues, and the narrow streets in the Jewish immigrant neighbourhood could easily evoke some of the small towns in the Russian Empire where the majority of the population was Jewish. In his poems, Segal depicted the tumult of Montreal's public spaces, the peacefulness of its residential neighbourhoods, the imposing presence of Christian places of worship, and the intimacy of social relationships, all reminders of the urban environment he had inhabited before crossing the ocean. These echoes of an older, Eastern European way of life managed to persist without much difficulty in the bowels of the large industrial city. Unmistakable signs of modernity and more traditional forms of sociality converged in Segal's Montreal, facilitating his movement from one universe to the other, as well as the preservation of a meaningful Eastern European Jewish space. The poet had even succeeded in including his Hasidic lineage in the Montreal section of his work, revealing how much the city for him seemed to lend itself to the expression of an intense and mystical religious piety, like the Christian Ville-Marie of the earliest European arrivals, a piety the *tsaddikim* themselves would not have rejected. In *Di drite sude*, Segal went so far as to compare the Mount Royal Plateau to the town of Medzhybyz[22] in the Ukraine, a holy place for the adherents of Hasidism because Israel ben Eliezer, the Baal Shem Tov, had died there in 1760.[23] Similarly, one snowy night, he saw in the gardens of a residence for priests' similarities to his Volhynian childhood.

Winter in Montreal

Soft silken snow
floats down over the ground
as though the pale grey were sowing
fresh peace on the earth.

Little trees grow luminous,
their branches—children's hands.

In their stillness I have seen
the land of distant silence.

They stand serene and calm
Silvery light and pensive.
In their stillness I have heard
My village home at dusk.

On the long balcony
the priests walk to and fro
reciting psalms held in their hands[24]
with pious peace of mind.

The white gardens lie warm
and the grey sky – nearby.
On the horizon the mountain
Dons a shawl of light mist.[25]

Segal was not the only poet to make reference to Montreal's land-scapes and its cultural symbols over the course of his career. Later on, other Yiddish writers did the same, including Yudika in a 1934 collection entitled *Vandervegn* (Migrant Roads), N. I. Gotlib in his eponymous collection of 1968, and Sholem Shtern in his 1982 memoirs entitled *Shrayber vos ikh hob gekent* (Writers I Knew). Segal, however, took this theme a step further by making the city more than a mere backdrop for the buildings and parks he saw every day. For the author of *Lirik* and *Di drite sude*, Montreal became the mirror image of his personal journey from Volhynia to the shores of the New World, and the embodiment of all his hopes. In Montreal his literary creativity flourished for the first time, and there he coherently articulated his irrepressible thirst for cultural modernity. There were enough pious Jews in the city for him to be constantly reminded of his indestructible, yet

Jacob Isaac Segal, 1940.
(Montreal Public Library.)

Invitation card for the booklaunch
in the Jewish Public Library of the
book *Lider un Loybn* by J. I. Segal,
published in 1944.
(Montreal Jewish Public Library.)

distant, attachment to traditional religious Judaism. A refuge from Eastern European arbitrariness, a place of creative freedom, and an intimate space within the Jewish community, Montreal for the poet held a multitude of expectations. Multicultural, multilingual, and in constant motion, the city, in all its complexity, still found room for the Yiddish language. In its streets, even in the shadow of its Catholic steeples, could be heard the melodies that Jews had carried with them from one exile to another for centuries. The mystery of this unexpected welcome and its concrete manifestations, elevated Segal's writing and ignited the emotions expressed in his poems about Montreal. Shtern, who had approached the theme of Montrealness from a very different perspective, often records in his memoirs the powerful impact of Montreal's cultural life on his New York guests. In the following passage, for example, the Yiddish poet Zishe Weinper, struck by the tolerant atmosphere in the neighbourhood snuggled at the bottom of Mount Royal, was amazed to discover a monumental cross that towered over the Jewish neighbourhood:

> We were near Horn's cafeteria, which was right next to the *Keneder Adler*. Through the clanging of the streetcars on St. Lawrence Boulevard (Main Street) could be heard the clamour of the Rachel Street Market[26] where Jewish immigrant women, some fresh off the boat, chatted and haggled with French farmers and their wives, half in Yiddish, half in English and French, the rest in sign language. . . Weinper was captivated by this scene. We joined the tumult of the market. . . Across the way the blinding sun was descending on the wooded mountaintop. The cross

that soared above the green-golden summit looked like a flaming torch. Shafts of light embraced the tree trunks, and their branches wrapped themselves in the fiery rays of the sunset.[27]

A Mystical Leap

Segal published three volumes of poetry during the 1940s and 1950s, all of whose titles invoked the Jewish tradition, namely, *Dos hoyz fun di poshete* [The house of the simple people] in 1940, *Lider un loybn* [Poetry and praise] in 1944, and *Sefer idish* [The book of Yiddish][28] in 1950. The crowning achievement of his career, almost 600 pages long, *Sefer idish* is a memorial to the Yiddish culture itself and the millions of victims of the Holocaust. In it, Segal confers upon Yiddish a holiness equivalent to that of biblical Hebrew. Furthermore, the poet compares his own literary work to books that deal with God's holiness and sing His praises. Segal's journey from the secular world to the realm of the divine could only be understood in the context of the near destruction of Ashkenzic culture, which had been brutally obliterated in Eastern Europe, where it had developed over many centuries. Confronting the silence that now hovered over the martyred communities and the disappearance of the places that were home to the most profound Jewish values, Segal held his breath, then turned to God. The poet had thus completed the long cycle which gradually made him leave the shores of introspective modernism, embraced so fervently by his New York colleagues, to undertake a journey increasingly suffused with the words and images of traditional Judaism, where the prayers had literary merit in their own right. This was consistent with the ideas of the Poalei Zion party, which found its way to Montreal at the beginning of the twentieth century. Although a totally secular movement that had distanced itself from religious practice of any kind, the Poalei Zion nonetheless considered the biblical and Talmudic literature a historical and cultural legacy. Segal strongly supported this view, which was shared by the directors of the secular schools, including the Jewish People's School where he had been teaching for many years. It was also the position of some garment worker activists who were not Zionists, a position that Sholem Shtern summarized very well in his memoirs:

> We were socialists, and we believed that the courageous militancy of the Communist Party would bring happiness to all people. At the same time, we were among a minority on the progressive

Jewish periphery which remained attached to the uniqueness of the Jewish cultural creativity that had developed over generations. In the restlessness of our longing we carried the spirit of traditional Judaism. We were not simply socialists, but Jewish socialists.[29]

The first of these three volumes, *Dos hoyz fun di poshete,* has a strong religious tenor. It returns to the idea of the people of God in exile for centuries, thrust into a life of dreariness and affliction, surrounded by a world of untold suffering and unrelieved sorrow. Amidst their interminable tribulations, the Jews recall the joy of the Sabbath and the light of the holidays. They recite the prayers bequeathed to them by their ancestors, unite to celebrate the glory of their heavenly father, and zealously obey the laws in their sacred books. Persecution, the loss of the earthly Jerusalem, and abject poverty reduced them to a life of unceasing simplicity while their hearts burned with the flame of Abraham and Moses in search of the divine presence. In his book, Segal shares the fate of his people, feels their despair, and listens to the chant of generations past, permeated by the melancholy of the Jews encamped on the shores of Babylon. He hears their lamentations following the destruction of the Second Temple and weeps at their helplessness under the yoke of the tsar. Projecting himself back to Eastern Europe, the author listens to the teachings of the *tsaddikim,* the Baal Shem Tov, Nachman of Bratslav, and the other great Hasidic rabbis. In their words and in the streets of the Korets of his childhood he seeks the consolation he does not find in his everyday life, in the monotony of the passing days and hours, interrupted only momentarily by the rhythm of the Jewish calendar. Like his father before him, Segal is in search of a divine blessing that would render his exile more bearable and his sadness less acute. His imagination wanders through the places where the founder of Hasidism once walked, where nature whispers the occasional divine allusion or hints of its impalpable presence. A sometime literary critic, Sholem Shtern made the following assessment of his friend Segal in the early 1940s: "He summoned the Baal Shem Tov in his thoughts, addressing him in an anxious voice, while experiencing pure and brilliant joy."[30] For a brief moment the poet joined the disciples of the Baal Shem Tov and drank in the words of this miracle rabbi, as in the following excerpt from *Dos hoyz fun di poshete,* which reveals the writer's excitement in retracing the steps of the great Jewish mystics and their followers across the Polish countryside (see Appendix 30):

From the Baal Shem Tov to Today

To the Baal Shem would come the poor --
The rich avoided his dwelling --
Jews from foreign lands and great distances,
And even from sorrowful and grey Lithuania.

After staying with him for three short days
They went home happy
With empty grey sacks slung over their thin shoulders
Through fields of golden corn.

Whoever has little bread and whoever has more
God's kindness the balance will restore.
When a person travels here from afar
He has come to do good.

Always repeating God's first words:
Let there be light, light on all his paths.
What is light? A tree here, a blade of grass there,
And the sweetly singing rivulets of rain.[31]

The poets J. I. Segal and Aaron Glanz-Leyeles (right), photographed at the corner of Mount Royal and Esplanade, Montreal, 1950. (Private collection of Sylvia and Annette Segal.)

In *Dos hoyz fun di poshete* (1940) Segal entered a new stage in his literary career by transporting himself body and soul into the familiar space of Eastern European Jewry, and shouldering the weight of the heritage of a still recent era, which his hurried departure for North America had not effaced. This time, although still under the spell of blazing modernity to which he aspired with all his being, Segal pursued his formal experimentations while incorporating into his poetry themes that would not have been rejected by even the most pious of the Baal Shem Tov's disciples—the echoes of God's word in pristine nature, blessings recited in a humble cottage, the afternoon prayer in a rustic house of worship. Even if finding refuge in the past was no longer possible, even if his faith had been precipitously snatched away by immigration and industrialization, images of an outmoded Jewish way of life peopled the poet's imagination: the simple gesture of lighting candles to usher in the Sabbath, a *chumash* lying open on a roughly hewn wooden table, and, above all, a melody suddenly drifting around the corner of a darkened street. In the 1940s, Segal vacillated constantly between a poetic approach rooted in a deeply religious traditional world, and an approach born of skepticism and modernity. This becomes evident in his 1940 book entitled *Dos hoyz fun di poshete*, which includes free-verse poems with the harsh and vengeful tone of prayers addressed directly to God. This book had a lasting impact on Yiddish literature at the time. Melekh Ravitch, who while in Mexico had received a copy from Segal, showered it with praise. In a letter dated December 1940, he stated that he was very moved by its contents:

> Your book strongly impressed me. In it are poetic masterpieces [. . .] I read many of these poems with a distinct feeling of envy – and that is the greatest compliment that one poet can give another – and also with a feeling of impotence – never, my little Ravitch, could you have done that – that is the highest praise that I can give you.[32]

In a book review which appeared in the *Tog* of New York, Sh. Niger did not hesitate to recognize and welcome the religious formalism, even if at times he found it disconcerting: "One of Segal's poems is entitled *Tkhine* (Yiddish prayer). This title is appropriate not only for this poem. One must read it exactly as if reciting a *tkhine*.[33]"

Tkhine [A Yiddish prayer] (excerpt)

Lord, kindle a new love
in our earthly congregation.
Choose a house on our humble street,
and usher in again your Sabbath day
and call the house: the house of rest.
From our cellar shops we are drawn to your threshold.
We shall once more open the panels in your walls
Where hourly confessions purified our bodies,

> And lightened our lonely souls,
> And to our errant judgment,
> extended a pure hand —
> To take us from one day to the next.[34]

Segal's Eastern European odyssey continued in *Lider un loybn* (1944), a book of over 500 pages, which was published only four years after *Dos hoyz fun di poshete*. When it appeared in print, the Nazis were in the process of destroying the Yiddish-speaking communities that had stretched across the former Russian Pale of Settlement. The more the world of Segal's childhood was consumed in the flames of the Holocaust, the more he turned inward to protect the surviving vestiges of his heritage. During the 1940s, these radiant symbols of an existence, which pulsated to the rhythm of the Five Books of Moses and the teachings of the great Hasidic rabbis, were beginning to fade even in Montreal, as a new Canadian-born generation began to find the essence of their identity in Canada. Except for the poet, who, in the recesses of his imagination preserved the devotion and inflections of yesteryear. Locked away in the vault of his memory were the streets and landscapes of Korets, incomparable in their profound significance and beauty, the refuge of all his poetry. David Rome noted this in reviewing the book in the Congress Bulletin in August of 1945, emphasizing its tone of nostalgia:

> That is Segal's memory of his parents and of his childhood. [. . .]
> In this regard Segal's happy age is not strangely dissimilar from
> those of other men in other times and environments. But Segal
> has not compromised, "adjusted". He has remained, as is given
> to few, youthful by remaining loyal to the society of his youth and
> to its ideals.[35]

The book, which seemed to fly in the face of contemporary trends, conjured up the presence of the God of Israel in every doorway, above each window, especially on the Sabbath Eve, when exactly at sundown the routines of everyday life grind to a halt, and the reign of the divine commences. Then, into the darkness of humble dwellings a peace descends, along with a joy that Segal was continuously seeking to recapture in boisterous America, and in a Montreal dizzy with ambition and prosperity.

Light of Old

How many good things remained in the old country
that we could not take with us.
To them I have written the quietest melodies,
Each word still so close it hurts.

But they are all over there in the distance,
and gradually perhaps already expiring.
The tips of the cornstalks have yellowed in the garden,
I look out through the lonely window –

The shopkeeper women walk home with their baskets,
A golden coolness frolics in the air
The weekday tumult, the weekday outdoors
Grows dearer and stiller and silenced.

The Sabbath illumines a faraway cottage,
Such sad and soothing light from God.
It seems as though someone in pure white
will soon appear in the streets of the town.

And all the windows of the houses will be lit
With sacred light and bless the world.
In all the houses your pious families will rest,
Hallowed Father in Your heavenly tent.[36]

A Chorus of Praise

Not all the modernist poets were delighted by Segal's predilection for nostalgia, for his dwelling on the past. Perhaps they had never pictured a twilight where God was enthroned in all His infinite splendour and boundless compassion. Yet the lyricism of Segal's writing and the loftiness of his sentiments succeeded in winning over even the most reluctant. Although it was a far cry from the Podolian fields of the Baal Shem Tov to the struggle of the immigrant workers and the hustle and bustle of the large North American cities, readers were affected by the Montreal poet's powerful imagery and the Hebraic cadences of his verse. In an era when an entire world had vanished forever, Segal was able to move them by his subtle allusions to the universe of Eastern Europe and his closeness to the melody of the prayers chanted in the ethereal stillness of Korets. By this time the echoes of Hasidic fervour and popular piety no longer resounded as powerfully in Yiddish literature as they once had, due to a lack of witnesses capable of recreating the requisite images and rhythms. When *Dos hoyz fun di poshete* appeared in 1940, Sholem Shtern, the Montreal poet dedicated to the struggle for socialism, mused that "J. I. Segal has the poetic power to make us believe in phenomena that we do not see around us. Like a true artist, he knows how to breathe life into a world which in reality we no longer feel."[37] Excited by the publication of *Lider un loybn*, Aaron Glanz-Leyeles, a founder of the American Introspectivist group *In Zikh* and one of the luminaries who would occasionally visit the Montreal Yiddish literary community, confided to Segal in 1945: "I enjoyed your book immensely. The sincerity of your poetry can leave no one indifferent. Over the years, in several volumes, you have created a great body of poetic work which clearly demonstrates that you are true to yourself."[38]

And Berish Weinstein, a member of the new generation of New York Yiddish writers, but also raised in an Hasidic environment, wrote candidly to Segal about *Dos hoyz fun di poshete*:

> It gives me pleasure to think that of all the poetry books that are in my book cabinet, your book has pride of place. And if a poet is destined to produce a book of poetry, it should possess the simplicity, sparseness, authenticity and poetic brilliance found in the poetry collection *Dos hoyz fun di poshete* by my beloved poet J. I. Segal.[39]

Thanks to *Lider un loybn*, in 1945 Segal was awarded the Louis Lamed Prize for Literature, an award established in the United States by the Louis Lamed Foundation for the Advancement of Hebrew and Yiddish Literature.[40] This prestigious organization was chaired by the great Yiddish literary critic, Shmuel Niger. At the time this particular honour was bestowed upon Segal, it represented the crowning achievement in the career of a North American Yiddish writer.[41] Segal had been nominated for the award by Hershl Novak, who had known the poet in the 1910s in Montreal when they both taught at the Peretz School, and had remained Segal's friend after leaving for the United States at the beginning of the 1920s.[42] In 1945 Novak was the administrator of the *Tsukunft*, a New York literary monthly influential in the Yiddish socialist world, while Shmuel Niger was its editor-in-chief. Through Novak, Segal was able to publicize *Lider un Loybn* in the United States, and make the acquaintance of influential people in Yiddish literary circles:

> Here in New York we are going to organize a few events, and make every effort to distribute the new book. Our colleagues have promised to help (Niger, Leivick, Bialostotzki, Glanz-Leyeles, Weinstein and probably others). It goes without saying that you will be our guest, in our home, and we will have the opportunity to revisit the old days in Montreal.[43]

Winning the Lamed prize contributed tremendously to making Segal known throughout the Yiddish-speaking world. In literary circles it was considered the highest endorsement of his work. Leib Wasserman, who had written the entry on Segal in the *Leksikon fun der nayer idisher liteatur*, the biographical dictionary of Yiddish literature by Niger and Shatsky, wrote the following: "[. . .] *Lider un loybn* helped to make famous one of the greatest Yiddish poets."[44] This event brought Segal a flood of congratulatory messages and greater visibility. To acknowledge his achievement, the Yiddish Writers' Association hosted a party in Segal's honour on November 10, 1945. The Jewish Public Library did the same on November 18 at the Jewish People's School. At the second and more intimate celebration, singer N. Mendelson delivered

Poets J. I. Segal and Joseph Rolnick (right) on Esplanade Avenue, in front of the home of Ida Maze, Montreal, c. 1950. (Private collection of Sylvia and Annette Segal.)

a solemn rendition of three of Segal's poems, followed by readings of selections from the poet's work.[45] Around that same time the New York Yiddish poet and essayist Abraham Ber Tabachnik wrote to Segal:

> First, let me congratulate you. You have more than earned that prize. And I'll let you in on a secret. I have known for a long time that you would receive the prize for poetry this year, not because anyone told me, but how could it have been otherwise? . . . I can only tell you that not a day goes by that I don't talk about you and your poetry.[46]

The Louis Lamed Prize was a turning point for the poet whose innate shyness and modesty had kept him out of the limelight. In his unpublished biography of Segal, H. M. Caiserman devoted a special chapter to this event, a chapter about literary creativity.[47] From then on, Segal was considered by his own community to be the most accomplished of the Montreal Yiddish writers, the very personification of the almost

prophetic figure of the modern poet, bearer of the loftiest aspirations as well as the deepest sufferings of his people. Several photos from this era show Segal, his face serious, his eyes restless, gazing into the distance in sorrowful contemplation. By assuming this pose, the poet was implying that for him art was as much an extraordinarily heavy burden, which he had to bear with equanimity, as it was a quest for meaning in an era traumatized by acts of genocide. A few months after having received the Louis Lamed Prize, Segal celebrated his fiftieth birthday, and again received hearty congratulations from many of his colleagues and faithful readers. On March 19, 1947, a large public celebration sponsored by the Montreal community

J. I. Segal and poet Itsik Manger (left), c. 1950. (Private collection of Sylvia and Annette Segal.)

Poets J. I. Segal and H. Leivick (left),
Montreal, c, 1950. (Private collection
of Sylvia and Annette Segal.)

was held at the Jewish People's School to publicly acknowledge this important new chapter in the poet's life.[48] On this occasion, once again Segal's poetry was recited and sung, and many people paid him tribute. The outpouring of accolades had begun two days earlier at the *Jewish Daily Eagle* when the editor-in-chief, Israel Rabinovitch, in his weekly column entitled "Day in, day out [*tog ayn tog oys*]," paid homage to the poet and his work.[49] In the same issue of the newspaper, the poet Melekh Ravitch compared Segal to a muezzin calling the faithful to prayer from the top of his minaret. Not everyone could hear his cry amidst the daily commotion of a Yiddish newspaper, but those who received the injunction retreated into a corner to release a deep, heart-felt sigh and recite the sacred texts aloud.[50]

In the United States, home to the last significant Yiddish readership, Segal was considered to be an American writer living in Montreal. In America Segal had received much attention in the Yiddish media in 1946–1947, as the *Keneder Adler* emphasized: "This birthday celebration was mentioned in every [American] Jewish newspaper, and dozens of articles were published about it."[51] The Yiddish daily the *Forward* ran several articles about Segal and the tributes he had received from a multitude of Yiddish cultural groups on this occasion.[52] At fifty years of age, the poet had become the artistic peer of the great New York Yiddish poets, whom he visited from time to time when he travelled to that great American metropolis, and whose ideal of literary modernism he ardently shared, among them Mani Leib, H. Leivick, Joseph Rolnick, Aaron Glanz Leyeles, Abraham Ber Tabachnik, Itsik Manger, Jacob Glatstein and Benjamin Jacob Bialostotzki. The latter had written a long article about Segal in honour of his fiftieth birthday in the *Fraye Arbeter Shtime* (Free Voice of Labour), where he declared Segal to

J. I. Segal and the actor Hertz Grosbard
(left), c. 1950 in front of the residence
of Melekh Ravitch on Esplanade
Avenue, Montreal. (Private collection
of Sylvia and Annette Segal.)

be one of the most accomplished lyric poets of his generation.[53] With his introspectivist sensibility and embrace of the triumphs of North American Yiddish poetry, Segal had managed to distance himself from both the Polish and Soviet Yiddish literary movements which had achieved recognition in Eastern Europe in the interwar period and as late as the early 1950s. Unlike the work of the Soviet Union's best Yiddish writers, Segal's writing gave no indication of a bias in favour of socialist ideology, nor any interest in socialist realism and the class struggle. On the contrary, his individualism, his preference for free verse, and his allusive style showed him to be a loyal follower of the American *In Zikh* movement. The major practitioners of this type of nauanced modernism had been the first to recognize this affinity by maintaining an ongoing relationship with Segal. In 1946 Glanz-Leyeles, at the time the president of the Yiddish Pen Club in New York, did not stand on ceremony when he relayed his heartfelt wishes to the poet on his fiftieth birthday:

> You have already achieved so much for the wonderful Yiddish poetry of our era—a magnificent edifice for future generations, and we wish you ever greater accomplishments on behalf of Yiddish poetry, Yiddish literature, and our eternal Jewish people. Among such a multitude of Yiddish poets—no evil eye!—produced by the American continent during our lifetime, it is a feat to maintain one's own voice and one's own personality. You have your own voice, and it is a noble, beautiful and original voice. I wish you long years of health and creativity, my dear colleague and cherished Yiddish poet![54]

The Contribution of the Holocaust Survivors

The publication of *Lider un Loybn*[55] and the events honouring its author took place in the immediate aftermath of World War II and the destruction of Eastern European Jewry. The poet was forced to resign himself to the fact that he would no longer receive any messages from his overseas colleagues, who had either vanished in the flames of the Holocaust or had fled, leaving everything behind. With the advent of peace, the world gradually began to discover the horrors of the concentration camps and the fate reserved for certain so-called racial minorities by the Nazis. Canadian Jews became aware that tens of thousands of survivors of the Nazi horrors remained stranded in refugee camps in Germany, Austria, and Italy, and they tried, whenever possible, to bring some of these displaced persons to Canada. The Canadian government, which had made almost no effort during the war to open its door to Jewish immigrants, fundamentally modified its immigration policies beginning in the late 1940s. Having been one of the countries least interested in admitting Jews living in desperate circumstances, Canada, during the post-war period, became one of the countries willing to receive a large influx of Holocaust survivors. Among the Yiddish-speaking immigrants who arrived in Montreal were scholars, teachers, and writers, some of whom had enjoyed illustrious careers in pre-war Eastern Europe and were able to contribute almost immediately to Jewish life in the city. In his early fifties at the time of this new influx, Segal emphasized the magnitude of their contribution in an interview with the *Forward* in May of 1951. "Here in Montreal there are now 5,000 refugees. Some of them have lent their support to the construction and consolidation of our school system, in addition to working in our cultural organizations."[56] For Segal's generation, which had been working since the end of World War I to develop Montreal Yiddish literature, the arrival of a new group of Eastern European writers, even in such tragic circumstances, was an unforeseen boon.

In contrast to the immigrants of the 1910s who had disembarked at Canadian ports fortified by their youth and unbridled optimism, Holocaust survivors entered the country after having endured terrible trials and tribulations and narrowly escaping death. Whereas Segal, Nepom, Maze, Matenko, and Shkolnikov had set foot in Canada at a young age, before having published a single line, many of the writers who came at the end of the 1940s had already enjoyed remarkable careers. Some of them were already well known in Yiddish artistic circles worldwide. This was especially true in the case of Rokhl Korn, born in Eastern Galacia in 1898, who settled permanently in Montreal in 1948. Korn had launched her career in the early 1920s by publishing poetry, first in Polish and then in Yiddish, in various Eastern European periodicals. In 1928, she published a small book entitled *Dorf* [Village] in Vilna, which helped make her reputation as one of the new voices of Polish Yiddish poetry,[57] followed by a collection of short stories in 1936 entitled *Erd* [Earth], depicting rural and agricultural life in her native Galicia. The following year, Korn published *Royter man, lider,* [Red man, poems] at a time when she was regularly contributing to Soviet publications and living in Russia. In his Lexicon, Chaim Leib Fuks states that

> after settling in Montreal, Korn began a period of intense literary activity. In addition to writing for the *Keneder Adler*, she contributed to almost every literary anthology at the time. She published poems and stories, essays about literature, articles about writers and books, and excerpts from her memoirs about her years of wandering.[58]

From 1948 to 1977, while living in Montreal, Korn published eight volumes of Yiddish poetry on three continents, and was the recipient of prestigious awards, including the Louis Lamed Prize twice, the H. Leivick Prize, the Manger Prize, the J. I. Segal Award and the Hayim Greenberg Award. Most noteworthy are her books entitled *Bashertkayt, lider 1928–1948* [Predestination, poems] and *Nayn dertseylungen* [Nine stories], published in Montreal in 1949 and 1957, respectively.

Although Korn herself had managed to escape into the Soviet hinterland after the German invasion of Poland, she was deeply affected by the horrors of the Holocaust and the suffering of the Jewish refugees during that dreadful period. However, the intensity of her pain did not diminish the tenderness of her emotions, the softness of her language, and her descriptions of nature, deemed exceptional by her contemporaries. Two years after having welcomed Rokhl Korn, Montreal opened its doors to another exceedingly talented woman. Born in Poland in 1923, incarcerated in the Lodz ghetto in 1940, interned in Auschwitz for a few months in 1944 before being sent to Bergen-Belsen where she remained until being liberated, Chava Rosenbfarb

The poets Melekh Ravitch, Jacob Glatstein, and J. I. Segal, c. 1950. (Private collection of Sylvia and Annette Segal.)

began her Yiddish literary career while still under the Nazi yoke. She arrived in Montreal preceded by a well-established reputation, due in large part to the publication in [296] London in 1947 of a collection entitled *Di balade fun nekhtiken vald* [The ballad of yesterday's forest]. This small book retraces the author's journey from her native Lodz to the concentration camps, describing a world stripped of its substance by the Holocaust. In 1948, the book was republished in Montreal by the bookseller Harry (Hirsch) Hershman, prior to Rosenfarb's arrival. A second edition appeared that same year in Montreal entitled *Geto un andere lider, fragmentn fun a tog bukh* [Ghetto and other poems, fragments from a diary]. Paradoxically, amidst the brutality of the genocidal Nazi universe, Rosenfarb began writing poetry with subtle and ethereal imagery to convey the impression of intractable pain. These were followed by a three-act play entitled *Der foygl fun geto* [The bird of the ghetto] published in Montreal in 1958, and the writer's major oeuvre, a trilogy that appeared in Tel Aviv in 1972, with the title *Der boym fun lebn* (The Tree of Life).[59] The latter is a work of unrelenting realism recounting the daily life of the Jews in the Lodz Ghetto. One of the main characters, a young girl who gives clandestine lessons to children and composes poetry to fortify the will of her loved ones to survive, as well as her own. Except for a few details, the description of this character and her experiences is autobiographical.

It was not long before other talented writers began arriving in Montreal in the aftermath of the Second World War, among them Mordechai Husid. Born in 1909, he published a collection of stories entitled *Formen in bren* [Forms in flames] in Vilna in 1937. After immigrating to Canada in 1950 and becoming a teacher at the Montreal Jewish People's School, Husid in 1969 published a volume of poetry called *Doyres shrayen mikh ariber* [Generations screaming over me] and in 1975 a second entitled *A shotn trogt mayn kroyn* [A shadow wears my crown] . One of the poets who came to Montreal during the post-war years was Simcha Simchovitch, who in 1950 published a collection of poems, including some written during his youth, which he called *Azoy iz a yugnt fargangen* [Thus passed my youth]. After 1955, Simchovitch pursued his career in Toronto where, in 1958, he published *In sho fun tfile, lider* [At the hour of prayer, poems]. Paul Trepman, a survivor of Majdanek and Bergen-Belsen, after settling in Montreal wrote short stories about Warsaw under the Nazi occupation, which appeared in 1949 in a book entitled *A gesl in Varshe* [A small street in Warsaw]. Several years later, Yehuda Elberg, a survivor of the Warsaw ghetto, moved to Montreal where he became known for his novels and short stories. In 1974, he published *Oyfn shpits fun a mast* (*Ship of the Hunted*),[60] a novel about daily life in the ghetto, and another novel, in 1983, entitled *Kalman Kalikes imperye* (*The Empire of Kalman the Cripple*),[61] about the tribulations of a young Orthodox Jew in a small Polish village in the early 1930s. In between, Elberg published a collection of short stories in Montreal entitled *Tsevorfene zangen* (Scattered Stalks), set within the Orthodox Jewish community during the Holocaust. Other Montreal authors who produced short stories based on their own personal experiences during World War II included Mina Volkovitch, Yerahmiel Weingarten, Paula Frankel-Zaltzman and Joseph Rogel. Frankel-Zaltzman, a survivor of the Stutthof Concentration Camp, in 1949 published a book entitled *Heftling number 94771*, which appeared in an English version in Montreal in 2003 under the title *Haftling (Prisoner) No. 94771*. Also in Montreal, two years later, Rogel published *Oyshvits numer A18260,* which appeared in English in 1972 as *Confessions of an Auschwitz Number (A18260).* Several other detailed descriptions of the dreadful conditions in the death camps were published after the war in the Yiddish press, especially in the *Keneder Adler,* or in privately distributed memorial books compiled through the efforts of survivor associations.[62]

The Ravitch Galaxy

Yiddish writers who settled in Montreal during the 1940s had not all experienced the horrors of the concentration camps, nor had they been forced to flee the German invasion of Poland in September of 1939, or the attack against the Soviet Union in June of 1941. There were Jews, who, alerted by their own morbid premonitions, had been able to leave Eastern Europe before the great upheaval, and Melekh Ravitch, as we have seen, was one of them. Born in a small town in Eastern Galicia in 1893, he had launched his Yiddish writing career as part of a group of modernist writers in Warsaw in 1921. Having made contact with Segal in the early 1920s, Ravitch had a special affection for his Montreal colleague. He had been able to follow the evolution of Segal's writing through critical reviews, which regularly appeared in the Polish press. Disgusted by the political and economic discrimination against Jews in Poland,[63] Ravitch decided to leave Warsaw forever in 1934. In August of that same year, he confided this to Segal and did not hide his desire to settle in Montreal: "I must leave Warsaw. Why? Warsaw is a tomb [. . .] Don't tell me, Segal, that Montreal is a tomb. That's just not true. But Warsaw, yes. [. . .] I must emigrate. I must leave this tomb. Perhaps it's possible to come to Canada, to Montreal?"[64] In his peregrinations in search of a haven in America, Ravitch first passed through Montreal in 1934, where he met face to face with Segal for the first time. He also had a few days to familiarize himself with the Canadian Yiddish literary milieu, visiting the premises of the *Keneder Adler* and the Jewish Public Library. At their first encounter, Ravitch played a little game with Segal by pretending to be a Canadian writer passing through the city, a claim which Segal did not take long to challenge. "And suddenly, Segal exclaimed: 'Don't try to fool me, Ravitch!' He had recognized me despite all my travels and the passage of time."[65]

Following this whirlwind visit, the two men exchanged letters regularly, notwithstanding Ravitch's subsequent sojourns on several continents. In January of 1936, Ravitch was living in Melbourne where he

was working on an anthology of Australian Yiddish literature entitled
Oystralishe shriftn [Australian writing] and founded a Yiddish-language
school for children. In 1938, he spent a year in Buenos Aires, Argentina,
after which he moved to New York, and then to Mexico. In August of
1941 he was finally admitted into Canada as an immigrant and moved
to Montreal permanently, no doubt thanks to the fact that the owners of
the *Keneder Adler* offered him a job as the newspaper's literary editor, a
position he shared for many years with his friend Segal. Once in Canada,
Ravitch's literary production was prodigious, particularly his contributions to Yiddish newspapers and cultural periodicals worldwide. Having
already published five poetry collections, as well as plays and travel
accounts in pre-World War II Poland, once in Canada he commenced a
remarkably productive period of writing in various literary genres.

In 1940, he published a volume of poetry entitled *Lider un baladn
fun di letste dray-fir-yorn* [Poems and ballads of the past three-four
years] in Mexico[66], followed by *67 lider* [67 poems] in Buenos Aires
in 1946. In 1953, Ravitch published *Di kroynung fun a yungn yidishn
dikhter in Amerike* [he coronation of a young Yiddish poet in America]
in New York and in 1954, in Montreal, *Di lider fun mayne lider* [The
songs of my songs], an anthology of poems from his first thirteen
poetry collections. At the same time, he began working on a series
of biographical sketches, which were eventually published in six volumes as *My Lexicon: Pen portraits of Jewish Writers and Artists in the
Americas and other Countries* (in Yiddish). The first volume appeared in
Montreal in 1945 and the final volume in Tel Aviv in 1982. Throughout
that period, Ravitch wielded tremendous influence in the Montreal
Yiddish cultural milieu, thanks to his outstanding literary ability and
the reputation he had already established abroad.

Like Rokhl Korn and Chava Rosenfarb, Ravitch chose to make
his home in Montreal primarily because he felt an affinity with the
literary and artistic goals of the city's most prominent Yiddish writers,
especially Segal. A smaller city than New York, but undoubtedly more
welcoming and hospitable to strangers, Montreal enjoyed the type
of Yiddish cultural and literary life that no longer existed in Eastern
Europe, and which was essential to Ravitch's career as a writer. As
early as August of 1934, after a brief visit to Montreal, Ravitch had
expressed to Segal his desire to establish roots in that city:

> By the way, you and I together could bring to life an entire
> Yiddish literary scene in Canada [. . .] Please try to set up a small

committee that could try to obtain the necessary immigration permits. Nothing else. Money is not necessary, nor will it become
necessary. Just the permits.[67]

A few months later, in January of 1936, Ravitch advised Segal to be
patient when the latter complained about the reception accorded to
his books by his Canadian co-religionists. Certainly, Segal's situation was not the most enviable from an economic standpoint, replied
Ravitch, but at least he did not have to contend with the arbitrariness of a government hostile to Jews like that of Poland. Furthermore,
Montreal's cultural milieu enjoyed the proximity to one of the greatest
centres of Jewish literature in the world, New York. Finding himself
far from Eastern Europe, the conviction that in Montreal he would
find an environment favourable to the pursuit of his literary work was
reinforced by the ravages of the Holocaust. Ravitch was not the only
one to perceive Montreal this way. Even American Yiddish writers
occasionally echoed this impression of the conviviality of Montreal's
literary circles. In 1948, the New York Yiddish poet Fishl Bimko wrote
to his colleague Segal:

> How are you doing there? By now everything must be fine in
> Montreal. You have a mountain there. And everything is friend-
> lier than here. Here everything is topsy turvy. You don't see a
> single soul who is stimulating.[68]

In Ravitch, Segal had found his equal—a great poet and writer capable of reaching artistic heights. His arrival in Montreal in 1941 brought
Segal unanticipated support at a very dark moment in his career,
when the bounteous springs of Eastern European Jewish culture were
drying up forever, while a new generation born in Canada was losing
the desire to produce Canadian Yiddish literature. The two men had
seen their writing take flight at the beginning of the century, during
an era when a revolutionary current of modernity had captured the
imagination of Yiddish artistic circles on both sides of the Atlantic,
and a large migratory wave had scattered a substantial part of Eastern
European Jewry to the four corners of the world. It did not take long
for Segal and Ravitch to become close literary collaborators, by adopting a plan, as early as 1941, to publish a five-volume anthology of
Yiddish poetry entitled "*Der oyster fun der idisher poezye* [A treasury
of Yiddish poetry]."[69] This work, which was to highlight Canadian

Yiddish literature, never came to fruition, most likely for lack of funding as well as the technology required for its production. Ravitch
and Segal differed, however, on one important aspect of their literary
work. During the 1930s and 1940s, Segal was increasingly gravitat-
ing toward ancient Hebrew, and a feeling of Hasidic piety emanated
from his poetry. Fascinated by biblical imagery and the fervour of the
Hasidic masters, Segal drew upon sacred Jewish texts for the rhythms
and melodies which gave his poetry an unmistakable Judaic flavour.
Ravitch, on the other hand, found his inspiration in a much more
expansive European cultural environment and drank deeply from
the wells of a universalism without cultural boundaries.[70] Whereas
Segal was driven by an increasingly powerful Hebraist impulse,
Ravitch did not hesitate to introduce into his writing concepts and
ideas from the Greco-Roman tradition found in all the great European
languages. While Segal's poetry sounded like a prayer that derived
from the psalms and the liturgy, that of Ravitch created the impression of philosophical contemplation grounded in rationalist thought.
For Ravitch, who was born in a small town in the Austro-Hungarian
Empire to a German-speaking family, Yiddish was the vehicle of
choice for spreading revolutionary ideas and the symbol of a Jewish
cultural renaissance free of religious constraints. However, when it
came to Orthodox Judaism, both poets shared the same attitude of
distrust and rejection, a distrust that resulted from their uncompro-
mising embrace of modernity.

The Yiddish Writers Association

In May of 1941, under the leadership of J. I. Segal, Melekh Ravitch,
H. M. Caiserman, Israel Rabinovitch, and Simcha Bunem Pretrushka,[71]
a new Yiddish Writers Association of Montreal was founded.[72] This
indicated that despite the dangerous developments threatening the
Jews of Europe, the Yiddish-speaking literary milieu had not yet
stopped growing in size and influence. In fact, the war years witnessed an intensification of Jewish cultural activity on the Mount
Royal Plateau, due in part to the arrival of refugees who had already
made their mark in Yiddish publishing elsewhere in the world, as
well as a terrible feeling of powerlessness vis-à-vis the situation facing
Poland and the Soviet Union. On June 22, 1941, the Germans invaded
Polish territory under Soviet control to launch their conquest of the
vast Soviet hinterland, thereby considerably enlarging the theatre of

military operations in Europe. There ensued a brutal confrontation between the two enemy regimes, which would determine the outcome of World War II, and, to a great extent, the survival of Yiddish-speaking communities in the old country. At that same time, the injection of new artistic energy was revitalizing Montreal's existing Jewish institutions and creating unexpected opportunities, including the founding of a Yiddish Writers Association that would represent Yiddish-speaking writers and endeavour to expand their readership. The primary purpose of this organization was to "create an environment in which Yiddish language, literature and culture could develop, advance and flourish."[73] The founders of the Association also wanted to establish ties with Jewish authors who were not writing in Yiddish, and to prepare for the arrival of new refugees once the war in Europe was over. To the first meeting were invited writers who had already published a book or at least twenty-five pieces of writing in Yiddish newspapers or periodicals, including essays, stories and journalistic articles. Of the forty-three official invitations, sent out mostly to Montrealers, twenty-three attended the first meeting on May 5, 1941. At the end of the year, the Association counted forty-nine members in good standing (see Appendix E), the majority of whom were Yiddish-speaking and lived either on the Mount Royal Plateau or the eastern part of Outremont. Until his death, Segal spared no effort in playing a major role in this community organization, and was, without a doubt, its most illustrious member.

The birth of the Yiddish Writers Association is a good indication that there was still a certain degree of optimism in Montreal's literary circles, and that despite the world situation, the most prominent writers regarded their future in Canada with confidence. At that time, the city boasted an incomparably large number of talented and promising Yiddish writers, some of whom had begun displaying their talents over forty years earlier, soon followed in the 1930s by new arrivals from several Eastern European countries. Established in a matter of weeks, the Association had set itself an ambitious program, with expectations of becoming a central institution in Jewish life in the long term. "The Association from the outset will be responsible for organizing [the Yiddish literary milieu], for structuring all its projects and undertakings, and bringing together those who wish to participate in meetings and literary events, and also for initiating a movement that can only grow with time."[74] Although the Canadian Yiddish writers were aware that the ongoing war would deal a severe blow to

Jewish cultural life in Eastern Europe, no one at that time would have suspected that the military conflict would destroy the very foundations of Jewish life in that part of the world. Meanwhile, Montreal's Yiddish-speaking artists and writers believed that they could count on a growth spurt, fed in part by immigration from Europe, once the war was over. Against all odds, they retained the hope that the city would long remain an important centre of Yiddish creativity, sustained by the wellspring of Ashkenazic Eastern European Jewry. In fact, the Association remained very active until 1948, when its membership had grown to sixty-nine people (see Appendix F). However, during the 1950s and 1960s the Association stopped attracting new members and slipped into a slow decline.

The arrival of Ravitch and a new cohort of Eastern European writers in Montreal also did much to boost Segal's stature as a literary critic, and encouraged him to increase his contributions to the Yiddish press. After having been "thanked for his services" in 1931 by the owners of the *Jewish Daily Eagle*, Segal resumed his place at the newspaper in 1935, and even increased the frequency of his contributions during the 1940s. The poet was especially interested in contemporary Jewish literary production, in Yiddish or other languages, with special attention to Canada and the North American continent. Once war had been declared, he switched genres to begin writing more comprehensive commentaries on [the political situation in Eastern Europe and the Nazi persecution of Jews. He was also interested in the consequences of this brutality on Yiddish culture around the world, and the vitality of his own Montreal community. After 1948, he wrote about the State of Israel and its influence on the Jewish Diaspora.[75] Among the Yiddish authors whom Segal critiqued at this time were Abraham Reisen, Joseph Rolnick, Aaron Zeitlin, Jacob Glatstein, Abraham Liessin, Peretz Hirschbein, Hayim Greenberg, David Ignatoff, and Menahem Boraisha. Closer to home the poet was also interested in H. M. Caiserman, Melekh Ravitch, Rokhl Korn, Israël Rabinovitch, Simon Nepom, and Benjamin-Gutl Sack. Thanks to his connections abroad, Segal's work was printed in the New York publications *Tsukunft*, *Yidisher kemfer* [Jewish fighter], *Epokhe* [Epoque], *Zayn* [Being] and *Getseltn* [Tents]. His literary reviews appeared in Mexico in *Der veg* [The way], and elsewhere in Canada, notably in *The Hebrew Journal* (*Der idisher zhurnal*) of Toronto. The poet also wrote essays on I. L. Peretz, Sholem Aleichem and even Romain Rolland, who had been translated into Yiddish a few years earlier (see Appendix C). In his biography of Segal, Ch. L. Fox claims that over the years the poet had written and published "forty-seven studies of various Yiddish writers, and twenty-five essays on literary and cultural issues"[76] in the Yiddish press. This evidently large body of critical writing, never republished after Segal's death, sheds light on the poet's aesthetic choices as well as his network of acquaintances across the North American Yiddish literary world. It also reveals the subtle elegance of his prose which, like his poetry, draws its inspiration from the ancient Jewish tradition, borrowing liberally, and with apparent ease, its images and symbols. Chaim Lieberman, editor of the New York *Forverts*, who had managed to read some of Segal's critiques in the *Keneder Adler*, wrote to him in the summer of 1948:

> I have to confess that I did not know you did this type of writing, and that I was very pleasantly surprised when I read it. It is literary criticism of the highest quality, infused with vision and lofty sentiments, and stylishly written. I know of no one here who can write a literary essay like you. Your article on Raboy is a true masterpiece, as is your article entitled *"Vegn an inyen* [About a certain matter]."[77]

As indicated above, the last book that Segal published, in 1950, was a volume of poetry entitled *Sefer idish*, which he intended both as a memorial to the martyrs of the Holocaust and an homage to the beauty of the Yiddish language, itself a victim of the Nazi persecution. Conceivably it was because he wished to mitigate the shock of a loss so immense and so deeply felt that the poet set out to produce a monumental work to serve as a counterweight to the terrifying years of the Nazi genocide, and rescue from oblivion the communities which had vanished forever. As the majority of literary critics recognized the moment the book appeared, in *Sefer idish* Segal had reached the summit of his art. The book garnered much attention in the Montreal Yiddish press and elsewhere in North America. A host of articles hailed it as an outstanding contribution.[78] Reactions flooded in from the vast network of contacts that the poet had maintained in the world of Yiddish literature and culture. Soon after the book appeared, Berish Weinstein, with whom Segal had corresponded for several years, told him how much it had moved him:

> When I received and opened your *Sefer idish*, I felt my hands (and my heart) tremble. This is not a figure of speech. I don't know

how to describe the emotion that overcame me: religious piety or wild enthusiasm. I felt that I was holding in my hands not a Yiddish book but a book of Yiddish pearls.[79]

In February of 1951, after a hasty first reading of the book, the poet Itsik Manger, who was preparing to visit Montreal at the invitation of Melekh Ravitch, wrote to Segal: "My first impression was your great love for Yiddish, and Yiddish not only as a language, but as a synthesis of a vision born of a thousand years of Jewish life."[80] In these years of profound grief, when the entire structure of Eastern European Jewry had collapsed under the force of the Nazi onslaught and racial hatred, Segal was singing his final tribute to the language that was both custodian of its historical continuity and symbol of is cultural vitality. For that reason, *Sefer Idish* sometimes sounds like a eulogy for a great departed, as in the following poem entitled *Idish lishmo* [For the sake of Yiddish].

For the Sake of Yiddish [excerpt]

In every word there's so much light,
You only have to free it
and the language is revived.
Congratulations, Yiddish!

How good I feel to be the one
Entrusted with this mission.
To you I'll give my share of grace
So you may live and prosper.

There's nothing that I would not do
to make you healthy, stronger.
I'd share with you my gold, my sun,
And preach to Jewish children

That Yiddish is so good for you
the doctors say to speak it.
Yet in my heart a silent wound —
Not everyone need know it.[81]

Twilight Reflections

While the Jews of Eastern Europe, brutally uprooted from their centuries-old communities, were being incinerated in the crematoria of Poland, the Yiddish language in Montreal and the rest of North America was gradually falling into disuse among newer generations. The cultural cornerstones that had buttressed its creativity on the North American continent were weakening. While the war and the suffering of Eastern European Jewry had been the centre of attention, within the Montreal Jewish community the use of Yiddish was in a slow decline, a decline which the sudden arrival of Holocaust survivors would delay for one more generation. The prospects for Yiddish culture were further narrowed by the day-to-day indifference of the Montreal Jews themselves, enticed by the possibility of full participation in Canadian society, and seduced by the attractiveness of English. By touting the power of a culture in which basic Eastern European Jewish values and cultural creativity had been expressed for centuries, Segal had wanted to raise the issue of identity among his co-religionists. Could it be that the land of Canada, in which Yiddish-speaking Jews from Russia, Poland, the Ukraine, and Lithuania had been transplanted for almost a half a century, was also sounding the death knell of Yiddish continuity? But *Sefer idish* was perhaps not the best vehicle for pleading the critically important case of the future of the Yiddish language in Montreal. The book seemed so dense that it sometimes suffered from an excess of spontaneity and the inclusion of less polished poems, as though, in an era marked by an incomprehensible apocalypse, the author had wanted to throw himself into the fray. *Sefer idish*, which was intended to illustrate the lasting power and poetic beauty of a beleaguered language, was barely accessible to readers raised in Canada who had never spoken Yiddish in an Eastern European context. This feeling of remoteness is reflected in the critical remarks of David Rome, publicist for the Canadian Jewish Congress, who had just begun translating Segal's poetry into English.

> Perhaps the present volume is the most lucid and rationally most mature of his published verse and the form of some of the poems bears the mark of a certain impatience with the externals of poetic form and of literary polish. Some of his poems approach his prose writing in the heaping up of ideas not always emotionally refined and clarified. Some poems are more nearly notations of ideas for poems to be written than completed poems.[82]

Henceforth, evening shadows would hover over the generation of Yiddish writers who had settled in Canada at beginning of the twentieth century, a century now battered by the Holocaust. In the fall of 1950, at a time when their principal representatives were searching, bewildered, for a way to heal their open wounds, a shipment arrived at the Montreal offices of the Canadian Jewish Congress containing Yiddish books that had belonged to Jews in Eastern Europe. Collected on the killing fields and miraculously saved from destruction, in Canada they would now serve as a memorial to the victims. Given their historical value and emotional significance, these orphaned books would be distributed by the Congress among the various Jewish communities in the country. Before embarking on their journey across Canada, they were inspected by a few specialists, including David Rome, Lavy M. Becker, and none other than J. I. Segal. Having published *Sefer idish* only a few months earlier, the poet was now confronting head-on the dreaded after-effects on Eastern European Jewish culture. In front of him lay stacks of books that only recently had been cherished by their owners, books they had used for the chanting of prayers in the synagogue, and books they had read in their leisure time. Segal, who had just written his own poetic testimony about the Holocaust, was now contemplating hundreds of books that no one would ever look at again, and which, after the catastrophe, had somehow landed on distant Canadian shores. Each of them reminded Segal of a part of his childhood. In the past they had found a place for themselves, perhaps in the library of a pious man, or on a shelf at the back of a classroom, or in a house of prayer. Never again would they serve the purpose for which they were intended, except in the diffuse recesses of an atrophied collective memory. After having produced *Sefer idish*, Segal was hearing the echo of all the books that would never be written because of the lack of writers capable of composing their content, of books that would no longer be read for lack of readers to turn their pages:

> As I entered the room I found it impossible to say anything. A strange speechlessness overcame me. There was nothing to ask. The origins of this Sinai of old books and the history of their wanderings here was all too familiar. The brown, old-leather volumes struck me with an almost physical reconstruction of old home, of chapel and of synagogue courtyard. Yet I knew by the presence of these volumes that these realities of old are no more. [. . .]

I wanted to be alone in my sorrow, in communion with these books, but I also remembered that the others in the room with me—who disturbed the quiet of the mourning—were also seized with the same thoughts and the same emotions. All of us in that library felt again the magnitude of the great destruction of the diaspora. It was a sight—not a vision—which is among those destined to remain ineffable, never to be given the dress of words or colour or sound, never to be completed through expression.[83]

Segal was not the only one to feel in his guts the shock of the Holocaust. Caiserman had been sent to Poland by the Canadian Jewish Congress in 1945 to assess the catastrophe that had befallen world Jewry. Caiserman, accompanied by Communist sympathizer Sam Lipshitz, had in fact been one of the first Canadian Jews to visit Europe once the war was over. For several weeks he travelled from one town to another, observing firsthand the incalculable consequences of the genocide. In Canada at that time, only a small number of well-informed people fully understood the grave extent of the maltreatment to which Polish Jewry had been subjected. Nor did many people have reliable information about the methods employed in the Nazi genocide. After having worked for over thirty years to build a Montreal Jewish community, Caiserman was now confronting the unimaginable and the inexpressible, to a point where this journey through Poland in the winter of 1945–1946 would radically change his perception of the future. He would also begin to consider the Jewish people's will to resist and the urgent need to construct its future on a new foundation. Nonetheless, on that trip Caiserman did not succeed in containing his heartache in the face of so much suffering. He was inundated by requests from survivors, often young orphans, who wanted to leave Eastern Europe at any cost, and make contact with their relatives around the world, including Canada. Wanting to do his part in the face of so much devastation, he personally adopted a young woman named Nella Gutman whom he met in Radom in early 1946, and succeeded in bringing her to Montreal a few years later. His reports in the press and his letters from this period convey the mournful nature of his mission, and reveal a man who, for a brief time, was on the brink of despair. At the beginning of January 1946, Caiserman visited the site of Auschwitz, which had been liberated only one year earlier and had not yet been the object of any investigation or plan for its preservation:

From there, we visited "Oshwienchin,"[84] the enormous concentration camp. It is a city composed of barracks, and approximately 40 square kilometres. The whole city was surrounded by
electrified wires so as to make exits impossible. Three cremato-
ries worked day and night to liquidate millions of people [. . .].
One cannot see the sleeping quarters without losing his personal
human dignity. Oshwienchin is the greatest inhumanity in the
imagination of human beings. There are no words to describe it.[85]

The friendship between Caiserman and Segal had one final moment
of intensity the late 1940s when the activist, despite all his onerous
administration responsibilities still cherished the dream of compiling a new anthology of Canadian Yiddish poetry. Nor had Caiserman
abandoned his plan to write a biography of the Montreal poet to
expressly draw attention to the originality of his writing and his
exceptional childhood in Korets. These literary ambitions seems very
much alive in a letter he received from Argentina a few days before his
death: "I am glad to note that, apart from your daily duties, you still
find the time and still have the spirit and energy to dedicate yourself
to spiritual work, [. . .] and that you are now working on an important
book on the poet Segal."[86] Although the book about Segal remained a
work in progress, this did not prevent the literary critic from following the poet's career to the very end, and repeatedly expressing his
admiration as he did when Segal obtained the Louis Lamed Prize in
1945: "I congratulate you from the depths of my heart, and I rejoice in
your success and the tremendous happiness of those who supported
you for so long, considered you a very great Yiddish poet, and fervently hoped for this important acknowledgement."[87] For Caiserman,
the hour of reckoning had arrived, and at times he began to reflect
about his almost forty years in Montreal. For him, the rise of Yiddish
literature in the city had been a providential bright spot in a career
devoted to union activism, to the creation of an institutional structure, and to the defence of the interests of Canadian Jews. An unre-
pentant traveller, consummate union organizer, and activist on behalf
of various causes, he had discovered in the poetry of his friend Segal
the promise of boundless Jewish creativity. Moved by its loftiness
and lyricism, Caiserman had wished to embrace with all his being
this literary awakening among a people exiled to a new continent,
the bearers of thousands of years of history. To celebrate this surpis-
ing renaissance of Yiddish letters in a land without any prior trace of

Jewish literature, he went so far as to reinvent himself as a critic and a biographer for the sake of continuity and bearing witness. Above all, however, Caiserman derived from Segal's work a sense of closeness to the Jewish God and heritage of Eastern Europe. "Today is the Sabbath. As always I am in the offices of the Congress—and I reread your pious, luminous and sad poems—but all of them marvellous—which appeared in the *Tsukunft* of January 1944."[88] Nor did the poet, who in his book *Lirik* had dedicated the following emotionally charged poem to Caiserman, take their friendship for granted:

To H. C.

> In you is the fresh coolness
> of dead leaves in the wind.
> Tell me about your weariness,
> Confide to me your fears.
> I shall sing pleasant songs to you,
> I shall be your brother,
> I shall make room for you in my house.
> I shall repair your day
> that you bring to me sick
> and discouraged.[89]

In the summer of 1946, at the invitation of the American Joint Distribution Committee, Caiserman set out on an international mission that was to take him to several countries in Lain America and Europe. This trip proved to be one of the most arduous of his career, as evidenced by one of his letters: "You can see, dear Miss Cox, the tremendous tour I dared to undertake, which, if I finish in good health, it will be after delivering near to 500 addresses during 6 months of traveling, after an exhausting trip to Poland, Germany, England."[90] All this hard work did not prevent Caiserman from undertaking another expedition at a time where the needs of Holocaust survivors were more urgent than ever, and the entire world was recovering from the ravages of war. His journey along roads previously unexplored is clearly outlined in a letter he sent to close friends in April of 1947. A few days before leaving Montreal, he had spoken at a small synagogue on Saint Urbain Street[91] in a working-class neighbourhood that was about to close its doors forever. "Among the audience in the synagogue were many former members of the Unions which 35 years earlier I helped organize. . . I cannot describe the deep emotional state in which I found myself, even hours after the service. At 8.40 p.m., the train departed from the Central Station and I again felt as if I have embarked on an endless journey."[92] To the very end, the Secretary General of the Congress remained true to the organization which he had founded almost thirty years before, and, a few days before his death, he returned from a tour of various Jewish communities in Quebec and the Maritimes. Caiserman died suddenly on December 24, 1950, at his residence in Outremont,[93] surrounded by his family. He was sixty-seven years old. Several community leaders and writers paid him tribute, including A. M. Klein who stated:

> The man has been a paradox; on the one hand, there had been about him an old-world courtesy, an incomparable warm-heartedness, a capacity for self-effacement, and on the other

Invitation to the book launch at the Jewish Public Library of *Letste lider* by J. I. Segal, published posthumously in Montreal in 1955. (Montreal Public Library.)

Title page of *Letste lider* by J. I. Segal, Montreal, published posthumously in 1955. (Canadian Jewish Congress Archives.)

—none like he could be so valiant and undaunted in the service of a cause, for principle an implacable polemicist, a champion without fear and without reproach.[94]

Segal, who was particularly affected by the death of his friend, commented on how distressed and devastated Caiserman had been by the spectacle of a world pervaded by extreme violence:

> Caiserman was a humanist par excellence. That is why he was so shattered by the brutality of our era. He was terrified not only of its bayonets, its guns, and its bombs, but even more so of its contemptuously vulgar language. He had always believed that there were limits to evil, just as there are limits to goodness.[95]

The Final Exile

It would not take long for Segal to join his friend Caiserman in the heavenly Jerusalem. He passed away on March 7, 1954, in the evening. There had been no prior indication that his departure was imminent. After experiencing some brief discomfort, Segal died of a

Hirsch (Harry) Hershman, Abraham Reisen
and J. I. Segal, studio Peter O. Gulkin, St. Lawrence Boulevard, Montreal c. 1950.
(Private collection of Sylvia and Annette Segal.)

cardiac arrest at the age of fifty-seven, surrounded by his family, and leaving uncompleted a number of manuscripts and other projects. Thus ended a chapter of Montreal Yiddish literary history. The death of the poet sent shock waves through the Montreal Jewish community, especially in Yiddish cultural circles, which had lost one of their most remarkable personalities. His funeral on the following day was the occasion for heartfelt tributes from the many organizations and institutions with which Segal had been associated over the course of his career. For over two hours people paid their respects at his coffin, which had been placed for that purpose in the Jewish Public Library, then at the corner of Mount Royal and Esplanade Avenue, mere steps from the Segal family home. This in itself was a sign of the extraordinary esteem in which he was held in the Jewish community.

After leaving the library, the funeral procession first stopped at the Labour Zionist Centre, and then at the Jewish People's School, where the poet had been working at the time of his death, before making its way to the Jewish cemetery,[96] where he was interred in

Reception in honour of the fiftieth birthday of Dan Wolofsky, owner of the Jewish Daily Eagle, c. 1950. At the head table, first row from left to right: Leon Cresthol, Dr. A. Stilman, Dan Wolofsky, Israel Rabinovitch, Max Wolofsky, Benjamin G. Sack, H. G. Halpern; second row, standing: I. Medres, A. M. Klein, Mordecai Ginzburg, Joseph Gally, J. I. Segal, Melekh Ravitch, N. I. Gotlib, and Hannah Widerman. (Montreal Jewish Public Library.)

the section belonging to the Jewish National Workers' Alliance.[97] The Yiddish Peretz and Jewish Peoples Schools closed their doors for a day, as did the Jewish Teachers Seminary (*Fareynikte Yidisher Lerer-Seminar*).

The report in the *Keneder Adler* emphasized the suddenness of the poet's death, seemingly unprovoked by any particular tension or stress. Despite the high regard for him in the Montreal Jewish community, Segal remained an enigma for most of his contemporaries, who could not hope to penetrate the writer's inner world or share his passion for poetry. Although Segal had lived with his family in a community, he had belonged to a universe unfathomable and inaccessible to mere mortals. At the time of the poet's death, the journalist Mordecai Ginzburg, who had known him at the *Eagle* for many years, wrote: "He lived in a completely different world, a world of dreams, symbols, and melodies. 'All my senses are drawn to poetry,' he declared in one of his writings. Therefore he did not have enough energy for those realities which he did not consider to be part of the world of poetry."[98] Segal's passing happened at a time when no one expected it. Too busy with his writing, he had not the slightest premonition that his hour had come:

> Thus, early Saturday evening [March 6], he was in the offices of the K. A. addressing all kinds of topics in his customary poetic and philosophical tone, unaware of his own physical condition, telling jokes and delighting those around him with his brilliant witticisms.
>
> How would Segal have been able to come to terms with the idea of death hovering over him at the very moment when he was preparing to publish a new book? How could he have imagined that this project would remain on the shelf? All his life, despite the many obstacles, he strove to accomplish this precise goal. He literally lived only to attain this single purpose, going about his daily routine with this sole aim which, in fact, was beyond his control, to the point of neglecting his health.[99]

Segal's death occurred just as a new group of Yiddish writers was attempting to settle in Montreal in the wake of the Holocaust, and resume their lives after a painful hiatus of several years. For these immigrants as well as those who had come to Canada during the inter-war period, Segal represented over forty years of Yiddish culture in this country. His prodigious literary output confirmed the durability of Yiddish writing on a continent which the Eastern European Jewish masses had barely explored, but where the impulse to preserve the heritage of past generations had blossomed from the outset. With Segal's departure, the first footsteps of a young literature still uncertain of its future and continually in search of affirmation in the Canadian context were also disappearing. The loss was even more profoundly felt because Segal had seemed to finally have attained the peak of his abilities and won universal recognition in places where Yiddish, after 1945, became especially revered—in New York, Paris, Buenos Aires, and even Tel Aviv. The link had been broken to a heritage that only Segal had been capable of embodying in all it splendour, a heritage that dated back to a time when the small communities of Eastern Europe reflected traditional Jewish values, those very values which the Russian Revolution, Pilsudski's Poland, and the Nazi scourge had done everything to suppress. Segal had preserved in his memory his undying recollections of the Korets of his childhood, the teachings of the Baal Shem Tov, and the green fields surrounding the *shtetl* as far as the eye could see. No longer would any Canadian Jew be able to conjure up and assimilate these images of a simpler and more primitive world, where piety intruded upon even the most trivial acts of daily life, and where innocence seemed to rule supreme. Along with Segal a large swath of Eastern European Jewish reality was precipitously disappearing, its memory growing fainter day by day. The prevailing optimism in the early days of the Montreal Yiddish-speaking community, which had witnessed the first literary experiments, had also disappeared forever after the incomprehensible horrors of the Holocaust and destruction of European Jewry. The hope, which had shone brilliantly for a few short years over the Montreal Jewish community during the great migratory wave and the first tentative steps of a young Canadian Yiddish literature, lay buried under the still-smouldering ashes of the Nazi concentration camps. The shock of Segal's departure was felt in the offices of the Canadian Jewish Congress which, in a rare gesture, issued a statement in Yiddish to underscore its significance:

> Mr. Samuel Bronfman, national president of the Canadian Jewish Congress, has sent a letter of condolence to the family of the late J. I. Segal, emphasizing that "the Jewish community of Canada has lost a prominent and important member, whose literary accomplishments have contributed so much to the splendour and substance of the cultural treasures of the Jewish people, and thereby

> highlighted the important place of the organized Jewish com-
> munity in Canada [. . .] The Canadian Jewish community values
> highly the contributions of J. I. Segal and his work that reflects his
> extraordinary mastery of the Yiddish language and culture."[100]

In addition to several hundred handwritten pages, which the Segal
family deposited in the archives of the Jewish Public Library in 1956,
Segal left behind an unpublished collection of poems, which Shlomo
Wiseman[101] and Mordecai Husid prepared for publication under the
title *Letste lider* [Last poems]. In this final volume of over 300 pages,
the poet returns to the four themes that predominated throughout
his career, especially from the 1930s, when he made the shift toward
Hasidic mysticism. In *Letste lider* Korets is the poet's principal source
of inspiration and the underpinning of his Jewish identity. The *shtetl*
thus appears as a utopian space, constantly revisited in his memory
and transferred in his writing to Montreal where it retained its physical appearance and its emotional impact. A second theme is that of
exile, disconnection and alienation, often symbolized by an ocean
liner, a harbour, or the strangeness of the Canadian landscape. The
loss of the *shtetl* and the immigrant condition, which the confluence
of historical events had inflicted upon a Segal powerless in the face of
adversity, were in fact a continuation of the wanderings of the Jews
over thousands of years, from country to country, from diaspora to
diaspora, except that God watched over his people and accompanied
them forever, providing his blessings and his consolation to those
who prayed for them and preserved the memory of his Law. A third
theme in *Letste lider* is the mystical contemplation of God whose principle cantor is the Baal Shem Tov roaming the Polish countryside in
search of His presence. Segal challenges this God of Abraham, Isaac,
and Jacob in his poetry and looks Him in the eye to ask for mercy and
inner peace, especially when reminded of the death of his first child
and the pain of his exile. Finally, *Letste lider* contains what are unquestionably the most beautiful of Segal's poems about his adopted city.
After living there for over forty years, the poet's bonds with Montreal
had deepened and the city assumed a more important role in his work.
Privileged witness of all his literary aspirations and a place of refuge
from the murderous rage of the Nazis, Montreal with its "mountain"
and its intense Jewish community life had become a new Jerusalem,
waiting for the inevitable coming of the Messiah. In this city reso-
nating with a unique Jewish presence, Segal discovered, along with

modernity, a Jewish society that was reminiscent of the *shtetl* of his childhood. It was an opportunity for the poet to present evocative images that captured the state of mind of the Yiddish-speaking immigrants, and portrayed their integration into the life of the city, such as this poem that alludes to the period of the great migration, a half-century earlier, by its references to the ocean liners and the docks that welcomed the newcomers to the New World:

Old Montreal

(translated by Miriam Waddington)

There's an old back street in Montreal
That was once the centre of town,
Now the stone walls are yellow and burnt out,
And there's a broken-down church which God forsook

When he moved away to a new cathedral;
Yet whenever I walk that way
I imagine I hear ghostly bells ringing
Behind those ash-gray walls.

A little way down is an oblong cemetery
With small headstones, and smack in the middle
Stands a tall stained marble column
Keeping its long watch.

Not far away is the harbour market
With high buildings, wooden and blind,
And you can see a dirty red flag
Hung out for no reason at all, teasing the wind.

Between these narrow streets and glimpsing walls
The chimney of a dockside ship pokes out,
And a midday thread of smoke goes curling up
As from some cozy winter house.[102]

After Segal's death, his family and friends hastened to preserve his literary legacy by creating a foundation in his name (see Appendix G). This project was launched in the summer of 1954 when a letter was sent out by the Jewish Public Library to raise funds for the purpose of perpetuating the poet's memory and publishing the remainder of his work. The signatories of this letter stressed the fact that Segal's contribution had gone well beyond the Jewish community of Canada: "Segal, of blessed memory, belonged to the world Yiddish literature. This gives us the courage, as well as the responsibility, to address ourselves to all friends of Yiddish literature."[103]

Thanks to their efforts, a second posthumous volume, this time a short anthology of some of his last children's poems entitled *Lider far idisher kinder* [Poems for Jewish children], was published in 1961 by the Segal Foundation. Illustrated by his daughter Annette Segal-Zakuta and edited by Yechiel Shtern, Hanna Wiseman, Mordecai Husid, and Rokhl Eisenberg,[104] this small volume revealed the poet's childlike innocence and his attachment to the world of childhood. Further projects were also proposed at this time, including a collection of Segal's poems already translated into Hebrew and English, a proposal to encourage various authors to produce new translations, and even another anthology of Segal's work, to be entitled *Sefer Yud Yud Segal* [The book of J. I. Segal].[105] A list of writers to be consulted, drawn up by Jacob Glatstein, was used by Melekh Ravitch in making the final selection of work to be included.[106] None of these plans, however, ever materialized. In 1957, on the anniversary of poet's death, a memorial evening was organized by the Jewish Public Library and the Yiddish Writers Association. In 1962 the Jewish Library inaugurated a space in its building on Esplanade Avenue dedicated to J. I. Segal, and, in 1968, it established a literary prize in his name, which to this day is awarded for creative and scholarly works relating to Jewish culture and education. Segal had died suddenly, without giving thought to his legacy. No doubt he was too busy memorializing his Volhynian childhood to imagine that his work might survive him in a very different era. In a review that appeared in November of 1953, following one of the poet's last public appearances, Bernard Wind remarked: "Segal, in all his poems, clings to the immediate and more distant past like a lover staring through the dust in the direction of a car that has already left."[107] Who would remember Korets now that the poet was gone?

Notes

1.   See Ian Kershaw, *Hitler, the Germans, and the Final Solution* (Jerusalem, International Institute for Holocaust Research, Yad Vashem and New Haven, Yale University Press, 2008); Lucy S. Davidowicz, *The War Against Jews, 1933–1945* (New York: Holt Rinehart and Winston, 1975); Raul Hilberg, *The Destruction of the European Jews* (New York: Holmes and Meier, 1985).

2.   Louis Rosenberg, Canada's Jews, *A Social and Economic Study of the Jews in Canada* (Montreal: Canadian Jewish Congress, 1939), 79.

3.   Hirsch Wolofsky, op. cit., chapters 20, 25 and 28. See also a previous work by the same author entitled *Eyrope un eretz yisroel nokh der velt-krig: fun Kanade biz eretz yisroel iber mizrekh un mayrev eyrope un tsurik, rayze-bashraybung* [Europe and Eretz Israel after the World War: from Canada to Eretz Israel through Eastern and Western Europe, a travel account], Montreal, *Keneder Adler*, 1922.

4.   David S. Wyman, *Abandonment of the Jews. America and the Holocaust, 1941–1944* (New York, Pantheon Books), 1984.

5.   Ibid., 52.

6.   In Yiddish, the *Idisher Arbeter Komitet*. Its offices were at 3838 Saint Joseph Boulevard.

7.   Letter from Michael Rubinstein, Chairman of the Jewish Labour Committee, Montreal, to the officials of the Canadian Jewish Congress, July 22, 1942, Caiserman Archive, Canadian Jewish Congress Archives, Montreal.

8.   Hirsch Wolofsky.

9.   Sholem Shtern, op. cit., 141–142 (French version); Sholem Shtern, op. cit., 41. (Yiddish version)

10.   Sholem Shtern, op. cit., 173 (French version); Sholem Shtern, op. cit., 77 (Yiddish version). See also Ben Lappin, "When Michoels and Feffer came to Toronto," *Viewpoints*, vol. VII, no. 2, 1972, 43–64.

11.   Letter from H. M. Caiserman, Montreal, to the editor of *Victoria-Inverness Bulletin*, Truro, Nova Scotia, January 12, 1943, Caiserman Archives, Canadian Jewish Congress Archives, Montreal.

12.   Sholem Shtern, op. cit., (French version), 260; Sholem Shtern, op. cit. (Yiddish version), 203.

13.   Chava Rosenfarb, "Yud Yud Segal," unpublished manuscript dated November 13, 1988, 17.

14.   J. I. Segal, "*Vayse velt* [White world]," *Sefer Yiddish*, Montreal, 1950, 204.

15.   Shtern, (French version) op. cit., 260–261, (Yiddish version) op. cit., 203–204.

16.   On this subject see Chantal Ringuet, "*A nayer landshaft*: Présence du paysage canadien dans la littérature Yiddish montréalaise," *Revue d'étude canadiennes*, Winter 2010, vol. 44, no. 1, 118–136.

17.   A.-B. Bennett, "Jewish Life through the Perspective of the Canadian Jewish Congress." Paper [in English] read at the Opening Session of Canadian Jewish Congress, Toronto, January 21, 1939, Canadian Jewish Congress Archives, Montreal, 1939.

18.   Chava Rosenfarb, op. cit., 5.

19.   J. I. Segal, "*Herbst*," *Lirik* (Montreal, 1930), 78.

20.   Translation by Miriam Waddington in Irving Howe and Eliezer Greenberg, eds., *A Treasury of Yiddish Poetry*. (Schocken, 1987), 153, of J. I. Segal, "*Shpet harbst in Montreal*," *Letste lider* [Last poems] (Montreal: J. I., Segal Committee and Canadian Jewish Congress, 1955), 106.

21.   J. I. Segal, "Montreal," *Mayn nigun* (Montreal, 1934), 284–285.

22.   Medzhybyz is a small town in the Khmelnytskyi province of western Ukraine.

23.   This reference to the death of the Baal Shem Tov can also be found in the poem "*Altmontreal* [Old Montreal]," *Di drite sude*, 1937, 46–47.

24.   La version hébraïque des psaumes.

25.   J. I Segal, "*Vinter in montreal*," *Lider un loybn*, Montreal, 1944, 103.

26.   Today the Parc des Amériques.

27. Shtern, op. cit., 66–67 (French version); Shtern, op. cit., 50 (Yiddish version).
28. The Hebrew word for book *"sefer"* when used in Yiddish, instead of the usual word *bukh*, means a religious book and "by extension any important book" (Y. Niborski and Bernard Vaisbrot, Dictionnaire Yiddish-Français, Bibliothèque Medem, Paris, 2002,) 414.
29. Shtern, op. cit., 203 (French); Sthern, op. cit., 310.
30. Sholem Shtern, *"Dos vunderleke vort* [The wondrous word]," New York, *Yidishe Kultur*, 1940–1941, 40–41. A photocopy of this article is in the Segal Archive of the Montreal Jewish Public Library Archives.
31. J. I. Segal, *"Fun Baal Shem Tov biz haynt* [From the Baal Shem Tov to today]," *Dos hoyz fun di poshete*, Montreal, 1940, 84.
32. Letter from Melekh Ravitch, Mexico, to J. I. Segal, December 29, 1940, Segal Archive, Montreal Jewish Public Library.
33. Sh. Niger, *"Yud Yud Segal a nayer shtrom lirik* [J. I. Segal, a new lyrical trend]." The *tkhine* was a prayer of supplication composed in Yiddish, generally intended for Ashkenazic women who could not read Hebrew. The first collections of *tkhines* were published in the 17th century.
34. J. I. Segal, "Tkhine," *Dos hoyz fun di poshete,* Montreal, 1940, 270.
35. David Rome, "The Loyal Poet," (*Congress Bulletin*, Montreal, Canadian Jewish Congress, August, 1945), 2.
36. J. I. Segal, *"Altlikht* [Light of old]," *Lider un loybn* (Montreal, 1944), 23.
37. Sholem Shtern, op. cit., around 1940–1941.
38. Letter from Aaron Glanz-Leyeles, New York, to J. I. Segal, July 12, 1945, Segal Archive, Montreal Jewish Public Library Archives.
39. Letter from Berish Weinstein, New York, to J. I. Segal, October 10, 1940, Segal Archive, Montreal Jewish Public Library Archives.
40. Established in 1940, this foundation awarded annual prizes for outstanding works published in both languages.
41. Other Montrealers to receive the Louis Lamed Prize included Simkha Petrushka, for his translations of the Mishnah into Yiddish (1950), Isaiah Rabinovitch for his Hebrew essays, and Rokhl Korn for Yiddish poetry (1950 and 1958).
42. See Hershl Novak's autobiography, op. cit.
43. Letter from Hershl Novak, New York, to J. I. Segal, March 8, 1945, Segal Archive, Montreal Jewish Public Library Archives, Montreal.
44. Wasserman, entry on Jacob Isaac Segal in Samuel Niger and Jacob Shatzky, *Leksikon fun der nayer idisher literatur* (Biographical Dictionary of Modern Yiddish Literature, New York, Congress for Jewish Culture, 1965), vol. 6, col. 397–403.
45. Mordecai Ginzberg, *"Yidishe Folks Biblyotek hot durkhgefirt ovent lekoved Yud Yud Segal* [the Jewish Public Library holds an evening in honour of J. I. Segal]," *Der Keneder Odler*, November 20, 1945, 3.
46. Letter from Abraham Ber Tabachnik, New York, to J. I. Segal, November 1, 1945. Segal Archive, Montreal Jewish Public Library Archive.
47. H. M. Caiserman, "Biography of J. I. Segal," undated manuscript, Caiserman Archive, Canadian Jewish Congress Archives.
48. The report that appeared two days later described the event as follows: "a fine large crowd." See *"Der 50-yoriker yubileum far Yud Yud Segal durkhgefirt oyf a zeyer shenem oyfn* [A grand celebration for J.I. Segal's 50th birthday]," *Der Keneder Odler*, March 21, 1947.
49. Israel Rabinovitch, *"Tog ayn, tog oys,"* Der Keneder Odler, March 19, 1947. See also on the same subject: B. G. Sack, *"Dikhter un proze kinstler* [Poet and prose artist]," *Der Keneder Odler*, March 16, 1947.

50. Melekh Ravitch, *"Yud Yud Segal. Makhshoves vegn a khaver – tsu zayn 50-tn geburt-stog* [J. I. Segal. Some thoughts about a friend and colleague – on his 50th birthday]," *Der Keneder Odler*, March 17, 1947.

51. *"Mitvokh, dem 19ten marts – der Yud Yud Segal yoyvl ovnt* [Wednesday, March 19 – birthday celebration for J. I. Segal]," *Der Keneder Odler*, March 14, 1947.

52. See *"Yud Yud Segal, prominenter dikhter a gast in Detroit* [prominent poet J. I. Segal invited to Detroit]" *(Forverts*, December 10, 1946), 4.

53. Benjamin Jacob Bialostotzki, *"Der liriker Yud Yud Segal* [The lyric poet J. I. Segal]," *(Di Fraye Arbeter Shtime*, New York, November 8, 1946), 5–6.

54. Letter from Aaron Glanz-Leyeles, President of the Yiddish PEN. Club in New York, to J. I. Segal, November 8, 1946.

55. According to the letter from Hershl Novak cited earlier, this book did not appear in 1944, as indicated on the title page, but in the spring of 1945. This delay was essentially due to the difficulty in printing and binding a book which the authorities did not consider essential to the war effort.

56. *"Montreal ken vern di shtarkste festung fun idisher kultur, zogt der dikhter Yud Yud Segal* [Montreal can become the strongest bastion of Yiddish culture]," says poet J. I. Segal, *Forverts* (Forward), New York, May 29, 1951.

57. In the interwar period, Vilnius, then called Wilno, was part of Poland.

58. Haim-Leib Fuks, op. cit., 316 [French version]; Ch. L. Fox, op. cit., [original Yiddish], 236.

59. This book was published in English as *The Tree of Life: A Trilogy of Life in the Lodz Ghetto* (Madison, Wisconsin, University of Wisconsin Press, 3 vols., 2004–2006).

60. *Ship of the Hunted* (Syracuse, N.Y., Syracuse University Press, 1997) was the author's own English translation.

61. *The Empire of Kalman the Cripple* (Syracuse, N.Y., Syracuse University Press, 1997). It was later translated into French as *L'empire de Kalman l'infirme* (Montreal, Leméac, 2001).

62. The memorial books (*yizkor bukh*, pl. *yizkor bikher*) were generally compiled through the collective efforts of former residents to recreate the life and history of their communities destroyed in the Holocaust. Written mostly in Hebrew and/ or Yiddish, these books also included eyewitness accounts of the fate of individuals and families who did not survive the years 1939–1945.

63. On this subject, see Chapter 29 in the autobiography of Hisrch Wolofsky, op. cit., cited on page 77 of this book.

64. Melekh Ravitch, Warsaw, letter to J. I. Segal, August 17, 1934, Segal Archive, Montreal Jewish Public Library.

65. Melekh Ravitch, *"Yud Yud Segal, portret fun a khaver* [J. I. Segal, portait of a friend]," *(Der Keneder Adler*, November 12, 1945), 5–6.

66. Mexico, *Der veg*, 1940.

67. Melekh Ravitch, Warsaw, letter to J. I. Segal, August 17, 1954, Segal Archive, Montreal Jewish Public Library.

68. Letter from Fishl Bimko, New York, to J. I. Segal, August 21, 1948, Segal Archive, Montreal Jewish Public Library.

69. The anthology was to have the subtitle *Der groyser baytrog fun kanadishn idishn yishuv tsu der alveltlekher idisher literatur* [The great contribution of the Canadian Jewish community to world Yiddish literature].

70. According to Chaim Leib Fuks, Ravitch, unlike Segal and many of the other Montreal Yiddish poets, never received a traditional religious education in his youth. See the entry for Ravitch in Haim-Leib Fuks, *Cent ans de littérature yiddish et hébraïque au Canada*, op. cit., 347–354, or in Ch. L. Fox, op. cit. (Yiddish), 264–271.

71.   Born in Poland, Petrushka arrived in Montreal in 1940 after having lived in Palestine for a number of years. He was the translator of the Mishna into Yiddish, published in Warsaw in 1924–1925 and the *Idishe entsiklopedya*, a Jewish Encyclopedia published in Yiddish in four volumes, also in Warsaw, between 1932 and 1935. This work was revised and reissued in Montreal in 1942 and in 1949 as *The Jewish Popular Encyclopedia* [*Yidisher folks-entsiklopedya*].

72.   See the *Keneder Adler*, "*Idishe shrayber farayn vet bekorev gegrindet vern in Montreal* [A Yiddish writers' association is about to be founded in Montreal], April 10, 1941, and "*Di grindungs farzamlung fun farayn fun idishe shrayber* [The founding meeting of the Yiddish Writers' Association]," ibid., April 27, 1941.

73.   Report on the meeting of May 5, 1941, Archive of the Yiddish Writers' Association, Montreal Jewish Public Library.

74.   Ibid.

75.   See among others "*Yisroel*" in *Dos Vort* (Montreal, June 1, 1953), 5–6. *Dos Vort* was a Montreal Labour Zionist newspaper.

76.   Haim-Leib Fuks, op. cit., 252 (French); Ch. L. Fox, op. cit., 182 (Yiddish).

77.   Letter from Chaim Lieberman, New York, to J. I. Segal, the month of Tishre, 1948, Segal Archive, Montreal Jewish Public Library.

78.   See, for example, Israel Rabinovitch, "*Yud Yud Segals nayer bukh Sefer idish* [J. I. Segal's new book *Sefer idish*]," *Keneder Adler*, March 31, 1950; Jacob Glatstein, "*In tokh genumen* [The heart of the matter]," (Idisher Kemfer, New York, November 24, 1950), 16–17.

79.   Letter from Berish Weinstein, New York, to J. I. Segal, spring 1950, Segal Archive, Montreal Jewish Public Library.

80.   Letter from Itsik Manger in English to J. I. Segal, February 14, 1951, Segal Archive, Montreal Jewish Public Library.

81.   J. I. Segal, "*Idish lishmo* [For the sake of Yiddish]," *Sefer Idish,* Montreal, 1950, 165.

82.   David Rome, "Yiddish Poems by J. I. Segal. The Value of Integrity," (*Congress Bulletin*, November–December 1950), 16.

83.   J. I. Segal, "Books in Exile. Old Friends in a New Setting Stir Deep Memories," (*Congress Bulletin*, November–December 1950), 13–14. Originally published in Yiddish in the *Keneder Adler*, September 5, 1950, 5–6, as "*Sforim in goles* [Books in exile]," and probably translated by David Rome.

84.   Oświęcim, the name of the Polish town where the Auschwitz death camp was located.

85.   H. M. Caiserman, "Polish Diary," January 9, 1946, Caiserman Archive, Canadian Jewish Congress Archives, Montreal.

86.   Letter from Tobias Bereljis, Buenos Aires, American Jewish Joint Distribution Committee, to H.M. Caiserman, November 9, 1950, Caiserman Archive, Canadian Jewish Congress Archives, Montreal.

87.   Letter from H. M. Caiserman, Toronto, to J. I. Segal, November 2, 1945, Caiserman Archive, Canadian Jewish Congress Archives, Montreal.

88.   Letter from H. M. Caiserman to J. I. Segal, January 15, 1944, Caiserman Archive, Canadian Jewish Congress Archives, Montreal.

89.   J. I. Segal, "*Tsu khet kuf* [to H.C.]," *Lirik*, Montreal, 1930, 151.

90.   Letter from H. M. Caiserman to Miss Dorothea Cox [English] Halifax, Canadian Broadcasting Corp., September 6, 1946, Caiserman Archive, Canadian Jewish Congress Archives, Montreal.

91.   This was the Tifereth Israel Synagogue at 5390 Saint-Urbain Street, today the Saints Irene and Markella Greek Orthodox Church.

92.   Letter from H.-M. Caiserman to Alexy, Dorris and Joseph [English], New York, April 14, 1947, September 6, 1946, Caiserman Archive, Canadian Jewish Congress Archives, Montreal.

93.   At the time of his death, Caiserman lived at 21 Maplewood Street West, Outremont.

94.   A. M. Klein, obituary, *The Canadian Jewish Chronicle*, December 29, 1950, 3. See also, Mordecai Ginzburg, *"H. M. Caiserman als mitboyer fun kanader yidisher kongres* [H. M. Caiserman, founder of the Canadian Jewish Congress]" *(Der Keneder Adler*, December 27, 1950), 4, 3; I. Medres, *"Dos kapitl Caiserman in Kanader yidisher geshikhte* [The Caiserman chapter of Canadian Jewish history]" *(Der Keneder Adler*, January 1, 1951); J. I. Segal, *"Dos groyse harts vos hot geplatst* [The great heart that broke]" *(Der Keneder Adler*, December 29, 1950), 4.

95.   J. I. Segal, *"H. M. Caiserman – der mentsh vos hot lib gehat* [H. M. Caiserman – the man who loved]" *(Der Keneder Adler*, January 1, 1951), 5, 6.

96.   The Jewish cemetery, located on de la Savane near Decarie Boulevard, is today known as the Baron de Hirsch or De la Savane Cemetery.

97.   H. M. Caiserman and J. I. Segal are buried next to each other in the section of the cemetery belonging to the Jewish National Workers' Alliance [*Yidisher Natsyonaler Arbeter Farband*], a Zionist mutual aid organization. See Danny Kucharsky, *Sacred Ground on de la Savane, Montreal's Baron de Hirsch Cemetery* (Montréal, Véhicule Press, 2008), 128–129 and 151–153.

98.   Mordecai Ginzburg, *"Plutsimdiger toyt fun Yud Yud Segal ruft aroys troyer in shtot* [City in mourning at the sudden death of I. J. Segal]" *(Der Keneder Adler*, March 8, 1954), 1.

99.   Ibid.

100. *"Toyt fun Yud Yud Segal* [Death of J. I. Segal]," *Inter Office Information*, Canadian Jewish Congress, no. 6, April 1, 1954. Internal document, Canadian Jewish Congress Archive, Montreal.

101. Since 1920, Shlomo Wiseman had been the director of the Jewish Peoples School, where Segal was still teaching at the time of his death. He also been one of the founders of the United Yiddish Teachers' Seminary.

102. J. I. Segal, *"Alt-Montreal* [Old Montreal]," *Letste lider* (Montreal, 1955), 105. English translation by Miriam Waddington in Irving Howe and Eliezer Greenberg, eds., *A Treasury of Yiddish Poetry* (New York, Schocken Books, 1969), 152.

103. Letter from the J. I. Segal Foundation, Montreal, June 21, 1954, Segal Archive, Montreal Jewish Public Library.

104. On this subject, see the report of the meeting of the publication committee, March 41, 1957.

105. See the report of the meeting of "The Friends of Segal," organized by the J. I. Segal Foundation, Montreal, January 11, 1957, Segal Archive, Montreal Jewish Public Library.

106. See the letter from Jacob Glatstein, *Folk un velt* [People and world], New York, to Melekh Ravitch, December 1, 1958, and the letter from Melekh Ravitch to Jacob Glatstein.

107. Bernard Wind, *"A novi vos gloybt nit* [A prophet who is a non-believer]" *(The Toronto Hebrew Journal*, Toronto, November 22, 1953), 4.

Conclusion

In Montreal, the death of J. I. Segal represented a breach in continuity with far-reaching historical and religious ramifications. The poet, who as a child had been nurtured on the teachings of traditional Judaism and the ideas of Hasidism, died in the aftermath of a genocide that had torn asunder the very fabric of the Eastern European Ashkenazic Jewish world. Raised in Korets, Segal for the rest of his life had dreamt about the fleeting years of his youth. By the time he died, however, the memory of a bygone era, when the daily life of the Jews was structured by their sacred texts and the veneration of righteous *rebbes*, had gradually begun to fade. The loss of the traditional Jewish way of life, inflicted by the relentless march of time, had now been compounded by an unexpected, murderous onslaught that had practically erased any trace of a Jewish presence in much of what is now the Ukraine. At the time of Segal's death, it was still difficult to grasp what the convergence of these two painful developments could mean for Jews born on the other side of the Atlantic. Of course, Segal was not the only one in the city to have lived during the distant era of the Russian Empire and to have an intimate knowledge of the traditional world of the *shtetl*. For a time, several members of his generation were still able to bear witness to the terrible rupture at the turn of the century occasioned by emigration to America and the sudden rise of modernity in the Jewish world. But Segal was the only one to have written such a large body of poetry. No one but he knew how to distil the emotions elicited by this faithfulness to the Old Country with its historic Ashkenzic roots. Furthermore, Segal was writing in Yiddish, a language that was the preferred vehicle for such obvious devotion, a tongue whose intonations had resounded over the vast steppes of Eastern Europe, from the foothills of the Carpathian Mountains to the borders of the Balkans. In March of 1954, A. M. Klein summed up the reaction of the Montreal Jewish community to the news of the poet's death:

> With the sudden snatching-away [. . .] of the poet J. I. Segal, Yiddish literature has suffered a loss most grievous — irreparable.

> For Segal was not just another rhymester toying with the echoes
> of sound, a bard by mere avocation. Poetry for him, the faithful
> guardian of an antique tradition, was not only a calling to be fol-
> lowed; it was a call to be answered. That call came to him across
> the generations by way of an unbroken sacred legacy, bequeathed
> at first by the Baal Shem Tov, cherished by the Bratslaver, and at
> last transmitted from his favorite Koretz to this latter-day Levite
> "making great song for a little clan."[1]

Segal's demise heralded not only the decline of the sublime form of
piety and surrender to God of traditional Ashkenazic Judaism, in particular in Hasidism, but also the gradual disappearance of an Eastern
European Jewish view of "Montrealness." The poet was part of the
great wave of Jewish immigration that brought to Canada's shores a
cohort of young idealists passionately devoted to the creation of a new
Yiddish culture in the New World. While plans were being hatched
for a socialist revolution to overthrow Russian absolutism and a rallying cry was raised for a new type of Jewishness dedicated to labour
militancy, a few newly arrived Yiddish-speaking intellectuals and
writers in Montreal had opened a new front of cultural activity. With
uncommon energy and determination, they devoted themselves to
this task, convinced that they were taking part in the social revolution now blazing through their country of origin, and which mysterious winds had blown to an unknown country. When he published
his first poetry collection, *Fun mayn velt*, in 1918, Segal had unwittingly been one of the principal architects of this creative upsurge.
For almost forty years he had remained the incarnation of a desire
to create a Canadian Yiddish culture and provide Montreal with a
robust network of Yiddish-language institutions, to serve a population profoundly attached to its Eastern European origins. Amidst
the ferment of ideas and clash of ideologies within the community,
Yiddish remained the cultural backdrop for all the Jews of Eastern
Europe, and a crucial rallying point for immigrants still bewildered
by their adopted country. The feverish drive to create and write in that
language, which had gripped a few individuals in Montreal in the
1910s and 1920s, now, with Segal's passing, was about to disappear
forever, and nothing could stop it. The editor-in-chief of the *Eagle*,
Israel Rabinovitch, conveyed the full impact of this development in
his column entitled *"Tog-ayn, tog-oys"* [Day in, day out] in December
of 1950, in which he had lamented the death of H. M. Caiserman. His

sober reflections were equally applicable to the shy but prolific author of *Sefer idish*, whose pen would run dry three years later.

> I know that it was a complete coincidence that it was so bitterly cold after the warmest person in our community closed his eyes forever. Nonetheless, it was very symbolic. I'm afraid that with the passing of the old guard, of which Chananiah Caiserman was perhaps the quintissential representative, a dramatic change has taken place in the climate of our local Jewish community.
> The climate of "Jewish life", in the fullest sense, is subtropical, like that of the Land of Israel.[2]

Their reverence for the Yiddish language as a vehicle for cultural continuity was reflected in the daily activities of the generation of activists and writers who had arrived in Montreal prior to World War I. Having experienced, during their Eastern European childhoods, the persuasive power of the Jewish religion, which they had forsaken on their way to the New World, these authors approached Yiddish writing with an intensity equalled only by the religious fervour of believers. Faithful to their origins to the point of venerating their unique culture, in particular the language that served as their channel of communication, Segal and Caiserman approached a Yiddish text with a mystical exaltation worthy of the greatest Hasidic masters. For them and all those who had accompanied them on their quest to reconstruct a Jewish identity, to read and write in Yiddish was the equivalent of a *mitzvah*, a religious commandment performed by pious Jews to be drawn closer to God, despite the fact that Segal and Caiserman in America were immersed in a milieu committed to secularism and modernity. Segal especially was constantly aware of the tension between his traditional Jewish upbringing and his irrepressible desire to embrace new freedoms and revolutionary ideas. This very difficult transition, repeated thousands of times over, was perfectly symbolized by the only Atlantic crossing which Segal experienced during his lifetime, when he abandoned the Korets of his childhood in favour of a large North American city. Although Segal never looked back, he was haunted by the memory, at times overpowering, of his Volhynian childhood, a preoccupation that would be further intensified by the events of World War II. Thus, although the poet reached out to the unfettered modernity of the New World, where he believed that he had discovered the ideal conditions for literary creativity and an inexhaustible source of inspiration, he never freed himself from the pangs of nostalgia and the sting of regret. In truth, Segal the man had lived between two worlds, one that had vanished forever, which only memory and writing could recreate, and the other material world from which he remained alienated by temperament and social status. In this unbridgeable gap that constantly gave rise to overwhelming feelings of absence and loss, Segal's poetry found a home. Bearing the imprint of biblical prophecy and submission to the power of Hasidic contemplation, only at moments did it touch upon the demands of the present, or lend a distracted ear to the hustle and bustle of North America.

Like the companions of his early days in Montreal, Segal was convinced that their Yiddish heritage had taken permanent root in that city, and that he would guide the steps of a new generation born in America. During the interwar period, while the city's Yiddish-speaking institutional network was developing and expanding, he was not alone in this conviction. In an entire Montreal neighbour-hood along St. Lawrence Boulevard and throughout the neighbour-ing streets, Yiddish was spoken openly, without any form of official censorship. At the time, this language seemed to have a bright future in Montreal, especially in a place that had been multilingual for over a century, and where each of the two dominant communities jealously guarded its own school system. Until the very end, Segal believed that Yiddish would work its way into Montreal's future, and continue to constitute a fundamental part of Jewish identity on the eastern slopes of Mount Royal. While visiting the offices of *Der Tog* in New York in 1951, Segal declared optimistically: "Jews are building a new library in Montreal, they're building synagogues, and Jewish children are reading—and really beautifully—our precious Yiddish language, literature and history."[3] The poet repeated the same words for journalists at the *Forverts* during this same visit: "In Montreal even more Jewish cultural institutions are being created, and could be created. Montreal could become a bastion of Yiddish culture."[4] How could it be otherwise, when half a century earlier the Yiddish language had established a foothold in the neighbourhoods near the harbour without encountering a single serious obstacle to its advancement, and had channeled a cultural impulse of great expressive power? In an article published in 1990, David Roskies posits the idea that, from the very beginning, the generation of Segal and Caiserman conceived the utopian project of creating a sustainable Yiddish culture in Montreal that would overcome the initial period of adjustment to the New World, and over time would go on to bear fruit in all spheres of activity.[5] The entire narrative which I have presented here corroborates this contention. Moreover, did the Jews not have the example all around them of the French Canadians who, every step of the way, had resisted British colonial rule and assimilation in North America?[6] What would prevent the Eastern European Jews from asserting their culture in a country where Canadian identity was still weak, and official patriotism for all practical purposes non-existent?

To achieve this result, the Ashkenazi Jews had the benefit of their long experience in the diaspora, as well as a rare capacity for institutional consolidation in the face of adversity. As a community that had always enjoyed a level of literacy unparalleled in Canada, they were able to take advantage of the available opportunities for social mobility. Despite these concrete advances and utopian projects explicitly promoting the Eastern European Jewish heritage, which could contribute to the realization of this miraculous objective, Yiddish in Montreal was essentially the affair of a single generation, a generation born and raised in Eastern Europe. Having left for Canada in three migratory waves, the first before World War I, the next in the inter-war period, and the final one after the Holocaust, consisting mainly of survivors, the Yiddish-speaking population of Canada did not succeed in transmitting its language, other than in a fragmented form. Among the four hundred and twenty-nine Yiddish and Hebrew authors included in the 1980 Lexicon of Ch. L. Fox, only six were born in Canada, and they were exceptional in that they were raised in immigrant families where Yiddish was spoken on a daily basis.[7] Segal himself was no exception to the rule. For his two daughters, Sylvia and Annette, the Yiddish language remained a cultural treasure that their father reserved exclusively for use with his friends and colleagues. The poet's children never breached the wall that Segal had erected around his work and his inner life. How could they have done so when Segal's world of meaning required a sophisticated knowledge, not only of the Yiddish language, but also of the age-old Eastern European cultural practices which had never taken hold in Canada? For those born in this country, even the daughters of the greatest Montreal Yiddish writer, the nostalgia which plagued Segal, his emotional fragility, and his insistence on straddling two worlds, could not make much sense in the long run.

One fine day a consensus was reached in the Montreal Jewish community that Yiddish, as wonderful as it was, and so full of precious cultural lessons, was no longer essential to the perpetuation of Ashkenazic Jewish culture in North America. Canadian Jews came to this realization only gradually, especially after 1945, when a world traumatized by six years of war was opening a new chapter. By the late 1940s it was evident that English would suffice to ensure the perpetuation of the great ethical principles of Judaism. The language of Shakespeare also provided Jews with sufficient community autonomy and cohesion within the open and diverse broader social Canadian context. At the same time, Montreal Jews had become aware that, after the eradication of the Ashkenazic world of Eastern Europe, North American Jewry, living in an English-speaking environment, had become the largest demographic entity within the Jewish diaspora. In this context, the transition of Jewish literature into English occasioned a radical change for Jewish writers in their mode of writing and relationship to language. In the 1930s when this shift started, the writers who turned to English, such as A. M. Klein, Vera Black and Shulamis Borodentsky Yelin, a kindergarten teacher at the Peretz School in Montreal since the 1920s, could still speak and read Yiddish fluently. Nevertheless, they treated Jewish themes in a very different way than their predecessors. Since Segal, Ravitch, Shtern, and Gotlib wrote in a language understood only by Jews, there could be no question as to their cultural and religious affiliation. No one could doubt their origins or their membership in the community, when most of the vocabulary they used, except perhaps for more modern and technical terms, belonged to the great Jewish tradition that began with the Hebrew alphabet. By adopting English as their literary vehicle, a language clearly situated outside the Jewish frame of reference, Klein and his colleagues had to make an extra effort to break away from the cultural influence of Anglican Protestantism dating back to the Elizabethan period. Wishing to reaffirm their loyalty to their own ancestral tradition, they felt they had no choice but to emphasize their allegiance by choosing uniquely Jewish subject matter and using specifically Jewish words which, at times, were incomprehensible to the average English-speaking reader. Who could have imagined at the beginning of the twentieth century that North American Jews would be able to create a large body of literature in a non-Jewish language without risking the loss of their identity altogether?

The fact that Yiddish speakers were turning to English as their literary language, and becoming open to other modes of cultural expression, represented an extraordinary change in perspective, which was further reinforced by factors specific to Quebec. After World War II, ethnic and religious compartmentalization was replaced by a more inclusive attitude on the part of the Catholic Church, fostered by the Second Vatican Council, and new ideas about the relationship of the God of Abraham and Moses with the chosen people. After having been directed exclusively to the English-language Protestant School system, Jews now found the doors to a French-Canadian society, in the throes of great structural changes, tentatively opening for them. In the post-war era, defensive Francophone nationalism gradually changed to the point of welcoming the cultural contributions made by recent immigrants. The profound social upheaval of the Quiet Revolution de facto raised the highly complex and interesting issue of the relations between Yiddish-speaking Montrealers and French Canada early in the twentieth century. After 1950, religious ecumenism, state secularism, and changing identities converged to finally allow an initial contact between Francophones and the Montreal Jewish community, but, undoubtedly, too late for Yiddish creativity to play a significant role. As mentioned earlier, since the 1910s Caiserman had taken an interest in French Canadian nationalist poetry. After 1929, he also worked energetically to forge links with certain members of the Catholic clergy, including Jesuits Joseph Paré and Stéphane Valiquette. Nevertheless, these initiatives were taking place in a kind of no man's land in terms of religious doctrine, and came to naught, despite the goodwill of the main participants.[8] Still, there were several signs of a significant change after the Second World War, notably thanks to *Le Cercle juif de langue française*, which was launched in Montreal in 1949–1950 by the Canadian Jewish Congress.[9] They were reported in an article by Benjamin Gutl Sack in the Jewish Daily Eagle at the end of 1950, and reproduced in English in the *Congress Bulletin*:

> "The goodwill of the Canadian Jewish Congress, carried out so faithfully and efficiently over a period of years, has borne fruit," he concluded. "It is not long since spokesmen of French Canada sought to poison the atmosphere of our country with anti-Semitism, since hatred of the Jews—the fire set by Arcand and his followers—inflamed the entire country and set the general French-Canadian public against us. The results of this hate brought no credit to French Canada. But today conditions have improved considerably. Today the leaders of French Canadian thought provide us with innumerable examples of friendship."[10]

Following World War II, contact was made in Montreal between Yiddish–speaking writers and their French-speaking counterparts. For the most part, these interactions took place in an atmosphere of goodwill. H. M. Casierman and David Rome redoubled their attempts at dialogue to the extent that personal friendships developed. Roger Nadeau, a journalist who wrote for *Le Canada*, eulogized Caiserman when he passed away, describing his activities in these words: "He was one of the pioneers in the work of establishing friendly relations between Jewish Canadians and French Canadians [. . .] For some time, the Jewish Canadians of Montreal have accorded an ever-growing importance to the French language and French culture."[11] In 1951, from February 11 to 25, a Jewish Book Exhibition was held under the auspices of the Jewish Public Library and the Canadian Jewish Congress, featuring for the first time the contributions of Raymond Douville, Gérard Malchelosse, and Jean Le Moyne to Canadian Jewish historiography. This event also made possible an informal and friendly discussion between the novelist Germaine Guèvremont, journalist Françoise Gaudet-Smet, and the poet J. I. Segal. On that occasion, demographer Louis Rosenberg and historian Léon Trépanier delivered speeches extoling the cultural and literary achievements of Canadian Jews.[12] That was in addition to the invitations which the *Le Cercle juif de langue française*[13] had extended to Germaine Guèvremont and Father Émile Legault, founder of the Compagnons de Saint-Laurent, among others, to speak during their 1950–1951 season. These early endeavours even included Yiddish culture and language when, on October 16, 1953, David Rome spoke about the work of J. I. Segal in French on a radio program hosted by none other than René Levesque. An opportunity to participate in a broadcast about Yiddish culture was so unusual that Rome reported it in a letter to Segal himself: "I would like to inform you that your work was recently discussed on the CBC radio's French-language station [. . .] in a program about the Jewish Public Library. The program was prepared by René Lévesque."[14] In March of that same year, the Montreal Yiddish Writers Association invited its first non-Jewish speaker, the Jesuit priest Father Edmond Desrochers, professor at Collège Sainte Marie, who addressed an audience of about twenty people about the principal cultural institutions in French Canada.[15] As early as May of 1951, S. D. Cohen who was in charge of the Joint Community Relations Committee of the Canadian Jewish Congress noted:

The continuing program of establishing and maintaining contacts with representative persons in various spheres of French-
Canadian life is continuing in a very gratifying manner. There
are contacts that we are constantly utilizing for the purposes of
deepening friendship and understanding for our group and for
the purpose of maintaining ourselves au courant with pertinent
developments in fields that interest us.[16]

There is no doubt that these developments came too late and were
too superficial to allow Yiddish literary achievements to have a lasting impact on the Montreal Francophone landscape at that time. In
the early 1950s, the Canadian Jewish Congress had established a strategy of cultural dialogue designed specifically to promote the poetry of
A. M. Klein, whose book *The Rocking Chair and Other Poems,* published
in 1948, won the Governor General's Award.[17] This English-language
collection seemed much more accessible to Francophone readers due
to its subject matter and sensibility, and even more so because it contained descriptions of rural traditions in French Canada. Yet, apart from

J. I. Segal with Germaine Guèvremont and Françoise Gaudet-Smet at the Jewish Book
Exhibition, Montreal, 1951. (Private collection of Sylvia and Annette Segal.)

a few excerpts from Segal's later collections, translated by David Rome, all published in the Congress Bulletin, the rest of Yiddish literature remained unavailable to Francophone readers in their own language. A.M. Klein had also translated a few of Segal's poems into English for the anthology *The Golden Peacock, An Anthology of Yiddish Poetry Translated into English Verse,*[18] published in 1939 by Joseph Leftwich. Gradually some of these poems were republished in Canadian Jewish publications during the 1940s. A few translations were included in the obituary that Klein wrote in 1954 for the *Canadian Jewish Chronicle,*[19] as well as in a short study by Miriam Waddington published in 1960,[20] but this was a drop in the bucket compared to the literary ocean that the poet had left for posterity. Segal's death in 1954, and the irreversible decline of Yiddish writing in Montreal beginning in the 1960s, sealed the fate of Montreal Yiddish literature in the Francophone world. Not only did the language barrier render any inroads in this regard practically impossible, but the culture which had generated this work eluded those who lived outside the Jewish universe.[21] Translations into French of Segal's work were slow in coming. In 1971, one solitary poem of Segal's appeared in a French-language anthology edited by Charles Dobzynski entitled *Le miroir d'un peuple, anthologie de la poésie yiddish (1870–1970),*[22] published by Éditions du Seuil. During the 1970s Sister Marie-Noëlle de Baillehache, with the assistance of David Rome, attempted to publish some twenty of Segal's poems that she herself had translated into French, but this project could not interest a single publisher.[23] Francophone readers had to wait until 1992 for a larger selection of Segal's poems to be published by Éditions du Noroît, enti- tled *Poèmes yiddish/Yidishe lider.* By that time, nearly forty years after the poet's death, translating Segal into the language of Molière had become a complicated venture, which required a long historical intro- duction, as well as footnotes explaining the basic concepts of Judaism.

Today, encountering Segal's work is like confronting a world that might at any moment disappear from view. The poet has not only vanished physically, but he seems to have fallen into oblivion, even in the Montreal community to which he had belonged and contrib- uted so much in terms of culture. The Eastern European world that filled his dreams, provided a refuge from adversity, and to which he had devoted most of his writing, was wiped off the map with weap- onry and racial hatred. As Melekh Ravitch noted in a 1954 article about Segal, the death of the poet foreshadowed the end of a world, a generation, and a language.

> The sun moves slowly across its enormous arc from east to west—
> but as soon as it touches the horizon, it quickly begins to fall, to
> sink—night descends—a generation has passed. That generation
> had believed that, like the sun, its day would move slowly—but
> now it has touched the horizon and is rapidly sinking—...[24]

A small number of activists and creators in Montreal were able to
carry on for a few more years after the Holocaust, assisted by a post-
war influx of writers, mostly from Poland. But they could delay the
inevitable for a short time only. Despite their best efforts and unshake-
able devotion, the days of Yiddish literature in Montreal, like everywhere else, were already numbered.

Yet the rapid decline of Yiddish in the shadow of Mount Royal
should not obscure the fact that, for almost half a century, this language had shone brilliantly in the city, and left a legacy of a magnitude inconceivable today. Yiddish writing, especially Segal's, had
attained such heights that it was impossible to suspect how few
Yiddish writers there actually were in Montreal, and how meagre
their earnings. The fact that Montreal Yiddish literature was essentially an immigrant venture aimed at a very limited audience, both in
the city and elsewhere on the planet, is astounding considering the
level of accomplishment and depth of poetic creativity. Segal had had
such a forceful and far-reaching impact that in other circumstances
he would have been propelled to the forefront of Canadian or Eastern
European literature. But, as Israel Rabinovitch remarked at the time
of the poet's death, Segal did not know how to go beyond Yiddish
Montreal, and probably had no desire to do so. He was too busy being
a great poet in the place where fate had led him, a city far from his
native Volhynia by the name of Montreal, amidst a French-speaking
people which, during his lifetime, had no inkling of the scope and
magnificence of his writing. The final word of this literary adventure
was written a few days after the poet's death by Israel Rabinovitch,
editor-in-chief of the *Keneder Adler*. His reflections marked the end of
a career launched several decades earlier on the pages of that same
Montreal newspaper, a newspaper which itself was now embarking
upon its final *dénouement*:

> J. I. Segal left behind a great cultural treasure for his people, and
> for all of humanity. Yet he died as he had lived—in great pov-
> erty... Bear in mind that during his lifetime our divinely gifted

poet was oblivious to the practicalities of life because all his energies were focussed on his poetry, and there was simply nothing
left for anything else. As hard as he tried "to be like everyone
else," he did not succeed. He could not be like everyone else
because his talent was too powerful, and at the same time he was
forced to pay a too high price for his divine gift.[25]

Notes

1.   A. M. Klein, "In Memoriam: J. I. Segal," (*The Canadian Jewish Chronicle*, Montreal,
     March 12, 1954), 3.
2.   Israel Rabinovitch, *"Tog-ayn, tog-oys"* (*Keneder Adler*, Montréal, December
     26,1950), 1.
3.   *"Barimter dikhter yud yud Segal git op freylekhn grus fun Kanade* [Famous poet J.
     I. Segal brings happy greetings from Canada]" (*Der Tog*, New York, May 29,
     1951), 7.
4.   *"Montreal ken vern di shtarkste festung fun idisher kultur, zogt der dikhter yud yud
     Segal* [Montreal can become a stronghold of Yiddish culture says poet J. I. Segal]"
     (*Forverts*, New York, May 29, 1951).
5.   Roskies, David G., "Yiddish in Montreal: The Utopian Experiment," in Ira
     Robinson, Pierre Anctil and Mervin Butovsky, eds., *An Everyday Miracle, Yiddish
     Culture in Montreal* (Montreal, Véhicule Press, 1990), 22–38.
6.   On this subject see the comments published in *Yidisher Kemfer* [Jewish fighter],
     March 14, 1919, cited in Simon Belkin, *Le mouvement ouvrier juif au Canada, 1904–
     1920* (Sillery, les éditions du Septentrion, 1999), 296; French version of *Di Poale-
     Zion bavegung in Kanade, 1904–1920* (The Labour Zionist Movement in Canada,
     1904–1920) [Yiddish] (Montreal, 1956), 193.
7.   Haim-Leib Fuks, op. cit., see figures 4 and 5, 437.
8.   See, for example, an article by H. M. Caiserman entitled *"A tip fun kanader frant-
     soyz* [A type of French Canadian]," *Keneder* Adler, October 19, 1936.
9.   On this subject see Jean-Philippe Croteau, *Les relations entre les Juifs de langue fran-
     çaise et les Canadiens français selon le Bulletin du Cercle juif, 1954–1968* (Montreal,
     University of Montreal, masters thesis in history, 2000).
10. "French-Canadians Appreciate Jews' Interest in French" [English] (*Congress
     Bulletin*, Montreal, November–December 1950), 5, 22.
11. Roger Nadeau, " Canadien juif que le Canada français ne doit pas oublier" (*Le
     Canada*, Montreal, January 20, 1951), 4.
12. "Exhibit Opens Here of Jewish Canadiana" (*The Gazette*, Montreal, February16,
     1951), 17. Roger Nadeau also commented on this event in *"La science prouve que
     tous les hommes sont frères et le bon sens montre qu'ils ont intérêt à l'être* [Science
     proves that all men are brothers and common sense would inidicated that that
     they have a vested in being so" (*Le Canada*, February, 22 1951), 4.
13. *Congress Bulletin*, op. cit.
14. Letter in Yiddish from David Rome, Director of the Jewish Public Library to
     J. I. Segal, November 10, 1953, Canadian Jewish Congress Archives, Montreal.
15. Internal note from David Rome to Saul Hayes and S. D. Cohen, Canadian Jewish
     Congress, March 12, 1953, Canadian Jewish Congress Archives, Montreal. The
     document did not specify whether Father Desrochers' lecture was delivered in
     French or English.

16. Internal note from S. D. Cohen to the Eastern Joint Public Relations Committee, Canadian Jewish Congress, May 1,1951, Canadian Jewish Congress Archives, Montreal.

17. See Pierre Anctil, "A.M. Klein: du poète et de ses rapports avec le Québec français," in the *Journal of Canadian Studies/Revue d'études canadiennes*, Peterborough, 1984, vol. 19, no. 2, 114–131.

18. The poems are "And This I Know," "Autobiographical," "King Rufus," and "A King." A new edition of this book published by T. Yoseloff in New York in 1961. Other translations of Segal's poems appeared in *America in Yiddish Poetry, an Anthology* (New York, Exposition Press, 1967), 528.

19. A. M. Klein, "In Memoriam: J. I. Segal," op. cit.

20. Miriam Waddington, "Yakov Yitzhok Segal, Canadian Jewish Poet" (*The Tamarack Review*, Toronto, autumn 1960), no. 17, 34–36. This is followed on pages 36 to 42 by five of Segal's poems translated by Waddinton and one by A. M. Klein. These translations were later included in *A Treasury of Yiddish Poetry*, edited by Irving Howe and Eliezer Greenberg (New York: Holt, Rinehart and Winston, 1969).

21. In 2011, Esther Weinschelbaum published translations of a number of Segal's poems, which were reproduced by Elieser Leoni in *The Korets Book: In Memory of Our Community That Is No More*, Tel Aviv, Azari Press, 1959, 284–296. These texts had appeared in *Korets, pirke yidish meturgamim l'ivrit* [Korets, Yiddish chapter translated into Hebrew], published by the Korets Association in Israel, Tel Aviv, 2011, 38–48.

22. The French translation of this poem was entitled "De Koretz." This book was republished by Gallimard in 2000 with the title *Anthologie de la poésie yiddish: le miroir d'un peuple*. At that time, Dobzynski added a second translated poem with the French title "Automne tardif à Montréal."

23. Undated typed manuscript containing twenty-one poems by J. I. Segal translated into French, David Rome Archive, Canadian Jewish Congress Archives, Montreal. Born in France, Sister Marie-Noëlle de Baillehache, a member of the Sisters of Our Lady of Sion, was one of the main participants in the Christian-Jewish Dialogue Group in Montreal in the 1960s and 1970s.

24. Melech Ravitch, portrait of "J. I. Segal" in *Mayn Leksikon. Idishe shraybers, kinstlers, aktyorn, oykh klal-tuers, in di amerikes un andere lender, (My Lexicon: Pen Portraits of Jewish Writers and Artists in the Americas and Other Countries)*, op. cit., 143.

25. Israel Rabinovitch, "Gut morgn." (*Der Keneder Adler*, Montreal, March 26, 1954), 1.

Appendices 1 to 33

J. I. Segal's responses to the questionnaire of the Jewish Writers Club (*Yud lamed peretz shrayber farayn*), New York, 1923

J. I. Segal Archive, Montreal Jewish Public Library

- To which newspapers, periodicals or other publications have you contributed your work, and which have you yourself published or edited?

  A – Contributed to:
  - ○ *Fraye Arbeter Shtime* (New York)
  - ○ *Keneder Adler (The Jewish Daily Eagle)* (Montreal)
  - ○ *Der yidisher zhurnal/The Daily Hebrew Journal* (Toronto)
  - ○ *Tsum Vort?* (Winnipeg)
  - ○ *Kanade* (Toronto)
  - ○ *Freiheit* (New York)
  - ○ *Fraynt* (Saint Petersburg)
  - ○ *Tsukunft* (New York)
  - ○ *In Zikh* (New York)
  - ○ *Feder* (New York)
  - ○ *Varshever Shriftn, Bikher-Velt* (Warsaw)
  - ○ *Kanade* (Montreal and Toronto)

  B – Published literary reviews and was a staff writer for:
  - ○ *Nyuansn* (monthly periodical, Montreal)
  - ○ *Epokhe* (literary journal, Montreal)
  - ○ *Royerd* (literary periodical, Montreal)

- What work—original or in translation—have you published, in what languages, who was the publisher, and where was it published?
  - ○ *Fun mayn velt* (poetry collection, Montreal)
  - ○ *Bazunder* (poetry, Montreal)
  - ○ *Fun mayn shtub un mayn velt* (poetry, New York).

In Shop [In Shop]

by J. I. Segal, *The Jewish Daily Eagle* (*Keneder Adler*) Montreal,
April 23, 1917, 4

In shop

Foyl un lang di teg zikh tsyen
in dem yokh bin ikh farshpant . . .
Imer, imer pratsn, myen
Es brekht un shmekht di mide hant.

Oyf di penemer fartsoygn
ligt der troyer shver un brayt
un fun yedns shtore oygn
kukt aroys di tifste layd.

Ikh trayb alts di mashin keseyder
un kayn rege nit gerut! . . .
Es darf di velt azoyfil kleyder —
un der trost azoyfil blut ! . . .

Helft [Help]

First poem published by J. I. Segal, *The Jewish Daily Eagle*
(*Keneder Adler*) Montreal, October 3, 1915

Helft

O brider, tse zet ir nokh alts nit di flamen.
Fun blut un fun treren di broyzende yamen.
fun ayere eygene vos ir hot tsuzamen
in layden un freyden gelebt mit zey yoren.

Tse filt ir nokh alts nit vi shreklekh der brokh iz
tse kent ir bagrayfen di beyze marokhes
fun ayere eygene fraynd un mishpokhes
vi zey kumen um dort un veren farloyrn! . . .

In shlakht falt der kreftiger, der shpayzer,
di alte fartraybt men fun zeyere hayzer . . .
Durkh mesires fun soynim tsum tsar un tsum kayzer
Di ere fun froyen un meydlekh beroybt . . .

Di idishe heym iz tsekrokht un tsebrokhn
Di foters geshosn, gehangen, geshtokhn.
Oyf aykh nor farblaybt di yesoymims betokhn . . .
Nit blaybt zshe tsu zeyer fartsveyflung vartoybt! . . .

Tse vet ir zey lozn dort vern tsuribn . . .
Gepaynigt, geyogt umetum un getribn
Nit helfen ot yene vos zaynen geblibn
zikh ranglen in blutigen shturm fun has . . .

Vi ken den aykh reyn blayben der gevisn
ven ir vet nit teylen mit zey ayer bisn
un lozn es zol zikh dem blut fargisn,
zey zoln fun hunger dort faln in gas! . . .

Nor ir kent zey helfen, nit lozn tsutretn
ir noente vayte . . . nor ir darft zey reten!
Zey shtreken tsu aykh di hent un zey beten:
"Erhalt unzer lebn mit vos nit ir kent! . . .

Retet dem tatn shikt hilf der mamen
kinderlekh! Helft, ir tort nit farzamen,
lesht oys di shreklekhe flamen
az nit veln mir ale do veren farbrent! . . .

In My Little Town

Second poem published by J. I. Segal, *The Jewish Daily Eagle*
(*Keneder Adler*) Montreal, November 22, 1916

In mayn shtetl

Mikh trogt mayn fantazye ariber aheym
in vayt-vayten shtetl in kleynem
Ikh zukh in di khorev gevorene erter
un ken nit gefinen dort keynem.

Es shteyen di shtiblekh vi groye aveylim
un glotsn mit pkhodim fun vaytn . . .
Azoy vi farumglikte nebekh on rakhmim
fun epes a shed a farshaytn . . .

Nor bloyz oyf a harbstikn boym oyf a hoyln
vos hot shoyn oyf zikh nit kayn bletlv
Shvebt umet a kro a shvartse un kroyet
(a kadish gevis nokhn shtetl . . .).

The Fundamental Principles of the Jewish Socialist Labor Party Poale-Zion

Flyer for the municipal election of April 1916

(Caiserman Archive, Canadian Jewish Congress, Montreal, [English version in Fineman, H., Poale Zionism: An Outline of its Aims and Institutions, Central Committee of the Jewish Socialist Labor Party Poale Zion of America, 266 Grand Street, New York, N.Y., 1918, pages 42 and 44].)

1. The Jewish Socialist Labor Party Poale-Zion aims, together with the working classes of all nations, to overthrow Capitalism and to establish the Socialist system of society.

2. The Jewish Socialist Labor Party Poale-Zion aims to concentrate the Jewish people in Palestine and to establish therein an autonomous Jewish commonwealth.

3. The Party takes an active part in the national work of the Diaspora to the end that the economic, national, cultural, and political condition of the Jewish people shall be raised in the lands of exile.

4. The Party strives to unite the entire Jewish proletariat into one world-wide Jewish Socialist Labor Party on these fundamental principles.

Autobiography of Hannaniah Meir Caiserman

Undated Yiddish document, Canadian Jewish Congress
Archives, Montreal

1. Given name: Hannaniah.
   Father's given name: Meir.
   Family name: Caiserman.

2. Day, month and year of birth: 19 March 1884.

3. Place of birth: Piatra Neamt, Roumania.

4. Date of immigration to Canada: 2 July 1910.

5. Date of first literary activity: in 1906 in Roumanian, *Vocea Dreptatei*, *Mevasseret Zion, Romanie Muncitoare*.

6. Contributor to *Nyuansn* and editor of the history of the Canadian Jewish Congress in *The Jew in Canada*. Published in *Folkstsaytung*, Canada, 1910; *Der Veg*, Canada; *Dos Folk*, Montreal; *Keneder Adler*; *Der yidisher zhurnal/The Daily Hebrew Journal*, Toronto; *Dos Yidishe Vort*, Winnipeg; also in *Le Devoir*, Montreal; *Yidishe Kemfer*; *Fraye Arbeter Shtime*; *Der Tog*; *Di Tsayt*, London; *Di Tsayt*, New York.

   Editor of *Nayland* (a magazine about immigration) and *Undzer Vort* (labour periodical) in Montreal. Also to *Dor Hayom* and *Hasodah*, in Eretz Israel. I write in Yiddish, English and French, and have translated into Hebrew and Russian (in *Mandchuria*, a Zionist periodical). I have used the pseudonyms H. M. Caiserman-Wittal and Moykil in a humorous publication called *Der Bezem*.

Jewish Immigration to Canada, 1901–1931

Adapted from Louis Rosenberg, *Canada's Jews, A Social and Economic Study of the Jews in Canada*, Montreal, Canadian Jewish Congress, 1939, Table 101, page 150, and documents in the Louis Rosenberg Archive, National Archives and Library of Canada

1901–1902	1,244
1902–1903	2,534
1903–1904	4,578
1904–1905	9,427
1905–1906	9,067
1906–1907	9,882
1907–1908	11,849
1908–1909	4,702
1909–1910	6,164
1910–1911	8,729
Total for the decade 1901–1911	68,176
1911–1912	9,099
1912–1913	11,624
1913–1914	18,031
1914–1915	7,677
1915–1916	6,539
1916–1917	6,533
1917–1918	1,311
1918–1919	2,316
1919–1920	3,785
1920–1921	7,045
Total for the decade 1911–1921	73,960

1921–1922	8,454
1922–1923	2,843
1923–1924	4,305
1924–1925	4,509
1925–1926	3,637
1926–1927	4,863
1927–1928	4,766
1928–1929	3,848
1929–1930	4,164
1930–1931	3,421
Total for the decade 1921–1931	44,810

Total Jewish Population in Canada, 1901–1931

From Louis Rosenberg, *Canada's Jews, a Social and Economic Study of the Jews in Canada*, Montreal, Canadian Jewish Congress, 1939, Table 101, page 150

1901	16,401
1901–1902	17,785
1902–1903	20,459
1903–1904	25,181
1904–1905	34,796
1905–1906	43,710
1906–1907	52,122
1907–1908	61,993
1908–1909	64,409
1909–1910	68,824
1910–1911	75,681
1911–1912	83,482
1912–1913	94,299
1913–1914	110,516
1914–1915	115,662
1915–1916	116,664
1916–1917	117,769
1917–1918	118,911
1918–1919	120,052
1919–1920	121,460
1920–1921	126,196
1921–1922	133,627
1922–1923	132,789
1923–1924	130,343
1924–1925	132,731
1925–1926	136,900

1926–1927	141,815
1927–1928	146,273
1928–1929	149,898
1929–1930	153,759
1930–1931	156,726

Figure 1
Jewish Population of Quebec According to the Census of Canada, 1871–1971

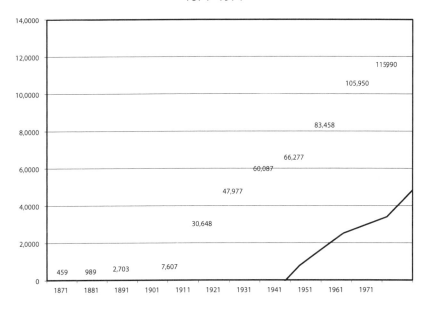

Figure 2
Jewish Population of Canada According to the Census of Canada,
1871–1971

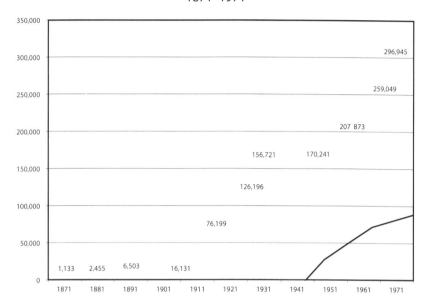

Figure 3
The Jewish Population of Canada by City, 1931

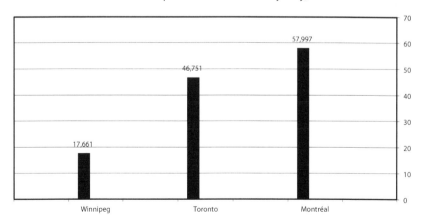

Di verk fun Yud Yud Segal
[the work of J. I. Segal]

Unsigned, undated document, J. I. Segal Archive,
Montreal Jewish Public Library

Fun mayn velt – 1918

Bazunder – 1921

Mayn shtub un mayn velt – 1923

Lider – 1926

Lirik – 1930

Mayn nigun – 1934

Di drite sude – 1937

Dos hoyz fun di poshete – 1940

Lider un loybn

Sefer yidish

Contributed to various periodicals and newspapers, and published poetry, essays, opinion pieces, etc. in:

Inzl, In zikh, Literarishe Bleter, Tsukunft, Shriftn, Oyfkum, Funken, Chicago, Nay-Idish, Kritik, Der Veg, Idishe Velt, Zamlbikher, Di Feder, Bikher Velt, 1925, Arbet, Nyuansn, Epokhe, Kanade, Der Kval, Royerd, Heftn, Idisher Kemfer, Idishe Velt, Vancouver, Di Prese, Di Folkstsaytung, Fraynt, Kinder Zhurnal, Grininke Beymelekh, Idishe Khrestomatyes, Keneder Adler (regular contributor).

"Biography of J. I. Segal"
by H. M. Caiserman

Unsigned, undated English manuscript, J. I. Segal Archive, Montreal Jewish Public Library

1. Childhood

2. Education

3. Parents and grand parents

4. Country of birth

5. Emigration

6. Arrival to Canada

7. Montreal – with mother and sister

8. Finding occupation

9. Years of early writing, first literary contacts

10. Creativeness

11. Transition to teaching

12. About 12 years Peretz School

13. 8 years in New York, – creativeness – Shalom Aleichem School – the new *svive* [milieu]– friendships – death of Charnela in New York at 7 years

14. Influence of her death in Segal's poetry

15. War years – 1919 back in Montreal

16. Contributing *Keneder Adler* since 1919 – literary page, essays, reviews

17. Teaching *Folks Shule* 6 years

18. Creativeness – Lamed *premye* [literary prize] – Congress *premye* [prize]

19. Works in Progess

20. Iteg

21. Caiserman's home

22. Friends in Montreal

Fun mayn mames shvel
[From my mother's threshold]
by J. I. Segal

Unsigned, undated manuscript, J. I. Segal Archive,
Montreal Jewish Public Library

1. friling in Korets [spring in Korets]

2. di mame [mother]

3. di mame

4. di mame

5. Shmuele der melamed [Shmuele the teacher]

6. di sheyne rebetsin [the pretty wife of the rabbi]

7. yaridn [markets]

8. Yehudit

9. Esther

10. Kkayke

11. Perl

12. Yankl Khaykes

13. di mume [the aunt]

14. Avraham

15. Feyge, Leah and Teme

16. der feter Aron [uncle Aron]

17. Genie

18. Batsheva Edelstein

19. Hinde

20. Elik dem . . . [Elik the]

21. khaverim [friends]

22. Koretse nayes [news of Korets]

23. talmud tora yorn, kapitlen 1, 2, 3 [Talmud Torah years, chapters 1, 2, 3]

24. lerer [teachers]

25. dem kayzer's yontef [the tsar's holiday]

26. bay Shmuelik dem shuster in . . . [at Shmulik the shoemaker's]

27. baym zeydn in shtub [in my grandfather's house]

28. dem zeydns toyt [grandfather's death]

29. Yonye Patantso

30. mume Dvora [aunt Dvora]

31. feter Arn [uncle Aaron]

32. in reb Ashers shulekhl [in Reb Asher's school]

33. der rebbe kumt . . . [the rebbe is coming]

34. vinterdiker shabes tsu nakhts [sabbath evening in winter]

35. di mume Brakha un der feter Moishe Yonas [Aunt Brakha and Uncle Moishe Yonas]

36. Yisroelik dem feter Moishe Yonas un milkhome [Uncle Moishe Yonas' Yisroelik, and war]

37. farnakht [dusk]

38. bay Reyze der . . . [at Reyze's . . .]

39. a khurbe [a ramshackle house]

40. protsesye [procession]

41. (. . .)

42. yom kippur [Day of Atonement]

Di shtot iz mayn dorf . . .
[The city is my village . . .]
by J. I. Segal

Bazunder lider, Montreal, 1921, 131

Di shtot iz mayn dorf . . .

Di shtot iz mayn dorf shoyn gevorn fun lang —
Mayn harts iz shoyn gut tsu der shtot.
Azoy gut vi tsu felder
azoy gut vi tsu taykhn un berg.
Un tsu shtilkayt far zshumende inzektn.
Vos huzhen nokh gold un nokh vaytkayt
nokh krishtolene opklangen . . .

Akh. Vifil likhtike felder un velder
es vakhn baytog un baynakht arum der shtot!
A shpil far di felder,
a shpil far di velder,
di tantsendik-glantsendike shtot!
Un fliglen un binen kumen zukhn gold un vaytkayt.
gold un vaytkayt un krishtolene opklangen
In shtot —
Di shtot iz mayn dorf shoyn gevorn fun lang.
Un di meydlakh, nayive fun arbet un midkayt
geyen vi tsign yedn ovent aheym . . .

Di shtot iz mayn dorf shoyn gevorn.
Ikh hob farshtikt ire griltsende koyles in zikh.
Un her nisht ir klapn un knaln:
durkhn vildstn geroysh ret ir shtilkayt tsu mir . . .
Shvaygt ir toytkayt tsu mir . . .

I

Poem by J. I. Segal (*Bazunder lider*, Montreal, 1921, 18

Ikh

Loyfn op di relsige lange shoen fun der fremd-gevorener velt,
altsding mitgeshlept un avekgevorfen ergets mistig.
Nem ikh zikh tsunoyf mit ale mayne letstigkayten in mayn nakht arayn,
zets avek zikh inem roykh fun zeyre luftn un reykhes,
Un ikh veg oyf shpinveb-vogsholn mayn shverkayt:
khvalyet laykht a shmeykhl arum mayne oygn:
vi di shtilkayt fun mayn farloren likht,
vos ligt ergets bahaltn nokh, bin ikh laykht . . .
Vi di vaytkaytn vos hobn nisht derzen mayn shotn nokh,
Un rufn mir nit, bin ikh laykht . . .
Glate himlen shvebn nokh iber mayn kop —
Unter glate himln groyen zikh eyntsike hor oyf mayn kop,
eyneyntsike tayere groye hor . . .

Ikh hob tsevorfn vegn krume oyf der harmonye fun der velt.
Flit nit iber zey kayn foygl, leygt zikh nit oyf zey kayn shotn
keyner vet tsu zey dervayl nisht benken un nisht garen,
afile shney vet iber zey nisht vaysn zikh fun ergets
ikh vel kayn zun tsu zey nisht rufen,
kayn levone nisht, kayn shtern.
In di nekht, ze ikh, falt oyf zey levone-shtoyb zamdig.
Glaykhn zey zikh oys un tsyen zikh tsu zunike vizyonen . . .
Ergets lign groyse shtet tsevorfn naket un tseshpreyt
un dreyen zikh tsu di krume vegn mayne vos ikh hob tsevorfn
iber der harmonye fun der harmonye fun der velt . . .

Kritik vegn Yud Yud Segal
[reviews of J. I. Segal's work]

Unsigned, undated manuscript, J. I. Segal Archive,
Montreal Jewish Public Library

Leksikon fun der idisher literatur, prese un filologye, Zalman Reisen, vol. 2,
625–629 (Vilna, 1928–1930).
Samuel Niger, *Der Tog*, May14, 1922 (New York).
Samuel Niger, *Der Tog*, 1932 (New York).
Samuel Niger, *Der Tog*, 1935 (New York).
Samuel Niger, *Di Tsukunft*, 1926 (New York).
Samuel Niger, *Oyfkum*.
Z. Lande, *Inzl* (New York).
S.-D. Singer, *Chicago* (Chicago).
N. Steinberg, *Chicago* (Chicago).
Alexander Kashin, *Kritik*, Vienne.
Yud Dorushin, *Emes*, July 27, 1928.
Aaron Glanz Leyeles, *Der Tog*, 1920 (New York).
Mordecai Jaffe, *Di Yidishe Velt*, Vancouver.
Menachem, *Di Vokh*.
Abraham Rheinvein, *Toronter Zhurnal*, Toronto.
Louis Benjamin (Montreal).
Daniel Leybl, *Der Tog*, Vila, February, 1922.
Leib Bercovitch, *Dos Vort*, Winnipeg, 1922.
N. Oyslender, *In Shtrom*, Mexico.
Moshe Olgin, *Di Frayhayt*, July 1922 (New York).
Moshe Olgin, *Di Frayhayt*, August 1924 (New York).
Chaim Talmatch, *Keneder Adler* (Montreal).
Samuel Niger, *Dos Naye Lebn*, 1922.
S. Dobrutsi, *Der Tog*, Vilna.
Saul-Joseph Janovsky, *Di Fraye Arbeter Shtime* (New York).
A. Almi, (Montreal).

Vinagrod, *Undzer Bukh*.

Moshe Gross, *Literarishe Bleter* (Warsaw).

Noah-Isaac Gotlib, *Literarishe Bleter*, 1932 (Warsaw.

Israël Rabinovitch, *Yoyvl bukh Keneder Odler*, 1932 (Montreal).

H. M. Caiserman, *Der Yidisher Arbeter*, 1919 (Montreal).

Benjamin Bialostotsky, *Esayen*.

H. Krul, *Di Fraye Arbeter Shtime* (New York).

David Bergelson, *In Shpan*, Berlin.

Jacob Zipper, *Lid*, Los Angeles.

Shalom Shtern, *Der Kamf* (Toronto).

Moshe Nadir, *Di Frayhayt* (New York).

B. Rivkin, *Di Tsukunft* (New York).

P. Kahan, *Oyfkum*.

Israël Rabinovitch, *Der Keneder Adler*, October 8, 1937 (Montreal).

H.-M. Caiserman, *Idishe dikhter in Kanade*, 1934 (Montreal).

Melekh Ravitch, *Di Fraye Arbeter Shtime*, 1936 (New York).

Baruch Katsenelson, *Oyfkum*.

Abraham Reisen, *Feder* (New York).

A. M. Klein, *The Jewish Chronicle*, Montreal.

Mount Royal, by J. I. Segal

Nyuansn, 1921, Montreal, vol. 2, 65

Mount-Royal

An emeser farnakht . . . a shtoltser hot der barg zikh oyfgeshtelt,
Un opgerukt zikh fun der shtot, farisn hoykh dem kop,
kayn beymer geyen shoyn fun im nisht vi in shayn arop . . .
Farglivert iz di loyterkayt fun himl un iz ful un ful mit kelt . . .

Di kelt iz dos fartroyert zunenshayn vos blaybt fun tog der nakht,
Un shtarbt fun finsternish un falt ven s'kon kayn oyg nisht zen;
Un fun dem faln kon amol groys vunder in der shtil geshen,
Un keyner zol nisht visn, es zol blaybn toyt un eybik-tsugemakht . . .

A makhne beymer in a ray, farglivert, fest un brav un shtark,
antkegn shtot fun barg arop, gegurt mit shverd un shpiz —
a blutige armey vos iz farzunken in der erd biz halbe fis,
Un kon kayn trot nisht ton, farayznt bay dem rand fun shvartsn barg . . .

In mayn shtub [In my room]
by J. I. Segal

Fun mayn shtub un mayn velt, New York, 1923, 51

In mayn shtub

Inem shtoyb fun mayn orimer shtub,
mayn shofl-anivesdik lebn shlaykht um.
Un mayn froy un mayn kind zaynen shtendik mit mir,
inem shtoyb fun mayn orimer shtub . . .

Baym fentster fun mayn orimer shtub,
groyt der shtoyb fun der eybiker velt.
Khotsh siz zun oyf der eybiker velt,
khotsh siz bloy in der eybiker hoykh!
Nor es shtoybt zikh durkh zun un durkh likht.
Fun eybiker hoykh un fun vayt.
Di groykayt, dos ash fun der tsayt . . .

Inem shtoyb fun mayn orimer shtub
trikt dos grin fun mayn oyg . . .
Krikht um a shpin in mayn oyg,
vebt shpinvebs a shpin in mayn oyg —

Un mayn froy un mayn kind in der groy fun mayn oyg . . .
Inem shtoyb fun mayn orimer shtub . . .

"O Montreal!" by J. I. Segal

Fun mayn shtub un fun mayn velt, New York, 1923, 62

O Montreal!

Di kleyne vinterdike teg mit shnay oyf der erd fun untn
Un mit a zun a kalt-un-varime fun oybn
vi toybn zaynen zey, di kleyne vinterdike teg!
Zey haltn zikh in loyterer luft mit tseshpreyte fliglen,
un sheyn zaynen zey, azoy sheyn biz gutskayt,
biz shpilndikayt far kleyne kinder.

Un oyf di hoykhe sheyne vinterdike teg,
oyf dem oysgeshpreytn, oysgezaytn shney,
shteyt a shtot, a shtot an oyfgeloykhtene.
Un di shtot iz shpilndik kegn dem tsorn-royt fun di keltn,

Ire moyern zaynen vaserfarbik un grin
Un konen koym shteyn . . . koym lebn
ibern kishef fun di kleyne sheyne vayse teg.

Di shtot heyst: Montreal. O, Montreal!
Fun dayne kleyne vayse teg glust zikh mir azoy nisht avekforn kayn New York,
ikh muz ober avekforn kayn New York
tsulib parnose, tsulib New Yorks groyskayt
un, vayl dakht zikh az in New York
zaynen faran nokh klenere teg vi in Montreal
O Montreal!

"Dayn ondenkn, mayn Tsharnele [*In your memory, my little Tsharna*]" by J. I. Segal

Lider, Montreal, 1926, 3

Dayn ondenkn, mayn Tsharnele

Unter kaltn himl, azoy eyntsik, azoy
eyntskik, iz a vayser feygl durkhgefloygn.
Vi durkh khulem bistu fun mayn oyg antrunen.
O, mayn farloshn likht.
Tsiternish hot mikh arumgenumen, biternish
hot mikh fartsert. Shtile sheynkayt fun
dayn reynkayt bloyt tsu mir fartrert.
O, mayn farloshn likht.
tseyl ikh, tseyl di mutne yorn mayne. Mit
farshtarte lipn, mit farshtumte oygn.
Ikh vel kumen, ikh vel kumen
krank zikh leygn nebn dir.
O, mayn farloshn likht.

In nayer voynung [In my new home] by J. I. Segal (excerpt)

Lider, Montreal, 1926, 87–88

In nayer voynung (excerpt)

Du bist geblibn azoy eyner aleyn.
Khbin gekumen in ovent aheym.
Bist gezesn baym tish un gevart,
getunklt tvishn di vent.
Du host mikh gezen.
Host mir gornisht gezogt.

Tsvey vokhn az mir hobn unzer voynung banayt.
Hart bay dem braytn fenster shteyt a shtik likhtker yam,
baytog iz er zilberdik-hel,
un er gayt in tsen lender avek
farnakht iz bloy,
un shteyt bay a heymishn breg.

Ikh nem on dayn hant.
Zetst zikh avek nebn dir un shvayg:

Durkh voser a veg zol ikh geyn makhn sholem mit got.
Durkh voser a shteg zol ikh firn dayn oysgeveynt harts.
Az du zolst derzen nokh,
in bloy funem vayt bay dem breg fun taykh,
dos kepl mit zaydene hor.
Dos hele bloye kol.

New York – Korets (excerpt)
by J. I. Segal

Unsigned, undated manuscript, J. I. Segal Archive,
Montreal Jewish Public Library

New York – Korets

Faran a kleynshtot heyst zi Korets,
faran a groysshtot, ushma New York.
Bin ikh in beyde der shtilster toyshev
mit mayne modne gang un zorg.

In mir iz Korets a ben hashmoshes
un hoykhe brayte New York arum mir.
A beyml mit glekldike bletlekh,
a Koretser beyml — gor mayn zumer.

Un shteyn tut shteyn dos dozike beyml
hinter a ployt lebn altn tsvinter —
In zaydenem shney a kind a beyml
a Koretser beyml — gor mayn vinter.

Vi heylung trift in mayn layb un beyner
der fridn fun a koretser ovnt.
New York dreyt toyznt shteyner-reder
un kumt nisht tsu tsu mir gor-noent.

Translation into yiddish of excerpts from the poetry of Pamphile Lemay by H. M. Caiserman

From an untitled, undated manuscript by H. M. Caiserman about Canadian poetry, Caiserman Archive, Canadian Jewish Congress Archive, Montreal, 21–22

Un vandert er iber di prairies un shnit-tsayt un vert yinger fun der imposanter natur-prakht, zingt er:

> O, di shtarke lider vos hoybn zikh fun di prairies
> Di vunderlikhe reykhes fun tsaytign hay
> O, di tsvaygn mit blondn, di grine draperayen
> Vos vign zikh un shvebn in bloyen azur!

Oder zet er dem mayestetishn St-Laurent taykh, filosofirt er:

> Oyb du volst gekent in dayn kishef vander
> O, vunderlikher taykh, O liber vagabond
> Volstu dertsteylt undz, farvos azoy noent fun dayn shtam
> farlirstu zikh in tifn yam…

Un zet er vi di frantsoyzishe yugend, farlozt dos land, krekhtst:

> Farvos farlozt ir unzer vunder land
> Ir yungen mit ayzn-shtarke orems?
> Darf zi ayer arbet shoyn nit mer
> Un ayer eydl blut?

> Un ir entlandet zikh aleyn! Iz oyf ayre brayte felder
> Kayn ort far aykh nishto?
> Shrekt aykh den der vinter mitn kaltn otem?
> Iz unzer zumer nit mild genug?
> Shmekt di blumen nit oyf unzere bayten?
> Zenen den on shotn unzere groyse velder.

(Original French)

Et il erre dans les champs au temps de la récolte et se sent rajeuni par
la grande beauté de la nature, il chante :

> Ô les vives chansons qui montent des prairies !
> L'exquise senteur du foin mûr!
> Ô les rameaux en fleurs, les vertes draperies
> Qui flottent sous un ciel d'azur!

Ou alors il voit le majestueux fleuve Saint-Laurent et il se prend à
réfléchir :

> Si tu pouvais parler dans tes vaillantes courses,
> O fleuve merveilleux! Ô fleuve vagabond!
> Tu nous dirais pourquoi loin, bien loin de tes sources,
> Tu vas enfin te perdre à l'océan profond . . .

Et il observe la jeunesse francophone qui abandonne son pays, il
gémit :

> Pourquoi donc fuyez-vois notre belle patrie,
> Jeunes gens aux bras vigoureux?
> N'a-t-elle plus besoin ni de votre industrie,
> Ni de votre sang généreux ?

> Et vous vous exilez! Mais dans nos vastes plaines
> N'est-il pas assez doux?
> Craignez-vous de l'hiver les rigides haleines?
>   L'été n'est-il pas assez doux?
> Sont-elles sans parfums les fleurs de nos charmilles?
> Sans ombres, nos grandes forêts?

Table of Contents
H. M. Caiserman
Idishe dikhter in kanade
(Jewish Poets in Canada)

Montreal, 1934, 221 pages

Tsum strayk [To the strike] (excerpt) poème de Moyshe-Leib Halpern

Folkstsaytung, Montreal, June 7, 1912

Tsum strayk (excerpt)

Shtey oyf, shtey oyf, genug geshklaft!
Genug gelitn hunger, noyt,
farkoyfndik dos blut far broyt,
di rod loz shteyn, di brust shtrek oys,
un kum mit undz in kamf aroys!
Farloz dem shap —di shklafn-shtayg,
— shtey oyf tsum strayk!

Azoy zingt mir Got in oyer
(This Is How God Sings in My Ear)
Jacob Isaac Segal

Lirik, Montreal, 1930, 259

Azoy zingt mir got in oyer —

Un in ayere gasn vel ikh ontsindn vider
mayne shabesdike eydele lamterndlekh.
Ayere yoselekh in sametene hitlen
veln geyen bay ayre zayt un mitrogn
di tales-zeklakh fun zayd in shtarkn vaynkulirn.
Di brayte tir fun der groyser shul shteyn ofn,
mayn groyse zun fargeyt iber der erd,
Un mayn himl iz klor un shtil.
Baym shtakhetn-ployt fun shulgortn
vaksn dare mokhike derner,
vildgeviks un shtekhelkes —
Ikh veys es zeyer gut.
Ikh veys es zeyer voyl.
Ikh hob aykh gelozt zikh bazetsn
in di bargike un tolike yishuvn
in skheynes mit a goyish folkl.
Zeyere kloysterlekh klingen tsu mir,
un der bloyer roykh fun zeyere tfiles,
geyt oyf un shlengt zikh far mayne oygn
Dershmek ikh oykh zeyer farvoglkayt
Un dem tsar fun zeyer farhorevet,
farhorevet shvarts shtikl broyt.

Footsteps
by J. I. Segal

Lirik, Montreal, 1930, 254

Trit

Farnakhtike velt.
Der Baal-Shem Tov zitst
baym breg fun a vald
dos royt fun zunfargang
tsugeyt un farveyt.

Der Baal-Shem-Tov shvaygt.

Arum un arum
iz nor shvaygn do.
Got shvaygt mitn vald,
Got shvaygt mitn groz.

Vi in boym un in groz
shvaygt oykh Got in mir.
Vet kumen a vintl,
vet royshn der boym,
vet royshn dos groz,
vet royshn mayn harts
mit loyb tsu im.

Oyfn vaytn vet
lign nokh goldene trit
fun der fargangener zun,
fun dem fargangenem tog,
un fun mayn gemit.

Tishre
by J. I. Segal

Di drite sude, Montreal, 1934, 109

Tishre

Ekhos, viderkoln,
heym un vaytn,
Un amoln.

A mide eyntsike bin,
broyngoldik,
zhumet arum der zun baytog
in shtiln gortn.

Letste varimkayt
iber kukuruze-shtekns
Shmekt di harbe psomim —
tishre-zafran.

Tilim-shtimung
iber himl un dekher.
A fenster brumt a parshe khumash:
fertsik yor in midber.

Tsankendik mid likht fun tishre.
Shtile kukuruze-shtekns.
Barg arop — a taykh,
lamedvovnike vaser-firers,
klapn in di inderfriyeke tirn:
vaser, vaser.

Sof yomtoyvm
frume troyrikayt lirisht
oyf di tsushoyberte kep fun sukes.

Loyterkayt [Purity]
by J. I. Segal

Lirik, Montreal, 1930, 28

Loyterkayt

Fun mayne shtile teg tut geyn a veg
arop in shotndikn kiln tol.
Un oysgeton fun shverkayt un fun shrek,
vel ikh mit dir zikh trefn dort amol.

In vayse kleyder, oyf der groyer erd,
mit oygn reyne, loytere in ru,
vest zitsn – fray fun alts vos erd bashvert
mit nokh azoyne likhtike vi du.

Ikh vel onnemen dayn kleyne vayse hant,
ir varimen bayn otem fun mayn moyl.
Hoykh iber unz — dos bargik-grine land,
di zun — tsu mayrev vi a goldener zayl.

In kranker roytlekhkayt iz durkhgeflekt di velt
nor du bist vays un ruik, vi farnakht.
Ikh loz dikh zitsn oyfn shvel fun dayn getselt
in zunikayt un shotn fun farnakht.

Vayse velt [White world]
by J. I. Segal

Sefer yidish, Montreal, 1950, 204

Vayse velt

Ikh vel dikh oyston fun dayn vundik layb
Un dir vet gringer vern.
Ikh vel dikh vi a shlofndike toyb
avektrogn fundanen oyf an ander shtern.

Nokh a tog, a nakht un tsvey
un kh'vel fun dayn farshmakhtn moyl arunterkushn
di shvartse biternishn fun dayn shtumen vey,
afirnemen dayn shteynerdikn kishn.

Gantsfri, az keyner vet nisht zen,
aroysshlaykhn mit dir zikh vi a gringer shotn.
Iber di gasn blit di ru fun ershtn shney
fun keynem nisht barirt un nisht batrotn.

Un mitn bloyen hoykh funem frimorgn veln mir avek
un oyf a vaysn gringn shlitn.
Keyn otem shrek, keyn shotn fun a flek
funem farklemtn payn vos host gelitn.

Nor a tog, a sho, a rege hot gevert
un ale vundikaytn hobn ayngedrimlt.
Gebentsh zol zayn di vayskayt fun der erd,
geloybt zol zayn di bloykayt funem himl.

Shpet herbst in Montreal (Late Autumn Montreal) by J. I. Isaac Segal

Letste lider, Montréal, 1955, 106

Shpet herbst in Montreal

Der vorim krikht avek in tunkl fun der erd,
es blankt der vint un shleyft zayn bloye shverd.
Vu zaynen di gefarbte bleter avekgfloygn?
Es shlofn shoyn in groen hartn shlof di tsvaygn.
Di himlen loytern un hoybn zikh hoykh un hekher
zeyer klorer kval trift likht un bloy iber di dekher.
Zeyer shtilkayt zalbt zey mit baruiktn genod;
frimer vert nokh unzer kloysterishe shtot
un zuntik finklen sharfer nokh di goldene tslomim,
Groyse gleker klingen halel, klenere entfern: omeyn.
Reyne, shtile gasn drimlen in baytogikn fridn,
shmeykhlen ruike oykh tsu mir — aza min idishn idn,
vos in zayn gang afile iz nokh nisht antshvign
der ritm un der klang fun an altn piet-nigun.

Fun bal-shem-tov biz haynt
[From the Baal Shem Tov to today]
by J. I. Segal

Dos hoyz fun di poshete, Montreal, 1940, 84

Fun bal-shem-tov biz haynt (excerpt)

Tsum bal-shem-tov flegn kumen orimelayt
di raykhe hobn zayne shveln oysgemitn.
Idn fun der fremd, fun zer vayt
afile fun der groyer umetiker Lite.

Opgeven bay im dray kleyne kurtse teg
zaynen zey shoyn freylakhe tsurikgeforn.
Oyf di dare pleytses groye leydike zek,
durkh di felder tsvishn gingoldenem korn.

Ver s'hot veynik broyt un ver s'hot mer —
s'vet gots gutskayt oysglaykhn dos krume.
Az a mentsh kumt oyf der velt aher,
iz er gutston do aher gekumen.

Tomid nokhzogn un nokhzingen gots ershte vort:
zol zayn likhtik, likht oyf ale zayne vegn.
Vos iz likhtikayt? A beyml do, a grezl dort,
un zingendikhe zise vasern fun regn.

Tkhine [A Yiddish prayer]
by J. I. Segal

Dos hoyz fun di poshete, Montreal, 1940, 270

Tkhine (excerpt)

Har, tsind-on a naye libshaft
in unzer eyde oyf der erd.
Kleyb op a hoyz in unzer nidergas,
un fir funsnay ahin arayn dayn shabesdikn tog
un ruf dos hoyz: dos hoyz fun ru.
Fun unzere keler-kleytn tsien mir zikh ale tsu dayn shvel.
In dayne vent tsuefnt mir di tovln vider
vu di vide fun yeder sho hot unzer layb gelaytert,
un unzer umetike zel gehelt,
un unzer blondzhendik farsthand
oysgeshtrekt a reyne hant—
fun eyn tog inem andern aribergeyn

Light of Old [Altlikht]
by J. I. Segal

Lider un loybn, Montreal, 1944, 23

Altlikht

Vifil gute zakhn zaynen in altheym geblibn
un mitnemen hot men zey nisht gekont.
Khob di shtilste nigunim tsu zey geshribn,
biz veytik iz nokh itlakh vort mit nont.

Nor zey zaynen ale in der vaytkayt dortn,
un tsankn shoyn oykh efsher bislekhvayz oys.
Gel leshn zikh di shpitsn kukurzun in gortn,
ikh kuk durkhn umetikn fenster aroys —

Kremerkes geyen shoyn aheym mit di koyshn,
a kaltlakhe goldikayt inderluftn shpilt.
Der vokhiker tuml, der vokhiker droysn
vert liber un shtiler un ayngeshtilt.

Der shabes loykht oyf in a vaytn shtibl,
aza troyrik treystndik likht fun got.
Dakht zikh: bald vet zikh eymitser in loyter vaysn
bavayzn ariber di gasn fun shtot.

Un ale fenster in di shtiber veln zikh tsindn
mit heylike likht un bentshn di velt.
In ale shtiber ruen dayne frume gezindn
geakhperter foter in himlgetselt.

Idish lishmo [For the sake of Yiddish] by J. I. Segal

Sefer yidish, Montreal, 1950, 165

Yidish lishmo (excerpt)

Faran in verter aza likht,
Du darfst es nor aroysbafrayen
Un gor dos loshn vert oyfgerikht.
Tiskhadesh, idish, tsu banayung.

Vi voyl iz mir, vos mir iz grod
Ot-di shlikhes shoyn ibergegebn,
Ikh zol mayn kheylek sheyngenod
Dir shenken — zol dir zayn tsum lebn,

Vos volt ikh far dir nisht geton
Dir shtarker makhn un gezinter.
Geshenkt dir fun mayn gold un zun,
Gehaltn droshes far idishe kinder,

Az redn idish is gezunt
Un az doktoyrim heysn redn.
Es trift in harts a shtiler vund
Un oysdertseyln — nisht far yedn.

Appendices A to I

Poetry Collections Published by J. I. Segal

1918 – *Fun mayn velt* [From my world], Montreal, 67 pages.

1921 – *Bazunder lider* [Various poems], Montreal, 199 pages.

1923 – *Fun mayn shtub un mayn velt* [From my house and my world], New York, 62 pages.

1926 – *Lider* [Poems], New York, 204 pages.

1930 – *Lirik* [Lyrical poetry], Montreal, 326 pages.

1934 – *Mayn nigun* [My melody], Montreal, 360 pages.

1937 – *Di drite sude* [The third meal], Montreal, 357 pages.

1940 – *Dos hoyz fun di poshete* [The house of the simple people], Montreal, 381 pages.

1944 – *Lider un loybn* [Poems and praise], Montreal, 507 pages.

1950 – *Sefer idish* [The book of Yiddish], Montreal, 584 pages.

1955 – *Letste lider* [Last poems] (published posthumously), Montreal, 332 pages.

1961 – *Lider far idishe kinder* [Poems for Jewish children] (published posthumously), Montreal, 111 pages.

J. I. Segal's Mailing Addresses

From his personal correspondence in the Montreal Jewish
Public Library Archives

March and April of 1917, August of 1917, and January and May of
1919: 85 Beaumont, Mile End, Montreal (east of Clark Street).

September 1919 to November 1920, January 1921: 619a Colonial,
Montreal (at Marie-Anne Street).

July 1921 to 4 August 1921: 1010 St. Lawrence Boulevard, Montreal
(north of Pine Avenue).

August to October of 1921 and December 1921 to January 1922: 1007
City Hall Street, Montreal (between Duluth and Rachel).

May, June, August and December 1923 and January 1924: 1017 Trinity
Avenue (at 165th Street, near Boston Road, New York (the Bronx).

August 1924: 1409 St. John's Place, New York (at Utica Avenue, in
Crown Heights, Brooklyn).

November 1924: c/o *Der Feder*, 49 East 7th Street, New York (at Second
Avenue, in Manhattan).

November 1925: c/o M. H. Yong, 2056 East 2nd Ave, New York (at
Avenue T, in Gravesend, Brooklyn).

June 1926: 1355 Cadieux Street, Montreal (today de Bullion, just north
of Rachel, north corner of Lionais Street).

June, August and September 1922, November 1928, January 1929: c/o
J. Rosen, 40 Mozart Street West, Montreal (at Clark Street, Mile
End).

August 1929: 80 Mozart Street West, Montreal (near Waverly, Mile End).

May 1931 to March 1954: 4540 Clark Street, apt. 4, Montreal (near
Mount Royal Avenue).

Published Articles by J. I. Segal Partial Chronological List of Archival Documents

"Durkh di ershte fir," [Through the first four], *Nyuansn*, Montreal, February 1921, no. 1, 55–60.

"Vegn Melekh Ravitch, an impresye," [About Melekh Ravitch, an impression], *Epokhe*, Montreal, January 1922, 3–7.

"Briv fun New York," [Letter from New York], *Kanade*, Montreal, no. 2, September 1925, 36–39; no. 3, December 1925, 24–29.

"In skhus fun undzer lid," [In the merit of our poem], *Der Keneder Adler (Jewish Daily Eagle)*, Jubilee Edition, August 30, 1927.

"Yud Lamed Peretz (tsum 16tn yortsayt)," [I. L. Peretz, on the 16th anniversary of his death], *Der Keneder Adler (Jewish Daily Eagle)*, Montreal, April 26, 1931.

"Der goyrl fun der idishn dikhter," [The fate of the Yiddish poet], *Literarishe Bleter*, Warsaw, no. 9, February 24, 1933, 133–134.

"Chaim Kruger," *Der Keneder Adler (Jewish Daily Eagle)*, Montreal, January 7, 1934.

"Tragedye: mentsh," [Tragedy: man], *Der Keneder Adler (Jewish Daily Eagle)*, Montreal, January 14, 1934.

"Chaim Krugers Rambam," *Der Keneder Adler (Jewish Daily Eagle)*, Montreal, January 28, 1934.

"Jonah Rosenfeld," *Der Keneder Adler (Jewish Daily Eagle)*, Montreal, February 4, 1934.

"Dos yom-tov-bukh," [The holiday book], *Der Keneder Adler (Jewish Daily Eagle)*, Montreal, February 11, 1934.

"Lamed Shapiro," *Der Keneder Adler (Jewish Daily Eagle)*, Montreal, February 18, 1934.

"Shtarb gikher! [Better to die], *Der Keneder Adler, (Jewish Daily Eagle)*, Montreal, February 23, 1934.

"Grigorii Gershuni," *Der Keneder Adler* (*Jewish Daily Eagle*), Montreal, February 25, 1934.

"*Yoshe Kalb*," *Der Keneder Adler* (*Jewish Daily Eagle*), Montreal, March 4, 1934.

"Hitleray (tsum Hitler-mishpet vos iz forgekumen in New York," [Hitleray: about the Hitler trial that took place in New York], *Der Keneder Adler*, (*Jewish Daily Eagle*), Montreal, March 11, 1934.

"Melekh Ravitch," *Der Keneder Adler* (*Jewish Daily Eagle*), Montreal, March 18, 1934.

"Vegn a literarishen ovent," [About a literary evening], *Der Keneder Adler* (*Jewish Daily Eagle*), Montreal, March 25, 1934, 4.

"H. M. Caiserman," *Der Keneder Adler* (*Jewish Daily Eagle*), Montreal, April 2, 1934, 5.

"Birger: Albert Einstein," [Citizen: Albert Einstein], *Der Keneder Adler* (*Jewish Daily Eagle*), Montreal, April 22, 1934.

"Der nayer literatur maskilizm," [The new literary enlightenment] *Der Keneder Adler*, (*Jewish Daily Eagle*), Montreal, April 29, 1934, May 6, 1934.

"Idish," [Yiddish], *Der Keneder Adler*, (*Jewish Daily Eagle*), Montreal, May 13, 1934.

"In shtiler aynzamkayt," [In quiet solitude], *Der Keneder Adler* (*Jewish Daily Eagle*), Montreal, May 28, 1934.

"Bazungene erd," [Celebrated ground], *Der Keneder Adler* (*Jewish Daily Eagle*), Montreal, June 3, 1934.

"Nay lider zamlungen," [New poetry collections], *Der Keneder Adler* (*Jewish Daily Eagle*), Montreal, June 10, 1934.

"Der driter numer 'Lid'," [The third issue of 'Lid'], *Der Keneder Adler* (*Jewish Daily Eagle*), Montreal, June 17, 1934.

"Literarishe ganeyve," [Literary theft], *Der Keneder Adler* (*Jewish Daily Eagle*), Montreal, June 24, 1934.

"Fun khaver tsu khaver: *Lider fun Shabse Perl*," [From one friend to another: poems by Shabse Perl], *Der Keneder Adler* (*Jewish Daily Eagle*), Montreal, July 1, 1934.

"In der shverer minut fun aveyde," [In the difficult moment of loss], *Der Keneder Adler* (*Jewish Daily Eagle*), Montreal, July 8, 1934.

"Chaim Nachman Bialik," *Der Keneder Adler* (*Jewish Daily Eagle*), Montreal, July 15, 1934.

"Der kanader idisher kongres," [Canadian Jewish Congress], *Der Keneder Adler* (*Jewish Daily Eagle*), Montreal, September 24, 1934.

"A vort," [A word], *Idishe dikhter in kanade* (Jewish Poets in Canada), Montreal, Farlag Nyuansn, 1934, 5–7.

"Geburt: fun lebn in raten-rusland in shpigl fun der dortiger literatur," [Birth: about life in Soviet Russia as reflected in its literature], *Der Keneder Adler (Jewish Daily Eagle)*, Montreal, October 11, 1935.

"Sukes," [Sukkoth], *Der Keneder Adler (Jewish Daily Eagle)*, Montreal, October 11, 1935, 5.

"David Einhorn: tsu zayn fuftsig-yorigen yubileum," [David Einhorn: on his 50th birthday], *Di Tsukunft,* New York, October 1936, 650–654.

"Der kanader idisher kongres," [The Canadian Jewish Congress], *Der Keneder Adler (Jewish Daily Eagle)*, Montreal, September 24, 1937.

"A idish kind," [A Jewish child], *Peretz Shuln Bukh*, Montreal, 1938, 41–43.

"Dos Peretz Shuln Bukh," *Der Keneder Adler (Jewish Daily Eagle)*, Montreal, 10 June 1938, 5.

"Der yunger dikhter Sholem Shtern," [The young poet Sholem Shtern], *Literarishe Bleter*, Warsaw, July 29, 1938, no. 31, 512–513.

"B. G. Sack—publitsist un historiker," [B. G. Sack—journalist and historian], *Der Keneder Adler (Jewish Daily Eagle)*, Montreal, around 1938, 4.

"Simon Nepom," *Der Keneder Adler (Jewish Daily Eagle)*, Montreal, June 20, 1939.

J. I. Segal and H. M. Caiserman, *Ershte reshime fun vikhtige verk in der moderner idisher literatur—prose, drame, poezye un literatur kritik*, [First list of major books in modern Yiddish literature—prose, theatre, poetry and literary criticism], Montreal, Canadian Jewish Congress, September 1940 (internal document).

"Shverd un pen," [Sword and pen], *St. Louis Jewish Record*, St. Louis, Missouri, November 29, 1940, 2, 4.

"Di velt vet nit fargebn . . .," [The world will not forgive . . .], *Der Keneder Adler (Jewish Daily Eagle)*, Montreal, September 30, 1941, 4.

"Az s'vet morgn zayn . . . shalom," [If tomorrow there's . . . peace], *Der Keneder Adler (Jewish Daily Eagle)*, Montreal, November 20, 1942, 4.

"Protestn," [Protests], *Der Keneder Adler (Jewish Daily Eagle)*, Montreal, December 11, 1942, 3, 4.

"Men hot zikh nisht gerikht . . . ," [We didn't budge . . .], *Der Keneder Adler (Jewish Daily Eagle)*, Montreal, December 18, 1942, 4, 3.

"Libe tsum mitmenshn . . . ," [Love for one's fellow man], *Der Keneder Adler* (*Jewish Daily Eagle*), Montreal, December 25, 1942, 4,3.

"Dos gelayterte folk un dos farmiyeste folk," [The refined nation and the demeaned nation], *Der Keneder Adler* (*Jewish Daily Eagle*), Montreal, January 29, 1943, 4, 3.

"Menahem Boraisha, tsu zayn kumen in Montreal," [Menahem Boraisha, on his visit to Montreal], *Der Keneder Adler* (*Jewish Daily Eagle*), Montreal, February 12, 1943, 4, 3.

"*Vider: hitler oder daytshland?*" [Again: Hitler or Germany?], Montreal, *Der Keneder Adler* (*Jewish Daily Eagle*), Montreal, February 19, 1943, 4, 3.

"Mir—di yesoymim . . . ," [We—the orphans], *Der Keneder Adler* (*Jewish Daily Eagle*), Montreal, April 9, 1943, 5.

"Vikhtike shlikhim mit a groyser shlikhes," [Important emissaries on a great mission], *Der Keneder Adler* (*Jewish Daily Eagle*), Montreal, September 3, 1943, 4.

"Romain Rolland," *Der Keneder Adler* (*Jewish Daily Eagle*), Montreal, November 5, 1943, 4, 3.

"Milkhome un nekome," [War and revenge], *Der Keneder Adler* (*Jewish Daily Eagle*), Montreal, November 19, 1943, 4, 6.

"Khurbn beys yisroel?" [The destruction of the House of Israel?], *Der Keneder Adler* (*Jewish Daily Eagle*), Montreal, December 10, 1943, 4.

"Oikh do," [Also here], *Der Keneder Adler* (*Jewish Daily Eagle*), Montreal, February 4, 1944, 4, 6.

"Vegn brutalitet," [On brutality], *Der Keneder Adler* (*Jewish Daily Eagle*), Montreal, February 11, 1944, 4.

"Me tseylt shoyn di korbones," They're already counting the victims], *Der Keneder Adler* (*Jewish Daily Eagle*), Montreal, February 18, 1944, 4.

"Moyre far nokh milkhome fashizm," [Fear of post-war fascism], *Der Keneder Adler* (*Jewish Daily Eagle*), Montreal, February 25, 1944, 4.

"Nokhamol: idn-sine," [Once again: Jew-hatred], *Der Keneder Adler* (*Jewish Daily Eagle*), Montreal, March 10, 1944, 4–5.

"Shkhites," [Slaughters], *Der Keneder Adler* (*Jewish Daily Eagle*), Montreal, March 17, 1944, 4, 3

"H. M. Caiserman, tsu zayn 60-yoriken yubilay," [H. M. Caiserman, on his 60th birthday], *Der Keneder Adler* (*Jewish Daily Eagle*), Montreal, 24 March, 1944, 4, 3; reprinted in the *Idisher Zhurnal* (*Daily Hebrew Journal*) Toronto, 2 April, 1944 and in *Dos Yidishe*

Vort (the *Jewish Press*, formerly the *Israelite Press*), Winnipeg, 4 April, 1944.

"Bikher, pinkosim—un shtet," [Books, chronicles—and cities], *Der Keneder Adler* (*Jewish Daily Eagle*), Montreal, April 17, 1944, 5, 6.

"Zey veln zikh nit rateven," [They will not survive], *Der Keneder Adler* (*Jewish Daily Eagle*), Montreal, April 28, 1944, 4.

"Take gornisht gelernt?" [Have we really learned nothing?], *Der Keneder Adler* (*Jewish Daily Eagle*), Montreal, August 18, 1944, 4–5.

"Erev yontef . . . ," [On the eve of the High Holidays . . .], *Der Keneder Adler* (*Jewish Daily Eagle*), Montreal, September 15, 1944, 4.

"Rosh hashana 5705," [Jewish New Year 1944], *Der Keneder Adler* (*Jewish Daily Eagle*), Montreal, September 17, 1944, 4, 6.

"Vegn yontef un vokh," [About holy days and ordinary weekdays], *Der Keneder Adler* (*Jewish Daily Eagle*), Montreal, October 13, 1944, 4.

"Idish lebn," [Jewish life], *Der Keneder Adler* (*Jewish Daily Eagle*), Montreal, October 20, 1944, 4, 6.

"Di tsayt fun rateven," [The time of rescue], *Der Keneder Adler* (*Jewish Daily Eagle*), Montreal, October 27, 1944, 4.

"Der barg-aroyf veg fun Yud Lamed Peretz," [The uphill journey of I. L. Peretz], *Der Keneder Adler* (*Jewish Daily Eagle*), Montreal, May 20, 1945, 4, 7 (on the 30th anniversary of his death).

"*Umru un shrek*," [Anxiety and fear], *Der Keneder Adler* (*Jewish Daily Eagle*), Montreal, November 24, 1945, 4, 8.

"*Der zeyde fun der idisher poezie*," [The grandfather of Yiddish poetry], *Epokhe*, New York, December 1945, no. 20, 89–92.

"Creative Freedom," *The Jewish Observer*, London, Ontario, December 1945, 74.

"Chaim Krul (1892–1946)," *Getseltn*, New York, January-February 1946, no. 7, 28–33.

"Yiddish Literature Turns to New Worlds," *Congress Bulletin*, Montreal, May 1946, 8ff.

"Mayn zeyde," [My grandfather], *Der Keneder Adler* (*Jewish Daily Eagle*), Montreal, September 29, 1946, 4; October 4, 1946, 4; October 9, 1946, 4; October 20, 1946, 4.

"Jacob Glatstein (tsu zayn 50th yoyvl)," [Jacob Glatstein (on his 50th birthday)], *Getseltn*, New York, October-December 1946, nos. 11–12, 199–204.

"I was not in Treblinka, Concerning H. Leivick's Most Recent Book of Poems Which Won the Lamed Prize, 1946," *Congress Bulletin*, Montreal, April 4, 1947, 2, 12.

"A naye vendung?" [A new direction?], *Der Keneder Adler (Jewish Daily Eagle)*, Montreal, May 27, 1947, 4.

"A shvartse simkhe," [A black celebration], *Der Keneder* Adler *(Jewish Daily Eagle)*, Montreal, May 30, 1947, 4.

"Avrom Reyzen," [Abraham Reisen], *Der Keneder Adler (Jewish Daily Eagle)*, Montreal, June 8, 1947, 5–6.

"A funk likht," [A spark of light], *Der Keneder Adler (Jewish Daily Eagle)*, Montreal, 25 July 1947, 4

"Finf un tsvontsik yoriker graduir-yoyvl in di idishe folks shuln," [Jewish People's Schools 25th annual graduation], *Der Keneder Adler (Jewish Daily Eagle)*, Montreal, March 28, 1948, 4, 6.

"Jacob Glatstein, der idisher kemfer," [Jacob Glatstein, the Jewish fighter], New York, April 23, 1948, 64–70.

"Geto-oifshtand," [Ghetto uprising], *Der Keneder Adler (Jewish Daily Eagle)*, Montreal, May 2, 1948, 4, 8.

"A Tribute to George Beurling," *The Canadian Jewish Chronicle*, Montreal, June 4, 1948, 6 (translation of an article which appeared in the *Jewish Daily Eagle*, May 27, 1948).

"Rokhl Korn (Tsu ir kumen un bazetsen zikh bay unz in shtot)," [Rachel Korn (on her coming and settling in our city)], Der Keneder Adler (Jewish Daily Eagle), Montreal, July 8, 1948, 5, 3.

"Der sidurl-got (vegn Melekh Ravitches a portret)," [The God of the little prayer book (about one of Melekh Ravitch's pen portraits)], *Der Keneder Adler (Jewish Daily Eagle)*, Montreal, September 27, 1948, 5–6.

"Joseph Rolnick geklibene lider," [Selected poems of Joseph Rolnick], *Der Keneder Adler (Jewish Daily Eagle)*, Montreal, October 11, 1948, 5–6.

"Menachem Boraisha—der dikhter," [Menachem Boraisha—the poet], *Der Keneder Adler (Jewish Daily Eagle)*, Montreal, February 21, 1949, 5–6.

"Yud Lamed Peretz," *Der Keneder Adler* (Jewish Daily Eagle), Montreal, April 10, 1949, 4 (about an event in honour of the I. L. Peretz presented by the Montreal Jewish Public Library at the Monument National Theatre).

"Pesakh 5709," [Passover 1949], *Der Keneder Adler (Jewish Daily Eagle)*, Montreal, 13 April 1949, s. 4, 3.

"H. M. Caiserman (tsu zayn 65 yorigen yoyvl," [H. M. Caiserman, on his 65th birthday], *Der Keneder Adler (Jewish Daily Eagle)*, Montreal, March 18, 1949, 6, 4.

"Heym un heymlozikayt," [Home and homelessness], *Der Keneder Adler (Jewish Daily Eagle),* Montreal, April 25, 1949, 5, 6.

"Geblibn natsis," [Nazis have remained], *Der Keneder Adler (Jewish Daily Eagle)*, Montreal, June 5, 1949, 4, 8.

"Vegn dem yungen idishn moler Yosl Bergner," [About the young Jewish painter Yosl Bergner], *Der Keneder Adler (Jewish Daily Eagle)*, Montreal, September 21, 1949, 4, 6 (on the opening of an art exhibit at the Workmen's Circle, September 17, 1949).

"H. Leivick (tsu zayn 60stn geboyrntog)," [H. Leivick on his 60th birthday], *Di Tsukunft,* New York, November 1949, vol. 54, no. 9, 524–530.

"Far 'guter oyffirung'," [For 'good behaviour'] *Der Keneder Adler (Jewish Daily Eagle)*, Montreal, December 23, 1949.

"Der nigun mitn pendzl," [Melody composed with a paintbrush], Introduction to Yosl Bergner's *59 Illustrations to all the Folk Tales of Itzchok Leibush Peretz*, Montreal, Hertz & Edelstein, 1950, 20 pages and 59 illustrations.

"Aaron Zeitlin (tsu zayn bazukh bay undz in shtot)," [Aaron Zeitlin (on his visit to our city)], *Der Keneder Adler (Jewish Daily Eagle)*, Montreal, February 10, 1950, 5.

"A bazukh leshalom tsum dikhter Shin Sholem," [A visit to poet Shin Sholem (Shalom Joseph Shapira)], *Der Keneder Adler (Jewish Daily Eagle)*, Montreal, April 27, 1950, 5–6.

Danville, a Tribute to its People and its Doctor, Montreal, 1950, 8 pages (English translation of an article published on August 18, 1950 in the *Keneder Adler (Jewish Daily Eagle)*.

"Sforim in goles," [Books in exile], *Der Keneder Adler (Jewish Daily Eagle)*, Montreal, September 4, 1950, 5–6.

"Books in Exile. Old Friends in a New Setting Stir Deep Memories," *Congress Bulletin*, Montreal, November–December 1950, 13–14.

"Dos groys harts vos hot geplatst," [The big heart that burst], *Der Keneder Adler (Jewish Daily Eagle)*, Montreal, December 29, 1950, 4.

"H. M. Caiserman — der mentsh vos hot lib gehat," [H.-M. Caiserman — the man who loved], *Der Keneder Adler (Jewish Daily Eagle)*, January 1, 1951, 5–6.

"Sholem Aleichem in Montreal (tsum 35tn yortsayt)," [Sholem Aleichem in Montreal, on the 35th anniversary of his death], *Der Keneder Adler (Jewish Daily Eagle)*, Montreal, June 4, 1951, 5–6.

"Hertz Bergner (tsu zayn bazukh bay unz in shtot)," [Hertz Bergner (on his visit to our city)], *Der Keneder Adler (Jewish Daily Eagle)*, Montreal, July 10, 1951, 5–6.

"Hitlers nore," [Hitler's lair], *Di Yidishe Velt*, August 31, 1951, 7.

"Avrom Reyzen (tsu zayn 75 yorign yoyvl)," [Abraham Reisen on his 75th birthday], *Der Keneder Adler* (*Jewish Daily Eagle*), Montreal, May 25, 1952, 5–6.

"Psikhologisher onheyb," [Psychological beginning], *Der Keneder Adler* (*Jewish Daily Eagle*), Montreal, August 3, 1952, 4, 6.

"Tog ayn, tog oys," [Day in, day out], *Der Keneder Adler* (*Jewish Daily Eagle*), Montreal, September 28, 1952, 1,7.

"Der Peretz Hirschbein gedenk-ovnt un Esther Shumiatcher-Hirschbein der gast fun ovnt," [Memorial evening for Peretz Hirschbein with Esther Shumiatcher-Hirschbein guest of honour], *Der Keneder Adler* (*Jewish Daily Eagle*), Montreal, November 25, 1952, 5–6.

"Moshe Yudl Shelubsky oif a fuler vokh," [Moshe Yudl Shelubsky on a full week], *Der Yidisher Kemfer*, New York, March 27, 1953, 9, 12.

"Yisroel," [Israel], *Dos Vort,* Montreal, June 1, 1953, 5–6.

"Unzer geshikhtlekher goyrl," [Our historic destiny], *Der Veg*, Mexico, June 13, 1953.

"Abraham Reisen," *Di Tsukunft*, New York, June-August 1953, vol. 58, no. 5, 307–310.

"Israel Rabinovitch (lekoved zayn hayntikn ovent)," [Israel Rabinovitch (in honour of tonight's evening], *Der Keneder Adler* (*Jewish Daily Eagle*), Montreal, January 18, 1953.

"Herbert Lehmans shtarke vornungen," [Herbert Lehman's strong warnings], *Der Veg*, Mexico, June 13, 1953, 7.

"*Tsu shtark*," [Too strong], *Der Veg*, Mexico, 4 August, 1953, 2–3.

"*Vizit in* Foehrenwald," [Visit to Foehrenwald], *Der Veg*, Mexico, August 18, 1953, 8.

"Fertsik tlies," [Forty gallows], *Der Veg*, Mexico, September 24, 1953, 2; reprinted in *Der Folksblat*, Montevideo, November 22, 1953, 4.

"Rokhl Blatshteyn," *Dos Vort*, Montreal, January 1, 1954, 5.

"England," *Der Keneder Adler* (*Jewish Daily Eagle*), Montreal, February 5, 1954, 4.

"Di epokhe fun sine," [The era of hatred], *Der Keneder Adler* (*Jewish Daily Eagle*), Montreal, February 12, 1954, 4, 6.

"Vegn unzer teater," [About our theatre], *Der Keneder Adler* (*Jewish Daily Eagle*), Montreal, February 15, 1954, 6, 3.

"Opgeshaft toyt-shtrof in yisroel," [Abolition of the death penalty in Israel], *Der Keneder Adler* (*Jewish Daily Eagle*), Montreal, February 19, 1954, 4.

"B. Rivkin," *Der Keneder Adler* (*Jewish Daily Eagle*), Montreal, February 22, 1954.

"A. Liessin un B. Vladeck," *Der Keneder Adler* (*Jewish Daily Eagle*), Montreal, February 26, 1954, 4, 6.

"Avrom Liessin," *Der Keneder Adler* (*Jewish Daily Eagle*), Montreal, March 1, 1954, 6, 2.

"Vaysruslekh," [About Byelorussia], *Der Keneder Adler* (*Jewish Daily Eagle*), Montreal, March 5, 1954, 4.

"David Ignatoff olevasholem," [David Ignatoff, may he rest in peace], *Der Keneder Adler* (*Jewish Daily Eagle*), Montreal, March 8, 1954, 6.

"Vaysrusland," [Byelorussia], *Der Veg,* Mexico, March 25, 1954, 2.

"Hayim Greenberg," *Der Yidisher Kemfer,* New York, April 2, 1954, 8–10. (on the first anniversary of his death).

"Yud Yud Segal vegn Yonas Meyerson," [J. I. Segal on Yonas Meyerson], *Der Keneder Adler* (*Jewish Daily Eagle*), Montreal, April 5, 1954, 5.

"Herendig Avrom Twersky redendig khasides," [On hearing Abraham Twerski talking about Hasidism], *Der Keneder Adler* (*Jewish Daily Eagle*), Montreal, May 30, 1954, 4, 8.

"Yeshayahu Spiegels velt," [The world of Yeshayahu Spiegel], *Der Idisher Kemfer,* New York, July 9, 1954, 9–11; reprinted in *Der Idisher Zhurnal* (*Daily Hebrew Journal*), Toronto, August 16, 1954, 5.

"Vegn an inyen," [On a certain matter], *Der Keneder Adler* (*Jewish Daily Eagle*), Montreal, December 14, 1954, 6, 2.

"Nokh alemen? Dovid Bergelson, fun zayne ibergeblibene ksuvim," [When all is said and done? From the posthumous writing of Dovid Bergelson], *Yoyvl bukh fun Keneder Adler* [The Jubilee edition of the *Jewish Daily Eagle*], Montreal, 1957, 81–82.

"Leyenendik Jacob Glatsteinen (fun zayn farblibene ksuvim, tsugeshikt fun dikhter A. S. Shkolnikov)," [Reading Jacob Glatstein (from his posthumous manuscripts, sent by the poet A. S. Shkolnikov)], *Zayn,* no.11, 1957, 30–32.

"Itsik Manger (fun zayne farblibene ksuvim)," [Itsik Manger (from his posthumous manuscripts)], *Zayn,* New York, August 1957, 3–4.

"Moishe Leib Halpern (farblibener fragment)," [Moishe-Leib Halpern (posthumous fragment)], *Zayn,* New York, vol. IV, no. 15, November 1957, 17–18.

"Yerushalayim d'kanade," [Jerusalem of Canada], *Idisher Zhurnal* (*Daily Hebrew Journal*) Toronto, January 17, 1960, 3, 5.

Published Articles About J. I. Segal
Partial Chronological List of Archival
Documents

Anon. "Yud Yud Segal geert bay intimen tsuzamenkunft tsu zayn fuftsik yorigen yubiley," [J. I. Segal honoured at a private gathering on the occasion of his 50th birthday]. *Der Keneder Adler (Jewish Daily Eagle)*, Montreal, December 3, 1946.

Anon. "Yud Yud Segal, prominenter dikhter a gast in Detroit," [Prominent poet J. I. Segal invited to Detroit]. *Der Forverts (The Forward)*, New York, December 10, 1946, 4.

Anon. "Mitvokh, dem 19ten marts – der Yud Yud Segal yoyvl ovent," [Wednesday, March 19th – birthday celebration for J. I. Segal]. *Der Keneder Adler (Jewish Daily Eagle)*, Montreal, March 14, 1947.

Anon. "Groyse Yud Yud Segal fayerung lekoved dem Sefer Idish haynt ovent in zal fun di folks shuln," [Large celebration in honour of J. I. Segal's book *Sefer Idish* this evening in the hall of the Jewish People's Schools]. *Der Keneder Adler (Jewish Daily Eagle)*, Montreal, January 28, 1951, 3

Anon. "Barimter dikhter Yud Yud Segal git op freylikhen grus fun Kanade," [Famous poet J. I. Segal sends happy regards from Canada]. *Der Tog*, 29 May, 1951, 7.

Anon. "Groyser oylem bay der levaye fun Yud Yud Segal," [Large crowd at the funeral of J. I. Segal]. *Der Forverts (The Forward)*, New York, March 9, 1954, 10.

Anon. "Troyer oysdrukn oyfn toyt fun dikhter Yud Yud Segal," [Condolences on the death of poet J. I. Segal]. *Der Tog*, New York, March 9, 1954.

Anon. "Dean of Jewish Writers in Canada Died Sunday." *The Canadian Jewish Chronicle*, Montreal, March 12, 1954.

Anon. "Yud Yud Segal zikhroyne-livrokhe," [J. I. Segal, of blessed memory]. *Argentiner Beymelekh,* Buenos Aires, no. 155–156, March-April 1954, 3.

Anon. "Nito mer Yud Yud Segal," [J. I. Segal is no more]. *Der Keneder Adler (Jewish Daily Eagle),* Montreal, 9 March, 1954 (editorial); reprinted in *Dos vort,* Montreal, April 1, 1954, vol. 7, no. 4, 1–2.

Anon. "Yud Yud Segals tsavoe-ruf vegn idish teater," [J. I. Segal's last wishes regarding the Yiddish theatre]. *Di Prese,* Buenos Aires, March 24, 1954,

Anon. "Yud Yud Segals bukh *Lider far idishe kinder* dershaynt in gikhn," [J. I. Segal's book *Poems for Jewish Children* to appear shortly]. *Der Keneder Adler (Jewish Daily Eagle),* Montreal, September 4, 1961, 6.

Anon. "Derefenung fun a Yud Yud Segal-vinkl in der idisher folks biblyotek (Jacob Glatstein – gast bay der fayerlekher derefenung)," [Opening of a J. I. Segal "corner" in the Jewish Public Library (Jacob Glatstein – a guest at the opening celebration)]. *Der Keneder Adler (Jewish Daily Eagle),* Montreal, March 19, 1962.

Alef Ayin. "Der 50-yoriker yubileum far Yud Yud Segal durkhgefirt oyf a zeyer shenem oyfn," [A fine celebration for J. I. Segal's 50th birthday]. *Der Keneder Adler (Jewish Daily Eagle),* Montreal, March 21, 1947.

Almi, A. (pseudonym of Elias [Eliyahu Chaim] Sheps), "Oyf dem velt tsu a velt, vegen Yud Yud Segals Fun mayn velt," [On the world to a world: I. J. Segal's *Fun mayn velt*]. *Der Keneder Adler (Jewish Daily Eagle),* Montreal, September 22, 1919, 5.

——. "Der zinger fun farheylikter oremkayt," [The bard of hallowed poverty]. *Undzer veg,* Toronto, May 1, 1954, 33–34.

Batashansky, Yakov. "Tsvishn yo un neyn: Yud Yud Segal—der dikhter fun di prost-poshet un orim," [between yes and no: J. I. Segal—the poet of the humble and the poor]. *Di Prese,* Buenos Aires, March 19, 1954.

Benjamin, Louis. "Segal's Poetry Reaches Profound Depths of Jewish Feeling." *The Jewish Standard,* Toronto, May 1, 1954, 4, 13–14 (obituary).

Bialostotzky, Benjamin Jacob "Der liriker Yud Yud Segal," [The lyric poet J. I. Segal]. *Di Fraye Arbeter Shtime,* New York, 8 November 1946, 5–6 (on the 50th anniversary of his death).

Caiserman, Hannaniah Meir. "Yud Yud Segal als poet (a kurtse retsenzye)," [J. I. Segal as poet (a brief review)]. *Der Yidisher Arbeter,* Montreal, February 1919, 3.

——. "*Royerd.*" *Der Keneder Adler* (*Jewish Daily Eagle*), Montreal, August 19, 1929 (on the initial publication of this journal).

——. "Yud Yud Segal," [The lyric poet J. I. Segal]. *Di Fraye Arbeter Shtime*, New York, 8 November 1946, 5–6 (on *Idishe dikhter in kanade*, Montreal, Farlag *Nyuansn*, 1934, 25–49.

Erdberg-Shatan, Mirl. "Yud Yud Segal in heyligen ondenk," [The lyric poet J. I. Segal] [J. I. Segal of blessed memory]. *Der Keneder Adler* (*Jewish Daily Eagle*), Montreal, April 6, 1954.

Friedman, Shari Cooper. *J. I. Segal: Between Two Worlds*. (Master's thesis, Department of Jewish Studies, McGill University, 1988.

——. "Between Two Worlds: The Works of J. I. Segal." In Ira Robinson, Pierre Anctil, and Mervin Butovsky, eds., *An Everyday Miracle: Yiddish Culture in Montreal*, Montreal, Véhicule Press, 1990, 115–128.

Fuks, Haim-Leib. "Yud Yud Segal, *Cent ans de littérature yiddish et hébraïque au Canada.*" Sillery, Septentrion, 2005, 250–254. The French translation by Pierre Anctil of Fox, Ch. L., *Hundert yor idishe un hebreyshe literatur in Kanade*, Montreal, 1980, 180–184.

Fuerstenberg, Adam G. "Transplanting Roots: J. I. Segal's Canadian Perspective." *Yiddish*, New York, Queens College Press, vol. 4, no. 3, 1981, 65–75.

——. "From Yiddish to Yiddishkeit: A. M. Klein, J. I. Segal and Montreal's Yiddish Culture." *Journal of Canadian Studies*, Peterborough, Ontario, September 1984, 66–79.

——. "Faithful to a Dream: the Proletarian Tradition in Canadian Yiddish Poetry," *Yiddish*, New York, Queens College Press, vol. 6, no. 1, (Spring) 1985, 84–95.

Gallay, Joseph. "Yud Yud Segal, olevasholem — der khaver un fraynt," [J. I. Segal, colleague and friend]. *Der Keneder Adler* (*Jewish Daily Eagle*), Montreal, March 12, 1954, 4.

Giladi-Gelbfarb, Joshua. "Yud Yud Segal, olevhasholem," [J.I. Segal, may he rest in peace]. *Der Keneder Adler* (*Jewish Daily Eagle*), Montreal, April 6, 1954, 4.

Ginzberg, Mordecai. "Idishe folks bibliotek hot durkhgefirt ovent lekoved Yud Yud Segal" [Jewish Publish Library hosts an evening in honour of J. I. Segal]. *Der Keneder Adler* (*Jewish Daily Eagle*), November 20, 1945, 3.

——. "Plutsimdiger toyt fun Yud Yud Segal ruft aroys troyer in shtot," [The city mourns the sudden death of J. I. Segal]. *Der Keneder Adler* (*Jewish Daily Eagle*), Montreal, March 8 , 1954, 1; reprinted in *Der Idisher Zhurnal* (*Daily Hebrew Journal*), Toronto, March 11, 1954, 4, 6.

——. "Der plutslinger toyt fun groysn idishn dikhter Yud Yud Segal," [The sudden death of the great Yiddish poet J. I. Segal]. *Der Keneder Adler* (*Jewish Daily Eagle*), Montreal, March 9, 1954, 4, 6.

——. "Yud Yud Segal haskore hot tsugetsoygn a riziker oylem," [J. I. Segal memorial draws a huge crowd]. *Der Keneder Adler* (*Jewish Daily Eagle*), Montreal, April 8, 1954, 6.

Glatstein, Jacob. "In tokh genumen arum bikher, menshn un zakhn," [About books, people and things]. *Der Yidisher Kemfer*, New York, July 13, 1945, 12–13 (on the publication of *Lider un Loybn*).

——. "Yud Yud Segals Sefer idish." *Der Yidisher Kemfer*, New York, November 13, 1950, 14–16 and November 24, 1950, 16–17 (On the publication of *Sefer Idish*).

——. "Yud Yud Segal." *Der Yidisher Kemfer*, New York, March 19, 1954, 11–12 (on the death of J. I. Segal).

——. "Prost un poshet," [Simply put]. *Der Tog*, New York, April 11, 1954.

——. "Yud Yud Segal 'Letste lider'." Der Yidisher Kemfer, New York, February 10, 1956.

——. "A tayere yerushe," [A precious legacy]. *Der Tog*, New York, December 31, 1961.

Gotlib, N. I. "Yud Yud Segal." *Literarishe Bleter*, Warsaw, vol. 9, no. 14, 1 April, 1932, 218–219.

——. "Yud Yud Segal." *Der Keneder Adler* (*Jewish Daily Eagle*), Montreal, March 9, 1959, 9 (on the 5th anniversary of his death).

Gross, Naftoli. "Der idisher dikhter Yud Yud Segal," [The Yiddish poet J. I. Segal]. *Der Forverts* (*The Forward*), New York, April 4, 1954.

Itchike. "Fun do un dortn—Yud Yud Segal," [Here and there—J. I. Segal]. *Vochenblatt* [weekly], Toronto, March 25, 1954, 4, 6.

Klein, A. M. "Baal Shemtov in Modern Dress." *The Canadian Jewish Chronicle*, Montreal, November 14, 1930, 14, 18.

——. "The Poetry Which is Prayer." *The Canadian Jewish Chronicle*, Montreal, November 2, 1945, 8, 16.

——. "Poet of a World Passed By." *The Canadian Jewish Chronicle*, Montreal, June 9, 1950, 5.

——. "In Memoriam: J. I. Segal." *The Canadian Jewish Chronicle*, Montreal, March 12, 1954, 3, 6.

Krant, Miriam. Vegn lebn un shafn fun Yud Yud Segal," [On the life and work of Yud Yud Segal]. *Folks-Shtime*, Montreal, September 11, 1985, 6.

Lamed Lamed [L.L.]. "Yud Yud Segal." *Kinder Zhurnal,* New York, April 1954, 12 (on the death of J. I. Segal).

Leoni, Eliezer. "Yakov Yitskhok Segal," [Jacob Isaac Segal] in *Korets (Wolyn); sefer zikaron le-kehilatenu she-ala aleha ha-koret* [The Korets Book: In Memory of Our Community That Is No More]. Tel Aviv: Azari Press, 284–296.

Maze, Ida. *"Lider far idishe kinder* fun Yud Yud Segal (aroysgegebn fun bildungs-komitet fun Arbeter Ring, New York, 1961, ilustrirt fun Chane Segal-Zakuta)," [Poems for Jewish children by J. I. Segal published by the Education Committee of the Workmen's Circle, illustrated by Annette Segal Zakuta]. *Der Keneder Adler (Jewish Daily Eagle),* Montreal, November 6, 1961.

M.R. [Mem Reysh]. "Tsum 10-tn yortsayt nokh Yud Yud Segal, zikhroyne livrokhe," [On the 10th anniversary of the death of J. I. Segal, of blessed memory]. *Der Keneder Adler (Jewish Daily Eagle),* Montreal, March 8, 1964.

Minkoff, Nahum Baruch. "David Ignatov, Yud Yud Segal," *Kultur un Dertsyung* [Culture and education]. New York, vol. 24, no. 3, March 1954, 4–5.

Mlotek, Chana and Joseph. "Leonard Bernsteins muzik tsu Yud Yud Segals a lid," [Leonard Bernstein's music to a poem by J.I. Segal]. *Der Forverts (The Forward),* New York, March 16, 1990.

Mukdoni, A. "Bikher un shrayber," [Books and writers]. *Der Idisher Zhurnal* (The Hebrew Journal), October 15, 1940 (review of *Dos hoyz fun di poshete).*

Niger, Sh. "A shoymer af a beys-oylem," [A guardian in a cemetery]. *Der Tog,* New York, July 8, 1934 (about *Mayn nigun).*

——. "Megn dikhter benken nokh amolige tsaytn?" [May poets long for the past?]. *Der Tog,* New York, July 22, 1934.

——. *"Altvort,"* [Words of old]. *Der Tog,* New York, February 13, 1938, 7.

Niger, Sh. "Yud Yud Segals a nayer shtrom lirik," [J. I. Segal's new lyrical departure]. *Der Tog,* New York, January 19, 1941 (?) (about *Dos hoyz fun di poshete).*

Niger, Shmuel and Shatzky, Jacob, eds. "Segal, Yankev-Yitskhok," [Segal, Jacob Isaac], *Leksikon fun der nayer idisher literatur*(Biographical Dictionary of Modern Yiddish literature),. New York, Alveltlekher Yidisher Kultur Kongres [Congress for Jewish Culture], 1965, vol. 8, 397–403.

Olgin, Moshe J. *"Idishe dikhter in Kanade,"* *Di Frayhayt,* New York, July 29, 1922, 5–6.

Rabinovitch, Israel. *"Dos hoyz fun di poshete,"* [The House of the Simple People]. *Der Keneder Adler (Jewish Daily Eagle)*, Montreal, October 2, 1940, 5–6 (on the publication of *Dos hoyz fun di poshete*).

——. "Tog ayn, tog oys," [Day in, day out]. *Der Keneder Adler (Jewish Daily Eagle)*, Montreal, March 19, 1947 (on the birthday of J. I. Segal).

——. "Yud Yud Segals nayer bukh *'Sefer idish',"* [J. I. Segal's new book, *Sefer idish*]. *Der Keneder Adler (Jewish Daily Eagle)*, Montreal, March 31, 1950, 17.

——. "Gut morgn," [Good morning]. *Der Keneder Adler (Jewish Daily Eagle)*, Montreal, March 8, 1954, 1 (obituary).

——. "Gut morgn," [Good morning]. *Der Keneder Adler (Jewish Daily Eagle)*, Montreal, March 9, 1954, 1, 3 (obituary).

——. "Di velt fun Yud Yud Segal," [The world of J. I. Segal]. *Der Keneder Adler (Jewish Daily Eagle)*, Montreal, March 15, 1954, 5–6; March 16, 1954, 5; March 17, 1954, 5–6 (about *Lider un loybn* and Segal obtaining the Lamed Prize).

——. *"Gut morgn,"* [Good morning]. *Der Keneder Adler (Jewish Daily Eagle)*, Montreal, March 26, 1954, 1.

——. *"Gut morgn,"* [Good morning]. *Der Keneder Adler (Jewish Daily Eagle)*, Montreal, April 6, 1954, 1.

Rappoport, Aaron. "Mit Mani-Leib in shop," [In Mani Leib's shop]. *Di Tsukunf*, New York, April 1957, vol. 62, no. 4, 167–169.

Ravitch, Melekh. "Yud Yud Segal, an intimer portret fun a khaver," [J. I. Segal, a personal portrait of a friend]. *Der Keneder Adler (Jewish Daily Eagle)*, Montreal, November 12, 1945, 5–6.

——. "Yud Yud Segal, makhshoves vegn a khaver – tsu zayn 50ten geburtstog," [J. I. Segal, some thoughts about a friend and colleague on his 50th birthday]. *Der Keneder Adler (Jewish Daily Eagle)*, Montreal, March 17, 1947, 5–6.

——. "Yud Yud Segals lider un poemen *'Sefer idish',"* [J. I. Segal's poems in *Sefer Idish*]. *Di Tsukunft*, New York, 1952, 32–34.

Ravitch, Melekh. "Yud Yud Segal," *Di Tsukunft*, New York, vol. 59, no. 4, April 1954, 149–150.

——. "J. I. Segal." In *My Lexicon: Pen portraits of Jewish Writers and Artists in the Americas and other Countries* [Yiddish]. Tel-Aviv, I. L. Peretz Publishing House, 1982, 141–144.

Rejzen, Zalman. "Segal, Yankev Yitzkhok," [Segal, Jacob Isaac]. In *Leksikon fun der Iidisher literatur, prese un filologye* [Biographical Dictionary of Yiddish Literature, the press and philology]. Vilna, Kletskin Farlag, 1927, vol. 2, 625–629.

Rome, David. "The Loyal Poet." *Congress Bulletin*, Montreal, August 1945, 2 (about *Lider un loybn*).

——. "Yiddish Poems by J. I. Segal: The Value of Integrity," *Congress Bulletin*, November–December 1950, 16.

Rosenfarb, Chava. "Canadian Yiddish Writers." In Pierre Anctil, Norman Ravvin, and Sherry Simon, eds. *New Readings of Yiddish Montreal / Traduire le Montreal yiddish*, Ottawa, University of Ottawa Press, 2007, 11–18.

Sack, Benjamin Gutl. "Yud Yud Segal nay bukh lider," [J. I. Segal's new poetry book]. *Der Keneder Adler (Jewish Daily Eagle)*, Montreal, November 3, 1940, 5, 7. (on the publication of *Dos hoyz fun di poshete*).

Sack, Benjamin Gutl. "Dikhter un proze—kinstler," [Poetry and prose—artists]. *Der Keneder Adler (Jewish Daily Eagle)*, Montreal, March 16, 1947, 5.

——. "Lekhaim, idish," [Here's to Yiddish]. *Der Keneder Adler (Jewish Daily Eagle)*, Montreal, January 28, 1951, 4, 6 (about an event honouring J. I. Segal on the publication of *Sefer Idish*).

——. "Vos mir hobn in Yud Yud Segaln farloyren," [What we lost in J. I. Segal]. *Der Keneder Adler (Jewish Daily Eagle)*, Montreal, March 14, 1954, 4, 8.

——. "Nusekh nekhtn zikhroyne-livrokhe," [Yesterday's melody, of blessed memory]. *Der Keneder Adler (Jewish Daily Eagle)*, Montreal, April 4, 1954, 4 (for J. I. Segal's 60th birthday).

——. "Baym shaar fun frumen sefer," [Opening the sacred book]. *Der Keneder Adler (Jewish Daily Eagle)*, Montreal, 6 March 1955, 4, 8 (on the first anniversary of J. I. Segal's death).

Segal, Esther. "Kinderyorn fun a idishn dikhter (bibliografishe notitsn vegn Yud Yud Segal)," [The childhood of a Yiddish poet (bibliographical notes about J. I. Segal]. *Far Unzere Kinder*, Paris, 1954, no. 25–26, 17–20.

Serlin. "Der umfargeslekher Yud Yud Segal," [The unforgettable J. I. Segal]. *Der Keneder Adler*, Montreal, March 1954.

Shishler, Hersh. "Opklang fun Zid Afrike vegn Yud Yud Segals toyt," [Reaction of South Africa to J. I. Segal's death]. *Der Keneder Adler (Jewish Daily Eagle)*, Montreal, June 1, 1954, 6.

Shkolnikov, A. S. "J. I. Segal, On the Occasion of His Fiftieth Birthday." *Congress Bulletin*, Montreal, November 1946, 2, 11.

Shtern, Sholem. "Dos vunderlekhe vort," [The amazing word]. *Yidishe Kultur*, New York, 1940–1941, 40–41 (on the publication of *Dos hoyz fun di poshete*).

——. "Yud Yud Segals aynflus oyf di yingere poetn in Kanade," [J. I. Segal's influence on the younger poets in Canada]. *Vokhnblat*, Toronto, July 18, 1973, 7.

——. "Tsum tsvantsikstn yortsayt fun dem dikhter Yud Yud Segal," [On the 20th anniversary of the death of poet J. I. Segal]. *Yidishe Kultur*, New York, October 1974, 40–44.

——. "Der dikhter Yud Yud Segal," [The poet J. I. Segal]. In *Shrayber vos ikh hob gekent, memuarn un esayn* [Writers I Knew, Memories and Essays]. Montreal, 1982, 262–270; translated into French by Pierre Anctil as "Le poète Jacob-Isaac Segal" in *Nostalgie et tristesse, mémoires du Montreal yiddish*, Montreal, Le Noroît, 2006, 273–293.

Shtiker, M. "Di tshikave velt," [The strange world]. *Der Tog*, New York, April 5, 1954, 2.

Shuster, Aaron. "Yud Yud Segal, olevasholem, als groyser makhnes-oyrekh fun idishe shrayber bay unz in shtodt," [J. I. Segal, may he rest in peace, the dean of Yiddish writers in our city]. *Der Keneder Adler (Jewish Daily Eagle)*, Montreal, March 16, 1954, 4.

Singer, S. D. "Yud Yud Segal," *Di Fraye Arbeter Shtime*, New York, June 4, 1954, 4.

Soroker, Shimele. "Argentiner opklangen vegn Yud Yud Segals toyt," [Argentinian reactions to J. I. Segal's death]. *Der Keneder Adler (Jewish Daily Eagle)*, Montreal, May 10, 1954, 4.

Vineberg-Krant, Miriam."Yud Yud Segal." *Der Keneder Adler (Jewish Daily Eagle)*, Montreal, March 18, 1963.

Vityes, Moshe. "Mitn ponim tsu Korets," [With his face turned toward Korets]. *Di Fraye Arbeter Shtime,* New York, November 8, 1946, 5–6.

Waddington, Miriam. "Yakov Yitzhok Segal, Canadian Jewish Poet." *The Tamarack Review*, Toronto, (Fall) 1960, no. 17, 34–36 (article includes six of Segal's poems translated into English by the author).

Wasserman, Leib. "*Segal, Yankev Yitskhok*," [Segal, Jacob Isaac]. In Samuel Niger and Jacob Shatzky, eds. *Leksikon fun der nayer idisher literatur Leksikon fun der nayer idisher literatur* (Biographical Dictionary of Modern Yiddish Literature). New York, Congress for Jewish Culture, 1965, vol. 8, 397–403.

Weinper, Zishe. "Yud Yud Segal." *Yidishe Kultur*, New York, October 1945, 23–37.

——. "Yud Yud Segal." *Yidishe Kultur*, New York, April 1954, 32–33.

Wind, Bernard, "A novi vos gloybt nit," [A prophet who does not believe]. *Der Toronter Zhurnal* (*Daily Hebrew Journal*), Toronto, November 22, 1953, 4.

Yafo, Mordecai. "*Yud Yud Segal*," *Der Tog*, New York, February 21, 1942.

Yungman, Moshe. "*Yud Yud Segal*," *Yung Yisroel*, 1956, 49–53, 56.

Members of the Yiddish Writers Association (*Yidisher shrayber farayn*) Montreal, c. 1941, with some addresses updated in 1945

Yiddish Writers Association Archive,
Montreal Jewish Public Library

1. H. M. Caiserman, 433 St. Joseph Boulevard West (1945)

2. Chaim David Miodek, 5316 Jeanne-Mance / 209 Bernard West (1945)

3. Chana Viderman, 4023 Laval (1945)

4. Shlomo Zalman Schneirson, 5158 Esplanade

5. Dr. Mordecai-B. Etziony, 4873 Park Avenue (1945)

6. Nehemia Segal, 647 de L'Épée

7. Moishe Yechiel Shatan 253 Villeneuve West / 4573 Jeanne-Mance (1945)

8. Mirl Erdberg-Shatan, 253 Villeneuve West / 4573 Jeanne-Mance (1945)

9. Shabse Perl, 159 St. Joseph Boulevard West / 811 Davar (1945)

10. N. I. Gotlib, 4013 St. Laurence Boulevard, 21 Cuthbert (1945)

11. Jacob Zipper, 4540 Clark, apt. 2 (1945)

12. Shloime Wiseman, 240 St. Joseph Boulevard (1945)

13. J. I. Segal, 4540 Clark, apt. 4 (1945)

14. Mme Chane Feinberg, 4945 Jeanne-Mance

15.   H. Hershon, 249 Villeneuve West

16.   Vera Black, 5362 Brodeur, Notre-Dame-de-Grâce

17.   Shmuel Kaplan, 4082 St. Urbain / 4841 Hutchinson (1945)

18.   Moishe Leib Hershunov, 125 Mount Royal Avenue West (1945)

19.   A. S. Zacher, 188 Querbes, Outremont

20.   Chaim Tolmatch, 31 Côte-Saint-Catherine Road (1945)

21.   Samuel Talpis, 5318 Snowdon Avenue(1945)

22.   Shimshon Dunsky, 5201 Waverly / 5226 Waverly (1945)

23.   Dr. Shlomo Gold, 205, Mount Royal Avenue West (1945)

24.   Dr Abraham Stilman, 4221 Esplanade / 261 Côte-Saint-Catherine Road (1945)

25.   Vladimir Grossman, 363 Sherbrooke West (1945)

26.   Moishe Mordechai Shaffir, 4228 St. Urbain (1945)

27.   Louis Benjamin, 20 Saint-Jacques East (1945)

28.   Hirsch Wolofsky, 1120 Bernard, apt. 24 (1945)

29.   B. G. Sack, 381 Saint-Charles / 1090 Laurier West (1945)

30.   Leon Cheifetz, 4075, St. Laurence Boulevard / 5696 Esplanade (1945)

31.   Mordechai Ginzburg, 5581 Jeanne-Mance (1945)

32.   Israel Rabinovitch, 1001, Mount Royal Avenue West (1945)

33.   Israel Medres, 4830 Hutchinson (1945)

34.   Sholem Shtern, 4472 Colonial (1945)

35.   Abraham S. Shkolnikov, 4654 St. Urbain/ 4614 St. Urbain(1945)

36.   Esther Segal, 4614 St. Urbain(1945)

37.   Ida Maze, 4479b Esplanade (1945)

38.   Simcha Pertushka, 1120 St. Joseph Boulevard West / 5017, Jeanne-Mance (1945)

39.   Melech Ravitch, 4099 Esplanade (Jewish Public Library) (1945)

40. A. M. Klein, 117, Mount Royal Avenue West / 4857 Hutchison (1945)

41. Yerachmiel Weingarten, 1081 Bernard West / 256 St. Joseph Boulevard (1945)

42. David Naymark, 747b de L'Épée, Outremont / 4288 St. Urbain (1945)

43. Kalman Karlinski, 4255 Esplanade

44. Hershl Metalowiec, 4813 Park Avenue / 5230, St. Joseph Boulevard (1945)

45. Nathan Szafran, 5308 Hutchinson Street

46. Jacob Grossman, 4137 Esplanade (1945)

47. Rabbi Harry J. Stern, Temple Emanu-El, 4128 Sherbrooke West

48. Sofie Dubnova-Ehrlich, 5579 Park Avenue

49. Victor Ehrlich, 5579 Park Avenue

List of New Members of the Montreal Yiddish Writers' Association (Yidisher shrayber farayn) 1942–1948, with addresses

Yiddish Writers' Association Archive,
Montreal Jewish Public Library

1942 – Sheyndl Garfinkle Franzus, 819 de l'Épée (1945)
1943 – Joseph Kagedan, 411 Saint Urbain (1945)
1943 – David Rome, 5715b Esplanade (1945)
1945 – Louis Rosenberg, 4890 Maplewood Avenue, apt. 7 (1945)
1946 – Yechiel Shtern, 6082 Jeanne-Mance
1946 – Melech Max Grafstein, London, Ontario
1946 – Charles M. Segal, 3987 Colonial
1947 – Braine Bercovitch, 4264 Saint-Dominique
1947 – Joseph Gallay, 5315 Jeanne-Mance
1947 – Aron Horovitz, 487 Park Avenue
1947 – Joseph Mlotek, Calgary
1947 – A. B. Bennett, Toronto
1947 – Joshua, Giladi-Gelbfarb, 5468 Saint Urbain
1947 – Irving Layton, 5391 Sherbrooke West
1948 – Martin Kleinfeld, 3430 Park Avenue
1948 – Bernard Wind, 4355 Saint Urbain
1948 – Joseph Rogel, 3700 Henri-Julien
1948 – Shlomo Mitzmacher, Toronto
1948 – Rokhl Korn, 4614 Saint Urbain
1948 – Paul Trepman, 5464 Waverly

Members of the Board of the J. I. Segal Foundation, Montreal, July 1954

Segal Archive, Montreal Jewish Public Library

Co-Chairmen
Shlomo Wiseman
Israel Rabinovitch

Treasurer
Sara Caiserman

Co-secretaries
Sheyndl Blumshteyn
Hertz Kalles

Members of the Executive
Itshe Akhtman
Joseph Berman
Rebecca Grossman
Sholem Harvey
Hannah Wiseman
Haim Talmatch
Hershl Metalowiec
Esther Segal Shkolnikov
Channa (Annette) Segal
Shivke (Sylvia) Segal Lustgarten
Harry Kon
Rokhl Korn
Melekh Ravitch

H. M. Caiserman
Partial Chronological List of Published Articles

According to Documents in Archival Holdings

"Tsayt notitsen," [Notes on current events], *Der Veg*, Montreal, October 22, 1915 and October 31, 1915.

"Yud Yud Segal als poet," [J. I. Segal as poet], *Der Yidisher Arbeter*, Montreal, February 1919, 3.

"The History of the First Jewish Canadian Jewish Congress," in Arthur Daniel Hart, *The Jew in Canada. A Complete Record of Canadian Jewry From the Days of the French Régime to the Present Day*, Toronto and Montreal: Jewish Publications Limited, 1926, 465–482.

"Idishe literarishe tetigkayt in Kanade, kronologisher iberblik," [Yiddish literary activity in Canada: a chronological overview], *Der Keneder Adler (Jewish Daily Eagle)*, Montreal, September 2, 1927, 5, 2.

"Royerd," [Virgin soil], *Der Keneder Adler (Jewish Daily Eagle)*, Montreal, August 19, 1929.

"Modern Art in Montreal: an Objective Appraisal of the Artist's Colony," *The Jewish Standard*, London, Ontario, vol. 2, no. 7, 1930, 183–184, 188.

"Fainmel and Paquet: Two Young Artists," *The Canadian Jewish Chronicle*, Montreal, March 28, 1930

"A Year of Failures and Achievements of Canadian Jewry," The *Jewish Standard*, London, Ontario, September 19, 1930, 307.

"N. I. Gotlibs bukh, Zeglen in zun," [N. I. Gotlib's book *Sails in the Sun*], *Der Keneder Adler (Jewish Daily Eagle)*, Montreal, February 3, 1932, 5.

"The Art of Bercovitch and Muhlstock," *The Jewish Standard*, London, Ontario, April 14, 1933, 169, 225–226.

"Yud Yud Segal," *Idishe dikhter in kanade* [Jewish Poets in Canada], Montreal: Farlag *Nyuansn*, 1934, 25–49.

(under the penname Hannaniah Ben Meir) "Komunistishe politik oyf der idisher gas [Communist politics on the Jewish street], *Der Keneder Adler (Jewish Daily Eagle)*, Montreal, October 13, 1936, 5–6.

"A tip fun Kanader Frantsoyzen," [A type of French Canadian], *Der Keneder Adler (Jewish Daily Eagle)*, Montreal, October 19, 1936.

"Di drite bilder oysshtelung fun der Y.W.H.A kunst shul," [The third exhibit of the Y.W.H.A. art school], *Der Keneder Adler (Jewish Daily Eagle)*, Montreal, December 28, 1936.

"*Shtile lebns* fun Pinchas Berniker," [Quiet lives by Pinchas Berniker], *Der Keneder Adler (Jewish Daily Eagle)*, Montreal, January 13, 1937

"Vegn dem tsveytn band *Zamlbikher*," [about the second volume of *Zamlbikher*], *Der Keneder Adler (Jewish Daily Eagle)*, Montreal, July 1 and July 2, 1937.

"A lumpige atak," [a shabby attack], *Der Keneder Adler (Jewish Daily Eagle)*, Montreal, February 9, 1938.

"Anti-Semitism in Canada", *London Jewish Chronicle*, London, Ontario, September, 23, 1938.

"A por verter vegn higen lerer farband," [a few words about the local teachers' association], *Der Keneder Adler (Jewish Daily Eagle)*, Montreal, December 13, 1938.

J. I. Segal and H. M. Caiserman, *Ershte reshime fun vikhtige verk in der moderner idisher literature – proze, drame, poezye un literatur kritik*," [first list of important work in modern Yiddish literature – prose, drama, poetry, and literary criticism], Montreal, Canadian Jewish Congress, September 1940, (internal document).

"Forshtayer fun der idisher literatur in Kanade," [representatives of Yiddish literature in Canada], *Der Idisher Zhurnal (Daily Hebrew Journal)*, Toronto, January 12, 1941, s. 5, 2.

"The Canadian Jewish Congress," *The Canadian Jewish Magazine*, Montreal, Passover 5701 (1941), 16–17.

"Jewish Educational Work of the Canadian Jewish Congress," *The Canadian Jewish Magazine*, Montreal, July 1941, 12–13.

"A vikhtige dertsyungs oysshtelung," [An important exhibit about education], *Der Keneder Adler* (Jewish Daily Eagle), Montreal, July 4, 1941, 5, 3.

"A vikhtige bilder oysshtelung fun a gast moler – Albert Rappaport, [an important exhibition by a guest artist – Albert Rappaport], *Der Keneder Adler* (Jewish Daily Eagle), Montreal, April 17, 1942.

"Is There a Canadian Jewish Literature?" *The Canadian Jewish Magazine*, Montreal, Passover 1942, 9–12, 14.

"A. Golombs *Umvegn un oysvegn*" [A. Golomb's book detours and exits], *Der Keneder Adler* (Jewish Daily Eagle), Montreal, July 19, 1942, 5.

"Vikhtiker idisher moler in mayrev Kanade," [Important Jewish painter in Western Canada], *Dos Yidishe Vort*, Winnipeg, November 26, 1942.

"Yud Weingartens bukh *A velt in flamen*," [Y. Weingarten's book a world in flames], *Der Keneder Adler* (Jewish Daily Eagle), Montreal, c.1942

"A bilder-oysshtelung fun Margaret Feinmel," [Margaret Feinmel's exhibition of paintings], *Der Keneder Adler* (Jewish Daily Eagle), Montreal, March 16, 1943.

"Finf yorhundert holendishe kunst oysshtelung in Montreal," [Exhibition in Montreal of five centuries of Dutch art], *Der Keneder Adler* (Jewish Daily Eagle), Montreal, April 11, 1944, s. 5, 4.

"Humanity at the Crossroads," *The Canadian Jewish Magazine*, Montreal, December 1944, 11–13.

"Di bashuldigte shrayen: khapt dem ganef! Arum senator Bouchards rede in senat," [The accused cry "catch the thief!" about Senator Bouchard's speech in the Senate], *Der Keneder Adler* (Jewish Daily Eagle), Montreal, July 19,1944.

"A. M. Kleins 3ter band lider [A. M. Klein's third volume of poetry], *Der Keneder Adler* (Jewish Daily Eagle), Montreal, April 3, 1945.

"*Germany and International Law*, book review of Germany's War Crimes and Punishment, the problem of individual and collective criminality, by H. M. Myerson, Toronto, Macmillan, 1944", *Congress Bulletin*, Montreal, May 1945.

"Mayn ershter blik oyf der khorever Varshe," [my first look at Warsaw in ruins], *Der Keneder Adler* (Jewish Daily Eagle), Montreal, June 4, 1946.

La obra del Joint en Palestina," [The work of the Joint in Palestine], Buenos Aires, Oficina latinoamerico del Joint, 1947.

"Baym keyver fun M. Shmuelsohn (a bletl kanader literarish geshikhte vos iz forgekumen in Montreal)," [At the grave of M. Shmuelsohn (a chapter of Canadian literary history that took place in Montreal)], *Der idisher Zhurnal* (*Daily Hebrew Journal*) Toronto, May 30, 1947, 4, 2.

Two Canadian Personalities, Lyon Cohen – A. J. Freiman, Montreal, 1948, 15 pages.

"Sholem Aleichem Panorama fun Melekh Grafstein [*Shalom Aleichem Panorama* by Melekh Grafstein]", *Der Idisher Zhurnal* (*Daily Hebrew Journal*) Toronto, 24 May 1948 (?).

"The Advance in Jewish Education in Canada," *The Canadian Jewish Chronicle*, Montreal, July 2, 1948, 2.

"Umfarantvortlekhe barikhten un komentarn," [Irresponsible reports and comments], *Der Idisher Zhurnal*, Toronto, October 28,1949, 5.

"Unzer arbet in di ramen fun kanader idisher lebn," [Our work in the context of Canadian Jewish life], *Dos Vort*, Montreal, September 30, 1950, 11.

"Di Val-d'Or gemaynde un dos problem fun kleyne idishe yishuvim in kanade," [the Val-d'Or community and the problem of small Jewish communities in Canada], *Der Keneder Adler* (Jewish Daily Eagle), Montreal, November 5, 1950.

"Antologye fun der kanader-englisher dikhter," [Anthology of English Canadian poets in Canada], *Der Keneder Adler* (Jewish Daily Eagle), Montreal, November 6, 1950.

"Di idishe gemayndes in Rouyn un in Noranda," [Jewish communities in Rouyn and in Noranda], *Der Keneder Adler* (Jewish Daily Eagle), Montreal, November 10, 1950.

"In di kleyne yishuvim fun der provints Kvibek," [In the small communities of the province of Quebec], *Der Keneder Adler* (*Jewish Daily Eagle*), Montreal, November 22, 1950, 5–6.

Articles and Books about
H. M. Caiserman

Partial Chronological List According to Documents
in Archival Holdings

Anon., "Montreal Bids Farewell to Prominent Worker," *The Canadian Jewish Chronicle*, Montreal, vol. VIII, no. 8, July 15, 1921, 1, 4.

Anon., "H. M. Caiserman geshtorben plutslim," [H. M. Caiserman dies suddenly], *Der Keneder Adler*, Montreal, December 25, 1950, 1.

Anon., "Idn fun ale rikhtungen baglayten H. M. Caiserman tsu zayn eybiger ru," [Jews of all shades and stripes accompany H. M. Caiserman to his eternal rest], *Der Keneder Adler* (*Jewish Daily Eagle*), Montreal, December 26, 1950, 1.

Anon., "Avek a kanader idisher pioner," [A Canadian Jewish pioneer is gone], *Der Keneder Adler* (*Jewish Daily Eagle*), Montreal, December 26, 1950 (editorial).

Anon., "H. Caiserman, Noted Jewish Leader, Dies," *The Montreal Star*, Montreal, December 26, 1950, 18.

Anon., "H. M. Caiserman, olevasholem," [H. M. Caiserman, may he rest in peace], *Dos Yidishe Vort*, Winnipeg, January 5, 1951.

Anon., "Kanader idn hobn farloyren a pioner fun idishen yishuv," [Canadian Jews have lost a pioneer of the Jewish community], *Der Tog* [the day], New York, January 10, 1951.

Anon., "Canadian Jewish Community Mourns Loss of H. M. Caiserman," Montreal, *Congress Bulletin*, vol. 6, no. 10, January 1951, 5.

Anon., "H. M. Caiserman General Secretary of Congress Died Suddenly, December 24, 1950," *Jewish Community Council Bulletin*, Windsor, Ontario, January 19, 1951, vol. 11, no. 1, 3.

Anctil, Pierre, "H.M. Caiserman: Yiddish as a Passion," 69–100, in Ira Robinson, Pierre Anctil and Mervin Butovsky, eds., *An Everyday*

Miracle, Yiddish Culture in Montreal, Montreal, Véhicule Press, 1990, reissued as "H. M. Caiserman ou le culte du Yiddish" in *Tur malka. Flâneries sur les cimes de l'histoire juive Montrealaise,* 75–107, Sillery: Septentrion, 1997.

Belkin, Simon, "H. M. Caisermans yubilay," [H. M. Caiserman's 50 birthday], *Dos Vort* [the word], Montreal, April 17, 1944.

— "H. M. Caiserman hot ongefangen zayn gezelshaftlikhe tetigkayt in der treyd-yunyen bavegung," [H. M. Caiserman began his community activism in the trade union movement], *Der Keneder Adler* (Jewish Daily Eagle), Montreal, December 27, 1950, 1, 19.

— "H. M. Caiserman, olevasholem," [H. M. Caiserman, may he rest in peace], *Der Keneder Adler* (Jewish Daily Eagle), Montreal, December 27, 1955.

Bennett, A. B., "H.M. Caiserman, Devoted Servant of Just Causes," *The Canadian Jewish Chronicle,* Montreal, April 13, 1944, 7.

Figler, Bernard, "Meet the Canadian Jewish Congress," *The Jewish Standard,* Montreal, April 1936, 21.

— "H. M. Caiserman: a Biography," in *The H. M. Caiserman Book,* Montreal: Northern Printing and Lithographing, 1962, 15–313.

Ginzburg, Mordecai, "In the Ashes of Warsaw, Jews Learn to Live (An interview with H. M. Caiserman, General Secretary, Canadian Jewish Congress)," *The Canadian Jewish Chronicle,* Montreal, March 15, 1946, 6.

— "H. M. Caiserman als mitboyer fun kanader idisher Congress," [H. M. Caiserman as a creator of the Canadian Jewish Congress], *Der Keneder Adler* (Jewish Daily Eagle), Montreal, December 27, 1950, 4, 3.

— "Kanader idn hoben farloyren a pioner fun idisher yishuv," [Canadian Jews have lost a pioneer of the Jewish community], *Der Tog* [day], New York, January 10, 1951.

Hershman, Harry (Hirsch) "H. M. Caiserman hot ongefangen zayn gezelshaftlikhe tetigkayt in der treyd-yunyen bavegung," [H. M. Caiserman began his community activism in the trade union movement], *Der Keneder Adler* (Jewish Daily Eagle), Montreal, December 27, 1950.

Klein, A. M., "In Memoriam: H. M. Caiserman," *The Canadian Jewish Chronicle,* Montreal, December 29, 1950.

Medres, Israel, "Dos kapitl Caiserman in kanader idisher geshikhte," [The Caiserman chapter in Canadian Jewish history], *Der Keneder Adler* (Jewish Daily Eagle), Montreal, January 1, 1951.

— "H. M. Caiserman – 10 yor nokh zayn toyt," [H. M. Caiserman – ten years after his death], *Dos Vort*, Montreal, 1961, 11.

Nadeau, Roger, "Canadien juif que le Canada français ne doit pas oublier," *Le Canada*, Montreal, January 20,1951, 4.

Rabinovitch, Israel, "Tog-ayn, tog-oys," [Day in, day out], *Der Keneder Adler* (Jewish Daily Eagle), Montreal, December 25, 1950, 1.

— "*Tog-ayn, tog-oys*," [Day in, day out], *Der Keneder Adler* (Jewish Daily Eagle), Montreal, December 26, 1950, 1.

Ravitch, Melekh, "H. M. Caiserman," *Der Keneder Adler* (Jewish Daily Eagle), Montreal, January 25, 1951, 4.

Rome, David, "H. M. Caiserman – a Tribute," in *Congress Bulletin*, Montreal, January 1951, 11, 22.

Rosenberg, Louis, "By the way," Winnipeg, *The Israelite Press*, April 21, 1944, vol. 34, no. 32.

Segal, J. I., "H. M. Caiserman," *Der Keneder Adler (Jewish Daily Eagle)*, Montreal, April 2, 1934, 5 (on his 50th birthday).

— "H. M. Caiserman (tsu zayn 60-yorikn yubilay)," [H.M. Caiserman on his 60th birthday], *Der Keneder Adler (Jewish Daily Eagle)*, Montreal, March 24, 1944, 4, 3; reprinted in *Idisher Zhurnal (Daily Hebrew Journal)*, Toronto, April 2, 1944 and in *Idishe Vort* [Jewish word], Winnipeg, April 4, 1944.

— "H. M. Caiserman, tsu zayn 65 yorigen yoyvl," [H.-M. Caiserman, on his 65th birthday], *Der Keneder Adler (Jewish Daily Eagle)*, March 18, 1949.

— "Dos groyse harts vos hot geplatst," [The great heart that burst], *Der Keneder Adler, (Jewish Daily Eagle)* December 29, 1950, 4.

— "H. M. Caiserman – der mentsh vos hot lib gehat," [H. M. Caiserman – the man who loved], *Der Keneder Adler (Jewish Daily Eagle)*, Montreal, January 1, 1951, 5–6.

Shrepman, Paul, "Oyfn frishen keyver fun H. M. Caiserman," [On Caiserman's fresh grave], *Der Keneder Adler (Jewish Daily Eagle)*, Montreal, December 28, 1950, 4.

Stern, Rabbi Harry J., "H. M. Caiserman," *The Canadian Jewish Review*, Montreal, vol. 33, no. 15, January 12, 1951, 12.

General Bibliography

Abécassis, Armand, *La pensée juive*. 4 vols. Paris: Livre de poche, 1978–1996.

Abella, Irving. *A Coat of Many Colours: Two Centuries of Jewish Life in Canada*, Toronto: Lester and Orpen Dennys, 1990.

Abella, Irving and Harold Troper. *None is Too Many: Canada and the Jews of Europe, 1933–1948*, Toronto: University of Toronto Press, 2012.

Anctil, Pierre. "A.M. Klein: du poète et de ses rapports avec le Québec français," *Journal of Canadian Studies*, 1984, vol. 19, no. 2, 114–131.

———. *Le rendez-vous manqué. Les Juifs de Montréal face au Québec de l'entre-deux-guerres*, Quebec: Institut québécois de recherche sur la culture, 1988.

———. *Le Devoir, les Juifs et l'immigration. De Bourassa à Laurendeau*, Quebec: Institut québécois de recherche sur la culture, 1988.

———. *Tur Malka. Flâneries sur les cimes de l'histoire juive montréalaise*. Sillery: Éditions du Septentrion.

———. Zakhor. Réflexions sur la mémoire identitaire juive et canadienne-française", in *Argument*, Quebec City, vol. 3, no. 1 (Fall 2000–Winter 2001) 76–84.

———. "Vers une relecture de l'héritage littéraire yiddish montréalais," in *Études françaises*, vol. 37, no. 3 (issue on the theme of "Écriture et judéité au Québec") Montreal: Presses de l'Université de Montréal, 2001, 9–27.

———. *Saint-Laurent, la Main de Montréal*, Sillery: Éditions du Septentrion and Musée Pointe-à-Callière, 2002.

———. "Finding a Balance in a Dual Society: The Jews of Quebec," in *Studies in Contemporary Jewry* (issue on the theme of "Jews and the State. Dangerous Alliances and the Perils of Privilege"), Oxford: Oxford University Press, vol. XIX, 2003, 70–87.

———. "Les communautés juives de Montréal," in Marie-Claude Rocher and Marc Pelchat, eds., *Le patrimoine des minorités religieuses du Québec, richesse et vulnérabilité*, Quebec: Les Presses de l'Université Laval (coll. "Patrimoine en mouvement") 2006, 37–50.

———. "Writing as Immigrants: Yiddish Belles-lettres in Canada," in *What is your Place? Indigeneity and Immigration in Canada*, Hartmut Lutz, ed., Augsburg, Germany: Wisner-Verlag, *Beiträge zur Kanadistik*, no. 14, 2007.

———. "À la découverte de la littérature yiddish laise," in *New Readings of Yiddish Montreal/Traduire le Montréal yiddish*, Pierre Anctil, Sherry Simon and Norman Ravvin, eds., Ottawa, University of Ottawa Press, 2007, 19–30.

——. "Traduire le Montréal yiddish," *A ruekh zhum/A Gentle Sound*, Faith Jones and Richard Menkis, eds., Vancouver, Association for Canadian Jewish Studies, 2008, 3–8.

——. "Préserver l'illisible: présences de Sholem Shtern dans la vie littéraire canadienne," in *Archivaria*, Ottawa, no. 67, 2009, 63–85.

——. *Fais ce que dois*. 60 *éditoriaux pour comprendre* Le Devoir *sous Henri Bourassa, 1910–1932*, Sillery: Éditions du Septentrion, 2010.

——. "Du Tur Malka au mont Royal, le poème yiddish montréalais," in Marie-Andrée Beaudet and Karim Larose (eds.), *Le marcheur des Amériques. Mélanges offerts à Pierre Nepveu*, Montreal, *Paragraphes*, no. 49, 2010, 45–62.

——. *Trajectoires juives au Québec*, Quebec: Les Presses de l'Université Laval, 2010.

Anctil, Pierre and Gary Caldwell. *Juifs et réalités juives au Québec*. Montreal, Institut québécois de recherche sur la culture, 1984.

Anctil, Pierre, Ira Robinson, and Gérard Bouchard. *Juifs et Canadiens français dans la société québécoise*. Sillery: Éditions du Septentrion, 1999.

Anctil, Pierre and Ira Robinson, *Les communautés juives de Montréal, histoire et enjeux contemporains*. Quebec: Éditions du Septentrion, 2010.

Baumgarten, Jean. *Le yiddish*. Paris: Presses universitaires de France, coll. "Que sais-je?", no. 2552, 1990.

——. *Le yiddish: histoire d'une langue errante*, Paris: Albin Michel, coll. "Présence du judaïsme," no. 26, 2002.

Bauer, Julien. *Les Juifs hassidiques*, Paris:Presses universitaires de France, coll. "Que sais-je?", no. 2830, 1994.

——. *Les Juifs ashkénazes*, Paris: Presses universitaires de France, coll. "Que sais-je?" no. 3623, 2001.

Belkin, Simon. *Di Poale Zion Bavegung in Kanade (The Labour Zionist Movement in Canada 1904–1920)*, Montreal, 1956. Translated into French by Pierre Anctil as: *Le mouvement ouvrier juif au Canada, 1904–1920*, Sillery: Éditions du Septentrion.

——. *Through Narrow Gates. A Review of Jewish Immigration, Colonization and Immigrant Aid Work in Canada, (1840–1940)*. Montreal: Canadian Jewish Congress and the Jewish Colonization Association, 1966.

Ben-Sasson, H. H. *A History of the Jewish People*. Cambridge: Harvard University Press, 1976.

Bernstein, Y. E. *The Jews in Canada (in North America): An Eastern European View of the Montreal Jewish Community in 1884*. Translated from Hebrew by Ira Robinson, Montreal: Hungry I Books, 2004.

Bialystok, Franklin. *Delayed Impact: The Holocaust and the Canadian Jewish Community*. Montreal: McGill-Queen's University Press, 2000.

Burnet, Jean R. and Howard Palmer. *Coming Canadians: An Introduction to a History of Canada's Peoples*. Toronto: McClelland and Stewart, 1988.

Caplan, Usher. *Like One That Dreamed. A Portrait of A. M. Klein.* Toronto: McGraw-Hill Ryerson Ltd, 1982.

Carroll, James. *Constantine's Sword. The Church and the Jews.* Boston: Houghton Mifflin, 2001.

Châteauvert, Julie and Francis Dupuis-Déri. *Identités mosaïques. Entretiens sur l'identité culturelle des Québécois juifs.* Montreal: Boréal, 2004.

Chouraqui, André. *Histoire du judaïsme.* Paris: Presses universitaires de France, coll. "Que sais-je?", no. 750, 2002.

——. *La pensée juive.* Paris: Presses universitaires de France, coll. "Que sais-je?" no. 1181, 1992.

Cohen, Richard I., Jonathan Frankel, and Stefani Hoffman. *Insiders and Outsiders: Dilemmas of East European Jewry.* Portland: The Littman Library of Jewish Civilization, 2010.

Corcos, Arlette. *Montréal, les Juifs et l'école.* Sillery: Éditions du Septentrion, 1997.

Croteau, Jean-Philippe. *Les relations entre les Juifs de langue française et les Canadiens français selon le* Bulletin du Cercle juif, *1954–1968.* M. A. thesis, Université de Montréal, 2000.

Davies, Alan. *Antisemitism in Canada: History and Interpretation.* Waterloo: Wilfrid Laurier University, 1992.

Dickinson, John Alexander and Brian Young. *Brève histoire socio-économique du Québec.* Sillery: Éditions du Septentrion, 1995.

Dobzyncki, Charles. *Anthologie de la poésie yiddish: le miroir d'un peuple.* Paris: Gallimard, 2000.

Donin, Rabbi Hayim Halevy. *To Be a Jew: A Guide to Jewish Observance in Contemporary Life.* New York: Basic Books, 1972.

Epstein, Isidore. *Le judaïsme, origines et histoire.* Paris: Payot, coll. "Petite bibliothèque," 1962.

Ertel, Rachel. *Royaumes juifs: trésors de la littérature yiddish.* Paris: Robert Laffont, 2008–2009, 2 volumes.

Fishman, David E. *The Rise of Modern Yiddish Culture.* Pittsburgh: University of Pittsburgh Press, 2005.

Francis, R. Douglas, Richard Jones, and Donald B. Smith. *Origins: Canadian History to Confederation* (6th edition) Toronto: Nelson Education, 2009.

——. *Destinies: Canadian History Since Confederation* (6th edition) Toronto: Nelson Education, 2008.

Frankel, Jonathan. *Prophecy and Politics: Socialism, Nationalism, and the Russian Jews, 1862–1917.* New York: Cambridge University Press, 1981.

——. *Crisis, Revolution and Russian Jews.* New York: Cambridge University Press, 2009.

Fox, Ch. L. *Hundert yor idishe un hebreyeshe literatur in Kanade* (One Hundred Years of Yiddish and Hebrew Literature in Canada). Montreal, 1980

Fuks, Haim-Leib, *Cent ans de littérature yiddish et hébraïque au Canada,* Sillery, Éditions du Septentrion, 2005. Translation into French by Pierre Anctil of Fox, Ch. L. *Hundert yor idishe un hebreyeshe literatur in Kanade* (One Hundred Years of Yiddish and Hebrew Literature in Canada). Montreal, 1980.

Goutour, David. "The Canadian Media and the 'Discovery' of the Holocaust, 1944–1945." *Canadian Jewish Studies*, 1996–1997, no. 4–5, 88–119.

Hart, Arthur Daniel. *The Jew in Canada: A Complete Record of Canadian Jewry from the Days of the French Regime to the Present Time*. Montreal: Jewish Publications Ltd., 1926.

Hazan-Brunet, Nathalie and Ada Ackerman, eds. *Futur antérieur. L'avant-garde et le livre yiddish (1914–1939)*. Paris: Musée d'art et d'histoire du Judaïsme and Skira Flammarion, 2009.

Hershman, Harry (Hirsch). *"25 yor idish arbeter bavegung in Montreal."* *Unzer Vort*, Montreal, December 23, 1927–March 2, 1928. Translated into French by Pierre Anctil as "À l'occasion des vingt-cinq ans du mouvement ouvrier juif à Montréal." In *Bulletin du Regroupement des chercheurs en histoire des travailleurs du Québec*, vol. 26 (Spring) 2000, no. 1, 42–60.

Hoffman, Stefani and Ezra Mendelshohn. *The Revolution of 1905 and Russia's Jews*. Philadelphia: University of Philadelphia Press, 2008.

Howe, Irving. *World of Our Fathers. The Journey of East European Jews to America and the Life They Found and Made*. New York: Harcourt Brace Jovanovich, 1976.

Howe, Irving, Ruth R. Wisse, and Khone Shmeruk. *The Penguin Book of Modern Yiddish Verse*. New York: Viking, 1987.

Hundert, Gershon David, ed. *The Yivo Encyclopaedia of Jews in Eastern Europe*. New Haven: Yale University Press, 2008, 2 volumes.

Hundert, Gershon David. *Jews in Poland-Lithuania in the Eighteenth Century: A Genealogy of Modernity*. Berkeley: University of California Press, 2004.

Kage, Joseph. *With Faith and Thanksgiving: The Story of Two Hundred Years of Jewish Immigration and Immigrant Aid Effort in Canada (1760–1960)*. Montreal: The Eagle Publishing Co., 1962.

Klein, A. M. *The Second Scroll*. Toronto: University of Toronto Press, 2000.

Kramer, Reinhold. *Mordecai Richler: Leaving St. Urbain*. Montreal: McGill-Queen's University Press, 2008.

Kucharsky, Danny. *Sacred Ground on de la Savane, Montreal's Baron de Hirsch Cemetery*. Montreal: Véhicule Press, 2008.

Lacoursière, Jacques, Jean Provencher, and Denis Vaugeois. *Canada-Québec 1534–2010*. Sillery: Éditions du Septentrion, 2011.

Langlais, Jacques and David Rome. *Juifs et Québécois français: 200 ans d'histoire commune*. Montreal: Fides, 1986.

Leoni, Elieser, ed. *Korets: sefer zikaron li-kehilatenu she-alah aleha ha-koret* [The Korets Book: In memory of our community that is no more]. Tel Aviv: Azari Press, 1959.

Linteau, Paul-André. *Histoire de Montréal depuis la Confédération*. Montreal: Boréal, 2000.

———. *Brève histoire de Montréal*. Montreal: Boréal, 2007.

Margolis, Rebecca. *Jewish Roots, Canadian Soil: Yiddish Culture in Montreal, 1905–1945*. Montreal: McGill-Queen's University Press, 2011.

Medres, Israel. *Between the Wars: Canadian Jews in Transition*. Translated by Vivian Felsen. Montreal: Véhicule Press, 2003.

Medres, Israel. "*Di idishe arbeter bavegung in kanade.*" *Der Keneder Adler*, Montreal, July 8, 1932, 25th Jubilee Edition, 79–80. Translated into French by Pierre Anctil as "Le mouvement ouvrier juif canadien." In *Canadian Jewish Studies*, 9 (2001).

———. *Montreal fun nekhtn (Montreal of Yesterday)*. Montreal: The Eagle Publishing Co. Ltd., 1947.

———. *Montreal of Yesterday: Jewish Life in Montreal 1900–1920*. Translated by Vivian Felsen. Montreal: Véhicule Press, 2000.

———. *Tsvishn tsvey velt milkhomes (Between Two World Wars)*. Montreal: The Eagle Publishing Co. Ltd., 1964.

Medresh, Israël. *Le Montréal juif d'autrefois*. Translated by Pierre Anctil. Sillery: Éditions du Septentrion, 1997.

———. *Le Montréal juif entre les deux guerres*. Translated by Pierre Anctil. Sillery, Éditions du Septentrion , 2001.

Menkis, Richard and Ravvin, Norman. *The Canadian Jewish Studies Reader*. Calgary: Red Deer Press, 2004.

Nadeau, Jean-François. *Adrien Arcand, führer canadien*. Montreal: Lux Éditeur, 2010.

Nefsky, Judith. "The Prehistory of the Founding of Canadian Jewish Congress, 1897–1919." *Canadian Jewish Historical Society Journal*, vol. 8, no. 2 (Fall 1984) 73–84.

Nepveu, Pierre. *Montréal l'invention juive*. Montréal: Université de Montréal, Groupe de Recherche Montréal imaginaire, 1991.

Novak, Hershl. *Fun mayn yunge yorn* [From my youth]. New York: Educational Committee of the Workmen's Circle, 1957.   Partial translation into French by Pierre Anctil as *La première école yiddish de Montréal, 1911–1914*. Sillery: Éditions du Septentrion, 2009.

Olazabal, Ignace. *Khaverim. Les Juifs ashkénazes de Montréal au début du xxᵉ siècle, entre le* shtetl *et l'identité citoyenne*. Montreal: Nota Bene, 2006.

Paris, Erna. *Jews, an Account of Their Experience in Canada*. Toronto: Macmillan of Canada, 1980.

Ringuet, Chantal. "Parcours et origines de la littérature yiddish montréalaise." *Voix et Images*, Montreal, no. 101 (Winter 2009) 121–137.

———. "*A nayer landshaft*, présence du paysage canadien dans la littérature yiddish montréalaise." *Journal of Canadian Studies*, vol. 44, no. 1, 2010, 118–136.

———. *À la découverte du Montréal yiddish*. Montreal: Fides, 2011.

Robin, Martin. *Shades of Right: Nativists and Fascist Politics in Canada, 1920–1940*. Toronto: University of Toronto Press, 1992; translated into French by Hélène Rioux and Christine Lavaill as *Le spectre de la droite: histoire des politiques nativistes et fascistes au Canada entre 1920 et 1940.* Montreal: Balzac-Le Griot, 1998.

Robinson, Ira, Pierre Anctil, and Mervin Butovsky. *An Everyday Miracle, Yiddish Culture in Montreal.* Montreal: Véhicule Press, 1990.

Robinson, Ira and Mervin Butovsky. *Renewing Our Days. Montreal Jews in the Twentieth Century.* Montreal: Véhicule Press, 1995.

Robinson, Ira. *Rabbis and Their Community. Studies in Eastern European Orthodox Rabbinate in Montreal, 1896–1930.* Calgary: University of Calgary Press, 2007.

Rome, David. "Sarah Caiserman is honoured by Pioneer Women's Organisation." Montreal, *Congress Bulletin,* October 18, 1963, 1, 14.

——. *The Strange Fate of Yiddish.* Montreal: Canadian Jewish Congress, 1969.

——. *The First Jewish Literary School,* in *Canadian Jewish Archives.* New Series no. 41, Montreal, Canadian Jewish Congress, 1988.

——. *Men of the Yiddish Press,* in *Canadian Jewish Archives.* New Series no. 42, Montréal, Canadian Jewish Congress, 1989.

——. *The Education Legend of the Migration,* in *Canadian Jewish Archives.* New Series no. 45, Montréal, Canadian Jewish Congress, 1991.

——. *Through the Eyes of the Eagle. The Early Montreal Yiddish Press 1907–1916.* Montreal, Véhicule Press, 2001. Translated into English from the Yiddish by David Rome; edited and annotated by Pierre Anctil.

Rome, David and Jacques Langlais. *Les pierres qui parlent/The Stones That Speak.* Sillery: Éditions du Septentrion , 1992.

Rosenberg, Louis. *Canada's Jews, a Social and Economic Study of the Jews in Canada.* Montreal: Canadian Jewish, 1939; reissued by Morton Weinfeld as *Canada's Jews: A Social and Economic Study of Jews in Canada in the 1930s.* Montreal: McGill-Queen's University Press, 1993.

Roskies, David. "Yiddish in Montreal: The Utopian Experiment." In Robinson, Ira, Pierre Anctil, and Mervin Butovsky, *An Everyday Miracle. Yiddish Culture in Montréal.* Montreal: Véhicule Press, 1990, 22–38.

——. *Yiddishlands.* Detroit: Wayne State University Press, 2008.

Sefton, Victor. "The European Holocaust—Who Knew What and When—A Canadian Aspect." *Canadian Jewish Studies,* 1978, no. 2, 121–133.

Segal, Jacob-Isaac. *Poèmes yiddish/Idishe Lider.* Selected and translated by Pierre Anctil. Montreal: 1992, Éditions du Noroît.

Shtern, Sholem. *Shrayber vos ikh hob gekent, memuarn oun esayn (Writers I Knew).* Montreal, 1982; partial translation into French by Pierre Anctil as *Nostalgie et tristesse, mémoires littéraires du Montréal yiddish,* Montreal: Éditions du Noroît, 2006.

Shuchat, Wilfred. *The Gate of Heaven: The Story of Congregation Shaar Hashomayim in Montreal, 1846–1996.* Montreal: McGill-Queen's University Press, 2000.

Simon, Sherry. *Translating Montreal: Episodes in the Life of a Divided City.* Montreal, McGill-Queen's University Press, 2006; translated into French by Pierrot Lambert as *Traverser Montréal: une histoire culturelle par la traduction.* Montreal: Fides, 2008.

Skolnik, Fred and Michael Berenbaum. *Encyclopaedia Judaica.* 22 vols. Detroit: Macmillan Reference USA, 2007.

Tauben, Sara Ferdman. *Shuln and Shulelakh: Large and Small Synagogues in Montreal and Europe.* Montreal: Hungry I Books, 2008.

——. *Montreal's Early Synagogues.* Montreal: Véhicule Press, 2011.

Trépanier, Esther. *Peintres juifs de Montréal, témoins de leur époque, 1930–1948.* Montreal: Éditions de l'Homme, 2008.

Tulchinsky, Gerald. *Canada's Jews: A People's Journey.* Toronto, University of Toronto Press, 2008.

Vaugeois, Denis. *Les Juifs et la Nouvelle-France.* Trois-Rivières: Éditions Boréal Express, 1964.

——. *Les premiers Juifs d'Amérique, 1760–1860. L'extraordinaire histoire de la famille Hart.* Sillery: Éditions du Septentrion, 2011.

Weinfeld, Morton. *Like Everybody Else—but Different: The Paradoxical Success of Canadian Jews.* Toronto: McClelland and Stewart, 2001.

Weinreich, Max. *History of the Yiddish Language.* Chicago: University of Chicago Press, 1980.

Weisbord, Merrily. *The Strangest Dream: Canadian Communists, the Spy Trials, and the Cold War.* Toronto, Lester & Orpen Dennys, 1983; translated into French by Jean Lévesque and Michèle Venet as *Le rêve d'une génération: les communistes canadiens, les procès d'espionnage et la guerre froide.* Montreal: VLB, 1998.

Wisse, Ruth R. *A Little Love in Big Manhattan.* Harvard University Press: Cambridge, 1988.

Wolofsky, Hirsch. *Mayn lebns rayze. Zikhoynes fun iber a halbn yorhundert idish lebn in der alter un nayer velt (Journey of My Life).* Montreal, 1946; translated into French by Pierre Anctil as *Mayn Lebns Rayze. Un demi-siècle de vie yiddish à Montréal et ailleurs dans le monde.* Sillery: Éditions du Septentrion, 2000.

Wyman, David S. *The Abandonment of the Jews. America and the Holocaust, 1941–1945.* New York: Pantheon Books, 1984.

Yelin, Shulamis. *Stories from a Montreal Childhood.* Montréal: Véhicule Press, 1983; translated into French by Pierre Anctil as *Une enfance juive à Montréal,* Brossard: Humanitas, 1998.

Yerushalmi, Yosef Hayim. *Zakhor: histoire juive et mémoire collective.* Paris: Gallimard, coll. "Tel," no. 176, 1991.

Zipper, Yaacov. *The Journals of Yaacov Zipper, 1950–1982: The Struggle for Yiddishkeit.* Translated by Mervin Butovsky and Ode Garfinkle. Montreal: McGill-Queen's University Press, 2004.

Canadian Studies

Series editor: Pierre Anctil

The *Canadian Studies* collection touches upon all aspects of Canadian society in all disciplines with a special focus on the situation of Canadian women, cultural and religious minorities, and First Nations. The collection is also devoted to regional studies, local communities, and the unique characteristics of Canadian society. Among the topics privileged in this collection are all contemporary issues, especially in the domain of the environment, with regards to large urban centres and new forms of art and communications.

Previous titles in this collection

Hugues Théorêt, *The Blue Shirts: Adrien Arcand and Fascist Anti-Semitism in Canada*, 2017.

www.press.uottawa.ca

Printed in September 2017
at Imprimerie Gauvin,
Gatineau (Québec), Canada.